MATERIAL MEMORY:

DOCUMENTS IN POST-CONFEDERATION HISTORY

Jeffrey Keshen

Department of History, University of Ottawa

Suzanne Morton

Department of History, McGill University

 Addison-Wesley

An imprint of Addison Wesley Longman Ltd.

Don Mills, Ontario • Reading, Massachusetts • Harlow, England
Melbourne, Australia • Amsterdam, The Netherlands • Bonn, Germany

Publisher:	Brian Henderson
Managing Editor:	Linda Scott
Editors:	Barbara Tessman, Muriel Fiona Napier, Madhu Ranadive
Production Coordinator:	Linda Allison
Manufacturing Coordinator:	Sharon Latta Paterson
Design:	Anthony Leung
Printing and binding:	Webcom Limited

Canadian Cataloguing in Publication Data

Material memory : documents in post-Confederation history
Includes bibliographical references.
ISBN 0-673-98480-X

1. Canada - History -1867- -Sources. I. Keshen, Jeff, 1962- . II. Morton, Suzanne, 1961- .

FC500.M37 1998   971.05   C98-930199-0
F1033.M37 1998

ISBN 0-673-98480-X

Printed and bound in Canada.

A B C D E -WC- 02 01 00 99 98

Preface

Both volumes of *Material Memory: Documents in Canadian History* are designed as companions to a general textbook. The second volume does not claim to provide an overview of post-confederation Canadian history—that would take several volumes of documents, and even then, a claim of comprehensiveness would undoubtedly spark considerable debate. Archival holdings in public institutions are vast—for example, at the National Archives of Canada in Ottawa, the papers of some government ministries and prime ministers can be measured by the kilometre. Because of this, many repositories have become extremely selective in their collection policies.

Therefore, to produce a manageable and intelligible selection we have focused on a number of specific issues or *caveats* that illustrate aspects of wider and typically covered themes in introductory survey courses on Canadian history. To establish context for the material chosen, a brief overview is provided for each topic; as well, short section introductions focus directly upon the different groupings of documents. Rather than suggesting conclusions, we have sought to stimulate classroom discussion by including—in many instances—documents that express opposing views. The aim is to encourage students to act as historians by examining and weighing primary sources, and producing a picture of the past. Through such an exercise, students will also become more adept at judging the often-contrasting arguments advanced by historians, as well as using evidence more effectively in their own work.

The topics selected reflect a *smorgasbord* of themes and issues. They present a mixture of political, social, cultural, and economic themes, to give you a 'taste' of issues that interest historians, and a chance to develop your skills as a scholar. Still, in reflecting current trends in Canadian history, as well as the dissemination of such information in survey courses, the topics and documents for this volume have been divided relatively equally between the broad areas of 'political' and 'social' history.

Certain political issues have had fundamental and ongoing importance in Canada, including: the constitutional power struggle between federal and provincial governments; relations between French and English Canada; and the attempt of Canadian leaders to forge a foreign policy that serves the nation's interests. Also clear from the documents is that political events have had different impacts on various segments of society. Therefore, this volume provides a synthetic approach—one that, like most recent narrative textbooks, weaves together different perspectives and experiences to demonstrate the complexity, but also the interconnectedness, of the past. For example, the documents demonstrate that 'provincial rights' was not simply a theoretical concept occupying the attention of politicians and the courts, but also came to serve the economic ambitions of entrepreneurs in Ontario's resource frontier; that the two World Wars not only generated patriotism, but also, from the perspective of certain minorities, troubling questions about Canada's commitment to liberty; and that the political and economic agendas of governments during the Cold War could bring prosperity and optimism, or fear and repression.

The documents range from state papers to personal diaries; from newspaper articles to excerpts from novels; from advertisements to illustrations; from electioneering radio broadcasts to so-called neutral statistics. Several topics that might initially be considered as political history soon cross over into the realm of social history. Likewise, a number of subjects suggesting a focus on so-called 'ordinary Canadians' also make clear that the political and economic decisions made by elites commonly had tremendous impact on the lives of practically all citizens.

The uneven distribution of power in Canadian society—whether along the lines of race, gender, class, religion, age, region, or language—fundamentally shaped, and continues to form, people's experience. Looking at the everyday life of 'marginal' groups allows us to understand the power structures shaping Canadian society, and the ways in which ordinary people responded to the challenges they faced. Therefore, although privileged members of society formally controlled politics and economics, and defined dominant morality, we must be careful not to exaggerate their complete control. Marginalized groups such as women, Native peoples, rural residents, immigrants, and the working class—who were excluded from formal politics and official decision making—have often been able to respond and shape their lives according to their own values and belief systems.

By examining such topics as provincial rights, native assimilation, rural idealism, or the post-World War II consensus, we hope you will come away with an understanding of what historians do, and begin the task of putting the story together yourself.

Several scholars provided valuable critiques for this volume. We would like to thank Ian Ross Robertson of the University of Toronto, Ken Cruikshank of McMaster University, W.J.C. Cherwinsk of Memorial University, John Kendle of the University of Manitoba, Michael Behiels and Garth Williams of the University of Ottawa, and John T. Saywell of York University (whose research on constitutional issues was invaluable for topic 1). J.L. Granatstein generously supplied pictures that appear in several sections. Finally, we would like to thank Barbara Tessman for her editorial assistance and Brian Henderson of Addison-Wesley for helping to develop and guide this project to completion.

PREFACE

Introduction

Historians try to bring the past to life and to explain why events followed certain patterns. To do this, they turn to evidence—principally primary sources that were created during the period in question, and are not later-day interpretations by people not directly connected with events. There are many primary sources available, including newspapers, state and personal papers, oral testimony, popular music, photographs, paintings, furniture, architectural styles, costumes, statistical accounts, personal wills, court reports, and novels.

But potential pitfalls as well as possibilities accompany evidence—a fact that should prompt you never to blindly accept the work of another scholar. Always consider, for example, whether an author interpreted particular sources according to the previous, and not present-day, meaning of the language. Was the author's documentation written by someone capable of making authoritative claims on the issues being analysed? Did the creator of the evidence (or the historian currently using it) have an affiliation—political, class, ethnic, or some other—that might have affected a point of view? Was the documentation generated close in time to the matter under investigation, or was it possibly clouded by increasing distance from the event? Studies undertaken by the U.S. military during World War II found that, after only six days, soldiers forgot significant details of battles in which they had participated.

Before approaching primary source material, a researcher must acquire a solid understanding of the salient issues and major players at the time. It is also critical to cast a wide net when gathering source material, for with more documentation there comes an increased ability to discover dominant patterns, to recognize anomalies and minority positions, and, by comparing different types of evidence, to acquire a more accurate assessment of what the source is really saying or attempting to accomplish. While government records will sometimes reveal underlying agendas, only the well-informed researcher can determine those cases where state papers are deliberately obscuring the truth. Similarly, candid accounts might be found in personal correspondence, but here too, the desire to convince and thus, inadvertently, to misrepresent will sometimes emerge; in certain circumstances, a writer may attempt to hold back potentially upsetting information. Diaries can also be suspect. While usually revealing much about the daily life and the psychological makeup of the writer, they also frequently lean toward rationalization or even self-congratulation, especially if composed by well-known people apt to think that their observations will be consulted by later generations.

Even if it is possible to 'pin down' the factors that guided decision making by an influential individual, it does not necessarily follow that that person's ideas permeated the 'body politic'—and it is no easy feat to take the pulse of a population. Public opinion polls can provide a snapshot, but their reliability can be affected by many factors, including the particular wording or order of the questions asked. Newspapers, and what has become the mass media, are among the most widely used primary sources for gauging popular trends. Considerable information on a variety of issues and social trends can be gleaned from news columns and editorials, and even from comic strips and classified ads. Yet, we cannot just assume that what the press reported, or the ideas that it conveyed, corresponded to those things that citizens considered significant in their day-to-day lives. It is important to bear in mind that the press does not speak with a single voice, that it sometimes sensationalizes in order to attract business, and that, in certain situations such as wartime, its opinions are curtailed.

Novels, paintings, photographs, music, and movies also provide the essence of an era. In some cases, such sources have influenced the way later generations have come to view a particular time—F. Scott Fitzgerald and Ernest Hemingway, for example, are largely responsible for the still influential perception that the 1920s were the time of a disillusioned, live-for-the-day, 'Lost Generation.' But often the artist stands as an outsider in society, whose ideas must therefore be rigorously tested as to the degree they represent reality. In fact, documentation on a number of issues during the 1920s does not reflect what Fitzgerald cast as the 'death of all Gods,' but rather paints it as an era when social and political conservatism were prevalent.

To obtain evidence beyond the written record, some academics have sought out oral testimony. For those who work in the area of Native history, this has been of particular value in trying to retrieve information from First Nations cultures, whose traditions were originally oral, not written. Oral recollections are a way of obtaining specific information from both paupers and princes, but we must be wary of them, and use other types of evidence to try and identify those that might be tarnished by a defective memory. People have a tendency to embellish their exploits; it is also possible that later events helped create interpretations distorting what the subject actually thought and did at the time. It is hard, too, for an interviewer to avoid asking leading questions. Yet oral history can challenge our reliance on the authenticity of the written word, and remind us of the need to be sceptical of *all* sources.

Material evidence—which can include artifacts ranging from barnyard equipment to *haute couture* fashions—has also been utilized to resurrect past lives and communities, especially where written records are unavailable. However, because no specified parameters, or written guidelines, accompany such objects, some scholars view the use of (and especially the reliance upon) material evidence as dubious because, they claim, such objects are too vague and open to too many interpretations.

Statistical data are perhaps most widely accepted as being accurate and value-free—but even facts can sometimes obscure. Certainly, a great deal of valuable information can be found in census and tax rolls, church records, personal wills, and similar fact-laden documents. However, many such sources, particularly older ones, contain numerous inaccuracies. Coverage of the population, especially in outlying areas, was uneven due to poor communications and relatively few or incompetent government employees; people often lied about their wealth in order to escape levies; and the questions asked in different locales were often not standardized. The ways in which statistical data have been formulated must also be taken into account—what biases, perceptions, and assumptions underlie the questions asked? Factual evidence usually provides only a skeleton of the times—missing, for example, its emotional temper—and by no means is it value-free.

Language, too, has its limitations. The meaning of specific words or phrases changes over time. Much exciting recent work has brought techniques or methodologies used in other disciplines such as literature to examine the ways that specific elements of language—metaphors, for example—are used by people at any given time. Canadian historians also face the challenge of sources being generated in a variety of languages. Even a knowledge of both English and French can be limiting when faced with the myriad of First Nations' languages (especially those that existed during the period of contact), or the numerous languages brought to Canada by different groups of immigrants. For example, a knowledge of Chinese characters is necessary to read Vancouver's *Dahan Gongbao* which began publishing in 1907. Hence, a great deal of the non-English or French language press remains unexplored. For the purposes of this volume, all documents have been translated into English.

Clearly, the documents that follow barely scratch the surface of Canadian history. The topics selected reflect the *smorgasbord* of the themes and topics that you might encounter in a university-level survey course on Canadian history. A mixture of political, social, cultural, and economic themes gives a 'taste' of issues that interest historians and a chance to develop your own skills as a scholar.

Some distinctions exist both between and within the two volumes comprising *Material Memory: Documents in Canadian History*. These can be attributed to, first, the differences in backgrounds and research interests of the various authors involved. Second, there are different kinds of sources available for the pre- and post-Confederation periods—there are, for example, far more mass media as well as government departments and commissions for the twentieth century. For historians who work in the pre-Confederation period, particularly prior to the nineteenth century, newspapers may be quite skimpy, have published erratically, have not survived, or simply not exist. How, then, do we take a public opinion poll of seventeenth-century New France? These facts have obviously helped shape the ways in which we approached our respective themes.

Several criteria were used in creating both volumes of *Material Memory: Documents in Canadian History*. These were: to introduce students to some of the sources from traditional political history as well as from newer social/cultural history; to include material covering all regions of Canada and as many population sub-groups as possible; to achieve some form of chronological balance; and to furnish examples of contemporary debates.

Guides to Primary Documents in Canada, and the Use of Historical Evidence

Canadian Periodical Index
Canadian Index
Union List of Manuscripts
Joyce Appleby, Lynn Hunt, and Margaret Jacob, *Telling the Truth About History* (New York: W. W. Norton, 1994)
Jacques Barzun and Henry F. Graff, *The Modern Researcher*, 3rd edition (New York: Harcourt, Brace, Jovanovich, 1977)

Norman F. Cantor and Richard I. Schneider, *How to Study History* (New York: Thomas Y. Crowell, 1967)

Kitson G. Clark, *The Critical Historian* (London: Heinemann, 1967)

James West Davidson, *After the Fact: The Art of Historical Detection* (New York: Knopf, 1982)

Louis Gottschalk, *Understanding History: A Primer of Historical Method* (New York: Knopf, 1950)

Marius Richard, *A Short Guide to Writing About History* (New York: Harper Collins, 1995)

Richard E. Sullivan, *Speaking for Clio* (Kirkesville, Missouri: Thomas Jefferson University Press, 1991)

John Tosh, *The Pursuit of History: Aims, Methods, and New Directions in the Study of Modern History*, 2nd edition (New York: Longman, 1991)

Robin Winks, ed., *The Historian as Detective: Essays on Evidence* (New York: Harper and Row, 1968)

Table of Contents

Canada's Real Constitution

Canada's first prime minister, John A. Macdonald, believed that a strong central government was essential for the new Dominion. Only such a government, he insisted, could weld together a widely scattered population, and prevent the type of Civil War that had recently engulfed the United States. But, because of the strong reservations expressed by Quebec and the Maritimes, Macdonald also realized that a Legislative Union, his preferred choice, was not possible. The result was a federal system that provided the central government with the power to plan for general needs, but also retained, in provincial governments, the principle of 'local autonomy.'

Although settling for a federal structure, Macdonald was determined to govern with a strong hand. He liberally applied the federal government's power to disallow provincial legislation seen as falling under Ottawa's constitutional jurisdiction. Inter-governmental disputes soon emerged because several key players, with a perspective on Dominion-Provincial powers significantly different from Macdonald's, entered the Confederation scheme.

In Ontario, Edward Blake, leader of the provincial Liberal party (and who served as premier for ten months in 1871 and 1872 before moving on to federal politics) accused Macdonald of balancing national interests in a way that compromised the power and potential growth of this most heavily populated province. He based his conclusion on such issues as the question of Ontario's boundary with the new province of Manitoba. Macdonald wanted the border set 300 miles east of Ontario's claim—partly because this land, if given to Manitoba, would, under the terms of the 1870 Manitoba Act, be controlled by Ottawa. After a fight that lasted nearly two decades, Ontario prevailed, but the boundary question represented only one of many disputes relating to two competing views of federalism.

The logic behind the 'Provincial Rights' philosophy was established by Blake. His 'Compact Theory of Confederation,' which was vigorously applied by his successor, Liberal premier Oliver Mowat (1872-1896), cast the 1867 union as a treaty between the colonies who granted specific, and limited, powers to a new federal government which was portrayed as equal in status to the provinces. This doctrine, along with the desire to lessen Prime Minister Macdonald's aggressive application of federal powers, was most clearly articulated at an 1887 Inter-Provincial Conference in Quebec City, where Mowat insisted that Ottawa's constitutional prerogative of disallowance be eliminated.

Given these divergent views, the courts often ended up exerting a major influence upon the power balance between federal and provincial governments. During this early period, the Supreme Court of Canada often leaned towards the federal government—claiming, for example, in the 1882 *Russell* case concerning the constitutionality of national temperance legislation, that the 'trade and commerce' powers of the federal government justified Ottawa's entry into this domain, and perhaps others. This decision was upheld on appeal to the Judicial Committee of the Privy Council in England (J.C.P.C.), the final court of appeal for Canadians until 1949. However, during the late nineteenth and early twentieth centuries, the J.C.P.C., under the direction of, first, Lord Watson, and, later, Viscount Haldane, changed direction and supported the Compact Theory of Confederation, claiming that this reflected the intent of most delegates to the original constitutional conferences, as well as the reality of Canadian politics over the following generation. And, bolstered in part by decisions from the J.C.P.C., Ontario's government increasingly pursued an activist role that often moved toward encroaching upon federal powers.

Section A

Views of Confederation

In 1865, delegates at Quebec City agreed upon Seventy-Two Resolutions that formed the basis of the British North America Act. However, different perspectives survived the negotiating process. Hector Langevin, an ally of John A. Macdonald, tried to convince Quebeckers to ignore warnings from Antoine-Aimé Dorion, the leader of the Rouges, who claimed that the proposed union represented a grave threat to the future of French-Canada. Christopher Dunkin, another opponent of Confederation, focusing upon the many unresolved and contradictory interpretations of the new union, predicted a frustrating, if not politically chaotic, future for Canada. Soon, competing views of federalism produced a number of court challenges in Canada and England, the outcomes of which, however, did not always point in the same direction.

John A. Macdonald — Leader of the Conservative Party

Now, as regards the comparative advantages of a Legislative and a Federal Union, I have never hesitated to state my own opinions. I have again and again stated in the House, that, if practicable, I thought a Legislative Union would be preferable. (Hear, hear.) I have always contended that if we could agree to have one government and one parliament, legislating for the whole of these peoples, it would be the best, the cheapest, the most vigorous, and the strongest system of government we could adopt. (Hear, hear.) But, on looking at the subject in the Conference, and discussing the matter as we did, most unreservedly, and with a desire to arrive at a satisfactory conclusion, we found that such a system was impracticable. In the first place, it would not meet the assent of the people of Lower Canada, because they felt that in their peculiar position—being in a minority, with a different language, nationality and religion from the majority,— in case of a junction with the other provinces, their institutions and their laws might be assailed, and their ancestral associations, on which they prided themselves, attacked and prejudiced; it was found that any proposition which involved the absorption of the individuality of Lower Canada—if I may use the expression—would not be received with favour by her people. We found too, that though their people speak the same language and enjoy the same style of law as the people of Upper Canada, a system founded on the common law of England, there was as great a disinclination on the part of the various Maritime Provinces to lose their individuality, as separate political organizations, as we observed in the case of Lower Canada herself. (Hear, hear.) Therefore, we were forced to the conclusion that we must either abandon the idea of Union altogether, or devise a system of union in which the separate provincial organizations would be in some degree preserved. So that those who were, like myself, in favour of a Legislative Union, were obliged to modify their views and accept the project of a Federal Union as the only scheme practicable, even for the Maritime Provinces...I trust the scheme will be assented to as a whole...As a matter of course, the General parliament must have the power of dealing with the public debt and property of the Confederation. Of course, too, it must have the regulation of trade and commerce, of customs and excise. The Federal parliament must have the sovereign power of raising money from such sources and by such means as the representatives of the people will allow. It will be seen that the local legislatures have the control of all local works; and it is a matter of great importance, and one of the chief advantages of the Federal Union and of local legislatures, that each province will have the power and means of developing its own resources and aiding its own progress after its own fashion and in its own way. Therefore, all the local improvements, all local enterprizes or undertakings of any kind, have been left to the care and management of the local legislatures of each province. (Cheers.) It is provided that all "lines of steam or other ships, railways, canals, and other works, connecting any two or more of the provinces together or extending beyond the limits of any province," shall belong to the General Government, and be under the control of the General Legislature. In like manner "lines of steamships between the Federated Provinces and other countries, telegraph communication and the incorporation of telegraph companies, and all such works as shall, although lying within any province, be specially declared by the Acts authorizing them, to be for the general advantage," shall belong to the General Government...The General Government assumes towards the local governments precisely the same position as the Imperial Government holds with respect to each of the colonies now; so that as the Lieutenant Governor of each of the different provinces is now appointed directly by the Queen and is directly responsible and reports directly to Her, so even the executives of the local governments hereafter be subordinate to the Representative of the Queen, and be responsible and report to him...

[Parliamentary Debates on the Subject of Confederation of the British North American Provinces. Quebec, 1865]

Antoine-Aimé Dorion — Leader of the Rouge

Now, sir, when I look into the provisions of this scheme, I find another most objectionable one. It is that which gives the General Government control over all the acts of the local legislatures. What difficulties may not arise under this system? Now, knowing that the General Government will be party in its character, may it not for party purposes reject laws passed by the local legislatures and demanded by a majority of people of that locality. This power conferred upon the General Government has been compared to the veto power that exists in England in respect to our legislation; but we know that the statesmen of England are not actuated by the local feelings and prejudices, and do not partake of the local jealousies, that prevail in the colonies. The local governments have, therefore, confidence in them, and respect for their decisions; and generally, when a law adopted by a colonial legislature is sent to them; if it does not clash with the policy of the Empire at large, it is not disallowed, and more especially of late has it been the policy of the Imperial Government to do whatever the colonies desire in this respect, when their wishes are constitutionally expressed. The axiom on which they seem to act is that the less they hear of the colonies the better (Hear, hear.) But how different will be the result in this case, when the General Government exercises the veto power over the acts of local Legislatures. Do you not see that it is quite possible for a majority in local government to be opposed to the General Government to disallow the laws enacted by the majority? The men who shall compose the General Government will be dependent for their support upon their political friends in the local legislatures, and it may so happen that, in order to secure this support, or in order to serve their own purposes or that of their supporters, they will veto laws which the majority of local legislature find necessary and good...

Sir, if a legislative union of the British American Provinces is attempted, there will be such an agitation in this portion of the province as was never witnessed before—you will see the whole people of Lower Canada clinging together to resist by all legal and constitutional means, such an attempt at wresting from them those institutions that they now enjoy. They would go as a body to the Legislature, voting as one man, and caring for nothing else but for the protection of their beloved institutions and law, and making government all but impossible...

Honourable members from Lower Canada are made aware that the delegates all desired a legislative union, but it could not be accomplished at once. This Confederation is the first necessary step towards it. The British Government is ready to grant a Federal union at once, and when that is accomplished the French element will be completely overwhelmed by the majority of British representatives. What then would prevent the Federal Government from passing a set of resolutions in a similar way to those we are called upon to pass, without submitting them to the people, calling upon the Imperial Government to set aside the Federal form of government and give a legislative union instead of it?

I am opposed to this Confederation in which the militia, the appointment of the judges, the administration of justice and our most important civil rights, will be under the control of a General Government the majority of which will be hostile to Lower Canada, of a General Government invested with the most ample powers, whilst the powers of the local governments will be restricted, first, by the limitation of the powers delegated to it, by the *veto* reserved to the central authority, and further, by the concurrent jurisdiction of the general authority or government. Petitions, with more than 20,000 signatures attached to them, have already been presented to this House against the scheme of Confederation. Numerous public meetings have been held in nineteen counties in Lower Canada, and one in the city of Montreal. Everywhere this scheme has been protested against, and an appeal to the people demanded...

[Parliamentary Debates on the Subject of Confederation of the British North American Provinces. Quebec, 1865]

Hector Langevin — Quebec Conservative

Under the new system there will be no more reason than at present to lose our character as French or English, under the pretext that we should all have the same general interests; and our interests in relation to race, religion and nationality will remain as they are at the present time. But they will be better protected under the proposed system, and that again is one of the strongest reasons in favour of Confederation. Not only indeed did we assure ourselves of that protection, but the provinces who were parties to the Confederation desired it also. All local interests will be submitted and left to the decision of the local legislatures. There will be other exceptions with respect to Lower Canada, and, in fact, all the exceptions in the scheme of Confederation are in favour of Lower Canada. These restrictions in favour of Lower Canada were obtained by the delegates from that province; but they seek no thanks for their conduct, as they consider that in so doing they only performed a duty—a duty incumbent on all true patriots and good citizens. All that they now come to this House and ask for, is its sanction to the measure which ensures these privileges to the populations which they represent. I may add that, under Confederation, all questions relating to the colonization of our wild lands, and the disposition and sale of those same lands, our civil laws and all measures of a local nature—in fact every thing which concerns and affects those interests which are most dear to us as a people, will be reserved for the action of our local legislature; all our charitable and other institutions will be protected by the same authority. There is also the question of education. Upon this question, as upon all others, the Lower Canadian delegates have seen to the preservation of certain privileges, and that question has been left to our Local Legislature, so that the Federal Legislature shall not be able to interfere with it...

[Parliamentary Debates on the Subject of Confederation of the British North American Provinces. Quebec, 1865]

Christopher Dunkin – Quebec Conservative

Representation by population is given to meet the grand demand of Upper Canada; but the people of Lower Canada are assured, in the same breath, that it will not hurt them; that their institutions and privileges are made perfectly safe; that they will even have as many members in the Lower House as before, and that they will, in a variety of ways, be really better off than ever... The postponement of the local constitutions is of the same character. Everyone is given to understand that the thing will be made to work to the satisfaction of all; each is promised that he shall have it as he wants...

Whoever prefers one legislative body, hears that it is beyond a doubt there very well may only be one; and those again who, even with one House, do not wish to see responsible government in the provinces, are assured that the machinery is likely to be very simple; that each province will probably have a lieutenant governor, with a few heads of needed departments, and one House, and that so, no doubt, the affairs of each province can be managed most economically and to the entire satisfaction of all. The appointment of lieutenant governors is again a bait, and perhaps not a small one for more than a few of our public men. The power of disallowance of local bills, and also that of reserving them for the sanction of the General Government, are on the one hand represented as realities— powers that will really be exercised by the General Government to restrain improper local legislation—to make everything safe for those who want a Legislative rather than Federal union; but on the other hand, to those who do not want a legislative union, it is represented that they mean nothing at all, and will never be exercised...

Literally, it sounds at every turn as a promise of everything for everybody; and yet, when each comes to ask how much it promises, and how, and where, and when, the whole is to be found ambiguous, unsubstantial and unreal. (Hear, hear.) I repeat, there is everywhere throughout this scheme a most amazing amount of that sort of cleverness which may characterize the astute politician, but which, I think, I shall be able to show is yet far from being the wisdom and foresight characteristic of the far-seeing statesman. (Hear, hear.) The game of all things to all men is a game that cannot be played with success in the long run. It can, under any circumstances, be but temporary in its success...

What are the relations to be established between our general and local governments? We are told to take for granted that no clashing of interest or feeling need be feared; that the Federal union offered us in name will be a legislative union in reality. Yet, whoever dislikes the notion of a legislative union is assured it will be nothing of the sort. Now, sir, I do not believe that you can have all the advantages of these two systems combined in one. (Hear, hear.) A Legislative union is one thing; a Federal union is another. The same system cannot be both at once. You cannot devise a system that shall have all the advantages of the one and of the other; but it is quite possible that you may devise one that will combine the chief disadvantages of both, and that is, I fear, pretty much what this system does. (Hear, hear.)...To be sure there is the grand power of disallowance by the Federal Government, which we are told, in one and the same breath, is to be possessed by it, but never exercised...

[Parliamentary Debates on the Subject of Confederation of the British
North American Provinces. Quebec, 1865]

The British North America Act:
Federal and Provincial Powers

91.   It shall be lawful for the Queen, by and with the Advice and Consent of the Senate and House of Commons, to make Laws for the Peace, Order, and good Government of Canada, in relation to all Matters not coming within the Classes of Subjects by this Act assigned exclusively to the Legislature of the Provinces; and for greater Certainty, but not so as to restrict the Generality of the foregoing Terms of this Section, it is hereby declared that (notwithstanding anything in this Act) the exclusive Legislative Authority of the Parliament of Canada extends to all Matters coming within the Classes of Subjects next hereinafter enumerated; that is to say,

1. The Public Debt and Property.
2. The Regulation of Trade and Commerce.

3. The raising of Money by any Mode or System of Taxation.
4. The borrowing of Money on the Public Credit.
5. Postal Service.
6. The Census and Statistics.
7. Militia, Military and Naval Service, and Defence.
8. The fixing and providing for the Salaries and Allowances of Civil and other Officers of the Government of Canada.
9. Beacons, Buoys, Lighthouses, and Sable Island.
10. Navigation and Shipping.
11. Quarantine and the Establishment and Maintenance of Marine Hospitals.
12. Sea Coast and Inland Fisheries.
13. Ferries between a Province and any British or Foreign Country or between Two Provinces.
14. Currency and Coinage.
15. Banking, Incorporation of Banks, and the Issue of Paper Money.
16. Savings Banks.
17. Weights and Measures.
18. Bills of Exchange and Promissory Notes.
19. Interest.
20. Legal Tender.
21. Bankruptcy and Insolvency.
22. Patents of Invention and Discovery.
23. Copyrights.
24. Indians and Lands reserved for the Indians.
25. Naturalization and Aliens.
26. Marriage and Divorce.
27. The Criminal Law, except the Constitution of Courts of Criminal Jurisdiction, but including the Procedure in Criminal Matters.
28. The Establishment, Maintenance, and Management of Penitentiaries.
29. Such Classes of Subjects as are expressly excepted in the Enumeration of the Classes of Subjects by this Act assigned exclusively to the Legislatures of the Provinces.

And any Matter coming within any of the Classes of Subjects enumerated in this section shall not be deemed to come within the Class of Matters of a local or private Nature comprised in the Enumeration of the Classes by this Act assigned exclusively to the Legislatures of the Provinces.

92. In each Province the Legislature may exclusively make Laws in relation to Matters coming within the Classes of Subject next hereinafter enumerated; that is to say,
1. The Amendment from Time to Time, notwithstanding in this Act, of the Constitution of the Province, except as regards the Office of Lieutenant Governor. [Repealed 1982]

2. Direct Taxation within the Province in order to the raising of a Revenue for Provincial Purposes.
3. The borrowing of Money on the sole Credit of the Province.
4. The Establishment and Tenure of Provincial Offices and the Appointment and Payment of Provincial Officers.
5. The Management and Sale of Public Lands belonging to the Province and of the Timber and Wood thereon.
6. The Establishment, Maintenance, and Management of Public and Reformatory Prisons in and for the Province.
7. The Establishment, Maintenance, and Management of Hospitals, Asylums, Charities, and Eleemosynary Institutions in and for the Province, other than Marine Hospitals.
8. Municipal Institutions in the Province.
9. Shop, Saloon, Tavern, Auctioneer, and other Licences in order to the raising of a Revenue for Provincial, Local, or Municipal Purposes.
10. Local Works and Undertakings other than such as are of the following Classes:
    (a) Lines of Steam or other Ships, Railways, Canals, Telegraphs, and other Works and Undertakings connecting the Province with any other or others of the Provinces, or extending beyond the Limits of the Province;
    (b) Lines of Steam Ships between the Province and any British or Foreign Country;
    (c) Such Works as, although wholly situate within the Province, are before or after their Execution declared by the Parliament of Canada to be for the general Advantage of Canada or for the Advantage of Two or more of the Provinces.
11. The Incorporation of Companies with Provincial Objects.
12. The Solemnization of Marriage in the Province.
13. Property and Civil Rights in the Province.
14. The Administration of Justice in the Province, including the Constitution, Maintenance, and Organization of Provincial Courts, both of Civil and of Criminal Jurisdiction, and including Procedure in Civil Matters in those Courts.
15. The Imposition of Punishment by Fine, Penalty, or Imprisonment for enforcing any Law of the Province made in relation to any Matter coming within any of the Classes of Subjects enumerated in this Section.
16. Generally all Matters of a merely local or private Nature in the Province.

[The British North America Act, 1867]

Provincial Rights: The Compact Theory of Confederation

The principal point, the proper construction of the B.N.A. Act, remains for consideration. There can be no doubt that the Act should be constructed with due consideration to the condition of different parties who entered into the compact of Confederation.

Here which it is intended to grapple with the conjunction of the four Provinces and the establishment of separate legislative powers, and when it has been attempted to deal with all the subject matters in a few printed pages, it would be a fatal error to stick to the letter of the Act. It is the duty of this Court to look around in order to get at the proper construction to be put on the different paragraphs of the Act. The rule of general intent and the rule of public convenience are of vital consequence in dealing with this Act.

There are some points which seem tolerably well admitted.

(1) We need to know what were the rights of the different Provinces before the Union, because it is necessary to apprehend where these rights have gone. If it is found that a subject matter was before Confederation a proprietary right of the Provinces, it must be found existing in one of the identities which were created. There was no intention to surrender what had been granted by England to the Provinces before Confederation, and all proprietary rights existing before Confederation must after Confederation exist in the Government either of Canada or of the Provinces...

There is another mode of constructing these motions; it is to interpret them as you would an ordinary grant. It is admitted that there is a general provision in favour of Canada, and that all matters not granted to the Province and relating to the peace, order and good government of Canada, the power is there, yet it is not a power more paramount than the local power is over subject matters granted to it. Within its range each has an exclusive power. Local authority is legislative in its character and exclusive in its bounds...

Therefore, reading these different sections together, it is manifest that Canada got such property as was expressly given to her and the Provinces kept what was not given to Canada...

> *[Edward Blake, Escheats for the Want of Heirs:* The Provinces are Entitled to Them. The Argument for the Provincial View in the Mercer Escheat Case Before the Supreme Court of Canada *(Toronto: C Blackett Robinson, 1881), pp. 5-7]*

Press Support for Provincial Rights

The Confederation has its origin in a bargain between certain Provinces, in which bargain the Provinces agree to unite for certain purposes and to separate or continue separated for others. The Provinces party to the bargain were at the time of the compact independent nations in the sense that they enjoyed self-government subject to the Imperial veto upon their legislation, to the Imperial appointment of their Governor General, and to the Queen's command of the Forces. The Dominion was the creation of these Provinces; or, in other words, was created by the British Parliament at the request of the Provinces. The Dominion being non-existent at the time the bargain was made, was plainly not a party to the bargain. It cannot, then be a party to a revision of the bargain. The power to revise the created body must lie in the hands of those who created that body. The overwhelming majority of those who created the Dominion being in favour of the revision of the Confederation compact, the British Parliament is not entitled to look any further or to consult the wishes of the Dominion Government in the matter. The resolutions of the Quebec Conference, after they have been approved by the Legislatures representing the Provinces party to the Conference, will therefore furnish the British Parliament exactly the reasons and the authority for a revision of the Confederation pact as was furnished to and acted upon by the same body twenty-two years ago and resulted in the British North America Act being passed.

[The Globe, 9 March 1888] Reprinted by permission of The Globe and Mail.

Decisions of the Judicial Committee of the Privy Council
I — Ottawa Prevails

Sir Montague E. Smith:

...The Lordships cannot think that the *Temperance Act* in question properly belongs to the class of subjects, "Property and Civil Rights." It has in its legal aspect an obvious and close similarity to laws which have restrictions on the sale or custody of poisonous drugs, or of dangerously explosive substances. These things, as well as intoxicating liquors, can, of course, be held as property, but a law placing restrictions on their sale, custody or removal, on the ground that the free sale or use of them is dangerous to public safety, and making it a criminal offence punishable by fine or imprisonment to violate these restrictions, cannot properly be deemed a law in relation to property in the sense in which those words are used in the 92nd section. What Parliament is dealing with in legislation of this kind is not a matter in relation to property and its rights, but one relating to public order and safety. That relation is the primary matter dealt with, and though incidentally the free use of things in which men may have property is interfered with, that incidental interference does not alter the character of the law. Upon the same considerations, the Act in question cannot be regarded as legislation in relation to civil rights. In however large a sense these words are used, it could not have been intended to prevent the Parliament of Canada from declaring and enacting certain uses of property, and certain acts in relation to property, to be criminal and wrongful. Laws which make it a criminal offence for a man wilfully to set fire to his own house on the ground that such an act endangers the public safety, or to overwork his horse on the ground of cruelty to the animal, though affecting in some sense property and the right of a man to do as he pleases with his own, cannot properly be regarded as legislation in relation to property or to civil rights. Nor could a law which prohibited or restricted the sale or exposure of cattle having a contagious disease be so regarded. Laws of this nature designed for the promotion of public order, safety or morals and which subject those who contravene them to criminal procedure and punishment, belong to the subject of public wrongs rather than to that of civil rights. They are of a nature which fall within the general authority of Parliament to make laws for the order and good government of Canada, and have direct relation to criminal law, which is one of the enumerated classes of subjects assigned exclusively to the Parliament of Canada...

[Russell v. The Queen, *[1882], Law Report Appeal Cases, House of Lords, 829]*

II — Support for the Compact Theory

Lord Watson:

The appellants...conceded that, until the passing of the *British North America Act, 1867*, there was precisely the same relation between the Crown and the province which now subsists between the Crown and the Dominion. But they maintained that the effect of the statute has been to sever all connection between the Crown and the provinces; to make the government of the Dominion the only government of Her Majesty in North America; and to reduce the provinces to the rank of independent municipal institutions. For these propositions, which contained the sum and substance of the arguments addressed to them in support of this appeal, their Lordships have been unable to find either principal or authority...

The object of the Act was neither to weld the provinces into one, nor to subordinate the provincial governments into a central authority, but to create a federal government in which they should all be represented, entrusted with the exclusive administration of affairs in which they had a common interest, each province retaining its independence and autonomy. That object was accomplished by distributing, between the Dominion and the provinces, all powers executive and legislative, and all public property, and revenues which had previously belonged to the provinces; so that the Dominion government should be vested with such of these powers, property and revenues as were necessary for the due performance of its constitutional functions; and that the remainder should be retained by the provinces for the purposes of provincial government. But, in so far as regards those matters which, by sect. 92, are specially reserved for provincial legislation, the legislation of each province continues to be free from the control the Dominion, and as supreme as it was before the passing of the Act...

It is clear, therefore, that the provincial legislature of New Brunswick does not occupy the subordinate position which was ascribed to it in the arguments of the appellants. It derives no authority from the Government of Canada, and its status is in no way analogous to that of a municipal institution, which is an authority constituted for the purposes of local administration. It possesses powers, not of administration merely, but of legislation, in the strictest sense of that word; and, within the limits assigned by sect. 92 of the Act of 1867, these powers are exclusive and supreme. It would require very express language, such as not to be found in the Act of 1867, to warrant the inference that the Imperial Legislature meant to vest in the provinces of Canada the right of exercising supreme legislative powers in which the British Sovereign was to have no share...

[Liquidators of the Maritime Bank of Canada v. The Receiver General of New Brunswick,[1] [1892], Law Report Appeal Cases, House of Lords, 437]

"Lord Watson": Written by Viscount R.B. Haldane, Judicial Committee of the Privy Council

He was an Imperial judge of the very first order. The function of such a judge, sitting in the supreme tribunal of the Empire, is to do more than decide what abstract and familiar legal conceptions should be applied to particular cases. His function is to be a statesman as well as a jurist, to fill in the gaps which Parliament has deliberately left in the skeleton constitutions and laws that it has provided for the British Colonies. The Imperial legislature has taken the view that these constitutions and laws must, if they are to be acceptable, be in large measure unwritten, elastic and capable of being silently developed and even altered as the Colony develops and alters. This imposes a task of immense importance and difficulty upon the Privy Council judges, and it was this task which Lord Watson had to face when some fifteen years ago he found himself face to face with what threatened

---

[1] The New Brunswick government deposited $35,000 in the Maritime Bank of Canada. When the Maritime Bank went into receivership, the provincial government demanded payment before other creditors, claiming the prerogative of the Crown as vested in the Lieutenant-Governor. The liquidators of the bank contended that such a prerogative rested only with the central government through the Governor General.

to be a critical period in the history of Canada. Lord Carnarvon's Confederation Act of 1867, which had given separate legislatures and executives to the Provinces, had by no means completely defined the relations of these legislatures and their Lieutenant-Governors to the Parliament and Governor-General of the Dominion. Two views were being contended for. The one was that, excepting in such cases as were specially provided for, a general principle ought to be recognized which would tend to make the Government at Ottawa paramount, and the Governments of the Provinces subordinate. The other was that of federalism through and through, in executive as well as legislative concerns, whenever the contrary had not been expressly said by the Imperial Parliament. The Provincial Governments naturally expressed this latter view very strongly. The Supreme Court of Canada, however, which had been established under the Confederation Act, and was originally intended by all the parties to be the practical final court of appeal for Canada, took the other view. Great unrest was the result, followed by a series of appeals to the Privy Council, which it was discovered still had power to give special leave for them, was commenced. I happened to be engaged in a number of these cases, and had to give such assistance as I could to the various Prime Ministers of the Provinces who came over to argue in person. Lord Watson made the business of laying down the new law that was necessary... He completely altered the tendency of the decisions of the Supreme Court, and established in the first place the sovereignty (subject to the power to interfere of the Imperial Parliament alone) of the legislatures of Ontario, Quebec and the other Provinces. He then worked out as a principle the other relation, in point of exercise of the prerogative, of the Lieutenant-Governors to the Crown. In a series of masterly judgments he expounded the real constitution of Canada...

Nowhere is his memory likely to be more gratefully preserved than in those distant Canadian Provinces whose rights of self-government he placed on a basis that was both intelligible and firm...

[John T. Saywell and George Vegh, eds., Making the Law: The Courts and the Constitution in Canada *(Toronto: Copp Clark, 1990), pp. 68-69]*

Section B

Province Building in Ontario

The desire of successive provincial governments to reap optimum potential from Ontario's natural resources both reflected and reinforced the doctrine of 'Provincial Rights.' Many Ontarians were inspired by Francis Hector Clergue, an American investor who established the Consolidated Lake Superior

Company, the forerunner to Algoma Steel, in late-nineteenth-century Sault Ste. Marie. Clergue beseeched Ontarians not to let their future, which he saw as contained in the province's natural resources, be sold off cheaply and in an unprocessed state to outsiders. Such ideas had an impact upon the Liberal governments of Arthur Hardy (1896-1899), and George Ross (1899-1905). To promote northern development and prevent the shutdown of Ontario sawmills, both administrations perhaps intruded into Ottawa's constitutional control over 'trade and commerce' by retaliating against America's 1897 Dingley tariff on processed logs with the introduction of a provincial export duty. Prime Minister Wilfrid Laurier, fearing defiance from Ontario's government, backed off from the threat of disallowance. However, the truce was short-lived; many other battles awaited between Ottawa and Queen's Park, as well as between Ottawa and several other provincial governments, over the matter of Canada's 'real constitution.'

Ontario's Capitalist Hero: Francis Hector Clergue
Immortalized in Fiction

Amongst the few who knew Robert Fisher Clark at all well, for there were not many of them, there was no question as to his beliefs. It was too obvious that his primary faith was in himself. Nor is it known whether, at any time, he gave any thought or study to the character of those with whom, in the course of his remarkably active life, he came into association. Always it appeared that there was laid upon him the responsibility of doing things which did not occur to the ordinary man, and he went about them with such supreme confidence and unremitting enthusiasm that he infused into his followers much of his communicable zeal...

It was chance that brought Clark to St. Marys, chance that he should be in a certain train at a given time, and above all it was chance that he should overhear a certain conversation, but it was not by any means chance that he should interpret the latter as he did.

The train was lurching over an uneven track that wound through the woods of western Ontario when, staring thoughtfully out of the window at the tangled bush, he caught from across the aisle the drift of talk that was going on between two strangers.

'And so,' said one of them, 'the thing went smash for lack of just two things.'

'And what were they?'

'Some more money and a good deal more experience.'

Clark raised his head ever so slightly. Money and experience—the lack of them had, to his personal knowledge, worked disaster in a wider circle than that of St. Marys. He had heard of the place before, but that was years ago. Presently one of the strangers continued.

'It was after the railway came that the people in St. Marys seemed to wake up. They got in touch with the outside world and began to talk about water power. You see, they had been staring at the rapids for years, but what was the value of power if there was no use to which to put it? Then a contractor dropped in who had horses and tools but no job.'

'So that's what started it?'

'Exactly. The idea was small enough to begin with and the town just wanted power for light and water works, so they gave the contractor the job, borrowed a hundred and thirty thousand dollars, and got the necessary land from the Ottawa government. I've an idea that if those rights ever get into experienced hands you'll hear a good deal more of St. Marys than you ever heard before.'

'And then?'

'The town went broke on the job. Mind you, they had a corking agreement with the government and a block of land alongside the rapids big enough for a young city. The mistake was they hadn't secured any factory. Also they needed about five times as much money.'

The other man smiled reflectively. 'The old story over again.'

'That's about it. Credit ran out and the work stopped and things began to rust, and now St. Marys has gone to sleep again and does a little farming and trade with the Indians.'

'In fact, it's a sort of rural tragedy?'

'Yes. You'll see the half-finished ditch just before we cross the bridge. I'm afraid St. Marys has that kind of a sick feeling that generally knocks the stuffing out of a municipality. Come on, let's have some lunch.'

The two disappeared toward the dining car, but Clark did not stir. His eyes, which were gray and keen, still fixed themselves contemplatively on the ragged wilderness. His lips were pressed tight, his jaw slightly thrust out. Water rights industries—unlimited power—land for an industrial city; all this and much more seemed to hurl itself through his brain...

A quarter of an hour passed when a long whistle announced the approach to the town. At the sound a new light came into the gray eyes, the traveler closed his bag with a snap and began to put on his coat. Just at that moment the porter hurried up.

'This isn't Minneapolis, sir.'

Clark drew a long breath. 'I know it—have changed my mind. I'm for St. Marys now.'...

'Now for my proposal. I believe in the future of this country, in its latent wealth and its possibilities, and I am prepared to take on the town's uncompleted enterprise and assume its one hundred and thirty thousand dollars of liability. Gentlemen, what I have in mind goes further than any of you have ever imagined, and it needs more millions than you have conceived. Millions will be forthcoming. In the financial markets of the world, capital must be assured of certain fundamentals. These fundamentals established, there is no difficulty whatever in securing as much money as may be required. That is my experience, and if you accept my proposition St. Marys will, within a year, begin to feel the influx of money which is seeking investment. Within that year you will hardly be able to recognize your town. Your property, your houses, your farm products will greatly increase in value, and local trade will experience a remarkable impetus. If you ask what are these basic industries which will mean so much, I need only point out that I am assured of an ample supply of pulp wood for very large mills which I propose to erect, and there is, without doubt, iron ore in these hills of yours. This is only a part of my plan.'

Again Clark paused, playing with all his power on those who had already grasped something of his vision. Ore had never been found in that part of the country, though innumerable prospectors had toiled through the hills in search of it, but now it seemed that the folk of St. Marys had cast aside their difference and unbelief, and were becoming incorporated in the speaker's high assurance. A little murmur of enthusiasm arose, to be hushed instantly.

'I only want your cooperation. I do not ask that you put in one dollar. There is ample money for the purpose, and I tell you frankly there is no room for yours. It is not my intention to bring in for the purposes of the work anything the town itself can supply, and the more you can organize to supply amongst yourselves, the better pleased I and my associates will be. All I hope is that you participate intelligently and profitably in that which will shortly take place. And first of all it will be my duty and pleasure to supply the town with water and light on terms to be arranged with your council. This will be the smallest and to me the least profitable of our undertakings, but I regard it as an obligation to the town. Ladies and gentlemen, a new era is dawning for St. Marys. Have I your support?'

Had he their support?... As though galvanized by an electric shock, the folk of St. Marys rose to their feet and began to cheer...

[Alan Sullivan, The Rapids (Toronto: University of Toronto Press, 1972; orig. pub. in 1922), pp. 6-8, 24-25]

A Rousing Address

...It is my opinion, after a residence of over five years in Algoma, and the expenditure of already more than five million of dollars, and having available fifteen million dollars more for investment in the same undertakings, it is my opinion—and it must be a pretty good one or it could not be so well backed up—that there is opportunity for a population in Northern Ontario equal to that of Southern Ontario, equal in number, equal in prosperity; and how it can be done I shall proceed to elucidate to you. You have only to go and follow the example we have set at Sault Ste. Marie...

Here in Ontario you do not know the extent of your own resources. You have more of mineral and chemical value available in Ontario than in all of British Columbia and Montana combined. (Hear, hear!) That is my judgment, and if my judgment was not worth something other people would not give me twenty million dollars to spend up here, and never look after it. I assure you that you have an asset up there that you do not appreciate, that you are neglecting. We have found, however, as every new country finds, that we cannot get on without a railway. You see I have not got through with my evolution yet. I do not know where it is going to end. We found that the water-shed of Hudson's Bay came down very close to Lake Superior; that the tributary streams to Lake Superior were so abrupt and rapid, and the region itself so rocky as to be very unproductive of timber, and it is a fact today that the Sault Ste. Marie Company, notwithstanding that it went up into a supposedly great pulp country, is drawing pulp wood by rail from North Bay. So you see how necessary it is for works of this character to be able to have access to their own raw resources.

We found plenty of wood up there, but it was not on the lake shores; we could not get it down the rivers; that in this inaccessible region there were plenty of forests, but we could not get at them. We found that it was necessary for the success of our works and for their establishment on so large a scale as we hoped and were planning, that it was necessary to have railway admittance into the region where the raw material exists; so we conceived the idea of building a railway into that region, and we began the investigation of the possible routes into the forest preserves...

We found it practicable, and we have now applied to the Government for certain concessions under which we expect to build during the next two years about 200 miles of railway through that country. I wish I had now before me a large map illustrating what that region is, because I want to impress on the gentlemen of the Board of Trade of Toronto the great importance to this city and to you as representatives of the Southern part of Ontario generally of railway systems centering towards Southern Ontario...

It is a never ending source of delight and pleasure and gratification to me. I am wholly and entirely absorbed in it, and I assure you that there is not a man of common sense who can come up and view what has been accomplished there without being inspired with an admiration and esteem for the resources of Canada which will make him a better citizen; he will cease to feel that he is dependent upon some other country or some other people's money for his daily bread. If, in my judgment, the inhabitants of Southern Ontario would insist upon such a development up there as logical and scientific attention to its resources requires, the value of your pine forests will be an insignificant item in your resources...

As long as the Canadians allow their raw materials, necessary to American industries, to go free of charge into the United States, consenting at the same time to allow a prohibitive import duty to be imposed by the United States on the manufactured product of those raw materials, just so long will that duty continue on the American boundary. But when the Americans find that the raw materials which they need, and which are possessed only in Canada, can only be had by a fair interchange of raw materials and manufactured products, then that fair interchange will be acquired and obtained. That is my judgment, gentlemen, and I am a business man of long experience in the United States, and I think I know how wise they are as business men. That is what I would do, and I am very sure that is what they will do. The conclusion to draw from that, of course, is that raw materials, of which Canada possesses a monopoly, should not be allowed to go out to those countries which impose a duty on the importation the manufactured product. (Applause.) When they allow the manufactured product to enter the United States as freely as the raw material then there is reciprocity, and I ask nothing better for Canada, as a pulp manufacturer, as a ferro-nickel manufacturer, as a sulphuric acid manufacturer, in all of these different lines I ask no favors from any American manufacturer; let him have all the raw materials he can get in Canada, and I am perfectly willing to meet him in the American markets, if it were not for the duty; but I assert that it is entirely unfair that products only procurable from the mines and forests of Canada should be allowed to go free into the United States to enable the manufactured result of that raw material to control the American market and to meet the Canadian manufacturer in the European markets. I call that unfair. (Applause.)

[Francis Hector Clergue, An Instance of Industrial Evolution in Canada:
An Address to the Toronto Board of Trade (Toronto: 1900),
pp. 5, 15-16, 18-20]

Invading Federal Jurisdiction to
Protect Ontario's Interests?

1. All sales of timber limits or berths by the Commissioner of Crown Lands which shall hereafter be made and which shall convey the right to cut and remove spruce or other soft wood, trees or timber, other than pine, suitable for manufacturing pulp or paper, and all licenses or permits to cut such timber on the limits and berths so sold, and all agreements entered into or other authority conferred by the said Commissioner by virtue of which such timber may be cut upon lands of the Crown, shall be so made, issued or granted subject to the condition set out in the first regulation of schedule A of this Act, and it shall be sufficient if such condition be cited as "The Manufacturing Condition" in all notices, licenses, permits, agreements or other writing...

SCHEDULE A

1. Every license or permit conferring authority to cut spruce or other soft wood, trees or timber, not being pine, suitable for manufacturing pulp or paper, on the ungranted lands of the Crown, or to cut such timber reserved to the Crown on lands leased or otherwise disposed of by the Crown, which shall be issued on or after the 30th day of April, 1900, shall contain and be subject to the condition that all such timber cut under the authority or permission of such license or permit shall, except as hereinafter provided, be manufactured in Canada, that is to say, into merchantable pulp or paper, or into sawn lumber, woodenware, utensils,

or other articles of commerce or merchandise as distinguished from the said spruce or other timber in its raw or unmanufactured state; and such condition shall be kept and observed by the holder or holders of any such license or permit who shall cut or cause to be cut spruce or other soft wood, trees or timber, not being pine, suitable for manufacturing pulp or paper, under the authority thereof, and by any other person or persons who shall cut or or cause to be cut any of such wood, trees or timber, under the authority thereof, and all such wood, trees or timber, cut into logs or lengths or otherwise, shall be manufactured in Canada as aforesaid. It is hereby declared that the cutting of spruce or other soft wood, trees or timber, not being pine, suitable for manufacturing pulp or paper, into cordwood or other lengths, is not manufacturing the same within the meaning of this regulation.

2. Should any holder of a timber license or permit, or any servant or agent of such holder, or any person acting for him, or under his authority or permission, violate or refuse to keep and observe the condition mentioned in the preceding regulation, then and in such case the license or permit to cut spruce or other soft wood, trees or timber, not being pine, on the berth, territory, lot or lots included in the license or permit, and on which or on any part of which such timber was cut, and in respect of which or any part of which there was a breach of such regulation or a refusal to observe or keep the same, shall be suspended and held in abeyance, and shall not be re-issued, nor shall a new license or permit issue unless and until so directed by the Lieutenant-Governor-in-Council, and then only upon such terms and conditions as the Lieutenant-Governor-in-Council may impose.

3. The Commissioner of Crown Lands, his officers, servants and agents may do all things necessary to prevent a breach of the aforesaid condition or regulation and to secure compliance therewith, and may for such purpose, take, seize, hold and detain all logs, timber or wood so cut as aforesaid, and which it is made to appear to the Commissioner of Crown Lands it is not the intention of the licensee, owner or holder, or person in possession of to manufacture or cause to be manufactured as aforesaid in Canada, or to dispose of to others who will have the same so manufactured in Canada, until security shall be given to Her Majesty satisfactory to the Commissioner that the said condition will be kept and observed.

[Statutes of Ontario, *Chapter 11, An Act Respecting the Manufacture of Spruce and Other Pulp Wood Cut on the Crown Domain, 30 April 1900*]

Cross-Border Disputes

Michigan contained originally not less than 120 billion feet of white pine timber. The amount now remaining uncut, based upon a census by the Supervisors of the State, is less than 5 billion feet.

The entire white pine supply for the mills on Lake Huron which has been the main source of production, is exhausted, not enough being left for half a year's cut.

More than 10 years ago, when the annual pine cut of the State was 5 billion feet, or more than it stands today, it became evident to Michigan lumbermen that they must look elsewhere for their log supply. They began to procure logs from the Georgian Bay, Canada. There was at that time an import duty on lumber of $2 per M. [thousand feet of sawed lumber], and Canada levied an export duty on logs of $2 per M...

It was pointed out that if the lumber duty was reduced to $1 per M., Canada would remove the log duty of $2 per M. and logs could then come in free, thus stocking the American mills and supplying American markets with the needed lumber...

After full deliberation a lumber schedule was adopted, providing that if Canada removed the log export duty, the duty on white pine lumber should be $1 per M...

The Dominion Government at once removed the log export duty, the duty on white pine was made $1, and relying upon a situation at once reasonable and apparently permanent, millions of dollars were invested by Americans in Canadian timber limits, their purchases covering an area of over 4200 square miles.

The Dingley Bill, reimposing a $2 duty on white pine, came like a thunderbolt to these American investors, for it destroyed the peaceable relations on which they were resting...

As a consequence many of the sawmills of Ontario have been idle, while the Michigan sawmill owner has up to the present been able to stock his mill at a profit with sawlogs cut from the Crown lands of Ontario.

It was plain to be seen that the government of Ontario must give to her own citizens the benefit of working the products of her great pine forests, a national industrial resource. So [Ontario] legislation has now been enacted that sawlogs out from Crown lands shall be sawed in Canada.

An eminent American lawyer has appeared before your Honourable Body [a federal Parliamentary Committee], protesting against this legislation as working the confiscation of the timber interests of the American Limit holders, and asking that it be disallowed or set aside.

The Premier of Ontario has on the floor of Parliament virtually replied to this contention to the effect that the regulation of the sale of public lands and timber is in the hands of the Province of Ontario and that the government stands upon the act complained of as protecting the interests of the Province and the people.

The American people look to you [Government of Canada] for a fair and peaceable settlement of such vexed questions, and they must naturally be appreciated in a spirit of equity and accommodation...

[NAC, MG26 G-1(a), Sir Wilfrid Laurier papers. Vol, 791-B, Reel C371, pp. 225046-225048]

QUESTIONS

1. Assess Christopher Dunkin's criticisms of the new Canadian union.

2. Where in the B.N.A. Act might jurisdictions between the federal and provincial governments overlap? Is it significant that 'residual powers' in the constitution fall under federal control?

3. Upon what basis did Sir Montague Smith of the J.C.P.C. support the federal government's right to pass national temperance legislation? How does his line of reasoning support the notion of a strong central government?

4. What can one learn from Allan Sullivan's portrayal of Francis Hector Clergue (aka Robert Fisher Clark)?

5. Should Ottawa have disallowed Ontario's legislation regulating the export of timber? Explain.

READINGS

Christopher Armstrong, *The Politics of Federalism: Ontario's Relations with the Federal Government, 1867-1942* (Toronto: University of Toronto Press, 1981)

David J. Bercuson, ed., *Canada and the Burden of Unity* (Toronto: Macmillan of Canada, 1977)

J. M. S. Careless, *Brown of the Globe: II, Statesman of Confederation* (Toronto: University of Toronto Press, 1963)

Ramsay Cook, *Provincial Autonomy: Minority Rights and the Compact Theory, 1867-1921* (Ottawa: Queen's Printer, 1969)

Donald G. Creighton, *The Road to Confederation: The Emergence of Canada, 1863-1867* (Toronto: University of Toronto Press, 1964)

Margaret Evans, *Sir Oliver Mowat* (Toronto: University of Toronto Press, 1981)

Charles W. Humphries, *"Honest Enough to Be Bold": The Life and Times of Sir James Pliny Whitney* (Toronto: University of Toronto Press, 1985)

Ged Martin, ed., *The Causes of Canadian Confederation* (Fredericton: Acadiensis Press, 1990)

H. V. Nelles, *The Politics of Development: Forests, Mines & Hydro-Electric Power in Ontario, 1849-1941* (Toronto: Macmillan Company of Canada, 1974)

Report of the Royal Commission on Dominion-Provincial Relations (Book 1) (Ottawa: J.O. Patenaude, Printer to the King, 1940)

P. B. Waite, *The Life and Times of Confederation: 1864-1867: Newspapers and the Union of British North America* (Toronto: University of Toronto Press, 1962)

——————, *Canada, 1874-1896: Arduous Destiny* (Toronto: McClelland & Stewart, 1971)

Attempts at Native Assimilation After 1885

It is easy to lose sight of the history of Canadian Native peoples in the period between the defeat of Riel in 1885 and the re-emergence of Native political movements in the 1960s. After the 1885 rebellion, Native peoples no longer were thought to pose any military threat, and the important economic contribution they had once played in the fur trade was no longer valued. Indeed, contemporaries understood that Native peoples were disappearing and their imminent extinction was widely predicted. This perception of decline was supported by numbers, as the population reached its lowest point after World War I. If Native people were really disappearing, assimilating them into the dominant society could be seen as an act of charity, as a paternal action by the majority for the good of the minority. European-Canadians would have had no doubt that their own culture was vastly superior to Native society. Therefore, the Victorian belief in progress meant that it was natural and inevitable that the so-called more 'civilized' European culture would supplant the so-called 'primitive' Native culture.

As in the case of the more than two million immigrants who arrived in Canada between 1896 and 1914, federal government policy toward Native peoples emphasized assimilation. The approach directed at Native people has been described as both protective and coercive. The primary tool of assimilation was the *Indian Act*, which defined an Indian as any 'male person of Indian blood reputed to belong to a particular band,' his children, and his lawful wife. The Act, consolidated in 1876 and revised thereafter, made certain government-recognized Native peoples wards of the state, and handed responsibilities for many aspects of their public and private lives to government officials.

The strategy for assimilation focused on transforming the economic basis of Native society by turning Native peoples into farmers, and thereby instilling a sense of private property, self-sufficiency, and a disciplined work ethic. In the opinion of some farmers and politicians, Native peoples stood in the way of development as the land they occupied was not put to productive use. Federal government policy emphasizing farming was supplemented and reinforced by the activities of church and schools (usually church-run schools) which sought to transform Native peoples into middle-class Christians who accepted their marginal role in society. Here lies one of the contradictions in assimilation policy—most European-Canadians did not want Native peoples to become like themselves, nor did they really believe they could. Assaults on Native culture by changing the economic basis, encouraging mission work by churches, and implementing the *Indian Act* were assisted by a range of prohibitions that barred Native peoples from participating in ceremonial dances, the West Coast *potlatch* or, in the twentieth-century, dressing up in Native dress to participate in exhibitions or parades.

Section A
Establishing Order

The use of military force to subdue the Métis and Native peoples of the Northwest Territories in 1885 was followed by a period in which Canadians tried to understand why violence had occurred, and how the Indian problem could best be resolved. A Methodist missionary, the Reverend John MacLean, who worked among the Blood peoples of Alberta, held to his beliefs in progress and civilization through the Protestant church and education. Prime Minister John A. Macdonald's response in the House of Commons to charges that the Indians of the prairies were suffering revealed both contemporary assumptions about the 'Indian character,' and that physical coercion was not the only means the government was willing to use to force Native peoples into compliance.

The impact of assimilation policies was complex. The example of Pauline Johnson, daughter of the chief of the Six Nations and an English woman, who was one of Canada's most popular poets and performers, illustrates this ambiguity. During her public readings—wearing formal evening dress during the first half, and the dress of a Mohawk Princess in the second—the celebrated poet might read a subversive romantic piece such as "A Cry from an Indian Wife."

Another form of subversion is evident in leaders of Six Nations' attempt to appeal to history as an argument for the fulfillment of treaty obligations. Certainly, contact with non-Native society led Native leaders to adopt tactics for change from the dominant culture, such as petitioning the courts and using the European-Canadian legal system.

A Missionary's View

The Half-Breed and Indian Insurrection

by the Reverend John MacLean, Blood Reserve, Fort Macleod, Alberta

There is an independent method of studying the Half-breed and Indian Question that will free us from the evils resulting from political prejudices and give us the true aspect of the whole matter. It is this method we shall pursue. Conversing some time ago with some Scotch half-breeds on the Riel rebellion, I learned more fully the true facts of the case. For some years the Scotch and French half-breeds in the Saskatchewan region have been agitating for the issue of land patents. Many of these men selected farm sites and by virtue of the "squatter's right" erected buildings and improved their farms. Petitions were prepared at different periods for the purpose of calling the attention of the Government to the necessity for granting their rights. The demands of the half-breeds were never distinctly refused, but they were indefinitely delayed. Many of these "squatters" became disgusted with their treatment by the representatives of the Government, and either sold their claims for a merely nominal value, or discarded their property and went to other parts of the North-West. Many of these have suffered for years on account of these grievances, and yet they are not amongst the insurrectionists. There are other minor burdens, but this is the source of all.

The immediate cause of the insurrection was the influence of the born agitator Riel. Professing a keen sympathy with the half-breeds in their trials, he spent over a year in devising his schemes, and in arousing the latent energies of the half-breed populace, to obtain their rights. He possessed a powerful influence amongst his own people, and there is no cause for surprise at his success. During his residence in Benton and other parts of Northern Montana, he was able to control the half-breed vote. His superior education, together with the prestige of his name, gave him pre-eminence, and the pain and poverty of the half-breed situation made them eager to accept any feasible means for deliverance. Revolt has taken place, and now there remains but one course to pursue. The rebellion having been suppressed, the leaders must be severely punished, and all the just claims of the half-breeds speedily and fairly settled.

The most serious part of the whole matter has been the co-operation of the Indians. It has been the boast of all true Canadians that the fair fame of Canada has never been tarnished by an Indian war. There have been strange mutterings amongst the Indians for the past two years. There has arisen the inevitable murmuring at the progress of civilization. Formerly the Indian was a hero—free, independent and wealthy—now he is inferior to the white man, confined to a reservation, and depending on the Government for his food. He is being forced backward and kept down, and his people are suffering through the vices of the pale face.

The excitement of the hunting days is gone. Idle hands make sad hearts, and many of them pine away and die. They see the great men dying, and they feel that the day is not far distant when they too shall pass away. The more numerous the white population living in close proximity to the Indians, the more rapidly the decrease of the red man. The glorious days of Indian valour are speedily passing away, and the vanquished smart under the gentle rod of their Christian conquerors.

The policy of the Indian Department has been at fault, but not to such a degree as certain politicians would declare. Many mistakes have been made through inexperience or a lack of knowledge. It is unjust to ascribe all the mistakes to the perverseness of one or two individuals, even though strong assertions may be sustained by the voice of the people. The good done by the Department seems to be lost sight of at the present time, as the evils arising from many causes are especially being ferreted out. Perfection in any system is not gained in a day. By the assistance of the Department, the Indians have made progress in agriculture. Men who in former years regarded labour as degrading have now learned to toil. Schools have been established and satisfactory progress made in education. The physical and mental well-being of the Indian has been attended to, with a good measure of success.

The causes of the prevailing discontent amongst the Indians are legion. Some of the men employed by the Department on the reservations have been granted their positions through political influence, even though they have been utterly incompetent for the respective duties of their office. They receive good salaries, and yet the Indians derive very little benefit from their services. Promises have been made to the Indians by Government officials that have never been kept. The Department has professed to give these people food enough to sustain them, yet at different times the rations have been cut down. They have been told that they were to remain on their reservations, but it was impossible for them to do so on their daily allowance. Since the half-breed outbreak some of them have had their supplies increased. A little judgment used in a proper distribution of food would help materially in allaying any angry feelings that may exist.

The Indians have had to suffer seriously at times, through not submitting to some pet scheme of a Department official. Coercive measures have been employed but have failed. There is no encouragement given to those who toil, as the loungers and workers are fed alike. Some of the chiefs are only learning the true nature of the treaties made in the years gone by. These causes do not all apply to one tribe, but they are given as veritable facts known to the writer to have been done on several reservations visited by him during the past five years. There does not exist a general feeling of disloyalty among the Indian tribes, but some have been induced by the solicitations of the half-breeds to join in the revolt, and a few have committed illegal acts with the hope of plunder. Hard has been the lot of some during the past two years, and as they have shared in the general excitement, they have raided farms and stores in expectation of enjoying a feast. We should not wonder if some of the young men who have never gained their laurels in an

Indian battle went out on the warpath to steal horses and commit other depredations. They have listened to the recital of the heroic deeds of their fathers, and they were desirous of following in the same old path. The Indian leaders in the revolt have ever been troublesome. The Indian Department and the various missionary societies have accomplished much good, but both kinds of organizations have fallen short of ultimate success through ignorance and a too narrow financial policy. The one true remedy for the existing dissatisfaction lies in the instituting of an Indian Council for the purpose of hearing the Indians' grievances, and the appointing of men of principle and courage as a committee to see that they receive their due. Let there be an Indian District Council held annually in each district, consisting of the agents, farm instructors, missionaries, and teachers, also the chiefs recognized by Government, from the reservations comprised in the district. Let there be an Indian Territorial or Provincial Assembly held annually at Regina or Winnipeg, the members of which consist of delegates sent from the District Councils and the Department officials of Regina. The district representatives would be able to state the "progress and poverty" of the representative tribes in their districts and to present the resolutions of the Councils respecting matters affecting the interests of the Indians. By this means the secret dealings of "cliques," "rings," and "officious individuals" would soon be at an end.

Competent men should be sent for every branch of the Department, selected by merit and not through political influence. The Indians have been encouraged in their farming operations, but they have had no market for their produce, and consequently many of them have been cheated by rascally white men, and are thereby disheartened. There should be an Indian Bureau which should attend to these and other matters. Let the Government buy the Indians' produce or open some kind of market for them.

To help the Indians more effectively in reaching the point when they can become self-supporting, a few ideas may be briefly given. To encourage the Indian farmers and their wives, prizes might be given annually for the best crops and neatest gardens, and for the most comfortable and cleanest homes. Only those who work should receive their full daily allowance of food. Married men possessing ability and principle should be sent as farm instructors. If possible all the farm labourers and men employed on the reservations should be married men, and the situations should be given chiefly, if not altogether, to men of sterling Christian character. Give the Indians cattle in exchange for their horses. Buy their guns, and stop supplying them with ammunition. Furnish them with enough food that they will not be tempted to go to towns and settlements to make money. It is a sad thing to say that the nearer a reservation is to a town the more immoral the Indians become, and the harder the work for the missionary. Let the Government put a stop to polygamy, gambling, and the selling of women to white men. If these men wish Indian wives, let them marry them. Sell part of the reservations, with the Indians' consent, and put the proceeds into a fund, the interest to be given annually to the members of each tribe or to be used in erecting substantial buildings for them. It has been assumed that all Indians can and will be farmers. Now there are many of them who have preferences for a trade, and are handy in using tools, and some means should be devised for cultivating the talents of these adult labourers. True, there are three Industrial Schools, but they are not sufficient for all the work. Adult Manual Labour Schools are a necessity, if we would effectively cope with all the difficulties of the Indian question.

In closing this article, let me make a statement and ask a question. There are three Indian Industrial Schools established in the North-West by the Government: one at Battleford, under the supervision of the English Church; another at Qu'Appelle, and the third at High River, thirty miles from Calgary, both of these under the care of the Roman Catholic Church. Is there justice in placing two of these schools under the jurisdiction of the Roman Catholics, and one only assigned to the Protestants? Give to the Catholics and Protestants equal rights, especially in a new country, and this would imply another Industrial School for those who in the past few years have been less favoured by the politicians and fathers of the State.

[Reverend John MacLean, "The Half-Breed and Canadian Insurrection," in The Canadian Methodist Magazine (July/December 1885), pp. 172-176]

Sir John A. Macdonald Responds to His Government's Indian Policy

Sir JOHN A. MACDONALD. I regret very much I was not able to be here when the hon. Member for West Huron (Mr. Cameron), made a long and elaborate attack on the Indian Department in regard to its North-West management...As regards the charges against Governor Dewdney, I would not be worthy of my place if I did not rise in support of my officers when I know they do their duty. That gentleman has a very severe and unpopular duty to perform, and there have been a set of influences brought against him which at one time brought undeserved unpopularity upon him. That he has surmounted, and the country and the North-West are rising to express views as to his merits just as strongly as originally they were prejudiced against him. I believe he is a good officer, a faithful officer. When the hon. gentleman states he was in Ottawa instead of being at his post, I may say that he was here because I summoned him myself for the purpose of going into the whole matter connected with arrangements in the North-West. It would be very easy for Governor Dewdney to throw away the money of the country upon Indians hanging round the various posts begging for food. It would be very easy to give them flour, beef and bacon, that would cause him no trouble and might give popularity. But he was told to husband the funds and the food placed at his disposal. With respect to the Indians that were camping in and about Fort Walsh, he was specially instructed by me to act as he did. Those Indians had left their reserves. They were told to go back to their reserves and to cultivate the land, and that they should have food if they did so. We had agricultural implements, cattle, seed grain and food for them there, but they would not go. They were near Fort Walsh, and almost immediately adjoining the boundary between the United States and Canada. There was then great danger of improper communications being had between the Indians of the two countries. They were, therefore, told that if they remained there they would not get any food. They were also told that if they would go to their reserves they would be fully supplied in every way, but they would not go. They were reduced from full rations to half rations, and then to quarter rations, but with the obstinacy of Indians they would not go, and they were told that if they refused they must take the consequences. It is only by using those means that you can get the Indians to work. There are police stations, scattered settlements, land agencies, all those are nuclei for white settlers, and their food is stored. The Indians hang round all those posts. So long as they can get the white men to feed them they will stay there. The mass of the population in the North-West is composed of young men, and the Indians hang round the posts because they want to stay there, and their women want to stay there, and because the Indians sell their women, and the greatest amount of demoralisation goes on in consequence of the degraded habits of the Indians, the barbarous and savage habits of the Indians. It is the policy, and it will be the policy of the Government so long as I have anything to do with this Department, to see that the Indians go on their reserves and work there, and the Government will then fulfil the treaty obligations and even more. By strictly carrying out that policy it has been in a degree successful. The Indians are going on their reserves, and this year the accounts are much more favourable as to the number of Indians on the reserves, the quantity of land broken and the quantity of roots and grain put in. The Indian will allow himself to run almost to death's door rather than move from the place where he is. It was only because with Christian feelings we could not see them starve that they were given quarter rations. That is the policy of the Government, and it is the correct policy. The committee must remember that the Government are under no obligations to furnish food to the Indians. He has got his hand and his head; he has the capacity for work if he chooses. The white immigrant goes there and he must "root hog or die"; he must work or starve.

Mr. PATERSON (Brant). We shut him up on a certain reserve?

Sir JOHN A. MACDONALD. The reserves are enormous.

Mr. PATERSON (Brant). We shut them up on reserves, and the reports of the hon. gentleman's own agents show that they have lost their crops through frost.

Sir JOHN A. MACDONALD. The Indians, by the strict, stern rule, are settling on their reserves. Why, Sir, before the buffalo disappeared, we gave no food to the Indians. Hon. gentlemen opposite, when they were in power, did not give food to the Indians. There were treaty obligations; a certain number of cattle and implements; a certain amount of seed grain and so on, were all given under treaty obligations, and that was all required to be given and all that was given until the sudden disappearance of the buffalo. Canada, or the Canadian Government, or the Canadian people, was under no obligation to feed these Indians, but as Christian men they could not allow them to starve; they supplied them with food; and every vote we asked for the purpose of feeding these Indians was opposed by hon. gentlemen on the other side, and especially by the hon. member for Bothwell, who said we were pauperising the Indians, and that they should work as well as the white men. Votes were taken year after year to feed the poor Indians while they were changing their habits of life, and changing their modes of acquiring their food. The buffalo was gone, and we fed them—sparingly, but sufficiently—until, by degrees, they could be got to go upon their reserves. I state distinctly that there has been a great amount of benevolence with prodigality or profusion; there has been great tenderness to the Indians. Although the Indian will keep himself in a starving condition, there has been the greatest tenderness on the part of Parliament to put money at the disposal of the Government, and there has been a careful and judicious disposition of the vote to the Indian, without letting him feel that he had enough for himself and his family without working. The great trouble is to get the Indians to work, for they can work and they are now working. But if they are told by pseudo-philanthropists, by men who are led more by their hearts than by their heads, that they are suffering, that it is the duty of the Government not to allow them to starve, then they will never work...

[Canada, House of Commons, Debates, 2 June 1886, pp. 1760-1761]

Preparation for Enfranchisement

If the Indian is to become a source of profit to the country it is clear that he must be amalgamated with the white population. Before this can be done he must not only be trained to some occupation, the pursuit of which will enable him to support himself, but he must be imbued with the white man's spirit and impregnated by his ideas. The end in view in the policy adopted for the treatment of our wards is to lead them, step by step, to provide for their own requirements, through their industry, and while doing so, to inculcate a spirit of self-reliance and independence which will fit them for enfranchisement, and the enjoyment of all the privileges, as well as the responsibilities of citizenship. For such a position, however, they must be gradually and carefully prepared; and if, as is understood to be the case, our neighbours are going from one extreme to the other, and freely enfranchising Indians, without the necessary preparation, the result will be anxiously looked for—for, if successful, the Indian problem will be more readily solved. No doubt the very system of banding Indians together on reservations militates against their conversion into citizens; however, a system which will supply every desideratum cannot in the circumstances of the case be devised, and it seems better to keep them together, for the purpose of training them for mergence with the whites, than to disperse them unprotected among communities where they could not hold their own, and would speedily be down-trodden and debauched.

[Canada, Sessional Paper (No. 12) Part I (1890), p. 165]

The Department of Indian Affairs and Morality

With regard to estimating the condition of morality, great care must be taken in the selection of a standard for purposes of comparison, and there is no direction in which it would be more unreasonable to gauge the progress of our Indians against the development of Christian civilization at the conclusion of the nineteenth century.

The Indian in his untutored condition probably has as well developed a sense of right and wrong, or what we call conscience, as any other class of man left to the unassisted guidance of his own nature. It is observed that the ideas as to what constitutes right and wrong entertained by the Indian are formed or deeply affected by his environment. For example, the Indian when he roamed the plains in his natural condition deemed it an entirely praiseworthy act to crawl through the grass as dawn was breaking and steal horses from the camp of another tribe. Yet theft between members of the same tribe was almost unknown and was regarded with far greater reprobation than in a civilized community. A wider consideration of the effects of the Indian's primitive condition on the development of his code of ethics would serve to explain why, when in contact with civilization he has been found to be so law-abiding on the whole, as also the direction taken by his errors in so far as he is prone to go astray. As I had occasion to point out at some length when reporting a year or two ago, the first effects of contact with civilization upon the physical condition of Indians are in some ways prejudicial, and the same thing may be predicted with regard to their moral state. The strongest factors in the improvement of the moral tone are, of course, education and example, and naturally the most powerful influence is that exerted by the missionaries of the various Christian denominations, who have done and are still doing so much to elevate the Indian. It is true that the Indians of Canada, at any rate those who have been overtaken by civilization within comparatively recent years, have been singularly fortunate, inasmuch as they have been taken hold of by the government and at the very outset protected, as far as possible, against debauchery through drink, and from being defrauded of their property.

Through time the Indians by direct education and contact with an improved class of settlement gradually learn to distinguish and thus get the moral benefits of civilization and improve their social tone in all directions.

It is obvious, therefore, that the moral condition of the Indians will vary in accordance with the length and intimacy of their intercourse with civilization, and, that under the most favourable circumstances, improvement must be slow. At the present day, notwithstanding the length of time during which the Six Nation Indians have been under missionary and other civilizing influences, about onefourth of their number remains avowedly pagan. Of course such paganism as theirs has been greatly modified through contact with civilization, but on the other hand, it undoubtedly not only affects their moral conduct but has a certain influence upon those of the professedly Christian members of the band.

The form of paganism which prevails among the Indians who have not been overtaken by settlement, nor reached in advance thereof by missionary effort, or who, like the Bloods, in Treaty No.7, have apparently resisted influences brought to bear upon them, is accompanied by far grosser vice, although even they have

The Department of Indian Affairs Displays "Progress": Father and Children Attending Qu'Appelle Industrial School. *[National Archives of Canada, C37113]*

reached the stage of being ashamed of flagrantly immoral practices and conceal them so successfully as to make it very difficult to ascertain the extent to which they still exist.

Speaking with such absence of exactness as the nature of the subject alone admits of, it may be said that as a consequence of their tribal customs there is a common hereditary tendency among them to what we would regard as laxity with regard to the marriage bond and the relationship between the sexes, and this laxity becomes more pronounced according to conditions hereinabove described, until a stage of gross vice is reached. On the other hand, there are communities in which an excellent tone prevails and it is no uncommon thing to find the Indians themselves requesting the intervention of the department in cases in which individual members may be guilty of conspicuous immorality.

The Sun Dance, the Tamanawas and the Potlach festivals help to keep alive habits and practices which are most objectionable, but, as they have their religious and economic features, the department's policy has been to suppress the worst features and wait for time and other influences to do the rest. This policy is having the desired effect as fast as could have been expected, although sometimes the embers which had been thought to be pretty well dead will flicker up fitfully, and some Indians who have abandoned these dances and festivals revive them for a year or so.

Among communities in the older provinces within easy range of places where liquor is retailed the majority of the Indians under the fostering protection of the provisions of the Indian Act have learnt to keep aloof from intoxicants, and among them the temperance sentiment is steadily growing. Among outlying bands the position is different and liquor is smuggled in by traders and others, resulting in orgies at certain seasons. In Manitoba and the North-west Territories the greatest trouble in this direction is experienced among the Indians who take hay or fire-wood into the settlements for sale or work in the vicinity of railroad towns and find half-breeds on the watch for them to take their earnings and convert them into liquor for them.

In the prohibition days, the North-west Mounted Police could, and did watch the points at which the smugglers made their ingress, but under the changed conditions they are comparatively helpless. In British Columbia the majority of the bands are at a distance from temptation, but the Indians who go to work at the mines and canneries are constantly exposed to it, and the constabulary force does not seem sufficiently strong to enforce the law in this respect. However, the department does all it can, and, without doubt, much is being accomplished in the way of restraint and the building up of character upon which after all the main dependence must be placed. From anything in the nature of serious crime there has been even a more marked absence than usual.

[Canada, *"Annual Report of the Department of Indian Affairs for the Year Ended 30 June 1900,"* Sessional Papers *No. 27 (64 Victoria A. 1901), pp. xxxi-xxxii]*

A Cry from an Indian Wife

My Forest Brave, my Red-skin love, farewell;
We may not meet to-morrow; who can tell
What mighty ills befall our little band,
Or what you'll suffer from the white man's hand?
Here is your knife! I thought 'twas sheathed for aye.
No roaming bison calls for it to-day;
No hide of prairie cattle will it maim;
The plains are bare, it seeks a nobler game:
'Twill drink the life-blood of a soldier host.
Go; rise and strike, no matter what the cost.
Yet stay. Revolt not at the Union Jack,
Nor raise Thy hand against this stripling pack
Of white-faced warriors, marching West to quell
Our fallen tribe that rises to rebel.
They all are young and beautiful and good;
Curse to the war that drinks their harmless blood.
Curse to the fate that brought them from the East
To be our chiefs—to make our nation least
That breathes the air of this vast continent.
Still their new rule and council is well meant.
They but forget we Indians owned the land
From ocean unto ocean; that they stand
Upon a soil that centuries agone
Was our sole kingdom and our right alone.
They never think how they would feel to-day,
If some great nation came from far away,
Wresting their country from their hapless braves,
Giving what they gave us—but wars and graves.
Then go and strike for liberty and life,
And bring back honour to your Indian wife.
Your wife? Ah, what of that, who cares for me?
Who pities my poor love and agony?
What white-robed priest prays for your safety here,
As prayer is said for every volunteer
That swells the ranks that Canada sends out?
Who prays for vict'ry for the Indian scout?
Who prays for our poor nation lying low?
None—therefore take your tomahawk and go.
My heart may break and burn into its core,
But I am strong to bid you go to war.
Yet stay, my heart is not the only one
That grieves the loss of husband and of son;

Think of the mothers o'er the inland seas;
Think of the pale-faced maiden on her knees;
One pleads her God to guard some sweet-faced child
That marches on toward the North-West wild.
The other prays to shield her love from harm,
To strengthen his young, proud uplifted arm.
Ah, how her white face quivers thus to think,
Your tomahawk his life's best blood will drink.
She never thinks of my wild aching breast,
Nor prays for your dark face and eagle crest
Endangered by a thousand rifle balls,
My heart the target if my warrior falls.
O! coward self I hesitate no more;
Go forth, and win the glories of the war.
Go forth, nor bend to greed of white men's hands,
By right, by birth we Indians own these lands,
Though starved, crushed, plundered, lies our nation low...
Perhaps the white man's God has willed it so.

[E. Pauline Johnson, Flint and Feather *(Toronto: Musson Book Co., 1912),*
pp. 17-19]

Chief Elliot Addresses the Ontario Historical Society

Admirable arrangements had been made by the Brantford Historical Society for the trip to the Council House of the Six Nations Indians at Oshweken.... On arriving at their destination the delegates were welcomed by the enlivening strains of the splendid brass band of the reserve.

Chief David John's Address

A special meeting was convened in the Council House at 10:30 o'clock, when the Indian Council was open in due form by Chief David John, Speaker of the Fire Keepers speaking in the Onondaga dialect:

"We are thankful to the Great Spirit for allowing such a large number of the chiefs to be present in good health to conduct the affairs of the Nation. We are pleased to welcome our distinguished visitors, the members of the Ontario Historical Society, and trust that their visit will be a happy one and that they will carry away with them pleasant recollections of the Six Nations.

"In the second place we thank the Great Spirit that there is no sickness of an alarming nature on the Reserve, that nothing of a disastrous nature has occurred since the last Council meeting, and that the affairs of the Nation are prosperous.

"And in conclusion we are pleased to see the Superintendent with us in his usual good health. We desire the chiefs to proceed with the business of the

Council with all earnestness and bring it to a successful and speedy conclusion."

Chief John then laid the wampum belt consisting of six strings of wampum, upon the table and the Council was then open and ready for business.

Address Read by Chief John W.M. Elliott (Deyenhehken, Double Life)

Chief J.W.M. Elliott read an address of welcome to the officers and delegates of the Ontario Historical Society, which was replied to by President Williams. The Chief addressed the Society as follows:

"Mr Chairman, Ladies and Gentlemen:

On behalf of the Six Nations' Council and of the Six Nations, we, the undersigned committee having been duly appointed at a meeting of the Six Nations' Council, beg to tender to you delegates of the Ontario Historical Society, our heartiest welcome and extend to you the right hand of friendship to our reserve.

"We feel that we can place you in the category of true friends, and we are pleased to welcome you and trust that your visit amongst us to-day may prove to be of interest and pleasure to you as well as profitable to us all. It is almost needless for us to point out to the well-informed members of the Ontario Historical Society the status of the Six Nations Indians. Yet in this modern epoch, it may be pardonable on our part to readvert to some of the achievements of the Six Nations in the past history of the North American continent. In the first place it may be a matter of interest to point out the fact that the Six Nations had a systematic government of its own long before the white men ever came upon the North American continent. The Six Nations Confederacy was formed one hundred years before Columbus discovered America... The confederacy was formed for the purpose of mutual protection of all those who took advantage of the league, and was composed at the time of its inauguration of the following Nations: Mohawks, Senecas, Onondagas, Cayugas, and Oneidas, and latterly the Tuscaroras joined the league, and other Nations followed. The Six Nations by means of this league became the most powerful nation and subdued nation after nation, and the name Six Nations became a synonym of dread amongst all other Indian nations of this continent. They conquered the great Neutral Nation and confiscated from these people this part of Canada in which our reserve is now situated. They absorbed the remnants of all the nations whom they conquered and built up an Indian empire which, but for the advent of the white man, would to-day have been great and mighty. They held dominion over a great territory embodying the states bordering on the St. Lawrence River, as well as those territories adjacent to the Niagara River and the Great Lakes, Ontario, Erie, Huron, from the outer confines of what is now New York and other adjacent states to Detroit, and beyond as historians state to the Mississippi.

"The Six Nations fought valiantly for the British Crown and the supremacy of British institutions against the French in the early history of this country at a time when Great Britain was weak and striving with a powerful European nation for a foothold in North America. They proved themselves loyal to their compact with the Imperial authorities and in the Revolutionary war with what is now the United States, in 1775-6, the Six Nations again took side with Britain, and again in 1812-14, they went forward in the firing line at Queenston Heights, Lundy's Lane and Niagara and in all the principal engagements fought at that time. The Six Nations lost their territories in the United States as a result of their having taken sides with the British in 1775-6 and in compensation for the losses which they sustained were granted this reserve upon the Grand River by General Haldimand, with the expressed will and pleasure of King George III. The Six Nations have ever been proud of their connection with Great Britain in the past as it has kept faith with them and honored its pledges made to them; but it is only 99 years ago since our forefathers were shedding their life's blood in defence of Canada and the people of Canada, and today in 1911, this same people find that their treaty rights granted to them together with this reserve, by the Imperial Government and the King of Great Britain, are being infringed upon and set aside by the Canadian Parliament in the drastic and unconstitutional amendments of the Indian Act. By our treaty rights as expressed in our deeds to this reserve, we were to enjoy these lands in the most free and ample manner in accordance with our several customs and usages, and we were to be free and immune from all fines and enfeoffments by the Crown. In these documents we are described as allies to the British Crown. Britain kept faith with us and honored its pledges to us, but the Canadian Government has gradually by intrusion robbed us of our conceded rights until to-day it has by its enactments reduced us to the state of minors. It has enacted laws which are remarkable for inconsistency. In one part of the code an Indian is held to be a man (in marriage) and in another part he is held as a minor (in the liquor clauses). It has enacted discriminating laws against us who are known as allies in our treaty with the Imperial Government. In the Indian Act we are cited together with the other Indians of Canada. As the Six Nations hold an unique position apart and different from any other Indian nation in Canada, in that they fought for their land rights and privileges, there should be special legislation made for them, and they should, as allies of the British Crown, have some say in the making of these laws, in the same manner as is the conceded right of the ordinary British subject. It has been for centuries the proud boast of Great Britain that its word once pledged is never broken. In all good faith and confidence the Six Nations entered into a league with Great Britain for mutual protection in war in the earliest period of the history of this country, and England has kept faith with us; but we are surprised to-day to find the Canadian Government by intrusion trampling upon our rights and privileges to such an extent that the Indian is reduced to a condition approaching slavery that the line of demarcation is hard to define. If the Six Nations chiefs and warriors were men enough to fight for Canada and the supremacy of the British Crown upon this North American continent against the... French leaders in the 17th century, and again in 1775-6 and

1812-15, and the British recognized them as a strong and valiant type of man-hood, why should the legislators of this country now place them in the category of minors?

"We trust in conclusion that the Ontario Historical Society will use its influence in advocating our cause, that our rights and privileges are not infringed upon and that we get full measure of our rights and privileges conceded by the Imperial authorities and the King of Great Britain, and that the pledged word and honor of Great Britain to us will be observed by the Parliament of Canada, and that it will cease to impeach the pledged honor of Great Britain and thereby accord us our rights, and step off the British flag. We know that many of you are descended from great, true and loyal United Empire stock and that your forefathers fought side by side with ours in the defence of this country, and, like our forefathers, they sacrificed their homes and their all in the United States for our King and country. We, their descendants, therefore, after the lapse of a century, meet here today in friendly confab, and discuss the achievements and traditions of our forefathers and our country. As they were comrades in arms in the fighting line, let us to-day fraternize as common brothers in peace and endeavor to accord to all the freedom which the British constitution grants to all under the British flag.

"In conclusion, God Bless the Rose of England, the Thistle of Scotland, and the Shamrock of old Ireland, and the Maple of Canada forever."

President William replied briefly, expressing the appreciation of the visitors at the cordiality of the welcome given them by their British fellow-subjects, the members of the Six Nations. It was indeed a pleasure to visit them in their homes and to see all sides the evidence of prosperity and progress that they were enjoying. The fine farms, the splendid homes and buildings, the churches and the school, which would be a credit to any town or village, were, to the members of the Ontario Historical Society, indicative of the advance made by the descendants of the first occupants of the land. These things manifested a determination to keep pace with modern times and maintain a position that would be an honor and credit to members of the Confederacy...

While the members of the Ontario Historical Society learned with pleasure of their past history and rejoiced with them at the present position, they regretted the one fly in the ointment, the grievance so forcibly and so ably presented by Chief Elliott. This was probably new to many and in response to the appeal made in the address presented, it would be placed before the Council..., when it would be carefully considered.

[*Ontario Historical Society,* Annual Report *1911, pp. 42-48*]

Section B
Maintaining Order

World War I marked an important shift in attitudes toward Native peoples, as their significant participation in the military raised questions about citizenship. The 1920s reports of the Deputy Superintendent General for Indian Affairs went out of their way to educate Canadians and their politicians about contemporary economic, health, and education conditions among Native peoples. Through the memoirs of Isabelle Knockwood, a Mi'kmaq who attended the Nova Scotian Shubenacadie Residential School in the 1930s, we see that residential schools, a strategy which moved Native children from their own cultural environment, inflicted pain, yet they also encouraged resistance.

The Canadian Indian and Citizenship

In a very logical letter to an American newspaper the Rev. Red Fox Skinhurhu (a full blooded Blackfoot Indian) urges the cause of his people to full citizenship in the United States. As in Canada the aborigine of the United States is a ward of the country and as such has no citizenship rights—he not being supposed to have sufficient intelligence to take up its responsibilities. If ever there was any suspicion in the minds of the present generation that the "Red" man was still the degenerate the framers of the Indian laws in both countries would have us believe, the splendid patriotism shown by him in this war of liberty and justice has entirely eliminated it. In Canada long before conscription came into force practically every single Red man of military age volunteered for military service—a record that was not near equalled by any other race in the country, either white or colored. Surely then he has the right to ask the question—if the Red man can fight why can't he vote?

It has always seemed an anomaly to us that any foreigner, be he black or white or yellow, can become a citizen of Canada after five years residence—without any examination as to his qualifications, which if given would have barred many present citizens—but that the real Native is penned up in reservations, without a voice in his own government, because in the early days of the white man's occupation of the country, he fell a victim to his conqueror's worst trait of character, drink, which he mistakenly thought produced the valor that overcame himself. The Dominion Government does not seem to realize that the very schooling given in the reservations has educated the Red man to a far more advanced stage of civilization than that of many foreigners now domiciled in Canada.

Now that peace has come after over four years of bloody war in which the Red man has taken his full share, the least the country can do, if even as a recompense for his sacrifice, is to give him the full privilege of citizenship, and we don't know of any other race that would make better citizens. After all no man is fit to become a citizen of Canada unless he is prepared to fight for her, and in this the Canadian Indian has set a splendid example to us all—and in particular to those many Europeans who have enjoyed our hospitality and protection, but who have done little or nothing, during the last four years to warrant that protection.

The Canadian Indian, in common with his American brother, has in this war proved his right to citizenship, and we have no right to keep him from it.

[Canadian Municipal Review, *January 1919, p. 13*]

Report of the Deputy Superintendent General of Indian Affairs, 1918-1919

Ottawa, December 1, 1919.
Hon. Arthur Meighen, K.C., B.A.,
Superintendent General of Indian Affairs,
Ottawa.

Sir,—I have the honour to submit the report of the Department of Indian Affairs for the year ended March 31, 1919.

POPULATION.

A quinquennial census is taken of the Indian population, the last census having been taken in 1917, prior to which a census was taken annually. The records of the department indicate that there is a slow but steady increase in the Indian population from year to year.

The following table shows the Indian population by provinces according to the census of 1917:—

Province—	Population
Alberta	8,837
British Columbia	25,694
Manitoba	11,583
New Brunswick	1,846
Nova Scotia	2,031
Ontario	26,411
Prince Edward Island	292
Quebec	13,366
Saskatchewan	10,646
Northwest Territories	3,764
Yukon	1,528
Total, Indian population	105,998
Eskimos	3,296
Total, number of Indians and Eskimos	109,294

...

AGRICULTURE

During the past two years the Department of Indian Affairs has shown great activity in opening up the reserves and developing their natural resources. In all the settled parts of the Dominion great care has been taken to encourage the Indians in agricultural pursuits and to afford them instruction in up-to-date methods of farming. The results of this policy are evidenced in larger and better crops on the great majority of the reserves.

In cases where reserves are too large to be cultivated by the number of Indians located on them, the surplus area is leased to whites for farming and grazing purposes, and in this manner extensive tracts that had hitherto lain idle are now being utilized...

Prairie Provinces

In view of the fact that only a small portion of land on the Indian reserves in the prairie provinces was under cultivation, and as these reserves are for the most part situate in the productive areas of the three provinces, it was considered necessary to take measures to have these idle lands brought under cultivation, and to organize the staff of the Department of Indian Affairs in the said provinces in the most advantageous manner possible for the effective carrying out of such measures. Accordingly, on February 16, 1918, an Order in Council was passed appointing Mr. W. M. Graham, Inspector of Indian agencies for the South Saskatchewan inspectorate, as Commissioner for the Department of Indian Affairs in Manitoba, Saskatchewan and Alberta, with the following duties and powers:—

(a) To make proper arrangements with the Indians for the leasing of reserve lands, which may be needed for grazing, for cultivation, or for other purposes, and for the compensation to be paid therefor;

(b) To formulate a policy for each reserve;

(c) To issue directions and instructions to all inspectors, agents and employees in furtherance of that policy;

(d) To make purchases and engage or dismiss any extra or temporary employees, and market the yield of grain and live stock, and in effect to have the sole management of this work subject to the approval of the Superintendent General of Indian Affairs, to whom he shall report fully at close and regular intervals;

(e) To make recommendations to the Superintendent General of Indian Affairs, looking to the greater efficiency of such of the Indian service in the said provinces as is not related to the said special work.

The greater production work on the Indian reserves is subdivided into three distinct branches, as follows:—

1. The establishment and operation of Government Greater Production Farms.—Mr. Graham began to make arrangements for the establishment of these farms as soon as possible after his appointment, and the work was well under way

early in the spring of 1918. Complete up-to-date equipment was secured at the most advantageous prices, and the necessary buildings, such as bunk-houses, cook-houses, stables, etc., were erected.

2. Farming by Individual Indians.—Every effort has been and is being made by the officers of the department, under the supervision of Mr. Graham, to stimulate, encourage and instruct the Indians in order that they may place larger areas under cultivation and materially increase their crops. This work has on the whole met with a great measure of success.

3. Farming and Grazing Leases.—As has been stated hereinabove, Mr. Graham was empowered by the Order in Council to make the necessary arrangements with the Indians for the leasing of reserve land to whites for farming and grazing purposes, in order to assist the greater production campaign. Mr. Graham has been particularly energetic in exercising the powers thus conferred upon him, and a large number of leases were granted and the result was a very valuable increase in the national food supply...

THE INDIANS AND THE GREAT WAR

In this year of peace the Indians of Canada may look with just pride upon the part played by them in the great war both at home and on the field of battle. They have well and nobly upheld the loyal traditions of their gallant ancestors who rendered invaluable service to the British cause in 1776 and in 1812, and have added thereto a heritage of deathless honour which is an example and an inspiration for their descendants. According to the official records of the department more than four thousand Indians enlisted for active service with the Canadian Expeditionary forces. This number represents approximately thirty-five per cent of the Indian male population of military age in the nine provinces, and it must be remembered, moreover, that there were undoubtedly cases of Indian enlistment which were not reported to the department. The Indian soldiers gave an excellent account of themselves at the front, and their officers have commended them most highly for their courage, intelligence, efficiency, stamina and discipline. In daring and intrepidity they were second to none and their performance is a ringing rebuttal to the familiar assertion that the red man has deteriorated. The fine record of the Indians in the great war appears in a peculiarly favourable light when it is remembered that their services were absolutely voluntary, as they were specially exempted from the operation of the Military Service Act, and that they were prepared to give their lives for their country without compulsion or even the fear of compulsion. It must also be borne in mind that a large part of the Indian population is located in remote and inaccessible locations, are unacquainted with the English language and were, therefore, not in a position to understand the character of the war, its cause or effect. It is, therefore, a remarkable fact that the percentage of enlistments among the Indians is fully equal to that among other sections of the community and indeed far above the average in a number of instances. As an inevitable result of the large enlistment among them and of their share in the thick of the fighting, the casualties among them were very heavy, and the Indians in common with their fellow countrymen of the white race must mourn the loss of many of their most promising young men. The Indians are especially susceptible to tuberculosis, and many of their soldiers who escaped the shells and bullets of the enemy succumbed to this dreaded disease upon their return to Canada as a result of the hardships to which they were exposed at the front...

Red Cross Work
The Indian women on many of the reserves formed Red Cross societies and Patriotic leagues. These organizations corresponded to similar societies in white communities. They carried on their work with energy and efficiency and were successful in the accomplishment of excellent results. They made bandages and provided various comforts for the soldiers, knitted socks, sweaters and mufflers, and also raised money for patriotic purposes by holding card parties, bazaars, and other social entertainments. The making of baskets and beadwork is a Native industry among the Indians, and the Indian women found a novel and very successful means of securing funds for war needs by the sale of these wares.

[Deputy Superintendent General of Indian Affairs, "Annual Report of the Department of Indian Affairs for the Year Ended 31 March 1919," Sessional Papers No. 27 (10 George VA 1920), 8, 10, 13-14, 25-26]

Report of the Deputy Superintendent General of Indian Affairs, 1925-1926

It cannot be too frequently stated that the Indian is self-supporting and that only those Indians are entirely dependent who belong to an indigent or improvident class which is also found in all white communities. The department must, in its capacity of guardian, take the place of all provincial or municipal organizations for the relief of such a class, and the expenditure in this direction is undertaken as much for the protection of the white people as for the benefit of the Indian. Epidemic conditions of disease are dangerous, no matter where they originate. The white population has a vital interest in the expenditure for the prevention of tuberculosis and for treatment of venereal diseases. This expenditure is upon the increase, as the fact becomes clear that these diseases among Indians must be dealt with by modern scientific methods.

INDIAN HEALTH PROBLEMS
Among the many important duties of the department, those associated with the conservation of the health of Indians must take a prominent place. Beginning in the residential schools, every effort is made to instil in the minds of the children at least a rudimentary knowledge of hygiene, particularly as related to the prevention of tuberculosis. The reserves in settled communities have physicians on part-time service, who come at the call of the agent, and in several large reserves the department

employs permanent physicians whose whole time is devoted to the work. Indians of outlying bands who gather at stated times to receive the annual treaty payments are given medical attention by a doctor who accompanies the Indian agent.

The health problem is assuming a very serious aspect among the Indians of the more outlying districts, particularly in the northern parts of Alberta, Saskatchewan, Manitoba, Ontario, and Quebec, where the question is closely associated with their economic condition. These Indians of the unsettled or sparsely settled regions are still in a primitive state and almost solely dependent upon hunting and trapping for their livelihood. In former times the Indians had a virtual monopoly of the chase and their physical wellbeing was reasonably assured. Now the situation is entirely altered. In recent years there has been an influx of white trappers, who are constantly moving northward in increasing numbers to an extent that is alarming from the point of view of the Indians. These white trappers are more astute and energetic than the aborigines, who cannot withstand keen competition to which they are utterly unaccustomed. Furthermore, it is the tendency of the whites to trap out an area until the game is completely exhausted, and then move on elsewhere, leaving the original Native population in a state of destitution. The effect of these new hardships upon the health of the Indians concerned is already becoming evident…

One of the great difficulties encountered in the past has been the fact that the older Indians are inclined to place their faith in the Indian medicine men, and refuse treatment by white doctors. The members of the medical staff of the department report, however, that they are gradually overcoming this difficulty, and that hospitals maintained on the various reserves are being more freely and confidently used by the Indians. Another difficulty is that even if willing to submit themselves for medical treatment, Indians as a general rule are very negligent in carrying out the instructions of the physician. Under such circumstances it is difficult to make headway, but where the inroads of disease have been checked it is considered good work has been done.

In past reports it has been pointed out that the great foe of Indians is tuberculosis. The struggle against this disease is most arduous, not alone owing to its prevalence but to the conditions under which Indians live, and it is extremely difficult to extend to this people any prophylactic system. The assertion may safely be made that Indians who have been for years in contact with civilization begin to show a certain resistance to this disease, and methods which have been successful in white communities can be more readily applied to them; but it becomes extremely difficult to apply the modern, scientific methods of prevention and cure to the nomadic element of the aborigines, where the Indians gain their living by hunting and fishing and where their habitations are primitive and inadequate. It is a known fact that some Indian bands entirely remote from civilization have displayed no trace of tuberculosis, but even slight contact with civilization sets up an epidemic condition which spreads with alarming celerity.

We have enlisted the interest and co-operation of a group of medical men who have specialized in methods of combating tuberculosis in all its phases.

Under their direction certain investigations are being carried out on the British Columbia coast among the fishing Indians, which will make available much interesting and valuable data which it is hoped will enable us to formulate a definite departmental policy.

As health conditions among the Indians affect the welfare of the contiguous white population, the health question as a whole is one of extreme importance, which the department has never sought to minimize. While generous expenditures have been made for tubercular Indians, these expenditures have been made largely in an effort to check the disease and to mitigate the suffering incident thereto. The cost of adopting an extensive system for the suppression of tuberculosis amongst the Indians would undoubtedly be very great, but until it becomes possible to remove the existing financial handicap, we cannot hope to take the radical steps necessary toward the elimination of tuberculosis.

The staff of travelling nurses, organized some years ago, has proved to be of great value. These nurses make regular inspection trips to the various agencies in several of the provinces, and it is their duty to make a thorough examination of all children in Indian schools, as well as to visit the homes on the reserves, giving assistance and advice. Simple talks on sanitation, diet and home-making are given, and many of the Indian women gratefully accept the advice of the nurses regarding the care of their children. Baby clinics are held wherever possible, and on some of the reserves, in addition to monthly clinics, baby shows are being established with a view to stimulating the interest of Indian parents in proper methods of caring for their children. Indian women and girls are encouraged by the nurses and field matrons to cultivate gardens, and they are instructed in methods of canning fruit and vegetables for the winter months. By such simple instruction in the art of living, coupled with the care given by the Indian agents and medical attendants, the health of the Indian people must be improved. Although it is realized that their condition still leaves much to be desired, it should be remembered that the true standard by which to judge a people undergoing evolution is, not the height they have reached, but the distance they have advanced...

ESKIMO AFFAIRS

During the session 1922-23 an amendment to the Indian Act provided that the Eskimos of Canada should be brought under the charge of the Superintendent General of Indian Affairs. These people, who, according to the best available census statistics, now number something over 6,000, were not, previous to this enactment, officially under the supervision of any government department. The Department of Indian Affairs, however, annually afforded them relief and medical attendance.

The Eskimos are widely scattered across the northern area of Canada, and only once a year can supplies be shipped in to certain central points, from which distribution is made by means of dog-sleds. The steamship which is sent annually by the Northwest Territories Branch of the Department of the Interior to Baffin Land and posts on the Hudson strait in Ungava, has proved to be of great value in the distribution of supplies to these points, and the Hudson's Bay Company boats, which also make annual trips to this isolated country, serve portions of Ungava and the Northwest Territories...

Supplies of relief rations, to be issued when necessary, have been sent to Mounted Police posts and to missionaries throughout the Arctic, and in ordering these supplies, special attention was given to the fact that foodstuffs containing an unusually high vitamine element are essential in the north. This department was fortunate in securing from the Canadian National Parks Branch of the Interior Department a quantity of slightly defective buffalo skins for distribution to destitute Natives, as well as a supply of pemmican made from buffalo meat, which is a strong and wholesome food particularly well suited for use in the north. It is felt that this and other highly nutritive relief rations will help to relieve the situation in districts where the depletion of the natural food supply has sometimes resulted in starvation. It is not anticipated that such relief will be necessary for any indefinite period, as the fishing operations which are being encouraged should gradually overcome the existing conditions to a very large extent.

It has not been possible to undertake extensive educational work in this inaccessible country, but the department has given assistance to Eskimo Mission schools at Aklavik, Shingle Point and Herschell Island in the MacKenzie District; and to the Lake Harbour and Cumberland Gulf schools in Baffin Land. It was reported that many of the Natives in the more remote districts have no conception of the laws of their country, it being taken as a matter of course by them that a man should resent injury or protect his property by killing the offender. Simply worded posters in the Eskimo dialects prevailing in the eastern and western Arctic areas, explaining the law in this connection, have been distributed in districts recommended by the Mounted Police and the missionaries, with a view to assisting in the gradual education of these Natives in adapting themselves to standards utterly foreign to their past mode of life...

EDUCATION

A special effort was made during the year to secure efficiency in both day and residential schools for Indian children. Many fully qualified teachers and instructors were engaged and much equipment was purchased with a view to better training for the younger generation of the department's wards. Parliamentary appropriation for the fiscal year ended March 31, 1926, was $1,918.000—nearly as large as the 1923-24 record vote for Indian education.

Residential school activity was particularly encouraging. The four Canadian churches, that are associated with us in the conduct of these institutions, have all adopted a measure of centralized control which, of course, makes for efficiency. This type of school offers both academic and vocational instruction; and the aim is to graduate Indian boys and girls so equipped that they will go to their respective communities prepared for lives of general usefulness...

The co-operation of the churches in the management of these residential schools is shown by the following table:

Roman Catholic	40	residential	schools:	enrolment,		3,514
Church of England	20	"	"	"		1,448
Methodist	7	"	"	"		794
Presbyterian	7	"	"	"		571
Total	74	residential	schools:	enrolment,		6,327

(As the figures are for the fiscal year ended March 31, 1926, they do not take into account a recent church union.)

The residential school enrolment by provinces for the fiscal year was as follows:-

Ontario	12	institutions with	1,094	pupils
Manitoba	10	"	"	1,024 pupils
Saskatchewan	12	"	"	1,290 pupils
Alberta	19	"	"	1,180 pupils
North West Territories	3	"	"	167 pupils
British Columbia	16	"	"	1,506 pupils
Yukon	2	"	"	66 pupils
Total	74	institutions with	6,327	pupils

Two hundred and fifty-four Indian day schools and 16 combined schools were in operation during the year. The Indian day schools are situated on reserves and are solely for Indian children. The combined schools are managed and financed jointly by the Department of Indian Affairs and local school boards and they are attended by both Indian and white pupils.

[Deputy Superintendent of Indian Affairs, "Annual Report of the Department of Indian Affairs for the Year Ended 31 March 1926," Sessional Papers No. 27 (Ottawa, 1927), 7-8, 10-11, 12-14, 15]

Isabelle Knockwood Remembers the Shubenacadie Residential School

As children at the school, we always had the feeling that the nuns and especially the principal, Father Mackey, had absolute power over us. But neither we nor our parents knew at the time that when they signed the paper the Indian Agent gave them they were appointing the school's principal as their children's legal guardian even during the summer vacations.

I was five years old and considered "under age" when I was admitted in 1936, so my parents wrote a "special reasons" letter to the Department outlining why I should be accepted: "I find it difficult to provide her with warm clothing, particularly as I am not able to work due to ill health. It will be a healthier environment for her. She will be with her (seven-year-old) sister who can help her in the work." It was signed by my father, though I think he had help with the wording as it was not in his handwriting. I knew nothing about this letter until over fifty years later when I came upon it in the Nova Scotia Public Archives and felt shocked to find that what my father had written as a pleading letter should be a public document for all to see. I also noticed my mother's careful and laborious handwriting of the address on the letter squeezed in at one side of the tiny scrap of paper. The fragmentary document spoke to me about my parents' struggle to teach themselves to read and write. My sister Rosie remembers something of the pain with which my parents reached the decision: "I remember when we were getting ready to go to school. Mom was combing my hair and she had tears in her eyes. She didn't want us to be separated."

Although Father Mackey was given such extensive legal powers, he had trouble with children not wanting to return to the school after summer vacations. Records show that every September he would send a list of missing children to the Department of Indian Affairs asking them to make arrangements for their immediate return.

The Department would send letters out to the Indian agents reminding them that when the parents signed the admission form they had given Father Mackey guardianship over their children even when they were home on vacation. My parents never understood this, which suggests that the Indian agents did not go out of their way to explain the real state of affairs. During the summer vacations and for the two Christmas vacations when we were allowed home, in our own and our parents' minds, we were released from the school's control. Some of the correspondence between Father Mackey and various Indian agents suggests that even some of the agents may not have known how matters stood. In November of 1936 Clarence Spinney, who was the Indian Agent for the Kentville area, wrote to Father Mackey about Pauline Phillips who had been admitted to the Victoria General Hospital in Halifax:

> It would appear to me that Pauline is going to be sick for some time and I do not think the hospital at Halifax is the place for her and I can have this little girl brought from the hospital there and have her removed to the hospital here in Berwick...I feel sure she will not be able to go back to school again this fall and winter and her grandfather Isaac Phillips has asked me to have his little girl brought back home... he has been to the Victoria General Hospital and seen his little girl and he tells me that all the little girl had on was a little cotton dress and was not getting the attention she should have. Mr. Phillips wishes to have his little girl sent home and placed in a hospital handy to home so he can go see her any time he wishes. Pauline is very homesick and wants to come home, and under these circumstances I have decided that Pauline be sent home and I will have her looked after from this end.

Father Mackey evidently disliked the suggestion that Pauline be transferred from the hospital to which he had sent her or that she should not return to the school, and he wrote to the Department of Indian Affairs insisting that the child would probably soon be well. A few days later the Department wrote to Clarence Spinney to inform him that, despite his position as Agent, he had no authority in this case:

> It is very possible that you may not know that the pupils of an Indian Residential School are wards of the principal during their residence at the school and even during the summer holidays when they are home. He is, in effect, their Indian Agent, and even more than that, their personal guardian.

The same day the Department wrote to Father Mackey confirming his absolute authority over the children in his charge. Despite Father Mackey's optimistic predictions of a speedy recovery, Pauline's illness was found to need a long convalescence and she was sent home.

There were several complaints to the Department of Indian Affairs both about the quality of education the children were receiving and the restrictions placed on holidays. Chief Dan Francis of Cambridge wrote a letter of complaint to the Department stating that the children from his reserve reported that they were not getting adequate education and spent most of their time working in the field and doing housework. He was given a tour of the school and apparently went away satisfied that the children would receive a good education. On January 1, 1939, Indian Agent Clarence Spinney of Kings County, wrote to the Department of Mines and Resources, Indian Affairs Branch, Ottawa:

> Dear Sir:
> The Indians here in Cambridge Reserve were determined to have their children who is attending the Shubenacadie Indian School—home during the xmas vacation.
>
> I refused to grant their request and advised them that this was against the rules of the Dept. These people went so far as [to] have a man go to the school for their children. They did not get the children. Father Mackey would not let them take the children.
>
> This Mrs. Nibby who you had the letter from thought by writing she would be able to get her children home for xmas.
>
> These people think they can have their own way and would like to do so and when they find out they cannot they get mad.
>
> I had your rules and regulations regarding this matter.
> I remain yours truly,
> C.A.Spinney, Ind Agt

In some cases parents or other relatives helped students avoid being sent back to school. Frank and Nancy Marble's parents kept them at home in 1935 after Frank had been whipped by Father Mackey and Edward Mcleod the year before.

Nancy Marble still remembers Father Mackey bringing the RCMP to the reserve to force her and her brother to return to the school:

> Father Mackey brought the cops up to New Town, [a section in Indian Brook] and the old man [Chief John Maloney] didn't allow them in. We seen them coming up through the woods and the old man said, "I'm not going to force you to go back N'tus (my daughter)," and Mom said, "Run. Run away, run in the woods." And I said, "No, I'm not going to run in the woods. If they grab me, alright." But Frank was more scared than I was and he said he didn't want to go back there because he was whipped and we didn't go back. We went to live with our grandmother in Pictou Landing.

A few parents engaged in time-consuming battles with Indian Affairs to try to free their children from the school. Doug Knockwood's father had to wait for two and a half years before he could get Doug out of the school:

> When my father came that Christmas, I had one big shoe on and one little shoe, and snots were running all over my face, and I had a jacket on that was too big for me. He took one look at me and called Father Mackey in and they got into an argument. I remember my father saying, "Take a look at him. When he was home, at least he was hygenically clean and even though we never had very much he had a decent pair of shoes on his feet and a jacket that fit. My boys are coming home with me." Father Mackey told him to get out so Dad began working on getting us out. His education at the Residential School helped him to write letters to the bureaucrats. It took him two and a half years. When you put something down on paper, it's stronger than words. ... I was so happy when summer vacation came and I could go home, but then I was brought back in my second year by the Mounties. I'm a little nine-year-old boy forced out of my home by the Mounties and my father is fighting for me not to go back to that school. My father was a troublemaker for the system and they took it out on us.

Everyone was keenly aware that it took courage to defy the authorities by helping truants and runaways stay away from the school. Sulian Hearney still remembers with gratitude how his older brother "literally saved my life" by insisting that he should not go back to school when he arrived home for Christmas in ragged clothes and suffering from an infected head wound: "He said I wasn't going back—he went against the agents, the Mounties, everybody. He saved my life."...

In the twelve years I was at the school, not one term passed without someone running away. In some years the same child would try over and over again despite the repeated punishments. Many tried to escape by using numerous ingenious ways to get out including: just walking away from the yard during play, jumping out of the second storey windows onto the roof of the back doors on both sides, tying sheets together and climbing down the walls from the third or fourth storeys, using a fire hose to climb down from the dormitory to the ground, using fire escapes, crawling out of basement windows, and in one case filing down a skeleton key to fit all the doors and leaving via the stairway in the middle of the night. Some boys even made keys and raided the storerooms for lunch to take with them...

Despite the fact that speaking Mi'kmaw was so absolutely forbidden, children would use their knowledge of the language to undermine the nuns' authority. Clara Julian could reduce us all to helpless laughter in church when she would take a line from one of the Latin hymns for Benediction, "Resurrecsit sicut dixit" [He said he would rise again]. But Clara would sing at the top of her voice, "*Resurrecsit kisiku piktit,*" which in Mi'kmaw means, "When the old man got up, he farted." The whole choir would start laughing and poor Sister Eleanor Marie thought we were laughing at Clara for mispronouncing Latin and she'd stop and patiently teach Clara the proper pronunciation. Clara would just stand there and grin. Even the holy ones had to laugh.

[Isabelle Knockwood, Out of the Depths: The Experiences of Mi'kmaw
Children at the Indian Residential School at Shubenacadie, Nova Scotia
(Lockeport, N.S.: Roseway Publishing, 1992), pp. 110-115]

The Application Form

To the Director of Indian Affairs, Ottawa, Canada

_____, 193-

Sir:

I hereby make application for admission of the undermentioned child into the _____ Residential School; to remain therein under the guardianship of the Principal for such term as the Minister of Mines and Resources may deem proper:

Indian name of child
_____

English name
_____

Age
_____

Name of Band
_____

No. of ticket under which child's annuity is paid
_____

Father's full name and number
_____

Mother's full name and number
_____

Parents living or dead
_____

State of child's health
_____

Religion
_____

Does the applicant speak English?
_____

Previously attended _____ school for ____ years

_____ (Signature of father)

Note: If mother or guardian signs, the agent must forward full explanatory note.

I hereby certify that the above application for admission has been read over and interpreted to the parent or guardian and that the contents were understood by him or her and that I witnessed his or her signature on this document:

I recommend the admission of the above child, who is of good moral character and is eligible to be admitted as a grant-earning pupil.

_____
Signature of Missionary or other witness (Principal or other official of the school must not sign as witness)

_____
Signature of agent

Note: All the above particulars must be fully given, especially the "Name of Band," "No. of ticket under which child's annuity is paid," and "Religion." The minimum age for admission is seven (7) years, except in the case of an orphan, destitute or neglected child. When application is made for the admission of such ages, full particulars should accompany the application.

QUESTIONS

1. What specific examples of the doctrine of progress appear in these documents?
2. How did John A. Macdonald characterize the Indian problem? Was this perception universally shared?
3. What did Chief Elliott (Deyenhehken) want?
4. What positive and negative effects did World War I have on Native peoples according to government reports? What health and education concerns were raised by the Department of Indian Affairs in the 1920s?
5. How did children and their parents respond to the Shubenacadie school?

READINGS

Sarah Carter, *Lost Harvest: Prairie Indian Reserve Farmers and Government Policy* (Montreal: McGill-Queen's Press, 1990)

Olive Patricia Dickason, *Canada's First Nations: A History of Founding Peoples from Earliest Times* (Toronto: McClelland and Stewart, 1992)

Daniel Francis, *The Imaginary Indian: The Image of the Indian in Canadian Culture* (Vancouver: Arsenal Pulp Press, 1992)

Gerald Friesen, *The Canadian Prairies: A History* (Toronto: University of Toronto Press, 1987)

J.R. Miller, *Shingwauk's Vision: A History of Native Residential Schools* (Toronto: University of Toronto Press, 1996)

_____, *Skyscrapers Hide the Heavens: A History of Indian-White Relations in Canada,* 2nd ed. (Toronto: University of Toronto Press, 1991)

Katherine Pettipas, *Severing the Ties That Bind: Government Repression of Indigenous Religious Ceremonies on the Prairies* (Winnipeg: University of Manitoba Press, 1994)

Frank James Tester and Peter Kulchyski, *Tammarniit (Mistakes): Innuit Relocation in the Eastern Arctic, 1939-63* (Vancouver: University of British Columbia Press, 1994)

Labour

By the late-nineteenth century, as the result of extensive economic reorganization associated with industrialism, an increasing number of Canadians were dependent on waged labour for their income. As this became more common, opportunities for self-sufficiency—such as keeping a cow or chickens or cutting firewood for home heating—declined in an urban environment. More people were living in towns and cities where wages—no matter how meagre—had to provide for all the necessities of life.

With the assistance of the protective tariffs of the National Policy (1879), manufacturing in Canada increased in terms of the number of establishments, wages paid to employees, and amount of capital invested. The scale of manufacturing also changed, as small family-owned enterprises were replaced by larger corporate concerns. With this came new methods of organizing labour, as certain male workers claimed power in the work process through their mastery of a specific skill—they joined together to form unions which controlled the work in their particular craft. Their acquisition of 'skill,' after a long period of apprenticeship, meant that they could not be easily replaced, and withholding their expertise led to work stoppages. Through the unions, skilled men used their specific knowledge of a craft to further their claims for decent wages and fewer hours.

Most workers, who did not possess specialized knowledge of a craft, were considered 'unskilled.' This group tended to include the most vulnerable members of Canadian society—immigrant men, minorities, women, and children. They did not have the leverage of 'expertise,' and found it almost impossible to organize into unions since they could easily be replaced as workers. In addition to low wages, the unskilled worker often suffered from irregular or casual employment.

Section A
Wages and Working Conditions

The 1880s were a time of industrial unrest, expressed by labour organization, strikes by workers, and lock-outs by employers. The federal government responded to labour strife with the creation of a Royal Commission on the Relations of Labor and Capital in 1889. This was a step on the road to increasing state intervention with the introduction of provincial factories acts, laws against child labour, workmen's compensation, and the creation of a labour holiday, the first Monday in September. In 1900, the federal Liberal government abandoned any pretence of distance in the relations between employers and employees with the establishment of a Department of Labour. This direct involvement increased in 1907, with the implementation of the *Industrial Disputes Investigation Act*, which prohibited strikes and lock-outs in certain occupational sectors before a process of government investigation could be undertaken. The deputy minister who was responsible for the establishment of this department, and generating this important legislation, was William Lyon Mackenzie King, the future prime minister.

Government was interested not only in employment, but also in unemployment among its citizens. The influence of contemporary social science is visible in the vast amounts of data the Department of Labour collected in the form of social surveys and statistics on wages and cost of living.

Investigating Working Conditions in Saint John, New Brunswick, 1889

George McAvity (T McAvity & Sons, Brass Founders), called and sworn. Questioned by Commissioner Freed.

Q. What class of goods do you manufacture? A. All classes of gasfitters' and plumber's supplies.

Q. How may men do you employ? A. I think we employ somewhere in the neighborhood of 110 and 115 at present.

Q. Are they all skilled hands? A. No

Q. What wages do you pay your skilled hands? A. They would average from $1.50 to $2 a day.

Q. And how much do the unskilled hands receive? A. According to what they are worth; we have always a number of apprentices on hand, and they start at

$1.50 a week, and after they have worked two or three years they command men's wages. We have some boys who have only been working for us for two years who are earning $8 a week and some who have been working five years that do not earn so much. There are so many machines used in our business now that we do not require so much skilled labor as we did years ago.

Q. At what age do you take on these apprentices? A. Fourteen or fifteen years.

Q. And what do unskilled laborers earn? A. One dollar and seventy-five cents a day. Such men as furnace men we could get at a little less, but we pay them the same; our men work fifty-two weeks in the year.

Q. Have you any unskilled hands earning less than $1.75 a day? A. We have a number of unskilled hands who only earn $1 or $1.25.

Q. Is your occupation considered unhealthy? A. I believe it is called unhealthy, but I do not think it is. The custom of considering the business unhealthy arose from the fact of foundries being carried on in the old English custom, where the moulding and finishing shops were not separated. Here, both in the United States and Canada, the moulding shops are separate from the finishing shops.

Q. Is that the case in your establishment? A. It is.

Q. Where do you sell your goods, as a general rule? A. We sell most of our goods in Ontario.

Q. Are not freights from here to there very high? A. Freight is high, but we offset that by our expenses being lower here. After the great fire of 1877 the only question we considered was whether we should locate ourselves here or go to Ontario.

Q. What determined you to stay here? A. The price of coal here, no labor troubles and fit material. We can buy a greater amount of old material here than we could get inland...

Q. Are wages lower in St. John than in Ontario—in your line? A. I think we can get men easier here than there.

Q. Were you workmen all St. John men? A. Yes.

Q. Do you educate most of your own men? A. Yes.

Q. When a boy finishes his time can you give him employment at his trade? A. When a boy finishes his trade we can give him employment, but most all of them, after their time is out, go away to the States. Every year we have perhaps half a dozen boys leaving us that way...

[Greg Kealey, ed., Canada Investigates Industrialism: The Royal Commission on the Relations of Labor and Capital, 1889 (Abridged) (Toronto: University of Toronto Press, 1973), pp. 317-318]

Labor Day by Edward Williams

The dawn of Labor's National Holiday will be welcomed by the toiling masses of our vast Dominion. Labor Day marks a new epoch in the history of the industrial classes, for till the end of time, once each year they will rest from toil and in countless thousands celebrate the progress of their industrial emancipation...

That Parliament has made Labor Day a national holiday is a tardy recognition of those noble beings who in the past, through vituperation and calumny, suffered persecution for defending the rights and liberties of men, and who claimed that the Trade Union was destined to develop the highest types of manhood in the march of civilization, and as feudalism allowed barbarism, so education and enlightenment would tend slowly but successfully bring about the freedom of thought and action which asserts the equality of rights before the law.

Trades unionism is not a visionary theory, to be spoken of contemptuously as an "ism." It is a fact, founded on principles of justice, law and truth. It is cosmopolite in tenet rather than dogmatic, and regards the interests of mankind, rather than of this own class or kind. It is open to the world, regardless of sex, color, nationality or political affiliation. In its organization it is as lawfully and holy as the church. It takes no private road; it seeks to guard the interests of the weak and helpless. It is not a secret oath-bound cabal, its councils being private only in the sense which is proper in conducting the affairs of a firm or corporation. The trades union typifies in the fullest and broadest sense the brotherhood of man...

Preamble

In order to better protect the workers, artizans and laborers in the struggle now going on in the civilized world between the oppressor and the oppressed, between the capitalist and the laborer, which grows in intensity from year to year, and will work disastrous results to the toilers if they are not combined for mutual protection and benefit;

It therefore behooves the representatives of the Trades and Labor Unions of this city in Council assembled to adopt such principles among the mechanics and laborers as will permanently unite them to secure the recognition of the rights to which they are justly entitled.

We therefore declare ourselves in favor of the formation of a central body embracing every Trade and Labor Organization in the city organized under the trades union system to be known as the Trades and Labor Council of Hamilton. Its work should be to bring all trades together in closer unity for the better protection of our interests as workmen and for the wider extension of the principles of trade unionism, so that all organized bodies of labor may make common cause, and that none may suffer for want of that practical and pecuniary assistance which isolated and detached, we cannot secure, and which united and consolidated, we are the more likely to obtain. It is the most natural and assimilative form of bringing the trade and labor unions together, at the same time preserving the industrial autonomy and distinctive character of each trade and labor union, and without doing violence to their respective constitution or traditions, blends them all in one harmonious whole—a federation of labor.

With such a body we should look to the organization of the unorganized working people in our city. Isolated labor in conflict with consolidated capital, in many cases has been driven to the wall, and defeated for a time, until thoroughly and permanently organized. A systematic propaganda can be inaugurated that would strengthen and enliven all the unions, by the distribution of trade union literature and creating a public demand for union goods and union labels, a reduction of the hours of labor so that the toiler may participate in the benefits of labor-saving machinery...

Declaration of Principles

1. While opposing to entering any political party as a body, we declare it to be our duty to use our influence with the lawmaking powers to secure the following objects: The adoption of proper laws regulating the hours constituting a day's work; reforms in prison labor so as to prevent the product of convict labor coming into competition with honest industry; and such other laws as may be beneficial.

2. We declare it the duty of every workingman to use his utmost endeavors to secure the amelioration of the condition of the laboring classes generally, and to accomplish this we believe that a central organization should exist, whereby all branches of labor may form allies to any particular one that may be oppressed.

3. We hereby pledge ourselves to assist each other in securing fair wages by honorable means, and we shall withdraw and use our influence to have others withdraw all patronage from any unfair employer, let his calling be what it may.

4. We declare that all existing beneficial labor laws should be rigidly enforced, and we pledge ourselves to take such measures as will secure their enforcement.

5. We are in favor of arbitration whenever differences exist between employers and employed.

6. We favor productive and distributive co-operation and the self-employment of labor, as only complete independence can be obtained when the laborer is no longer dependent on other individuals for the right to work; and especially do we recommend that whenever trades strike for the accomplishment of any just purpose, if the funds of the organization will allow it, the resistance, instead of being passive, should become active and aggressive, by using the funds productively instead of unproductively.

7. That we favor day labor in preference to contracts on all works of a public character.

8. We favor the ownership and operation by municipalities or by the provincial or national governments of all natural monopolies such as electric light works, street railways, the postal, telephone and telegraph systems, steam and electric railways, etc.

[Official Program and Souvenir of the Labor Day Demonstration Held at Dundurn Park, Hamilton, Ont., September 6th, 1897, pp. 3-5]

Average Weekly Expenditures on Staple Foods, Fuel, Lighting, and Rentals by a Family of Five; Income $750 per Year; 1897-1907

Commodity	Quantity	Price, 1897	Price, 1907
MEATS,			
Beef,			
Sirloin steak	2 lbs	.25	.36
Chuck roast	2 "	.20	.30
Boiling beef	3 lb	.15	.24
Mutton,			
Forequarter	2 lb	.15	.25
Pork,			
Fresh	1 "	.10	.14
Salmon (tinned)	1 tin	.13	.17
Fresh fish	1 lb	.10	.15
Bacon	1 "	.14	.20
Lard	2 lb	.20	.30
Eggs,			
Fresh	1 doz.	.20	.30
Packed	1 "	.15	.22
Milk	6 qts	.30	.36
Butter,			
Creamery	1 lb.	.22	.28
Dairy	2 "	.40	.52
Bread	12 loaves	.60	.84
Cheese	1lb	.13	.18
Flour,			
Pastry	2 "	0.04.5	.06
Strong bakers'	6 "	.12.6	.13.8
Rolled oats	6 "	.18	.21
Rice	3 "	.30	.37.5
Sugar			
Granulated	4 "	.18	.20
Yellow	2 "	.08	.09
Teas			
Black	1/4 "	.10	.10
Green	1/4 "	.08	.10
Coffee	1/4 "	.09	.10
Potatoes	2 pecks	.16	.30
Wood	1/4 cord	.70	1.00
Coal	1/8 ton	.80	.90
Coal oil	1 gal.	.30	.30
Rent	per week	2.50	3.50
Total		$9.05	$12.17

* At average price the year round. The commodities and quantities included in this budget are a modification of those employed by the United States Department of Labour as applied to the working classes.

[Labour Gazette, *August 1907, p. 172*]

Wages and Hours of Labour

Table showing in average wages per week, and hours of labour, in Toronto; also numbers of days idle

Title of Organization	Av Wages per Week	Av Hrs per Week	Days Idle per Yr
Bakery and Confectionery Workers' Intern. Union, No.204	14.00	57	-
Bartenders' Union and Benefit Society No.280	12.00	70	-
International Alliance Bill Posters and Billiers, No.40	9.00	76	90
Bookbinders' International Union, No.2	15.00	48	14
Boot & Shoe Workers' Intern. Union No.233 (Male)	12.00	49	21
" " " (Female)	8.00	49	21
Brass Moulders' Union of North America, No.5	14.85	55	0
United Brewery Workers' International Union, No.304	12.00	52	-
Bricklayers' International Union, No.2	15.00	44	221
Intern. Asso. of Bridge & Structural Iron Workers, No.4	13.94	50	100
Amalg. Soc. of Carpenters & Joiners, 1st Branch, No.836	14.52	44	30
" " " " " " 2nd Branch, No.837	12.50	44	-
" " " " " " 3rd Branch, No.838	-	44	100
" " " " " " 4th Branch, No.839	14.52	44	-
" " " " " " 5th Branch, No.840	14.52	44	90
" " " " " " 6th Branch, No.841	14.52	44	60
" " " " " " E Toronto Br 835	14.00	44	18
United Bro of Carpenters & Joiners of America, No.27	16.25	44	60
" " " " " " " " No.1799	14.00	44	62
Carriage & Wagon Makers' International Union, No.85	10.00	50	60
Cigar Makers' International Union, No.27	10.00	44	40
Civic Employees' Union, No.1	13.50	50	0
" " " No.2	13.25	55	-
Coopers' International Union, No.180	14.00	55	-
International Bro. of Electrical Workers, No.114	14.30	44	50
National Association of Marine Engineers of Canada, No.1	20.00	84	60
International Union Marine Engineers, No.338	20.00	60	150
Intern. Union Steam Engineers, No.152, Stationary Eng	15.00	66	-
International Association of Fur Workers No.2 (Male)	15.00	44	-
" " " " " (Female)	6.00	44	-
Intern Ladies' Garment Workers' Un of Am No.48 (Male)	8.00	50	90
" " " " " " " (Female)	4.00	50	90
United Garment Workers of America, No.185	14.00	49	55
Glass Bottle Blowers of U.S. & Canada, No.68	30.00	53	100
Amalgamated Glass Workers' Intern Asso of Am, No.21	14.00	50	30
International Union Journeymen Horseshoers, No.49	14.25	50	-
Intern. Union of Wood, Wire and Metal Lathers, No.97	17.00	44	50
Lithographers' Intern Protection & Benefit Asso, No.12	18.00	49+$\frac{1}{2}$	-
Internat. Longshoremen's M.& T. Association, No.767	10.00	varies	200
International Association of Machinists, No.235	14.00	50	-
Malsters Union, No.317	12.50	60	160
Marble Workers' International Union, No.12	13.00	49+$\frac{1}{2}$	30
Metal Polishers, Buffers' &d Platers' Intern. Un No.21	15.00	52+$\frac{1}{4}$	45

Title of Organization	Av Wages per Week	Av Hrs per Week	Days Idle per Yr
Iron Moulders' & Core Makers' Union No.25	12.50	49+1/2	80
Bro. of Paint's, Decor't'rs & P'p'rhang's of Am. No.3	14.30	44	60
" " " " " " " " No.219	13.00	44	90
Photo Engravers' Union, No.35	18.00	46+1/2	-
Piano, Organ & Musical Instrument Workers' In Un. No.39	14.00	50	36
" " " " " " " " No.41	13.50	50	18
Operative Plasterers' Int Assoc No.48	22.00	44	75
Plasterers' Labourers' Association No.1	9.00	44	90
Printing Pressmen's International Union, No.10	16.50	48	-
Web Pressmen's Union, No.1	18.00	45	12
Printing Press Assistants' & Feeders' Int Un No.1	10.50	48	-
Toronto Typographical Union, No.91	16.00	48	15
Saw-smith Union of North America, No.10	17.50	50	20
Sheet Metal Workers' International Assoc No.30	16.00	44	-
Bro. of Silver Workers of America No.13	11.00	44	-
Stereotypers & Electrotypers Intern Union of N.A. No.21	18.00	45	-
Journeymen Stonecutters' Association of North America	22.00	44	100
National Stonecutters' Society of U.S & Canada, No.12	19.00	44	varies
Amalg. Assn. Street & Electric Rlwy Emp of Am., No.113	12.00	60	0
Journeymen Tailors' Union of America, No.132 (Male)	13.00	54	90
" " " " " (Female)	7.50	54	90
International Brotherhood of Teamsters, No.409	12.50	60	-
" " " " No.457	12.00	60	12
" " " " No.495	10.00	72+1/2	12
Teamowners' Assoc of Toronto, No.1 (2 Horses)	27.00	54	-
Commercial Telegraphers' Union of America (Male)	12.00	51	-
" " " " " (Female)	10.50	51	-
Theatrical Stage Employees' Intern Union	10.00	-	100
Tobacco Workers' International Union No.63 (Male)	10.00	50	50
" " " " " (Female)	7.00	50	50
Travellers' Goods, Leather Novelty Workers In U No.5	10.50	52+1/2	12
Upholsterers' International Union of North America No.30	14.00	50	100
Brotherhood of Railway Carmen of America No.372	7.59	45	-
Brotherhood of Local Firemen & Engineers, No.596	15.00	-	-

[Ontario Report of the Bureau of Labour, Sessional Papers Vol. 4, Part 8, 1909 (Appendix 30), pp 168-177]

Help Wanted

MALE

COMPETENT, ENERGETIC GENERAL store clerk with some capital to manage and take interest in good Sask. business. Apply Box 275, Globe

DRUG CLERK WANTED — IMPROVER — must be telegraph operator; references required. Box 244 Globe

EXPERIENCED TRAVELLING SALESMAN wanted for the Maritimes Provinces by biscuit and confectionery firm; must be first-class salesman, with good address; energetic and able to sell and retain the best trade; single man 29 to 35 with good connection on the above territory preferred; good salary to the right party; address immediately, stating experience, references, age and salary expected. Box 222 Globe

WANTED — AT ONCE — EXPERIENCED male attendants. Apply stating age, height, weight and experience with reference to the Chief Attendant. Homewood Sanatorium, Guelph

WANTED — AN A1 HARDWARE CLERK — must be strictly temperate; married man preferred; give age, experience and send references and salary wanted. Campbell & Ferguson, Limited, Waskadn, Man.

HELP WANTED — FEMALE

APPLICATIONS FOR THE POSITION of matron of the Neepewa General Hospital will be received up to December 31; duties to commence as soon as possible after appointment is made; initial salary will be $45.00 per month. Fred Leach, Hon, Sec., Box 384 Neepewa, Man.

A WELL QUALIFIED DRESSMAKER — Manitoba, department store; salary starting $25.00 weekly. Apply by letter or personally to Mr Blair, Debenhams Canada, Limited, Toronto

COMPETENT LADY BOOKKEEPER must be bright, intelligent and painstaking rather than of long experience; splendid opportunity for the right applicant; advertiser will interview; state salary. Milton Screw Co., Limited, Milton, Ontario.

DINING-ROOM GIRLS WANTED — At once — highest wages. Apply City Hotel, London, Ont.

GIRL WANTED — WITH EXPERIENCE; for groceries and ice cream parlor in morning. 392 Yonge Street

GIRLS TO WORK IN UNDERWEAR AND HOSIERY mills; experience not necessary; highest wages paid; drop a postcard for full particulars. Penmans Limited, Paris, Ont.

WANTED BY WELSH WESTERN widower of 30; no children; on farm, a housekeeper between 25 and 30 or widow with one child who would prefer a permanent home to big wages. Apply David Nicholls, Sweet Valley, Alta.

MECHANICS WANTED

BARBER WANTED — A FIRST CLASS barber; must be a good hockey player; eighteen dollars per week and percentage. Address Sam Matthews, Phoenix, B.C.

GOOD MACHINE MAN FOR SMALL planing mill who can make knives and run and look after all classes of planing mill machinery used for making ordinary building material; steady work; reasonable wages; pay weekly; none but first-class men need apply. Apply stating wages and experience to Box 750 Globe

[Selected from The Globe, *Saturday, 16 December 1911]*

Section B
Responses of Society

Labour issues were of interest to a larger circle of society than just employer and employees. Reformers, such as Montreal businessman Herbert Ames, concentrated their efforts on the moral aspects of working conditions—the issues of child labour, toilet facilities, and concerns that young women's work might destroy the reproductive capacity of Canada's future mothers. In 1891, Pope Leo XIII issued the *Rerum Novarum,* which offered Catholic social relations as a solution to industrial unrest and socialism, and firmly placed women within the home. The ideas of the encyclical were put into practice in the Catholic Unions formed in Quebec after 1907.

Both skilled and unskilled labour generally opposed immigration. An expanded labour pool depressed wages and weakened solidarity, as labourers were forced to compete with one another for the few jobs available. Labour was therefore among the strongest supporters of legislation such as a head tax on Chinese immigration. Women, like immigrants, could also undermine working conditions as they were always paid less, and therefore were additional unwelcome competition. But immigrants and women were not the only menace for labour. Skilled men were particularly vulnerable to the introduction of new technologies, as well as to industrial organization in which a task was altered by a new machine or broken down into small components which could be mastered quickly. The importance of the campaign for reduced hours—first for nine hours and, later, the eight-hour day—reflected new difficulties that emerged with an intensification of the work experience.

When dealing with labour there is almost always a problem of sources. Most of the evidence we can collect about the working-class experience comes from outside observers. Working people were less likely than the educated elite to leave the sorts of documents historians value, such as diaries or letters. Even if they created such records, they were unlikely to be kept and deposited in an archive. This section, therefore, also includes some folk songs as a way of catching a glimpse of the working-class experience 'from below.'

Rerum Novarum

On the Condition of the Working Classes *Rerum Novarum* Encyclical Letter of His Holiness Pope Leo XIII issued on May 15, 1891. To Our Venerable Brethren the Patriarchs, Primates, Archbishops, Bishops and other Ordinaries of Places Having Peace and Communion with the Apostolic See:

1. Once the passion for revolutionary change was aroused—a passion long disturbing governments—it was bound to follow sooner or later that eagerness for change would pass from the political sphere over into the related field of economics. In fact, new developments in industry, new techniques striking out on new paths, changed relations of employer and employee, abounding wealth among a very small number and destitution among the masses, increased self-reliance on the part of workers as well as a closer bond of union with one another, and, in addition to all this, a decline in morals have caused conflict to break forth...

4. The problem is difficult to resolve and is not free from dangers. It is hard indeed to fix the boundaries of the rights and duties within which the rich and the proletariat—those who furnish material things and those who furnish work—ought to be restricted in relation to each other. The controversy is truly dangerous, for in various places it is being twisted by turbulent and crafty men to pervert judgment as to truth and seditiously to incite the masses...

5. In any event, We see clearly, and all are agreed that the poor must be speedily and fittingly cared for, since the great majority of them live undeservedly in miserable and wretched conditions.

6. After the old trade guilds had been destroyed in the last century, and no protection was substituted in their place, and when public institutions and legislation had cast off traditional religious teaching, it gradually came about that the present age handed over the workers, each alone and defenseless, to the inhumanity of employers and the unbridled greed of competitors. A devouring usury, ...and in addition the whole process of production as well as trade in every kind of goods has been brought almost entirely under the power of a few, so that a very few rich and exceedingly rich men have laid a yoke almost of slavery on the unnumbered masses of non-owning workers.

7. To cure this evil, the Socialists, exciting the envy of the poor toward the rich, contend that it is necessary to do away with private possession of goods and in its place to make the goods of individuals common to all, and that the men who preside over a municipality or who direct the entire State should act as administrators of these goods. They hold that, by such a transfer of private goods from private individuals to the community, they can cure the present evil through dividing wealth and benefits equally among the citizens.

8. But their program is so unsuited for terminating the conflict that it actually injures the workers themselves. Moreover, it is highly unjust, because it violates the rights of lawful owners, perverts the function of the State, and throws governments into utter confusion...

23. ...[I]t is perceived that the fundamental principle of Socialism which would make all possessions public property is to be utterly rejected because it injures the very ones whom it seeks to help, contravenes the natural rights of individual persons, and throws the functions of the State and public peace into confusion. Let it be regarded, therefore, ...that private ownership must be preserved inviolate. With this understood, we shall explain whence the desired remedy is to be sought...

28. It is a capital evil with respect to the question We are discussing to take for granted that the one class of society is of itself hostile to the other, as if nature had set rich and poor against each other to fight fiercely in implacable war... Each needs the other completely: neither capital can do without labor, nor labor without capital...

29. And first and foremost, the entire body of religious teaching and practice, of which the Church is interpreter and guardian, can pre-eminently bring together and unite the rich and the poor by recalling the two classes of society to their mutual duties, and in particular to those duties which derive from justice.

30. Among these duties the following concern the poor and the workers: To perform entirely and conscientiously whatever work has been voluntarily and equitably agreed upon; not in any way to injure the property or to harm the person of employers; in protecting their own interests, to refrain from violence and never to engage in rioting; not to associate with vicious men who craftily hold out exaggerated hopes and make huge promises, a course usually ending in vain regrets and in the destruction of wealth.

31. The following duties, on the other hand, concern rich men and employers: Workers are not to be treated as slaves; justice demands that the dignity of human personality be respected in them, ennobled as it has been through what we call the Christian character... It is shameful and inhuman, however, to use men as things for gain and to put no more value on them than what they are worth in muscle and energy. Likewise it is enjoined that the religious interests and the spiritual well-being of the workers receive proper consideration. Wherefore, it is the duty of employers to see that the worker is free for adequate periods to attend to his religious obligations; not to expose anyone to corrupting influences or the enticements of sin, and in no way to alienate him from care for his family and the practice of thrift. Likewise, more work is not to be imposed than strength can endure, nor that kind of work which is unsuited to a worker's age or sex.

59. ...The length of rest interval sought to be decided on the basis of the varying nature of the work, of the circumstances of time and place, and of the physical condition of the workers themselves...

60. Finally, it is not right to demand of a woman or a child what a strong adult man is capable of doing or would be willing to do. Nay, as regards children, special care ought to be taken that the factory does not get hold of them before age has sufficiently matured their physical, intellectual, and moral powers... Certain occupations, likewise, are less fitted for women, who are intended by nature for

work of the home—work indeed which especially protects modesty in women and accords by nature with the education of children and the well-being of the family...

65. If a worker receives a wage sufficiently large to enable him to provide comfortably for himself, his wife and his children, he will, if prudent, gladly strive to practice thrift; and the result will be, as nature itself seems to counsel, that after expenditures are deducted there will remain something over and above through which he can come into the possession of a little wealth...

81. The condition of workers is a subject of bitter controversy at the present time; and whether this controversy is resolved in accordance with reason or otherwise, it is in either event of utmost importance to the State. But Christian workers will readily resolve it in accordance with reason if, united in associations and under wise leaders, they enter upon the path which their fathers and their ancestors followed to their own best welfare as well as to that of the State... It is remarkable how much associations of Catholics can contribute to the welfare of all such men if they invite those wavering in uncertainty to their bosom in order to remedy their difficulties, and if they receive the penitents into their trust and protection.

82. ...Everyone according to his position ought to gird himself for the task, and indeed as speedily as possible, lest, by delaying the remedy, the evil, which is already of vast dimensions, become incurable. Let those in charge of States make use of the provision afforded by laws and institutions; let the rich and employers be mindful of their duties; let the workers, whose cause is at stake, press their claims with reason. And since religion alone, as We said in the beginning, can remove the evil, root and branch, let all reflect upon this: First and foremost Christian morals must be re-established, without which even the weapons of prudence, which are considered especially effective, will be of no avail, to secure well-being...

84. As a pledge of Divine favor and as a token of Our affection, most lovingly in the Lord We bestow on each of you, Venerable Brethren, on your clergy and on your people, the Apostolic Blessing.

85. Given in Rome, at St. Peter's, the 15th day of May, in the year 1891, the fourteenth of Our Pontificate.Leo XIII.

A Montreal Reformer on Casual Labour

One of the matters investigated in our special census was this irregularity of work. Although as families in receipt of regular incomes were regarded such as possessed at least one worker employed without intermission, and also all families which receiving ten dollars or more per week for part of the year, might be reasonably expected to put aside sufficient to enable them to get through the remainder without hardship, yet even with these regarded as 'regular' there still remained 1724 families, or 23 per cent of the total number, whose small incomes could not be depended upon as constant and regular throughout the year. Of course this included many instances of alternative trades, as for example, when a man is a brick-layer in summer and a furnace-man in winter, but still the ratio of *nearly one family in every four without steady work*, seems alarmingly high and explains much of the poverty. The relative proportion of irregularity in employment varies greatly with the locality, but increases as one approaches the water front. In the belt above St. James street, the proportion is but one family in eight, between St. James and William streets it is one family in every five, beyond the canal it is one family in four, while between William street and the canal the proportion is *two* families out of every five. Think of it, of fifteen hundred families in all 'Griffintown,' six hundred do not know what it is to have a regular income and steady work. It is not at all improbable that these six hundred families could furnish nearly an equal number of able-bodied men to any local enterprise which, during the winter, would offer a living wage. With most of the wage-earners of these families the programme for the year is as follows: Work upon the wharves in summer and odd jobs of any sort during five long winter months. When spring arrives, overdue rent and debt at the corner grocery have so mortgaged the coming summer's earnings that saving becomes impossible. This irregularity of work is doubtless the main cause of poverty, for the prolonged idleness unfits many a man for steady work even when he at length succeeds in getting it. Once irregular always irregular is apt to be true, and irregularity, demoralization and poverty is the order of descent.

[*Herbert Brown Ames,* The City Below the Hill *(Toronto: University of Toronto Press, 1973; orig. pub. 1897), p. 73]*

Children in the Labour Force

I have found but few children illegally employed this year. The "Compulsory School Attendance Act" being locally looked after by the school trustees, is having the effect of assisting the factory inspectors in this respect. Besides, the majority of employers are law-abiding and law-respecting, and, when they know what the law requires, will conform to it; at least, such is my experience with them. When the "Compulsory School Attendance Act" first became law, it led to considerable misunderstanding in some localities. Many persons had the idea that children not going to school during holidays could then work in factories, and as a consequence the first year or two after that law was enacted, I found quite a few children at work during the summer holidays. Then there are some would-be public guardians who, seeing a small child on the streets near a factory, infer that because the child is small it is under the factory age. I have seen whole families quite small, though old; and size is not always a criterion of age. In Toronto there may be many children seen in the streets near factories, but it does not follow that they are workers in them. I am glad to say that in regard to the employment of children the law is very well observed, and without much friction to parents or employers.

[*Twelfth Annual Report of the Inspector of Factories 1899, Western District, Ontario*, Sessional Papers Vol. 32, Part 2, 1900 (Appendix 8, 4)]

Results of the Immigration upon Canadian Workingmen

The evidence shows that the arrival of such a large number of immigrants interfered with the wages of the working men in Montreal. Mr. Honore Gervais, member of Parliament, representing the Division of St. James, Montreal, being asked what in his opinion would be the results on resident labourers in Montreal of the bringing in of such a large number of labourers stated:—

"I would think it would be most detrimental to the interests of resident labourers, because having to accept fixed salaries they have to make a scale that would cover the cost of living, and by the coming of these Italian labourers in such large numbers without a moment's warning to our shores, the scale of wages is destroyed because there are too many willing to work at reduced rates, and thus our resident labourers are bound to suffer. Accordingly, on account of the sudden fall or decrease in wages generally, it is most detrimental to the workmen of Canada, to the workmen of Montreal, that at any moment some ten thousand men shall be thrown on our shores and come in competition with our workmen resident in Montreal."

Mr. Hannaford, engineer of the Montreal Street Railway Company, stated that they had 300 Italians in their service, and that they paid the ordinary labourers 12 cents per hour, and that the sub-foremen received as high as $1.37 a day, that the rate of wages in Montreal to ordinary labourers in other departments is $1.50 per day, that they have no trouble in obtaining labourers; and in answer to the question "Well, you can get any number you wish at $1.25 per day," he replied. "They come to us, we do not have to look for them."

Mr. J. B. Mack, upon being asked: "Will you state your opinion of the effect on the scale of wages in a city like Montreal, caused by the bringing in of large numbers of foreign labourers at one time," answered, "The effect of bringing in large numbers of foreign labourers, in my opinion, would be a reduction in wages, and probably prolonged hours of labour. When the labour market is flooded, wages are not liable to increase, rather to decrease, and it is a benefit to capitalists or companies who employ large numbers of unskilled labourers to have a large immigration in order to have work performed at less cost.

Q. Can you tell the commission of certain classes of labour wherein the wages did go down?—A. I have been told that in various classes wages have been reduced."

Mr. Charles Hodgson Osler, superintendent of mains and services in the Montreal Light, Heat and Power Company, stated that out of 250 or 260 men employed by the company 100 were Italians.

Q. You remember the influx of Italian labour last April and May?—A. Yes.

Q. Would that affect the scale of labour for labourers?—A. Yes, I think it would.

Q. These Italians only received from $1.25 to $1.35 a day?—A. Yes.

Q. Are there others besides Italians only receiving that amount?—A. Yes, quite a number.

Q. Who are they?—A. Well, some English and French speaking men.

Q. You get as many men as you require on your work without difficulty?—A. We have done it so far, we have had no trouble at all; we had a little trouble last year, but we increased the wages to $1.45. We got lots of men this year at $1.25, whereas we had to pay $1.45 last year.

Q. I suppose there are the same number employed this year as last?—A. No, I have nearly double the quantity this year.

Q. The wages then dropped 20 cents?—A. Yes, there was a large influx of men, and we took advantage of labour as it came in.

> [Report of the Royal Commission on Immigration of Italian Labourers to Montreal and the Alleged Fraudulent Practices of Employment Agencies, Canada, Sessional Papers 1905 (36 b), pp. xxxvii-xxxviii]

The British Columbia Premier Writes to Laurier

THE GOVERNMENT OF THE PROVINCE OF BRITISH COLUMBIA
Premier's Office
Victoria, October 1900

Rt Hon Sir Wilfrid Laurier.
Prime Minister,
Ottawa, Canada

Dear Sir Wilfrid - There are several matters affecting the mutual interests of the province of British Columbia and the Dominion of Canada concerning which the government is anxious that I should make representations to you...which I may say, are shared by a large majority of the people of British Columbia. The matters in question have for some time past been under discussion in the legislature, on the public platform and in the press, and I have no doubt that on account of the increasing interest felt in the east in the affairs of this western country they have already been brought under your notice...

In the first place, you will have observed by the various expressions of opinion, and, particularly from the attitude of the legislative assembly, that there is a strong and growing feeling regarding the immigration of Mongolians. In the opinion of the government the time has fully arrived when some decisive steps should be taken by the authorities having complete and effective jurisdiction to permanently end the state of affairs complained of...

Owing to the geographic relation of British Columbia to the continent of Asia this province is the landing place for Oriental immigration to the Pacific coast and consequently the competition to which the labouring classes here are exposed is keenly felt in a way that cannot be appreciated in other parts of Canada. This applies to Japanese and Chinese alike.

...

If the people against whom we desire a measure of protection were in their standard of living on par with our own the competition of Japanese and Chinese would be a legitimate one, but I need not point out to you what has been contended so often and with so much force against an indiscriminate and unrestricted immigration of Mongolians, that, without lowering the general standard of living necessary to meet the decrease in wages, it is not possible for white labour to exist in the face of a system that has grown up under conditions entirely foreign to Anglo-Saxon communities, wholly inapplicable in this country and out of harmony with our institutions. I am not prepared to say that there are not at the present time and that probably for a little time to come there will not be some avocations in which the Chinese and Japanese may be employed with actual benefit to the whole community. I believe there are. These, however, are limited, and even respecting these it is desirable to change the conditions as soon as possible. The introduction of machinery will in time in all probability afford very largely a substitute for such labour, and, in any event, if the employment of Mongolians in a limited way may be justified it certainly is very undesirable that any increase in the demand for their services should take place or that their employment should not be reduced to an absolute minimum.

A good deal has been said about public sentiment being educated to discourage the employment of Mongolian labour wherever possible, and while that may be commendable in itself it will fail in practice to meet the case; because in large industries, more particularly, the temptation to obtain the cheapest form of labour and to utilize it whenever and wherever available will undoubtedly exist.

In my opinion, the only satisfactory way to deal with the whole subject is by the increase of the per capita tax in such a measure as to surely limit the number of immigration and by the enactment of legislation similar to the Natal Act to regulate their employment while in the country. It is true that the Dominion government has increased the tax from $50 to $100 per head, but as you will have already ascertained the consensus of opinion, so far as this province is concerned, is that it fails to meet the requirements. Sentiment throughout British Columbia is absolutely opposed to any temporizing with the question. The opposition of the Imperial authorities must not be allowed to stand in the way of the interests of this, an integral and most loyal part of the Empire, and if sufficient remedies have been permitted to be exercised in the other colonies they cannot consistently be refused in Canada, our case being all the stronger from the fact that by our direct geographical relation as a highway of traffic to the Orient we are particularly exposed to the evils of such immigration...

The numbers of Chinese who find their way to Eastern Canada are small and the effect on the labour market in consideration of the largeness of the total population is in the aggregate so insignificant as not to be appreciable. On the other hand our population is so comparatively limited that any influx of Chinese is felt in a correspondingly increased ratio.

James Dunsmuir,
Premier.

[Return to Addresses of the House of Commons, dated the 12th and 18th December, 1907, for a copy of all correspondence between the Government of Canada and the Imperial authorities, and a copy of all correspondence between the Government of Canada and any person or persons, and of all reports communicated to the Government in respect to the Anglo-Japanese convention regarding Canada; also relating to the immigration of the Chinese and Japanese into Canada, Sessional Papers *1907-08 (74b), pp. 55-57]*

The Yellow Peril

The citizens of British Columbia are protesting against the proposal to allow, on a large scale, the importation of Chinese labor under indenture. They take the stand that there is already a yellow peril in their midst without making it worse by augmentation. Strong protests are also being made by organized labor for the particular reason that with the lower standards of living the Oriental works for long hours at a wage the white man could not start to compete with. The British Columbians have a special right to protest against the importation into their fine province of Chinese or Japanese alien labor for even under the best conditions they are undesirable as citizens, and when it is considered that under the duty of a $500 head tax against Chinese immigrants, supposed to be prohibitive because of the large amount, but what in reality has become an excuse for working a system of trade in human beings obnoxious to all sense of decency, their protest is more than justified. The usual procedure is for an agency to advance the $500 head tax, the emigrant in time becoming the slave for a long period of the agency that either uses the man for its own purposes or lets him out at a profit on every hour he works. Long before the tax is repaid with compound interest and profits that Chinese immigrant has acquired the worst traits of western civilization because of his environments and is taught to look upon the better characteristics of the white race as something to be exploited for his own ends.

Such a system of demoralized immigration is bound to have a bad affect on the morals of any immigrant, whatever his race, but on the Chinese immigrant with no moral code of his own and absolutely ignorant, even of his own country the results are disastrous to himself, and when many of him, positively dangerous to the country inflicted with him. British Columbia suffers most because of numbers, but throughout Canada the Chinaman is known, usually in the laundry, and if an investigation was made it would be startling to our sense of decency to find the number of white women living in prostitution in these same laundries—often one woman co-habiting in turn with each of the inmates of a laundry. And this in Christian Canada.

From the report of a private investigation made some time back we find that the conditions under which the Japanese laborers, engaged at the salmon fisheries in British Columbia, live are anything but conducive to health and clean living. What chance then have white workers against such people whose very squalor and filth have been brought about by the nature of their work—the cleaning of the fish—and the miserably poor pay. The Jap at home—in Japan—is of a cleanly nature and it is only by exploitation by white parasites that he has degenerated.

The native of India is by nature and temperament very different to either the Jap or Chinaman. The East Indians in Canada—about 2,000—are Sikhs, who will not be exploited knowingly, and no doubt the agitation against them a few years back was instigated by those who have exploited too well the other Orient races. In their native India these people have, since the mutiny, set a splendid example to the other races in loyalty to the Empire. They are cleanly and industrious in spite of assertions to the contrary, and they cannot understand why they have been discriminated against in a part of the Empire which harbors other colored races. Of one thing we are certain, whatever yellow peril there is or may be in Canada the East Indian will never be part of it.

The difficulty is this: Canada is not a white man's country in the sense that Australia is—where no colored immigration is allowed—and our system of immigration is not conducive to the best form of Canadian citizenship; the principal objective of the alien immigrants being to make money rather than to found homes and become responsible citizens. This in particular applies to the immigrant from the Orient. The consequence is that we have a slum life, which in comparison to that of other countries is out of all proportion to our population. In other words it is the foreign element that has built up our slums. For this state of affairs the local councils are largely to blame for not enforcing more strictly their own by-laws regarding over-crowding and hygiene, and this moral cancer is not confined to our urban centres by any means, for slum life is to be found in our rural communities.

[Canadian Municipal Journal, *Vol. XIV, No. 3, March 1918*]

Campaign Songs

Composed by Rev. A.E. Smith, June 1920

We Are Going to Vote

(Tune: Work for the Night Is Coming)
Not for the man of silver,
Not for the man of brass,
Nor for the man of glitter,
Not for the man of gas,
Not for the old line party,
Led by the same old tote,
Not in the former fashion
Are we going to vote.

Not for the Liberal platform,
Not for their politics,
Not for the Tory Minstrels
Not for their cunning tricks,
Not for the old Grit party,
Not for the Tory note,
Not in the former fashion
Are we going to vote.

But with a clearer vision,
Seeing the peoples' need:
Heeding the cry for justice
Under the heel of greed.
And for the cause of children,
Calling with plaintive note,
Right with the Labor Party,
We are going to vote.

We Will Make the Party

(Tune: Onward Christian Soldiers)
Onward social workers,
Working out the creed,
Looking to the ages
For the workers' meed:
Striking hands together
Standing firm and true,
We will make THE PARTY
That will make things new.

Chorus
Onward social workers, marching as ye fight:
Making conquest ever in the cause of right.

Onward sturdy workers,
Brighter grows the day,
Stubborn greed opposing
In the age long fray.
Striving ever upward,
Forward to the light
We will make THE PARTY
That will will put things right.

Chorus
Onward, then, ye workers,
Marshalled for the fight
Making conquest ever
In the cause of right.

[The Confederate *(Brandon, Manitoba),* 3 June 1920]

Work Songs

The Grand Hotel

There's a place in Vancouver the logger's know well,
It's a place where they keep rotgut whiskey to sell,
They also keep boarders and keep them like hell,
And the name of that place is the Grand Hotel.

Oh the Grand Hotel when the loggers come in,
It's amusing to see the proprietor grin,
For he knows they've got cash and he'll soon have it all,
So, "Come on, boys, have a drink, you'll will hear Tommy call.

In the mornin' Tom Roberts comes up to the door,
And there he sees loggers all over the floor,
He shouts as he hauls them up onto their feet,
"Drink up you bums or get out on the street".

We're going back to work and we're still pretty high,
With a bottle of rum and a mickey of rye,
A dozen of beer and a two gallon jar,
And passes for camp on the old "Cassiar".*

* A coast steamship which used to serve logging camps and small ports.

So Long to the Kicking-Horse Canyon

So long to the Kicking-horse Canyon,
Our shovel and pick days are through.
We'll bid farewell to the old cement mixer
And that rotten old foreman we knew.
Good-bye to that old dusty box-car
Where we froze our tootsies away,
Oooooooohhhhh send our mail to the end of the trail,
So long to the Kicking-horse Canyon.

We'll roll up our beddin' and pack up our clothes,
And lighten our hearts with a song.
But where we'll be travellin' nobody knows,
We just gotta be driftin' along.

*["Bunkhouse and Forecastle Songs of the Northwest," Folkways Records,
New York, 1961]*

QUESTIONS

1. What assumptions underlay the 1897 Hamilton Labor Day Program?
2. Which occupations had the best wages, hours, and regularity in Toronto in 1909? Which had the worst? How did this relate to the federal Department of Labour's budget?
3. What do these documents say about the sexual division of labour?
4. What, according to Ames, were the causes of poverty among the working class of Montreal?
5. What were the specific arguments against Asian labour?

READINGS

Bettina Bradbury, *Working Families: Age, Gender, and Daily Survival in Industrializing Montreal* (Toronto: McClelland and Stewart, 1993)

Edmund Bradwin, *The Bunkhouse Man: A Study of Work and Play in the Camps of Canada, 1903-1914* (Toronto: University of Toronto Press, 1972; orig. pub. 1928)

Paul Craven, *"An Impartial Umpire": Industrial Relations and the Canadian State, 1900-1911* (Toronto: University of Toronto Press, 1980)

Craig Heron, *Working in Steel: The Early Years in Canada, 1883-1935* (Toronto: McClelland and Stewart, 1988)

Gregory S. Kealey, *Toronto Workers' Respond to Industrial Capitalism, 1867-1892* second edition (Toronto: University of Toronto Press, 1991)

Gregory S. Kealey and Bryan Palmer, *Dreaming of What Might Have Been: The Knights of Labour in Ontario, 1880-1900* second edition (Toronto: New Hogtown Press, 1987)

Mark Leir, *Where the Fraser River Flows: The Industrial Workers of the World in British Columbia* (Vancouver: New Star Press, 1990)

Bryan Palmer, *Working-Class Experience: Rethinking the History of Canadian Labour, 1800-1991* second edition (Toronto: McClelland and Stewart, 1992)

_____, *A Culture in Conflict: Skilled Workers and Industrial Capitalism in Hamilton, Ontario, 1860-1914* (Montreal-Kingston: McGill-Queen's University Press, 1979)

The Rural Eclipse

By 1921, half of all Canadians lived in towns or cities. Canada could no longer be considered a nation of farmers. The 1911 census revealed a number of rural districts in Central and Eastern Canada where the population had not only failed to keep up through natural increases, but also the number of inhabitants had dropped absolutely. By 1900, all good land in southern Central and Eastern Canada had long been settled. Younger sons who would not inherit, frustrated farmers on marginal lands, and farmers' daughters, poured into Canadian and American cities, or joined thousands of immigrants in staking a homestead in the 'last best west.' In the first decade of the twentieth century, farmers also settled the Clay Belt of Northern Ontario and Quebec, and opened up the Lac St. Jean region. The pull of the towns and cities was in large part the attraction of new employment opportunities created through rapid industrialization. For young men and women, paid labour provided steady wages—unlike their unpaid work on the family farm. The six-day work week and the ten-hour day were seen as improvements over the never ending labour of farming.

Farms and farming were also changing. Successful farms benefited from technological innovations, improved techniques, and crop specialization, as less labour was required to produce greater crop yields. Marginal farms were restricted by a general tightening of farm credit, as banks could make more money in the cities and in industry. The farmers themselves had an increased dependency on towns and cities. New expectations of health and education services meant that proximity to professionals such as doctors or high school teachers was seen as being advantageous. Improved transportation facilities transformed the distribution of goods in rural areas, and manufacturers had no need to locate near their consumers. The accessibility of daily metropolitan newspapers through rail networks and improved roads meant current information was readily available on products and urban prices. Retail catalogues—such as Eaton's, or Quebec's Dupuis Frères—abounded, and eroded the profitability of rural storekeepers.

Section A
Decline and Responses

The fact that fewer Canadians were gaining their livelihood from the land had social as well as economic consequences. Social and moral regulation in rural society had been maintained by an effective combination of church, family, and informal community supervision. A life of farming was idealistically thought to encourage self-reliance, hard-work, and 'purity,' with the family operating as a co-operative economic unit. It had special importance in francophone Catholic Quebec, where many political and religious leaders believed the French-Canadian people had been called by God to live rural life—'*une vie chrétienne, française et rurale.*' A vibrant agrarian society would preserve what was unique about French Canadian culture, and protect it from assimilation—a real threat as hundreds of thousands left Quebec's rural parishes, at least temporarily, for the factories of New England where they formed 'Little Canadas.' Independent and collaborative efforts by governments and the Roman Catholic Church attempted to repatriate *Canadiens* who had moved to the United States, and assisted new farmers through the establishment of colonization societies. In 1938, Montreal doctor Philippe Panneton, writing under the pseudonym of 'Ringuet,' published a novel *Trente Arpents* (*Thirty Acres*) which chronicled the decline of rural Quebec and its impact on one family.

Diminished economic, demographic, and social power, and the corresponding reduction in political and cultural strength, meant that farmers organized their own newspapers, co-operatives, self-education programs, and political organizations. Before World War I, Ontario farmers came together as the United Farmers of Ontario and, as a political movement, went on to win the 1919 provincial election. A history of political discontent directed at the federal government's tariff and railway policies led to the formation of a Grain Growers' Association in each of the three prairie provinces, and the establishment of the influential *Grain Growers' Guide*, prior to World War I. These powerful associations promoted producer and consumer co-operation, improved rural education and health care, and brought about better roads. Women's economic partnership on prairie farms led these organizations to be early supporters of woman's suffrage, and they played a role in the success of this campaign on the prairies. Like their Ontario counterparts, at the end of World War I, they transformed themselves into political parties, and co-operated in the creation of the National Progressive Party.

Agricultural Production in Canada

Field Crops, 1891, 1901 and 1910

	1891 (Bushels)	1901 (Bushels)	1911 (Bushels)
Wheat	42,223,372	55,572,368	139,989,600
Barley	17,222,795	22,224,366	45,147,600
Oats	83,428,202	151,497,407	323,449,000
Rye	1,341,325	2,316,793	1,543,500
Corn in ear	10,711,380	25,875,919	18,726,000
Buckwheat	4,994,871	4,547,159	7,243,900
Peas	14,823,764	12,348,943	6,538,100
Beans	800,015	861,327	1,177,800
Flax seed	138,844	172,222	3,802,000
Grass and clover seed	346,036	288,275	
Potatoes	53,490,857	55,362,365	74,048,000
Field roots	49,679,636	76,075,642	95,207,000
Hay (in tons)	7,693,733	7,852,731	15,497,000
Tobacco (in pounds)	4,277,936	11,266,732	
Hops (in pounds)	1,126,230	1,004,216	
Mixed grains (in bushels)			19,433,600
Sugar beets			155,000

[Canada, Commission of Conservation, Lands, Fisheries and Games, Minerals (Ottawa: The Mortimer Co., Ltd, 1911), p. 22]

Census of Canada, 1911

Rural and Urban Population of Canada in 1911 and 1901 by Province and the increase in the decade

	Population, 1911 rural	urban	Population, 1901 rural	urban	Increase rural	urban
Canada	3,924,394	3,280,444	3,349,516	2,021,799	574,878	1,258,615
Alberta	232,726	141,937	52,399	20,623	180,327	121,314
British Columbia	188,796	203,684	88,478	90,179	100,318	113,505
Manitoba	255,249	200,365	184,738	70,473	70,511	129,892
New Brunswick	252,342	90,517	253,835	77,285	-1,493	22,262
Nova Scotia	306,210	186,123	330,191	129,383	-23,981	56,745
Ontario	1,194,785	1,328,489	1,246,969	935,978	-52,184	392,511
PEI	78,758	14,970	88,304	14,955	-9,546	15
Quebec	1,032,618	970,094	992,667	656,231	39,951	313,863
Saskatchewan	361,067	131,365	73,729	17,550	287,338	113,815
Yukon	4,647	3,865	18,077	9,142	-13,430	5,277
Northwest Territories	17,196	—	20,129	—	-2,933	—

[Canada, Census of Canada 1911, Volume I, Table IX, p. 530]

Regarding the Vocation of the *Canadien* People to Devote Themselves to Agriculture

The goal which brings us together today directly concerns religion and the nation.

The presence here today of so many distinguished guests who have come to discuss the question of colonisation, is proof that the subject deserves the serious attention of all *Canadiens* who love their country. I believe it to be one of the most important political questions of all, because our future as a nation and our influence in Confederation depend on finding the correct answer.

Having been invited by the Colonisation Society to speak at this congress, I have chosen to address the following subject: *The vocation of the* Canadien *people to devote themselves to agriculture.*

Discovering the role assigned to a nation by divine Providence is very important, since the greatness and continuance of that nation depend on its fulfilment. This specific vocation, like all others, can be discovered through recognizing certain signs, signs that are like the manifestation of God's will.

Through the study of history, we find proof that each nation has a special role, evident in the qualities and aptitudes given by God to different peoples, as to each individual...

I wish to speak to you about the providential role given to the *Canadien* people (a role it must fulfil in order to enjoy material well-being). By studying it we can avoid the mistake of undertaking work which is not ours to accomplish, thereby undermining the plans of the Divine Architect.

Gentlemen, we care constantly being told that we are not prepared for life's battles; that we lack the practical knowledge necessary to find the path of fortune, while our countrymen who hail from abroad have all that it takes to become respected leaders in commerce and finance. I believe that these complaints regarding the education of our youth are ill-founded and that they are the result of a lack of understanding of the divine mission which the *Canadien* nation is called to accomplish in this country.

Here, in Canada, we find ourselves alongside a people highly skilled in commerce, aided by the strength of its capital and favoured by the world of finance. Gifted in this manner, they encounter no obstacles on the road to riches, arriving more easily and more rapidly than us at success in commerce and industry.

Gentlemen, is this a great disaster for us? Is it a disaster which we must complain of greatly? I do not believe so, and I think we are wrong to complain when we have a much more important mission to fulfil.

Unlike the *Anglais* and the Yankees, we lack the desire to pursue commercial endeavours. Is that to say that we have no business sense and that mathematics are beyond us? Not at all. If French Canadians are inferior to the *Anglais*, it is only in terms of money. If we had the money, we would rival all other nations in the realm of commerce. We are not lacking in intelligence in any domain. French Canadians have excelled in industry, the arts, science, literature and high commerce; we have always come out on top when we have applied our spirit and talents to different endeavours. If I had to give you a list of names, I would not know where to begin. The present leader of our federal government and our lieutenant governor are proof of the rich intellectual tradition we are able to pass on to our children.

Despite all of this, I repeat that the aptitude and spirit of our people do not lead us to the world of commerce; though I must add that this is not what places us in an inferior position *vis-à-vis* our countrymen of foreign origin. They have their merit, which we are pleased to recognize, but we also have our own, which we can claim with pride.

...

Let us praise God for having placed in the hearts of French Canadians modest tastes and a love for rural life and, given this, let us recognize and accept our important role as a nation of farmers.

...

What were we 136 years ago when the fortunes of war tore us from our motherland and put us under the care of a stranger? We were but a handful of helpless families, unprepared and ill-equipped for what is called the "struggle for life [English in original]." Nevertheless we were able, through sacrifice and hard work, to grow unnoticed and unheeded, all the while excluded from commerce and all government employment. One day, we surprised our conquerors by standing up like people long experienced in doing business, and we took our place at the head of society. From where within ourselves did this sudden improvement come? Where is the well from which flowed so many blessings promised to God's people? ... In the calm of rural life, in the humble yet noble life of farmers, in fulfilling, like the Sons of Jacob, the important role assigned to us by divine Providence.

Today, there would be few traces of our French families of 1763 if, instead of retiring to the calm and silence of the countryside and the forest, they had sunk their energies into careers in business and commerce. In mixing with foreigners, they would have risked losing their language, probably their Faith, and most certainly their traditions.

The situation will be the same for us in the future as it was in the past. We will be saved by staying true to our vocation, which is to be a nation of farmers.

...

What our youth lacks in order to fulfil its role is not practical education as we understand it (or even a higher quality of instruction), which is available to all those who seek it. What it lacks is what it has always lacked, practical help and intelligent guidance to take possession of the land and to exploit the endless riches, passed on to us from ancestors, which lay at our feet. It is because we have been thus ill-equipped for the last thirty years that emigration to the United States has, like a terrible plague, depopulated our countryside and cluttered the cities with idle and delinquent masses.

For thirty years we have searched in vain for a way to stem the tide of emigration. Today, we have found the answer to the problem, and it is an obvious one: well organized and government supported Colonization Societies. We have already seen what they are capable of accomplishing. The Montreal Colonization Society, in spite of its limited financial resources and the apathy it has encountered, has succeeded in doing a great deal of good, thanks to the dedication of those who oversee its operations. You will be astounded when you see what it has accomplished over the last two years. Emigration to the United States has almost completely stopped, and a good number of *Canadiens* have been able to return home. Most importantly, the society must be credited with awakening the entire country to the resources possessed by the province of Quebec through its numerous publications and its constant appeals for help...

We have enough space for seven or eight million inhabitants before we even have to begin subdividing lands as they do in Europe...

I repeat that we must, as our divine mission, take control of the land! Let us become a great people; fill up the country, and when the beautiful province of Quebec is populated like the countries of Europe, when all of our land is exploited, we will find ourselves almost magically prepared for life's battles...

> *[Speech by M. l'abbé Georges Dugas, formerly a missionary to the*
> *Canadian North-West, at the opening session of the Congress on*
> *Colonisation, Montreal, 22 November 1898. Trans. Steven Watt]*

Change on the Quebec Farm

"I can't help it, Pa, there's no work round here. My carpentering doesn't even bring me in enough to eat. And farming's worse still. I'm going to Quebec, where I can get three dollars a day right at the start."

Here was another one going off to answer the call of the city, dazzled by the winking lights of the electric signs, by easy money easily earned and easily spent. Napoléon had chosen the daily round of factory life with its humdrum safe security.

He meant to leave, as the farm could no longer support those who worked it, the very people who had faith in it. Not that it had lost its fertility; it was more prodigal and generous than ever, though this very abundance had become a source of poverty. Prices were slowly subsiding under the curse of a succession of rich fat harvests. What was the good of reaping a hundred-fold if the buyer had only to wait until the farmer, in his anxiety to empty his overflowing barns to make room for the new crop outside, was ready to sell at prices that sank lower and lower?

There were now nine members of Etienne's family on the Moisan farm; and, in addition, there were Euchariste, Marie-Louise, Napoléon and his wife, the latter already pregnant. The farm was more than able to feed these thirteen mouths. But they needed money and still more money to clothe these thirteen bodies and provide shoes, both big and little, for these thirteen pairs of feet.

But seeing the prices meat, vegetables, eggs, and butter fetched, they might just as well be eaten on the spot. The farm could no longer produce enough to satisfy all the new human needs. Besides clothing and boots and shoes, there was gasoline for the engine and spare parts for the farm implements. All too often a horse or a cow fell sick and you can't always do without the veterinary; sometimes people were ill too, and brews and herb remedies won't always cure them...

It was bad enough that he hardly knew where he was, there had been so many changes about the farm. He could hardly recognize anything any more. Not even Etienne, who was less and less willing to give in to his father's wishes and decisions. Not even his grandchildren, who merely thought of him as their grandfather, not as the master of the house, the fields and the stock, which is what he would have liked. Even the animals were different. Etienne had sold Brilliant, and Rougette had to be finished off when she broke her leg. Inspectors had been sent by the government to examine the herd and perfectly healthy-looking cows, that Euchariste was proud to own, had been listed as diseased and slaughtered. Of course, they had received compensation and with the money Etienne had bought pedigreed stock, black and white Holsteins, whose heavy dignified gait made Euchariste think rather longingly of his lively little Canadian cows.

Even the methods of working the farm had changed and each innovation seemed to Moisan to separate man from the soil and break that healthy contact that made for husky men and a friendly fertile earth. Gasoline engines had come in and replaced the horses, but they ruined the pastures with the fumes from their exhaust. Farmers were being urged on every side to give up mixed cultivation with its handy routine. Young upstarts, who had lots to do with books but nothing or hardly anything with the land, tried to teach the old farmers their business...

The evenings brought him some peace of mind, because then he could be with Etienne's children, his grandchildren. In their company he didn't mind forgetting he was head of the family and boss of the farm; he was content to be just a grandfather. Though he wouldn't allow anyone else to think of him as an old man at sixty, he took a quiet delight at making himself seem older than his age for the benefit of the latest batch of youngsters.

"Grandpa, tell us a story."

"All right!... Once upon a time, when I was no bigger than you are Bernard ..."

He told them stories of bygone days he had heard from his elders, all the old tales of adventure from the heroic age of the shanty-men and the lumber-camps: the "Flying Canoe," the "Banshee of the Saint-Maurice," the exploits of Joe Montferrand who, to point out his house to a bully who had come to fight him, just lifted his plough up by the handles. And then there was Felix Poutré, the Patriot, who escaped from Colborne's prisons by pretending to be mad. That brought him straight to the glorious days of the Rebellion of '37 and to its heroes, some of whom he had actually known. And the children's eyes lost their sleepy look when he told them for the hundredth time how, when he was seven years old, he saw Louis-Joseph Papineau.

"Yes, children, you can take it from me, things wouldn't be the way they are if the Patriots had won in '37. We French-Canadians would be our own bosses and farmers' boys wouldn't have to go off to the States to make a living."

But he never mentioned the name of Ephrem, his favourite son.

"We wouldn't have the English sitting on our necks all the time and French-Canadians would stay good French-Canadians like in the old days."

Though he couldn't have explained it, this summed up his innermost feelings, all his horror of the changes that had come about little by little and that left him completely bewildered. People no longer measured in leagues but in miles; money was reckoned in dollars and cents instead of in shillings and pence. Etienne and those of his generation were always using English words they picked up from city people and tourists. Even the newspapers and particularly the catalogues of the big Toronto mail-order houses were crammed with foreign expressions that were speedily incorporated into the impoverished speech of townspeople and countryfolk alike. Their games were affected too. They had started a baseball team in the village and all the special terms used were, of course, in English. Every Sunday afternoon you could hear the umpire, who couldn't even say "Good morning" in English, yelling "Strike two," "Ball one," and "Safe" with all the swank he could muster.

Like everybody else, Euchariste sometimes went to watch the matches played against neighbouring villages. On fine summer Sundays they all turned up by car or truck and, while the youngsters aped American baseball stars to the best of their ability, the old people exchanged the week's meagre news and hankered after the past. Perched on the fence surrounding the field, like a row of swallows on the telegraph wires, the young girls in their print dresses from Dupuis Frères flirted shyly with the tourists, who sometimes stopped their cars for a moment along the side of the road under the dusty beech trees.

It was a far cry from those Sundays of long ago, with the quiet empty afternoons spent on the veranda. The coming of the automobile had changed all that. There was one in every cart-shed now. The less prosperous farmers ran an old jalopy picked up on a second-hand lot, while in families where the sons were allowed to show off as much as they liked there were more pretentious cars. Every Sunday in summer the whole family would climb in, while the eldest son took his place sitting bolt upright behind the steering-wheel. In this way it took no longer to drive from one parish to the next than it used to take to go and visit a neighbour.

"Say, look who's here!"

Euchariste leaned over to see who it was. Under the haw trees, which the caterpillars had covered with their grey tents, a car had drawn up.

"Well! Hullo... How are you?"

"Pretty fair, 'Charis. How are you?"

"Doing fine. How are the folks? They all well?"

"Thanks. They're fine."

"What's new?"

"Oh! Nothing special."

Conversation lagged. In days gone by they would have swapped news about their farms and about the haying, which had just begun. What was the use now? What was the use of finding out what they all knew, of asking about work that was the same everywhere: the ploughing, seeding, reaping and harvesting of their disastrous riches?

"Say, 'Charis, is it true you..."

There was a shout from the crowd of onlookers, thrilled by a spectacular play of the home team.

"What happened?" asked one of the old men.

"Don't know."

"Is it true, 'Charis, your boy down in the States got married?"

"Why, sure. He wrote us about it a while back."

"He must be getting on all right."

"Looks like it."

What Euchariste did not mention was that Ephrem had married an Irish-American girl at White Falls. Wasn't it bad enough that events had proved him wrong and Ephrem right? His son had been successful ever since his desertion, while the farm had betrayed those who gave it their confidence. It wounded the farmer in him more than anything else could that the farm hadn't placed a curse on Ephrem. He had refrained from doing so himself as he was sure his son would come back repentant.

"They're better off in the States than we are here," said young Bertrand, who was in mourning for his wife and wore a heart-shaped patch of black cloth on his left sleeve.

"No wonder," replied Moisan with sudden bitterness. "It was bound to happen with all these fine modern inventions: gasoline engines, machinery, imported stock. That's not all, neither; farmers think they've got to live like city folk now. Young fellows these days have to have an automobile to go and see their girls; and every cent they earn goes to buy clothes and things good enough for a millionaire."

[Ringuet, Thirty Acres *(Toronto: McClelland and Stewart, 1940),*
pp. 185-191; orig. pub. Trente Arpents *(Paris: Flammarion)]*

The Grain Growers' Guide

Winnipeg, June, 1908

Our Paper

The Guide is by no means our ideal of what a Farmers' Paper should be. It is, in fact, but the first step towards the ideal we have in mind. How soon it takes the second step depends in a very great measure upon the Farming Public.

It is almost inconceivable that a great agricultural country inhabited by a class of more than ordinarily progressive farmers should not support an enterprise of this kind to the extent of making it the largest, strongest and most influential paper in Canada. We are giving them the chance to do so and we think they will.

Our ideal of a paper, and one which we hope to see realized in a comparatively short time, is that of a great weekly newspaper containing authentic accounts of all matters and movements of importance to the farmers and other workers, who are in 'the same boat as the farmers, so far as being slaves of the capitalist classes who control the natural resources, the means of production and transportation and medium and avenues of exchange.

This newspaper would help in the work of freeing the people from this slavery by assisting them to organize and get a clear insight into the causes of the present unsatisfactory conditions, and the nature of the remedies, educational, legislative and co-operative, to be applied. It would also try to teach them to escape from the slavery of selfishness, petty greed and the crime of disloyalty in their relations with one another.

This great newspaper would naturally replace in the lives of our people the organs of machine politicians, public service corporations and other capitalistic interests, which, content with preaching false doctrine on economics, repressing or distorting the truth about the success of advanced legislation in other countries, systematically employ inspired articles disguised as news items to confuse public opinion...

Its Editorials would be written from the stand-point of the producers and its news columns would contain all that could be found out respecting progressive legislation, the growth of Co-operative Associations and the progress of the public ownership and co-operative idea as applied to public utilities and natural resources.

It would be a great educational force and would the more quickly operate upon the public intelligence, because as well as supplying "good medicine" through its circulation, it would cut off the supply of "dope" by reducing the circulations of the plutocratic organs, which it would naturally replace in the homes of the people.

So long as partisan and capitalistic organs are the only media of publicity which we have, it is practically impossible to carry on a campaign of education which affects the interests of a party or of a capitalistic institution.

By a conspiracy of silence a popular agitation can be kept from spreading, a prosecution of a vicious corporation can be made to appear as a persecution, or an effort to show the strength of popular discontent with existing conditions or the conduct of our legislators can be rendered abortive by declining to publish the communications of the malcontents.

We recognize that our paper in its present form is not capable of efficiently discharging the functions of an opinion paper, an official organ for an Association, a reporter of markets, or a newspaper, and therefore we speak of it as being only the initial step in the creation of a more efficient publication which will succeed it so soon as the support given it by the public will warrant.

So soon as it becomes self-supporting as a monthly, it will be converted into a semi-monthly and after making good in that form will become a weekly. New features appropriate to its changed form will be added as the changes are made...

The paper will deal with crop conditions throughout the world. It will not yell itself hoarse, however, about a crop that is just peeping through the ground, thus enabling the "bears" to pound down the price of our commodity. For the same reason it will discount all exaggerated accounts of wonderful crops. It will not conceal the fact of a frost that greatly lessens our yield or depreciates its quality for the sake of helping the miller to get wheat cheaper than he should, or to enable the land speculators to continue to secure high prices for land from those who are going to sweat the price out during the coming years.

It will not tell whether the price is going to be higher or lower from time to time, at least not so long as the speculators rule and can "rig" the markets, because not being in touch with the speculators, it don't know what they are going to do, and consequently don't know what prices will do. For example: cables come higher from Europe and prices fall here or "bear" news comes from across the line and prices go up here. In the wheat market it is the unexpected that happens and the "favorite" rarely wins.

Card gamblers cannot live on one another. It is necessary that a green-horn should sit into the game from time to time to supply the funds.

So with gambling in futures. The public must come into the game for the professionals to make money. When enough of the outside public, including many farmers, who have sold their real wheat, have bought the option, it is necessary that the price should be put down in order that the professional should rake in the margins. When enough of the public sell short then is the time for the price to go up.

The best this paper can do then is to tell what prices would do if there was nobody to "monkey" with the market. But even this is difficult, as those who speculate in grain are able to manufacture "bull" and "bear" news, commonly called "dope," from time to time that is hard to distinguish from genuine crop news, and this is a plan greatly resorted to by speculators.

A feature of the paper will be cartoons illustrating interesting situations in public affairs or driving home important truths which the farmers need to learn.

In later issues there will be regular departments such as current events, proposed legislation here and elsewhere, news on public ownership of public utilities, co-operative news, opinions of noted publicists, words of great thinkers on economic, social and ethical subjects, etc.

There will also be pages specially for women and young people.

It is hoped, however, our women and youths will read the paper from cover to cover. Woman suffrage is near at hand and with it the promise of better laws. Some people are afraid to trust women with the franchise. Well, the man who deliberately thinks that women are as bad and as selfish as men are, and would make as silly a use of the franchise as most men do, must have a very low estimate of women's morals and intellectual ability, that's all.

There will be plenty of room for correspondents who have something to say for the public good.

Then there will be the "Cranks Corner." To the editor the word "Crank" is a title of honor. It is by means of cranks that the world is moved forward. So if anybody's letter appears in this corner he must take it as a compliment, as the Corner will admit the ideas of men who are thinking things out for themselves and striving to find solutions to the problems which individual and social life presents.

[The Grain Growers' Guide *(Winnipeg, Manitoba), June 1908]*

The Girl and the Farm

One of the most startling features of the census is the recorded drift of women from the farms to the cities. While their adventurous brothers go west the sisters are crowding into the cities and towns to take places in whitewear factories, in departmental stores, and as stenographers and clerks. The migration of young men from the farms of Ontario has been going on for many years. In some measure the drain has been made good by the influx of male immigrants from Great Britain and other European countries.

The migration of the young women is a more serious thing for the future of the Province, because the place of the migrants is not being taken by anyone. In Bruce there are 1,875 more males than females, in Grey 1,719, and in a small county like Welland 2,381. There is scarcely a county in Ontario devoted chiefly to agriculture in which there are not many more men than women, while in the single constituency of North Toronto there are 7,500 more women than men.

Why is rural Ontario unable to keep the girl on the farm? In what respect do the cities and towns present superior attractions? The steady drain upon the country to supply school teachers for the west accounts for only a few hundred girls yearly. Ontario sends them forth joyfully, knowing that their career as teachers will be short, and that in their prairie homes they will become the mothers of the best type of Canadians, Godfearing, patriotic and educated.

But what happens to the girl who leaves the farm for a place in a whitewear factory or behind the counter? What of her future? Why should she prefer the discomfort of a hall bedroom and the physical weariness of factory life to the freedom and the healthy conditions of a country home? It would be worth the while of the Young Women's Guild and the Y.W.C.A. to get a few hundred answers to these questions from farmers' daughters in the stores and factories of Toronto. It would probably be found that the desire for pocket-money and the instinct of gregariousness are the two chief causes for the drift of the girls from the farm. Too many comfortable Ontario farmers think their daughters have no need of money, and that for their services an occasional dollar grudgingly doled out is ample recompense. Many a girl becomes a wage-earner in the cities so that she may sometimes have a dollar to spend, even though in earning it she must live under conditions that are not nearly so agreeable as life on the farm.

The desire for social intercourse is another potent reason for the country girl's migration. It seems to be generally agreed that there is not so much social life in the country as there was a generation ago. The spelling bees, the Templar meetings, and sleighing parties, and occasional dances of the earlier days have in many cases been refined out of existence, and the church socials are not nearly so useful a means of bringing the sexes together in the intimacy that makes for life partnerships.

Political and fiscal changes will not keep the girls on the farm. The telephone, with its facilities for arranging social gatherings; good wide roads that would permit women and girls to drive about more without danger of being crowded into the ditch by every passing motor car; the making of regular, systematic money allowances to the girls to be spent on their own initiative, and the introduction of sanitary conveniences into farm buildings would do much to prevent rural Ontario from becoming a country of elderly and middle-aged people, while the cities are swarming with pallid and restless girls who should be the life and the joy of the farms of this fertile Province.

[The Globe, *23 December 1911*]

The Country Guide

VOL XXI   WINNIPEG, APRIL 2, 1928   NO.7
It only requires a rapid glance over the past 20 years of agricultural development on the prairies to understand why at this time we have changed the name of The Grain Growers' Guide to The Country Guide. In 1908, when The Guide was established, this prairie country was still largely in the pioneer stage and grain growing was the only important industry. The Grain Growers' Associations, then in their youth, were engaged in the struggle for freedom in marketing the grain crop. But as the country developed and a wider range of problems confronted the farming community the Grain Growers' Associations recognized that their names were no longer appropriate and they have all been changed. The same causes which led to a change in the name of the associations have brought about the change in the name of The Guide. Both changes have been made to keep abreast of the times.

Following the change of name of the associations many readers suggested a change in the name of The Guide. Many new names for this journal have been submitted and considered. Finally the name The Country Guide was selected as the most appropriate for the type of farm magazine service which The Guide is now rendering to its readers. We have retained the words "The Guide" by which this journal has been familiarly known for 20 years and have added the word "Country" indicating the rural field to which this journal is devoted. While there is always a sentimental attachment to a name which has been familiarly known for such a long period, yet we believe the new name will be welcomed by our wide circle of readers. The change of name involves no change in policy. "Equal Rights to All and Special Privileges to None" still flies at the editorial masthead and The Country Guide will be as thoroughly devoted to the interests of its readers under the new name as it has been for 20 years under the old.

During the past 20 years agriculture and rural life on the prairies have undergone many changes. The farming area has spread far to the north and the farm population has doubled, yes nearly trebled. Agricultural methods have changed and farming is slowly but steadily becoming more diversified. Country life has been profoundly affected by such modern developments as the telephone, the automobile and the radio. The telephone and the automobile have brought the farm closer to the town while the radio is steadily bringing the whole world to the ears of the farm home. The old isolation of 20 years ago is rapidly disappearing and the relationship between town and country is undergoing a revolution. In no similar period of 20 years has country life been so deeply affected. Never before has rural public opinion been such a factor in determining public policies. Never before has country life afforded such opportunities.

The problems which face agriculture and rural life have not by any means been all solved, but the farm population today is in better shape to solve them than ever before. The various farm organizations of men and women are studying the vital problems of the day. Their representatives sit in all the provincial legislatures and in the House of Commons. There is no part of the world where agriculture is better represented in educational organizations, business organizations and political organizations than here on the prairie. We have all the machinery necessary to carry on a great educational program for the highest development of rural civilization.

We believe that the new conditions surrounding our country life call for the very highest type of farm magazine. Farming is not merely a business, but a business and a living combined. The farm is not merely a factory for the production of food stuffs, but a home for the family and the centre of the family life. In no other important industry is this the case, consequently a journal giving service to the modern farm home must take into consideration conditions as they now exist. This is the reason why the pages of The Guide are devoted in part to the wide range of problems confronting agriculture, which is not only the mainstay of this part of the country but the greatest single factor in Canada's development. It is also the reason why the pages of The Guide are devoted in part to political affairs, social and economic development, fiction, literature, science, art, travel, etc. Our readers have demonstrated that they are as deeply interested in world problems as are the urban dwellers. The farmer and his wife and family are today interested in everything in which the town and city people are interested. The future of Canada, will largely be molded by those boys and girls now growing up in the farm homes. It is therefore our aim and purpose to devote The Country Guide not only to those things which go to make farming more profitable, but also to those things that go to make living more comfortable and satisfying and to supply a wide range of information as well as entertainment necessary to the development of good citizenship in a modern democracy.

Thus it is in keeping with the development of country life in the West that we have changed the name of this journal to The Country Guide. We hope to make other improvements and mark steady progress from time to time in the development of the highest type of farm magazine. Our best hope is that we shall continue to merit the large volume of generous commendation that has poured into this office from our readers during the past twelve months.

[The Country Guide *(Winnipeg, Manitoba), 2 April 1928]*

Keep the Boy on the Farm

by Nina Moore Jamieson

In all our talk about keeping the boy on the farm, do we pause to consider the possibility of overdoing even a good thing? Is there such a thing as keeping him there unadvisedly? For farms differ as widely as humans differ, and there is no chance to deal with the situation in generalities. What is back of this cry "Keep the boy on the farm?" Why do we so readily accept it as the solution of our agricultural difficulties?

In the first place, perhaps it is because we realize that farming is a business that takes a lot of learning, and comes best when we grow into it. The child who learns to milk, at eight, never has any particular trouble in milking. Wait till twenty-eight, however, and see how the little untrained, undeveloped muscles will rebel! How the back will ache, how the hands will cramp!

That which is learned easily in early youth, grows to be instinctive as years advance. So we know that the boy who has grown up to a familiarity with grains and implements and cattle and horses will have much of this work mechanically by heart. He will know how to coddle a balky binder, how to get the very last shred of service out of much-mended harness, how to rig up a makeshift when something goes wrong with the useful little gasoline engines. He knows a lot about applied mechanics. Knows it, and doesn't guess how he came to know it.

As he grows up, he becomes more and more of value to the farm. What a pity to let him drift away to some other line of work, with all that specialized knowledge wasting the back of his mind! It is, indeed. Yet it happens day after day, and there is nothing much that can be dome about it. Because knowledge is specialized it does not necessarily become the finger of destiny.

Keep the boy on the farm—but not to such a condition as this! If he is worth wages, pay him, and pay him on the first of the month, as though he were a hired man—but see that he earns his money! Even though it is not possible to scrape up more than five or ten dollars a month—scrape it, and then let him buy his clothes, and his gas, and his postage stamps and his long distance calls.

Don't put him to the humiliation of going to his mother saying:

"I want some money, mother."

"How much?"

Most of us have had the "How much?" fired at us, and we know the strange inner reluctance to state a sum. We also know the rebellion that follows "What did you do with what I gave you last week?"

Why do we feel like that? I wonder! Yet most of us feel that it is quite the right thing to go to our husbands for cash. It is their business to provide for us, to support us. We have a right to be proud of them if they are generous, and to resent it if they are stingy. But we sometimes fail to appreciate the demoralizing effect on a man's self-respect when the position is reversed, and he has to ask some woman for money, or let her give it to him as a matter of course.

If the boy stays on the farm, let him stay as an independent citizen, free to go if something better offers, but warmly free to stay if his heart and his chosen work dictate that to him.

Little is ever said about the way some sons are coaxed to remain and give the best years of their lives to building up a farm, under the promise that it will be theirs, some day. Perhaps the father says, "Yes, by all means get married and bring your wife here. The house is big enough—you take one side, we'll take the other. We're getting old. It'll all be yours some day."

The daughters are married and away, their portion with them—or at work somewhere, having taken out their share in the cost of their training. So the boy stays on. It is a loose arrangement. Who is to pay the taxes? Who is to look after the fuel? Who is to pay for repairs to buildings, new fences? Son sees the importance of one thing, father of another. Theoretically, both know that there can't be two moons in the sky. Also that there is no sense in taking two bites of one cherry.

Presently the father dies—and then, what? There may be no will—no record of business dealings. Daughters claim their share. He has no statement in writing of his own standing. Or there may be a will, which all these years his father has meant to change—But the boy was kept on the farm and what a lovely thing it was!

A regular muddle. All his life dictated to him, his wife serving just as he was, for something which never arrived. Would he not have been better if he had gone and worked in the same way for some stranger? At least there would not be the bitterness that these family arrangements invariably cause...

[Family Herald and Weekly Star, *8 April 1931*]

Section B
Rural Schools

Rural change and urbanization were a source of great anxiety, and concerns about rural depopulation focused on young people. Responses came from farmers themselves, from traditional leadership in the churches, schools, and legislature, and from a new breed of experts—social scientists—who addressed the problem with the help of new intellectual disciplines. The nascent field of sociology was used to identify the social and economic "causes" of rural depopulation, and solutions were proposed after a gathering of facts in the form of a social survey. Educators sought to shape rural society by using the public school system to transmit values and enhance the role of agriculture.

To Centralise Rural Schools

The opening at Middleton, N.S., of the first school in Canada which embodies the much-discussed principles of consolidation and transportation is naturally of interest to the citizens of the Dominion, more especially as next year will see the establishment of similar institutions in Ontario, Quebec, and other eastern provinces. The experiment at Middleton will, therefore, be closely watched by all who take more than a passing concern in the problems of education.

The credit of introducing the consolidated school into Canada belongs principally to two men. These are Sir William C. McDonald, the millionaire philanthropist of Montreal, and Prof. J.W. Robertson, the Commissioner for Agriculture and Dairying, Ottawa, and the leading Canadian advocate of practical, as opposed to merely theoretical education. Sir William's earlier gifts for the improvement of education went to the universities. Following these was a princely donation for the establishment and maintenance for three years in each of the older provinces of a school for instruction in mechanical and domestic science. The result was the multiplication of such schools in Canada. The philanthropist next turned his attention to the cause of rural education. It was the opinion of Messrs. McDonald and Robertson that in addition to mechanical and domestic sciences the country schools should give instruction in the natural sciences, especially those intended to improve horticulture and agriculture, that such instruction could only be provided at centralised schools, and that consolidation could only be effected by transporting the children. The outcome was an offer by Sir William to provide the money, and Prof. Robertson offered to superintend the inauguration of a comprehensive scheme for the introduction of nature study, manual training, and household science into the rural educational system of Canada. The scheme included the establishment of a training school in nature study and household science in connection with the Ontario Agricultural College at Guelph, the establishment and maintenance for three years in each of the five Eastern Provinces of a group of schools having school gardens and an instructor in nature study, and also the establishment and maintenance for three years in each of these provinces of a consolidated school with school garden and departments of manual training and domestic economy...

As the great majority of the people of Canada are engaged in agricultural pursuits, a scheme for the improvement of rural education must create widespread interest. The close relation which in the United States the transportation of pupils has borne to the good roads movement and the free rural mail delivery movement gives additional importance to the experiment now inaugurated at Middleton. Those who have studied the question say that the inadequate educational privileges and isolation of country life are leading causes of the exodus from the farms. If through this scheme a new attractiveness can be added to farm life, one of the greatest economical problems before the people of Canada will be solved...

When Sir William McDonald's offer was published in 1901, the advantages of Middleton as a location for one of the schools was urged upon Prof. Robertson. The Middleton Board of Trade appointed a committee to act in the matter. This committee attended meetings in Middleton and seven adjoining school sections, and induced them to apply for the McDonald grant, each section pledging itself to enter the consolidation if the financial conditions proved satisfactory...

Each individual section retains its identity and elects a school board, who through a secretary, collects the school taxes as formerly. In addition, there is a consolidated board composed of three members for Middleton and one for each of the other sections. This board has full control of the central school, and arranges for the transportation of the children living outside of Middleton section. The eight sections for the next three years will contribute the average amount paid by them in the year 1899, 1900 and 1901, and all other expenses of buildings, equipment and maintenance, are to be contributed by the McDonald fund.

A fine brick and stone building, 87 x 62 feet, with basement and three floors, is being erected at Middleton. This is to be finished by Jan. 1 next. The old school-house, which has just been completely remodeled and repaired, contains four well-ventilated rooms. A large barn is being built to shelter the vans and horses during school hours, ground is being prepared for school gardens. The school is to be equipped with the best apparatus obtainable. Until the new building is completed the old building and four halls will accommodate the school. The ceremony of laying the cornerstone of the new building took place on Monday, September 7th, in the presence of a large number of spectators and the leading educationists of the province.

Among the by-laws adopted by the board are these:—The school will open at 9.30 a.m. and close at 3 p.m., with one hour intermission at noon and 15 minutes in the forenoon. No non-residents will be carried in the vans. Non-resident students giving certificate of character from a clergyman or justice of the peace, and certificate of studious habits from their last teacher, will be admitted to the grades 1, 2, 3 and 4 upon the payment of $6 per year tuition, to grades 5, 6, 7 and 8 on the payment of $8, and to the High School grades on payment of $10 per year tuition. Van drivers are to wait not longer than two minutes for any one child, and arrive at the school-house in the morning not more than 30 minutes, nor less than ten minutes before the time for opening the school. The vans are to be ready within five minutes and start not more than fifteen minutes after the school closes for the day. The drivers are to exercise the same care for the children's physical and moral welfare while in the vans as the teachers while they are in the school-room, and are each held in bonds to the amount of $500.

The consolidated district has been divided into eleven van routes, and the contracts awarded for the year. The length of routes ranges from $2^{1}/_{2}$ to $6^{1}/_{2}$ miles, and the amount paid the contractors from $300 to $600. As the drivers had this year to purchase horses, harness, and robes, it is probable that next year the cost of transportation will be materially reduced. By picking up the children at gathering stations, instead of in front of their homes, the cost might be further reduced.

The teachers have prepared themselves, and the school will be equipped with the object of making the study of the natural sciences and practical educational work leading features, indeed nature study will dominate the whole course. Much of the work will be done in the garden, field, by the brooks, and in the forest. The purpose is to train the child by doing rather than by hearing; and the pupil's education will be measured by what he can do rather than by what he knows.— *Toronto Mail and Empire.*

[*The Educational Monthly of Canada, 25 October 1903, pp 375-377*]

The Middleton School, 1904
The Middleton Consolidation

The progress of this great experiment has been kept continuously before the public in the *Journal of Education*. The institution is now fully equipped...The old building near by has been completely transformed within, and contains the laboratories—chemical, mechanic science, and domestic science. The school grounds, garden, and van stables, are complete. The school has a greater number of teachers than the original sections, and they all rank among the best qualified in the profession. The town and the rural sections have more than all the privileges and advantages of the most expensive city school system in the province, where the people pay a high rate for their privileges. But according to the agreement entered into with the ratepayers, they need contribute no more than 35 cents on the $100 for the three years of the experiment. Not till this term is completed can we be sure of the mettle of the privileged ratepayers of this beautiful region in the Annapolis Valley. They may have, as has been stated on good authority, the finest consolidated school in the world. It is certainly the finest in Canada. The people are as yet, however, doing nothing more for it than for their old schools. Their leaders, however, are preparing for the time when the complete administration of this model establishment will devolve upon themselves. That they will be equal to the crisis when it arrives we have good reason to expect; for it will involve no greater proportionate exertion than is now being made in some less favored sections of the province where the people cannot obtain similar educational privileges at five times the rate of taxation.

The running expenses of the school will be greater during the second year on account of the increase of the teaching staff—due to the addition of the departments of mechanic and domestic science. On the other hand, there will be an increase in the Manual Training grant and a decrease in the cost of driving the vans... Again, there is hope for the cheapening of this service when the drivers with their horses can discover some profitable way of passing the time between 9 a.m. and 4 p.m. Sir William's experiment has already proven very many valuable principles; and the people of the first consolidations which have just been effected in the Island of Cape Breton are practically applying them. But while doing so they are voting their own money for it also, thus practically demonstrating that the poorer rural sections may be rich in the possession of patriotic and intelligent citizens, who are quick to see an advantage, public spirited enough to act promptly even when the effort costs.

The cost of the first year's work in the Macdonald Consolidated is as follows:
The new Macdonald buildings, the
reconstruction of the old building into
Laboratories or a Practical Science
building, and the general equipment of
the whole with grounds and school garden $21,183.72

The Vans, Stable and Ground 4,289.29
      Total expenditure on Capital Account.. $25,473.01
      General (annual) running expenses......   10,623.13
      Grand Total Expenditure 36,096.14

From regular ordinary sources received 3,957.85
From Sir Wm C Macdonald received................. 32,138.29
      Grand Total Receipts $36,096.14

Analysis of General Running Expenses
(First School Year)

Expenditure.

Salaries of Van Drivers	$5,462.40
Salaries of Teachers	2,796.28
Provincial Aid of Teachers	1,055.93
General Expenses (Fuel, Janitor, Insurance	
Annual Repairs and Supplies)..............	1,308.52
Total	$10,623.13

Receipts.

Sectional Assessment...	$1,760.00
Provincial Aid to Teachers................................	1,055.93
Municipal School Fund	596.67
Manual Training Grant	221.25
Raise by School Entertainments........................	220.00
Fee from Pupils from outside Sections	104.00
Sir Wm C Macdonald Fund...............................	6,665.28
Total..	$10,623.13

Further improvements on the building and equipment have been authorised, which during the second year may add about $1,000 to the original cost. That the teachers and pupils are enthusiastic in their efforts to aid the work is shown by their contribution of $220, applied specially to the purchase of a piano. Experiments are being tried in many practical directions, among them being the preparation of lunches in the domestic science department for the pupils...

It will be admitted by all who visit the school and note the excellence of the equipment, that the school board of the consolidation sections has exacted of Sir William Macdonald no ordinary educational outfit. The liberal gift of these desiderata is a public ratification of the implied determination of the beneficiaries to conduct the school in future themselves on the same effective plan on which they have asked that it should be founded and started. The honor, not only of their public men, but every individual in the communities concerned, is pledged to the world for the successful carrying out of the experiment on the scale agreed upon. Failure would not only tarnish the honor of these communities, but it would arouse the indignation of the province against them in case of failure for the asking of what is nearly a national opportunity, from other communities whose patriotism and intelligence might be assumed to make the experiment a success locally, and a credit to the province. The Middleton sections are running this risk; the jealous school sections should clearly see that the Middleton good fortune is heightened with a responsibility which few honorable communities would venture to seriously undertake. This responsibility the consolidated school board has taken well to heart, we have good reason to think, and are providing ways and means for the future administration of the school on practically the same lines.

[Nova Scotia, "Annual Report on the Public Schools of Nova Scotia 1903-4," Journal and Proceedings of the House of Assembly of the Province of Nova Scotia, *Appendix 5, (1904), pp. xxiii-xxxvii]*

The Middleton School, 1906

Division No. 4—Digby and Annapolis

L.S. Morse, M.A., *Inspector.*

...The greater number of the schools were found to be in fairly satisfactory condition. Some were classes superior, some good and some poor. The same classification applies to the teachers employed inasmuch as it may be considered an axiom that the "teacher makes the school." That some poor schools are to be found should not be considered strange when the large number of inexperienced and untrained teachers entering the profession each year is considered. This year forty-six new and untried teachers entered the profession in this division. During the proceeding year fifty-two teachers entered upon this work for the first time. It would be strange, if out of so many untried teachers a few should not be found to be comparative failures. As nearly all new teachers are from sixteen to eighteen years of age, the wonder is that there are so few failures. More maturity and a little experience most commonly make fairly good teachers of those at first classed as poor. It is to be regretted that the short period which most teachers remain in the profession makes so large an influx of new teachers each year necessary. The salaries are so low that there is but little inducement for teachers to remain long in the school-room. This condition has driven many young men to other occupations who would otherwise engage in teaching, and has left this sphere of labor largely to young women. Of the two hundred and fifty-five teachers and substitutes employed in this division this year, forty-seven only were males. The remedy for this state of affairs lies with the ratepayers. The Government cannot reasonably be expected to do more than it has been doing. An increase of salaries to good teachers, and the enactment of a good pension law, would probably induce more of the young men to adopt teaching as a life profession. A pension scheme should derive some of its income from the Government. The small remuneration received by the great majority of the teachers will not permit them to contribute largely towards a pension fund. Their salaries will barely suffice for present necessities. A pension fund is necessary to make provision for sickness and old age.

It might, perhaps, be considered invidious to eulogize the work done in particular schools to the exclusion of others, but space will not permit me to mention all. As the Macdonald Consolidated School at Middleton was established as an object lesson for the whole Province, it is quite proper that I should refer to that specially. In my report last year I referred to this school as an unqualified success from an educational point of view. It has still continued to be such, and has fully demonstrated the benefit of bringing pupils from outlying sections to a central school. Eleven teachers were employed during the year, with Mr George B McGill as principal. Three of these taught the High School Grades, six taught the Common School Grades, and one in each of the Mechanic and Domestic Science departments. The whole staff proved to be efficient teachers and did excellent work. It would be surprising if such were not the case with the facilities for work which they enjoyed. Three of the teachers held Agricultural diplomas, and did effective work in that line by means of the excellent school garden on the premises. The attendance was even better than during the previous year. A larger county grant was obtained as a consequence, and the cost of conveyance of pupils slightly reduced. The ultimate fate of the school is problematical. Another year will tell the tale. It cannot be maintained without the aid of the Macdonald Fund, unless the sections submit to a much higher rate of taxation than at present.

[Nova Scotia, "Annual Report on the Public Schools of Nova Scotia, 1906," Journal and Proceedings of the House of Assembly of the Province of Nova Scotia, *Appendix 5, (1906), pp. 92-93]*

The Middleton School, 1908

Division No. 4 – Digby and Annapolis
L.S. Morse, M.A., *Inspector*
... I am sorry to be obliged to report, however, that the consolidated school as such ceased to exist at the close of the year. The outside sections, at the annual meeting, voted to maintain independent schools during the ensuing year. This adverse vote was, I believe, caused by the decision of the trustees of the Macdonald Fund to grant no further special aid to this consolidated school. This of necessity would place a heavier burden upon the individual sections than the ratepayers were willing to assume.

[Nova Scotia, "Annual Report on the Public Schools of Nova Scotia, 1908," Journal and Proceedings of the House of Assembly of the Province of Nova Scotia, *Appendix 5, (1908), p. 146]*

Rural Schools in Manitoba

CHART 4.

Teaching Experience.

NUMBER OF TEACHERS	YEARS OF EXPERIENCE	PER CENT
9 teachers	Under 1 year	29%
8 teachers	1-2 years	26%
8 teachers	3-5 years	26%
1 teacher	5-10 years	3%
3 teachers	11-20 years	10%
2 teachers	over 20 years	6%
31 teachers	—TOTAL—	100%

The teaching profession is the most migratory of all the professions. Of thirty-two cases considered, 59% had been less than six months in their present schools; 13% had been in their present positions between six months and one year; 19% between one to two years, and 9% from two to five years. The length of time in their previous school was almost as short. Thirty per cent held their positions for less than six months; 20% for one year or less; 30% from one to two years, 15% from two to three years, and 5% over three years. One school reports having had ten different teachers during the past six years.

When the inadequate training of teachers and the short time they spend in each school is taken into consideration, it is not hard to understand why the country school has not its right place in rural leadership. While we might not agree with Mabel Carney, in her book "Country Life and the Country School," when she says, "The greatest single need for the improvement of country life at the present time, therefore, is for a corps of properly prepared country teachers who will enter our existing country schools, and, through vitalized teaching and tactful social leadership, convert them into living centres for the instruction of both children and adults and the complete upbuilding of country community life," nevertheless the country school has a great opportunity, and in the days that are to come will make a still larger contribution toward rural reconstruction.

One of the difficulties the teacher must face in the newer sections of the Valley is the problem of securing suitable lodgings within reasonable distance of the school building. The following figures dealing with twenty-five teachers show that 52% live within less than a mile of their school; 24% are distant from one to two miles; 8% are distant from two to three miles; 8% from three to five miles; one teacher, or 4%, is distant six miles, and another (4%) resides ten miles from the school building. It is not fair, however, to infer that all of these of necessity reside at such distance. Those who live more than three miles, it can safely be said, do so to meet their own convenience. A number who desire to live with their parents are willing to drive a considerable distance. In the case of two town schools the teachers are married men, who live on their own farms.

The teachers were asked what games the pupils played. From the number of games mentioned it is clear that play-life is receiving at least some attention, for 82% specified some of the games played. Baseball is the most popular, 47% of the schools reporting it. Thirty-six per cent play hide-and-seek; 29% play tag; 25% play football; 21% pull-away; 18% prisoners' bar; 11% circle games; 7% basket-ball; 3% anti-over, croquet, marbles, wicket and swinging. Fifty-seven per cent of the schools mentioned other games not included among these. The weakness of the play-life among the school children is not that it lacks variety so much as supervision and organization. The work that is being done in this regard at Bowsman school is much to be commended.

It is true the games requiring team-play, such as baseball, football, basket-ball, are among the most popular. All such games should be played and encouraged in the country. If co-operation is to develop, as it must, for the strengthening of rural life, the boys and girls, too, must learn the value of team-play while at school. Many of life's problems are prepared for on the playground.

The goal of the rural school too often has been the entrance examination. No sacrifice has been too great in order that one or two pupils might be coached for this *summum bonum* of rural education. The training of the many—who will remain on the farm—is neglected that the few may take the "entrance" stepping-stone from the farm. Sixty-seven per cent of the schools report having had pupils pass their entrance examination during the last five years. Thirty-seven per cent of the schools report these pupils as having gone to high school; 6% as having gone to agricultural school or college; 13% as having gone to business college; 12% as having gone to towns and cities to work.

School Gardening

Elementary agriculture, school-gardening, and nature study, are beginning to have a recognized place in the school curriculum. The Department of Education is to be commended for the interest it is creating and fostering in country life through its leadership in elementary agriculture, nature study and school-gardening. Of thirty-two schools considered, 75% teach elementary agriculture, 91% teach nature study and 55% have school gardens.

As to how effectively elementary agriculture and nature study is being taught, there was little means of ascertaining. From a few observations, however, one felt that much of it was bookish. As one teacher said, "It is an easy thing to teach English literature because we have been trained to, but trying to teach nature study is a different matter." There are few places in the West where nature offers to hand such abundant material for her study.

As stated above, in over half the schools, gardening is carried out by the pupils. There is no doubt that the school garden has come to stay, but in Manitoba it is still in the experimental stage. The idea is excellent, and is appreciated by both the children and their parents. In Swan River questionnaires were filled out from interviews with one hundred and thirty farmers. One of the questions asked was, "In what is the school making its largest success?" And of those who answered, 56% gave first place to nature study and the school garden. This percentage is considerably smaller because of the overwhelming appreciation of consolidation where it is in operation. If we omit the opinion of the farmers in the consolidated school districts, the percentage of those in the other districts who consider nature study and the school garden the most noteworthy success is increased from 56% to 80%.

One hundred and three farm household questionnaires were filled out. Two of the questions asked of mothers were these—"Do your children show a greater interest in plant life and agriculture because of the training they are receiving in nature study, agriculture, and school gardening?" "Do you consider the teaching of these subjects in the school helpful?" Eighty-nine per cent of the mothers said they thought that their children did show greater interest, and 96% considered the teaching of these subjects helpful.

An attempt also was made to find out how the pupils liked nature study and the school garden. From one hundred and eighty replies from seven schools, including two consolidated, three rural and one town school (Bowsman), 81% of the pupils said they liked nature study. Eighty per cent of the pupils would like to have a school garden next year.

The enrolment in the above schools is very largely rural, and accounts for their keen interest in nature study and the school garden. Swan River village, with a population of over five hundred, represents more the urban interest, which is strongly reflected in the attitude of the pupils toward the teaching of these subjects. Fifty per cent of the pupils say they do not like nature study, and 83% do not want a school garden next year.

These figures are the strongest argument that the attempt to ruralize the curricula of the country school is appreciated by country people. When it is remembered that these subjects are still very imperfectly taught in many schools, and that the school garden is usually inferior to the farm garden, this showing is most remarkable. In 70% of the school gardens the soil had received no previous preparation, and at only 12% of the schools were the gardens cared for during the summer vacation. Two improvements in the school garden are essential—first, the physical conditions, such as fencing and preparation of the soil, must be as carefully attended to as in the best home gardens; and second, during the vacation period uniform care must be provided independent of the pupils. The Department of Education might very profitably meet the expense of such care, providing always that at the beginning of vacation the gardens came up to the Department's standard. The local agricultural society might give encouragement by offering prizes for the best collection of school garden products, and to individual pupils for school plot exhibits. If the prizes for individual pupil exhibitors were conditioned by a home plot, as well as a school plot, so that part of the pupils' interest was centred in the garden at home, they might accomplish even better results.

Consolidation of Rural Schools

The most convincing argument in favor of consolidation where it has been tried in the Benito and Durban schools, is the enthusiasm with which it is endorsed by parents living in these districts. Twenty-three farmers were interviewed. Among these not one questioned the benefits of consolidation, and in reply to the question, "In what way is the school making its most noteworthy success?'" 65% said "consolidation." During the years 1913-14 there were enrolled in the consolidated schools of Manitoba, 6,255 pupils, the average attendance being 4,084, or 65.8% of the enrolment, or 9.9% higher then in the one-roomed schools. If the same increase in attendance were to obtain in Swan River Valley through consolidation, it would mean *50 more* children in our schools every school day.

[Departments of Social Service and Evangelism of the Methodist and Presbyterian Churches, Rural Survey of Swan River *(Manitoba, August-September 1914), pp. 44-47] Used by permission of the United Church of Canada; prepared for the Swan River Survey Committee.*

QUESTIONS

1. Which provinces experienced the greatest shift in population? How did those at the time understand the causes of the rural exodus and what solutions did they propose?

2. What concerns around rural decline were specific to French Canadians?

3. Why were young people targeted in attempts to fight rural 'outmigration'?

4. How did the Macdonald Consolidated School in Middleton, Nova Scotia, try to address the problem of rural education?

5. What do school inspectors' reports and the findings of the Methodist/Presbyterian Manitoba rural survey tell us about the problems of staffing rural schools?

READINGS

Marjorie Griffin Cohen, *Women's Work, Markets and Economic Development* (Toronto: University of Toronto Press, 1988)

Gerald Friesen, *The Canadian Prairies* (Toronto: University of Toronto Press, 1987)

John MacDougall, *Rural Life in Canada: Its Trends and Tasks* (Toronto: University of Toronto Press, 1973; orig. pub. 1913)

Ian MacPherson, *Each for All: A History of the Co-operative Movement in English Canada, 1900-1945* (Toronto: Macmillan, 1979)

Paul Voisy, *Vulcan: The Making of a Prairie Community* (Toronto: University of Toronto Press, 1988)

Aubrey Wood, *A History of Farmer's Movements in Canada: The Origins and Development of Agrarian Protest, 1872-1924* (1924, Toronto: University of Toronto Press, 1975; orig. pub. 1924)

Canadian Imperialism and Canadian Nationalism

Canadian participation in the South African War brought policy issues concerning imperial defence, political organization, and economics into widespread public debate. The dispute between the United Kingdom's Cape Colony and two neighbouring Afrikaner republics went to the centre of Canadian politics in 1899, dividing both the Liberal cabinet and the country when the British government formally requested the assistance of Canadian troops. This would be the first official Canadian contingent to go overseas, and the action thus generated much enthusiasm and opposition.

Most French Canadians saw the war as an example of clear imperial aggression on the part of Britain. An opposition led by Henri Bourassa, an important French-Canadian nationalist politician, argued that by sending troops, Canada had reversed the process of gradual evolution toward self-government.

The search for an appropriate response to the South African War starkly revealed that Canadians were imagining different futures for their country. Certainly, most French Canadians and many English-speaking Canadians hoped for a future of greater autonomy for Canada within the British Empire. This did not mean they wished to sever all British ties, but wanted a relationship based on independence and equality.

Other English-speaking Canadians favoured stronger British connections through greater imperial unity. This idea assumed that English Canadians shared a political, economic, social, and spiritual heritage. Imperial unity, it was said, would free Canada from economic depression, ethnic tension, provincialism, and any threat of American annexation. It offered Canadians increased importance as the centre of the British empire, a perception that was reinforced by global maps which showed a 'pink' Canada in the centre, with the rest of the British Empire in matching pastels on either side. When the editor of *La Vérité* made the claim in 1904 that the French-Canadian people were the true and better Canadians since their loyalties were never divided between countries, this reasoning made no sense to imperialists. They did not understand how loyalty to Canada could be separated from British allegiance.

Section A
Imperialism as English-Canadian Nationalism

Military victories, such as that at Pretoria in the South African War, brought celebrating crowds into the streets of Toronto. The origins of this excitement are suggested in a speech on Canadian history, given by Toronto amateur historian Mary Agnes FitzGibbon to the most important female, middle-class, dominion-wide organization—The National Council of Women. While some turned to history, others were preoccupied by contemporary concerns such as the United States' expanding cultural influence, aggressive foreign policy, and economic protectionism. As an alternative to North American 'continentalism,' economic relations within the empire were put forward by the protagonist, Lorne Murchison, in Sara Jeannette Duncan's 1904 novel, *The Imperialist*. Another perspective is provided by McGill professor, Stephen Leacock, an influential political-economist and satirist, who promoted imperialism as a solution to Canadian domestic politics. The question of imperialism and Canadian identity also encouraged proposals and revisions to national symbols.

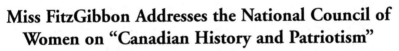

Miss FitzGibbon Addresses the National Council of Women on "Canadian History and Patriotism"

I want to speak to you, first, of why a woman should take an interest in Canadian History, and then of something of what Canadian History is to the Empire. We, Canadians, know less of our own history than we should, but it is only lately that the means of knowledge has been within our reach,—within the last few years. I, as a girl, often wondered how a small yellow book of thirty or forty pages could contain the history of a country like ours, while so much time was spent in the study of large volumes devoted to the Roman and Grecian affairs,—but so it was. If my words to you to-night can bring to you a tenth, or even a hundreth part of the appreciation of the knowledge of our history which I feel, but can never express, I shall realize that my coming to Victoria has not been without some good results...

I am privileged to stand here to-night,—because I represent the Women's Historical Society, who are affiliated with the National Council of Women. Throughout all our work in the Historical Society, we have found everywhere a lamentable ignorance of Canadian History, but we have also found an intense desire to know more about it. A very excellent book on Canadian History is that written by Charles G. D. Roberts. It was not accepted by the judges appointed for the competition because of some minor inaccuracies and on the ground that it read too much like a novel. To my woman's mind that is what we want. Canadian History has been made too dry and uninteresting; this should not be. But, nevertheless such is the case and I know many of the schoolmasters will agree with me that for this reason it is a very difficult lesson to teach. Just think of what Canadian History has been! Take the achievements of the last one hundred and fifty years. In one hundred and fifty years, what has Canada done? A conquered race has been made happy and content; two nations, two religions, two creeds, which in former days were occasions for persecution, fire and other terrible things, now live side by side on Canadian soil in peace. From Canadian shores sailed the first steamship; the greatest railway that ever spanned a continent has been built in this Dominion from ocean to ocean. Canada has held her own,—her many miles of frontier,—with less than five thousand soldiers against three armies of upwards of eight thousand each. Her women stayed at home in the forest guarding the hearthstone while the men went out against the invaders. She has done what no other nation has ever done:—she has obtained responsible government without separation from the mother country. To-day, on Canadian shores, we have every language, every nation, every climate, and every product, and we are all united under one flag, the Union Jack, the flag which has ever carried with it civilization and Christianity.

But why is Canadian History of such importance to the Empire? Trace it back to the earliest days, when Cabot sailed from the British shores, believing that through the West he would reach the great riches of the East. Canada has been called "The keystone of the arch of Imperial Federation", for without Canada the English Empire would not encircle the globe. One of your last governors, in speaking of the joining of British Columbia to Canada, said that it was your privilege to consent to the most important event in Canadian History, and that it was you who had succeeded in striking the last blow which would make Canada one of the most important countries in the world. The West has its heroes within its own shores as on the veldt, for what a history of daring lies in the survey and building of the Canadian Pacific Railway! Just think of that great achievement, in the building of this line; the engineering skill which has overcome such difficulties! Shall we leave it to the grandchildren of to-day to realize what the C. P. R. is to the world?

British Columbia has been for long sheltered behind its mountains, and it will take some time for it to entirely fulfil its noble destiny as part of Canadian Confederation. But things were not built in a day. Federation was born in 1783. There is a book extant by Governor Pownall of Virginia, outlining exactly what our confederation is to-day. His letters were to Lord Granville, that statesman who said at his dying hour that the Treaty of Paris was one of the noblest and most just treaties of peace that was ever signed between two nations. But the time was not then ripe. I could talk for hours, and never weary, though I fear I'd weary you, of the stories in Canadian History. We have heard to-night of the flags and their histories, and all the technicalities of the formation of each. There are other stories of our flag, and had I time I could tell you of no less noble deeds, than those related, which have happened under the flag of Canada, and which are like gems on the pages of Canadian History. I want to rouse your curiosity; I want you to be so interested in Canadian History, that you will leave no stone unturned, no book unread, that will give you an idea of what it is.

It is an old, but trite saying, that "the hand that rocks the cradle rules the world," but it is none the less true, though trite. Women have every power to influence for good or evil. It is women's hearts and women's love that make men what they are. It is women who make men heroes; it is women who strengthen men to strike the blow for their Queen and country. If women could only realize what power they have to do good! There are many indications that this is woman's age, and it is for us to do our duty in it nobly and well. We must live for truth, for honesty, for all things lovely, for all things pure. It is recognized that the rise and fall of nations was due to their women. Cast your eyes over the history of other nations,—over the history of Rome, and you will read plainly there how the women were the reason of the fall. And if we do not do our duty, keep our literature pure, our homes lovely, and our men content, we will have lost the greatest opportunities that have ever been given to women in the world before.

Our men are fighting now for the Empire on Afric's shores, and when the war is over and our soldier boys return, how many a heart will be aching, how many a home will be empty, but through it all, will not the Canadian woman's heart rise in grateful acknowledgment of the fact that to them has been given the privilege of giving their best and dearest to the Empire? Nothing was ever gained except by sacrifice. You will recognize this, that "by blood all things were purified, and out of the woman came the salvation of the world." So we should claim our heritage; we should take up our duties and do them, no matter how little they appear to be—if it is only to teach our children love and loyalty to their country, only to wipe out the provincialisms, the narrow lines that divide the parts of this great land of Canada—this Canada of ours. The word "Colony" has to be wiped forever off the page of history. We are all Imperialists; we are one with the greatest Empire the world has ever known, or will ever know, because it is our desire to make it so. We will know that we are all one in heart, loyal to our homes, to our cities, to our provinces, to our country and, above all, to the Empire. Wipe out those provincialisms! Forget that we are Ontario, Manitoba, or British Columbia; make the Canadian Pacific Railway a greater bond than it is to-day—make it a bond in reality between Imperial Canada and Britain...

[Report of the Seventh Annual Meeting of the National Council of Women of Canada, *Victoria, BC, July 1900 (Ottawa: Taylor and Clarke, 1900),* pp. 28-33]

Pretoria Day in Toronto 5 June 1901. *[Archives of Ontario, OA 51243]*

Lorne Murchison's Speech to the Voters of Elgin on the Virtues of the Imperial Idea

"I claim it my great good fortune," the young man was suddenly telling them in a note of curious gravity and concentration, "and however the fight goes, I shall always claim it my great good fortune to have been identified, at a critical moment, with the political principles that are ennobled in this country by the imperialistic aim. An intention, a great purpose in the endless construction and reconstruction of the world, will choose its own agency; and the imperial design in Canada has chosen the Liberal party, because the Liberal party in this country is the party of the soil, the land, the nation as it springs from that which makes it a nation; and imperialism is intensely and supremely a national affair. Ours is the policy of the fields. We stand for the wheat-belt and the stock-yard, the forest and the mine, as the basic interests of the country. We stand for the principles that make for nation building by the slow sweet processes of the earth, cultivating the individual rooted man who draws his essence and his tissues from the soil, and so, by unhurried, natural, healthy growth, labour sweating his vices out of him, forms the character of the commonwealth, the foundation of the State. So the imperial idea seeks its Canadian home in Liberal councils. The imperial idea is far-sighted. England has outlived her own body. Apart from her heart and her history, England is an area where certain trades are carried on—still carried on. In the scrolls of the future it is already written that the centre of the Empire must shift—and where, if not to Canada?"

There was a half comprehending burst of applause, Dr. Drummond's the first clap. It was a curious change from the simple colloquial manner in which young Murchison had begun and to which the audience were accustomed; and on this account probably they stamped the harder. They applauded Lorne himself; something from him infected them; they applauded being made to feel like that. They would clap first and consider afterwards. John Murchison smiled with pleasure, but shook his head. Bingham, doubled up and clapping like a repeating rifle, groaned aloud under cover of it to Horace Williams: "Oh, the darned kid!"

"A certain Liberal peer of blessed political memory," Lorne continued, with a humorous twist of his mouth, "on one of those graceful, elegant, academic occasions which offer political peers such happy opportunities of getting in their work over there, had lately a vision, which he described to his university audience, of what might have happened if the American colonies had remained faithful to Great Britain—a vision of monarch and Ministers, Government and Parliament, departing solemnly for the other hemisphere. They did not so remain; so the noble peer may conjure up his vision or dismiss his nightmare as he chooses; and it is safe to prophesy that no port of the United States will see that entry. But, remembering that the greater half of the continent did remain faithful, the northern and strenuous half, destined to move with sure steps and steady mind to greater growth and higher place among the nations than any of us can now imagine— would it be as safe to prophesy that such a momentous sailing-day will never be more than the after-dinner fantasy of aristocratic rhetoric? Is it not at least as easy to imagine that even now, while the people of England send their viceroys to the ends of the earth, and vote careless millions for a reconstructed army, and sit in the wrecks of Cabinets disputing whether they will eat our bread or the stranger's, the sails may be filling, in the far harbour of time, which will bear their descendants to a representative share of the duties and responsibilities of Empire in the capital of the Dominion of Canada?"

It was the boldest proposition, and the Liberal voters of the town of Elgin blinked a little, looking at it. Still they applauded, hurriedly, to get it over and hear what more might be coming. Bingham, on the platform, laughed heartily and conspicuously, as if anybody could see that it was all an excellent joke. Lorne half turned to him with a gesture of protest. Then he went on—

"If that transport ever left the shores of England we would go far, some of us, to meet it; but for all the purposes that matter most it sailed long ago. British statesmen could bring us nothing better than the ideals of British government; and those we have had since we levied our first tax and made our first law. That precious cargo was our heritage, and we never threw it overboard, but chose rather to render what impost it brought; and there are those who say that the impost has been heavy, though never a dollar was paid."

He paused for an instant and seemed to review and take account of what he had said. He was hopelessly adrift from the subject he had proposed to himself, launched for better or for worse upon the theme that was subliminal in him and had flowed up, on which he was launched, and almost rudderless, without construction and without control. The speech of his first intention, orderly, developed, was as far from him as the history of Liberalism in Fox County. For an instant he hesitated; and then, under the suggestion, no doubt, of that ancient misbehaviour in Boston Harbour at which he had hinted, he took up another argument. I will quote him a little.

"Let us hold," he said simply, "to the Empire. Let us keep this patrimony that has been ours for three hundred years. Let us not forget the flag. We believe ourselves, at this moment, in no danger of forgetting it. The day after Paardeburg, that still winter day, did not our hearts rise within us to see it shaken out with its message everywhere, shaken out against the snow?...

"So long as no force appeared to improve the trade relations between England and this country Canada sought in vain to make commercial bargains with the United States. They would have none of us or our produce; they kept their wall just as high against us as against the rest of the world: not a pine plank or a bushel of barley could we get over under a reciprocal arrangement. But the imperial trade idea has changed the attitude of our friends to the south. They have small liking for any scheme which will improve trade between Great Britain and Canada, because trade between Great Britain and Canada must be improved at their expense. And now you cannot take up an American paper without finding the report of some commercial association demanding closer trade relations with Canada, or an American magazine in which some far-sighted economist is not urging the same thing. They see us thinking about keeping the business in the family with that hard American common sense that has made them what they are, they accept the situation; and at this moment they are ready to offer us better terms to keep our trade."

Bingham, Horace Williams, and Mr. Farquharson applauded loudly. Their young man frowned a little and squared his chin. He was past hints of that kind.

"And that," he went on to say, "is, on the surface, a very satisfactory state of things. No doubt a bargain between the Americans and ourselves could be devised which would be a very good bargain on both sides. In the absence of certain pressing family affairs, it might be as well worth our consideration as we used to think it before we were invited to the family council. But if any one imagines that any degree of reciprocity with the United States could be entered upon without killing the idea of British preference trade for all time, let him consider what Canada's attitude toward that idea would be to-day if the Americans had consented to our proposals twenty-five years ago, and we were invited to make an imperial sacrifice of the American trade that had prospered, as it would have prospered, for a quarter of a century! I doubt whether the proposition would even be made to us...

"But the alternative before Canada is not a mere choice of markets; we are confronted with a much graver issue. In this matter of dealing with our neighbour our very existence is involved. If we would preserve ourselves as a nation, it has become our business, not only to reject American overtures in favour of the overtures of our own great England, but to keenly watch and actively resist American influence, as it already threatens us through the common channels of life and energy. We often say that we fear no invasion from the south, but the armies of the south have already crossed the border. American enterprise, American capital, is taking possession of our mines and our water-power, our oil areas and our timber limits. In to-day's *Dominion*, one paper alone, you may read of charters granted to five industrial concerns with headquarters in the United States. The trades unions of the two countries are already international. American settlers are pouring into the wheat-belt of the Northwest, and when the Dominion of Canada has paid the hundred million dollars she has just voted for a railway to open up the great lone northern lands between Quebec and the Pacific, it will be the American farmer and the American capitalist who will reap the benefit. They approach us to-day with all the arts of peace, commercial missionaries to the ungathered harvests of neglected territories; but the day may come when they will menace our coasts to protect their markets—unless, by firm, resolved, whole-hearted action now, we keep our opportunities for our own people."

They cheered him promptly, and a gathered intensity came into his face at the note of praise.

"Nothing on earth can hold him now," said Bingham, as he crossed his arms upon a breast seething with practical politics, and waited for the worst.

"The question of the hour for us," said Lorne Murchison to his fellow townsmen, curbing the strenuous note in his voice, "is deeper than any balance of trade can indicate, wider than any department of statistics can prove. We cannot calculate it in terms of pig-iron, or reduce it to any formula of consumption. The question that underlies this decision for Canada is that of the whole stamp and character of her future existence. Is that stamp and character to be impressed by the American Republic effacing"—he smiled a little—"the old Queen's head and the new King's oath? Or is it to be our own stamp and character, acquired in the rugged discipline of our colonial youth, and developed in the national usage of the British Empire?...

Dr. Drummond clapped alone; everybody else was listening.

"It is ours," he told them, "in this greater half of the continent, to evolve a nobler ideal. The Americans from the beginning went in a spirit of revolt; the seed of disaffection was in every Puritan bosom. We from the beginning went in a spirit of amity, forgetting nothing, disavowing nothing, to plant the flag with our fortunes. We took our very Constitution, our very chart of national life, from England—her laws, her liberty, her equity were good enough for us. We have lived by them, some of us have died by them...

"And this Republic," he went on hotly, "this Republic that menaces our national life with commercial extinction, what past has she that is comparable? The daughter who left the old stock to be the light woman among nations, welcoming all comers, mingling her pure blood, polluting her lofty ideals until it is hard indeed to recognize the features and the aims of her honourable youth..."

"...Let us not hesitate to announce ourselves for the Empire, to throw all we are and all we have into the balance for that great decision. The seers of political economy tell us that if the stars continue to be propitious, it is certain that a day will come which will usher in a union of the Anglo-Saxon nations of the world. As between England and the United States the predominant partner in that firm will be the one that brings Canada. So that the imperial movement of the hour may mean even more than the future of the mother land, may reach even further than the boundaries of Greater Britain..."

[Sara Jeanette Duncan, The Imperialist, (Toronto, 1990; orig. pub. 1904), pp. 262-269]

Stephen Leacock's Appeal to a Greater Canada

Now, in this month of April, when the ice is leaving our rivers, the ministers of Canada take ship for this the fourth Colonial Conference at London. What do they go to do? Nay, rather what shall we bid them do? We—the six million people of Canada, unvoiced, untaxed, in the Empire, unheeded in the councils of the world,— we, the six million colonials sprawling our over-suckled infancy across a continent,—what shall be our message to the motherland? Shall we still whine of our poverty, still draw imaginary pictures of our thin herds shivering in the cold blasts of the North, their shepherds huddled for shelter in the log cabins of Montreal and Toronto? Shall we still beg the good people of England to bear yet a little longer, for the poor peasants of their colony, the burden and heat of the day? Shall our ministers rehearse this worn-out fiction of our 'acres of snow,' and so sail home again, still untaxed, to the smug approval of the oblique politicians of Ottawa? Or, shall we say to the people of England, "The time has come; we know and realize our country. We will be your colony no longer. Make us one with you in an Empire, Permanent and Indivisible."

This last alternative means what is commonly called Imperialism. It means a united system of defence, an imperial navy for whose support somehow or other the whole Empire shall properly contribute, and with it an imperial authority in whose power we all may share. To many people in Canada this imperialism is a tainted word. It is too much associated with a truckling subservience to English people and English ideas and the silly swagger of the hop-o'-my-thumb junior officer. But there is and must be for the true future of our country, a higher and more real imperialism than this—the imperialism of the plain man at the plough and the clerk in the counting house, the imperialism of any decent citizen that demands for this country its proper place in the councils of the Empire and in the destiny of the world. In this sense, imperialism means but the realization of a Greater Canada, the recognition of a wider citizenship.

I, that write these lines, am an Imperialist because I will not be a Colonial. This Colonial status is a worn-out, by-gone thing. The sense and feeling of it has become harmful to us. It limits the ideas, and circumscribes the patriotism of our people. It impairs the mental vigor and narrows the outlook of those that are reared and educated in our midst. The English boy reads of England's history and its glories as his own; it is *his* navy that fought at Camperdown and Trafalgar, *his* people that have held fast their twenty miles of sea eight hundred years against a continent. He learns at his fire-side and at his school, among his elders and his contemporaries, to regard all this as part of himself; something that he, as a fighting man, may one day uphold, something for which as a plain citizen he shall every day gladly pay, something for which in any capacity it may one day be his high privilege to die. How little of this in Canada! Our paltry policy teaches the Canadian boy to detach himself from the England of the past, to forget that Camperdown and Copenhagen and the Nile are ours as much as theirs, that this navy of the Empire is ours too, ours in its history of the past, ours in its safe-guard of the present.

If this be our policy and plan, let us complete our teaching to our children. Let us inscribe it upon the walls of our schools, let us write it in brass upon our temples that for the Navy which made us and which defends us, we pay not a single penny, we spare not a solitary man. Let us add to it, also, that the lesson may bear fruit, this "shelter theory" of Canada now rampant in our day; that Canada by some means of its remoteness from European sin and its proximity to American republicanism, is sheltered from that flail of war with which God tribulates the other peoples of the world, sheltered by the Monroe Doctrine, by President Roosevelt and his battleships, sheltered, I know not how, but sheltered somehow so that we may forget the lean, eager patriotism and sacrifice of a people bred for war, and ply in peace the little craft of gain and greed. So grows and has grown the Canadian boy in his colonial status, dissociated from the history of the world, cut off from the larger patriotism, colourless in his ideas. So grows he till in some sly way his mind opens to the fence-rail politics of his country side, with its bribed elections and its crooked votes—not patriotism but 'politics,' maple-leaf politics, by which money may be made and places and profit fall in a golden shower.

Some time ago Theodore Roosevelt, writing with the pardonable irresponsibility of a Police Commissioner of New York and not as President of the United States, said of us here in Canada, that the American feels towards the Canadian the good natured condescension that is felt by the free-born man for the man that is not free. Only recently one of the most widely circulated of American Magazines, talking in the same vein, spoke of us Canadians as a "subject people." These are, of course, the statements of extravagance and ignorance; but it is true, none the less, that the time has come to be done with this *colonial* business, done with it once and forever. We cannot in Canada continue as we are. We must become something greater or something infinitely less. We can no longer be an appanage and outlying portion of something else. Canada, as a *colony*, was right enough in the days of good old Governor Simcoe, when your emigrant officer sat among the pine stumps of his Canadian clearing and reared his children in the fear of God and in the love of England—right enough then, wrong enough and destructive enough now. We cannot continue as we are. In the history of every nation as of every man there is no such thing as standing still. There is no pause upon the path of progress. There is no stagnation but the hush of death.

And for this progress, this forward movement, what is there first to do? How first unravel this vexed skein of our colonial and imperial relations? This, first of all. We must realize, and the people of England must realize, the inevitable greatness of Canada. This is not a vain-glorious boast. This is no rhodomontade. It is simple fact. Here stand we, six million people, heirs to the greatest legacy in the history of mankind, owners of half a continent, trustees, under God Almighty, for the fertile solitudes of the west. A little people, few in numbers, say you? Ah, truly such a little people! Few as the people of the Greeks that blocked the mountain gates of Europe to the march of Asia, few as the men of Rome that built a power to dominate the world, nay, scarce more numerous than they in England whose beacons flamed along the cliffs a warning to the heavy galleons of Spain. Aye, such a little people, but growing, growing, growing, with a march that shall make us ten millions to-morrow, twenty millions in our children's time and a hundred millions ere yet the century runs out. What say you to Fort Garry, a stockaded fort in your father's day, with its hundred thousand of to-day and its half a million souls of the to-morrow? What think you, little river Thames, of our great Ottawa that flings its foam eight hundred miles? What does it mean when science has moved us a little further yet, and the wheels of the world's work turn with electric force? What sort of asset do you think then our melting snow and the roaring river-flood of our Canadian spring shall be to us? What say you, little puffing steam fed industry of England, to the industry of Coming Canada. Think you, you can heave your coal hard enough, sweating and grunting with your shovel to keep pace with the snow-fed cataracts of the north? Or look, were it but for double conviction, at the sheer extent and size of us. Throw aside, if you will, the vast districts of the frozen north, confiscate, if you like, Ungava still snow-covered and unknown, and let us talk of the Canada that we know, south of the sixtieth parallel, south of your Shetland Islands, south of the Russian Petersburg and reaching southward thence to where the peach groves of Niagara bloom in the latitude of Northern Spain. And of all this take only our two new provinces, twin giants of the future, Alberta and Saskatchewan. Three decades ago this was the 'great lone land,' the frozen west, with its herds of bison and its Indian tepees, known to you only in the pictured desolation of its unending snow; now crossed and inter-crossed with railways, settled 400 miles from the American frontier, and sending north and south the packets of its daily papers from its two provincial capitals. And of this country, fertile as the corn plains of Hungary, and the crowded flats of Belgium, do you know the size? It is this. Put together the whole German Empire, the republic of France and your England and Scotland, and you shall find place for them in our two new provinces. Or take together across the boundary from us, the States of Maine, New Hampshire, Vermont, Massachusetts, Rhode Island and Connecticut—all the New England States and with them all the Middle States of the North—New York, New Jersey, Pennsylvania, Delaware, Ohio, Indiana, Michigan, Illinois, and Wisconsin, till you have marked a space upon the map from the Atlantic to the Mississippi and from the Ohio to the lakes—all these you shall put into our two new provinces and still find place for England and for Scotland in their boundaries.

This then for the size and richness of our country. Would that the soul and spirit of its people were commensurate with its greatness. For here as yet we fail. Our politics, our public life and thought, rise not to the level of our opportunity. The mud-bespattered politicians of the trade, the party men and party managers, give us in place of patriotic statescraft the sordid traffic of a tolerated jobbery. For bread, a stone. Harsh is the cackle of the little turkey-cocks of Ottawa, fighting the while as they feather their mean nests of sticks and mud, high on their river bluff. Loud sings the little Man of the Province, crying his petty gospel of Provincial Rights, grudging the gift of power, till the cry spreads and town hates town and every hamlet of the country side shouts for its share of plunder and of pelf. This is the tenor of our politics, carrying as its undertone the voice of the black-robed sectary, with narrow face and shifting eyes, snarling still with the bigotry of a by-gone day. This is the spirit that we must purge. This is the demon we must exorcise; this the disease, the canker-worm of corruption, bred in the indolent securities of peace, that must be burned from us in the pure fire of an Imperial patriotism, that is no theory but a passion. This is our need, our supreme need of the Empire—not for its ships and guns, but for the greatness of it, the soul of it, aye for the very danger of it.

Of our spirit, then, it is not well. Nor is it well with the spirit of those in England in their thoughts of us. Jangling are they these twenty years over little Ireland that makes and unmakes ministries, and never a thought of Canada; jangling now over their Pantaloon Suffragettes and their Swaddled Bishops, wondering whether they shall still represent their self-willed Lords nose for nose in the councils of the Empire or whether they may venture now to scale them down, putting one nose for ten. One or ten, what does it matter, so there is never a voice to speak for Canada? Can they not see, these people of England that the supreme English Question now is the question of Canada: that this Conference of the year of grace 1907 might, if it would, make for us the future of the Empire? Or will they still regard us, poor outlying sheltered people of Canada, as something alien and apart, sending us ever of their youngest and silliest to prate in easy arrogance of 'home,' earning the livelihood their island cannot give, still snapping at the hand that feeds them?

And what then can this Colonial Conference effect after all, it is asked? Granting, for argument's sake, the spirit of the people that might prove it, our willingness to pay, their willingness to give us place and power, what can be done? Hard indeed is the question. Hard even to the Ready Man in the Street with his glib solution of difficulties; harder still to the thoughtful; hardest of all to those who will not think. For if we pay for this our Navy that even now defends us, and yet speak not in the councils at Westminster, then is that Taxation without Representation; straightway the soul of the Anglo-Saxon stands aghast; the grim deaths-head of King John grins in the grave, while the stout ghost of old Ben Franklin hovers again upon our frontier holding in its hand the proffer of independence. But if you admit us to your councils, what then? Ah, then indeed an awful thing befals! Nothing less than the remaking of your constitution, with a patching and a re-building of it, till the nature-growth of precedent and custom is shaped in the clumsy artifice of clause and schedule, powers and prohibitions, measured and marked off with the yard-stick of the *ultra-vires* attorney. This surely is worse than ever. This perhaps you might have done, save for the bare turn of a majority, for Irksome Ireland. But for Uncomplaining Canada, not so.

So there we stand, we and you, pitched fast upon the horns of a dilemma. You cannot tax us, since you will not represent us. We cannot be represented because we will not be taxed. So we stand stock still, like the donkey in the philosophic fable, balanced between two bales of hay, nibbling neither right nor left. So are we like to stand, till some one of us, some of you and us, shall smite the poor donkey of our joint stupidity there where it most profits that a donkey shall be smitten, and bid it move!

Yet is the difficulty perhaps not impossible of solution. The thing to be achieved is there. The task is yours to solve, men of the council table. Find us a way whereby the burden and the power shall fall on all alike; a way whereby, taxed, we shall still be free men, free of the Imperial citizenship, and your historic constitution unshattered in the progress. Is it then so difficult? We come of a race that has solved much, has so often achieved the impossible. Look back a little in the ages to where ragged Democracy howls around the throne of defiant Kingship. This is a problem that we have solved, joining the dignity of Kingship with the power of democracy; this, too, by the simplest of political necromancy, the trick of which we now expound in our schools, as the very alphabet of political wisdom. Or look back to where the scaffolds of a bigot nation run with blood for the sake of rival creeds that know not yet the simple code of toleration, to be framed now in an easy statute with an artful stroke of a pen. Have we done all this and shall we balk at this poor colonial question? At it then, like men, shrewd representatives of Ottawa and Westminster, trained in the wisdom of the ages. Listen not to those who would block the way with a *non possumus* on this side, a *non volumus* on that. Find us a way, shew us a plan, a mere beginning if you will, a widow's mite of contribution, a mere whispering of representation, but something that shall trace for us the future path of Empire.

Nor is guidance altogether lacking in the task. For at least the signs of the times are written large as to what the destiny of Canada shall *not* be. Not as it is,—not on this *colonial* footing, can it indefinitely last. There are those who tell us that it is best to leave well alone, to wait for the slow growth, the evolution of things. For herein lies the darling thought of the wisdom of the nineteenth century, in this same Evolution, this ready-made explanation of all things; hauled over from the researches of the botanist to meet the lack of thought of the philosopher.

Whatever is, is: whatever will be, will be,—so runs its silly creed. Therefore let everything be, that is: and all that shall be, shall be! This is but the wisdom of the fool, wise after the fact. For the solution of our vexed colonial problem this profits nothing. We cannot sit passive to watch our growth. Good or bad, straight or crooked, we must make our fate.

Nor is it ever possible or desirable that we in Canada can form an independent country. The little cry that here and there goes up among us is but the symptom of an aspiring discontent, that will not let our people longer be colonials. 'Tis but a cry forced out by what a wise man has called the growing pains of a nation's progress. Independent, we could not survive a decade. Those of us who know our country realize that beneath its surface smoulder still the embers of racial feud and of religious bitterness. Twice in our generation has the sudden alarm of conflict broken upon the quiet of our prosperity with the sound of a fire bell in the night. Not thus our path. Let us compose the feud and still the strife of races, not in the artificial partnership of an Independent Canada, but in the joint greatness of a common destiny.

Nor does our future lie in Union with those that dwell to the Southward. The day of annexation to the United States is passed. Our future lies elsewhere. Be it said without concealment and without bitterness. They have chosen their lot; we have chosen ours. Let us go our separate ways in peace. Let them still keep their perennial Independence Day, with its fulminating fireworks and its Yankee Doodle. We keep our Magna Carta and our rough and ready Rule Britannia, shouting as lustily as they! The propaganda of Annexation is dead. Citizens we want, indeed, but not the prophets of an alien gospel. To you who come across our western border we can offer a land fatter than your Kansas, a government better than Montana, a climate kinder than your Dakota. Take it, Good Sir, if you will: but if, in taking it, you still raise your little croak of annexation, then up with you by the belt and out with you, breeches first, through the air, to the land of your origin! This in all friendliness.

Not Independence then, not annexation, not stagnation: nor yet that doctrine of a little Canada that some conceive,—half in, half out of the Empire, with a mimic navy of its own; a pretty navy this,—poor two-penny collection, frollicking on its little way strictly within the Gulf of St. Lawrence, a sort of silly adjunct to the navy of the Empire, semi-detached, the better to be smashed at will. As well a Navy of the Province, or the Parish, home-made for use at home, docked every Saturday in Lake Nipigon!

Yet this you say, you of the Provincial Rights, you Little Canada Man, is all we can afford! We that have raised our public charge from forty up to eighty millions odd within the ten years past, and scarce have felt the added strain of it. Nay, on the question of the cost, good gentlemen of the council, spare it not. Measure not the price. It is not a commercial benefit we buy. We are buying back our honour as Imperial Citizens. For, look you, this protection of our lives and coast, this safe-guard from the scourge of war, we have it now as much as you of England: you from the hard-earned money that you pay, we as the peasant pensioners on your Imperial Bounty.

Thus stands the case. Thus stands the question of the future of Canada. Find for us something other than mere colonial stagnation, something sounder than independence, nobler than annexation, greater in purpose than a Little Canada. Find us a way. Build us a plan, that shall make us, in hope at least, an Empire Permanent and Indivisible.

[University Magazine, Vol. VI, April 1907, pp. 133-142]

The Maple Leaf Forever

Words and music by Alexander Muir

In days of yore, from Britain's shore,
Wolfe the dauntless hero came,
And planted firm Old England's flag,
On Canada's fair domain!
Here may it wave our boast, our pride
And joined in love together,
The Thistle, Shamrock, Rose entwine,
The Maple Leaf forever!

Refrain
The Maple Leaf, the Maple Leaf,
The Maple Leaf forever!
The Thistle, Shamrock, Rose entwine,
The Maple Leaf forever!

At Queenston Heights, and Lundy's Lane
Our brave fathers, side by side,
For freedom, homes, and loved ones dear,
Firmly stood, and nobly died;
And those dear rights which they maintained,
We swear to yield them never!
Our watchword evermore shall be
The Maple Leaf forever!

Refrain

May our Dominion still extend
From Cape Race to Nootka Sound;
May peace forever be our lot,
And plenty in store abound;

And may those ties of love be ours
Which discord cannot sever,
And flourish green o'er Freedom's home,
The Maple Leaf forever!

Refrain

On Merry England's far famed land
May kind Heaven sweetly smile;
God bless Old Scotland evermore,
And Ireland's Emerald Isle!
Then swell the song, both loud and long,
Till rocks and forests quiver,
God save our Queen, and Heaven bless
The Maple Leaf forever!

[Queen's University Song Book, 1903]

Section B

"Canadian" Nationalism

Most French Canadians were hostile to the idea of imperialism, and there was no agreement among all English-speaking Canadians. There was, however, no consensus among anti-imperialists as to how Canadians should proceed. Political commentator Goldwin Smith supported a continental union with the United States, while André Siegfried, observing Canadian politics from France, concluded that Americanization was inevitable whatever Canada's aspirations.

Two opposing visions of an independent and autonomous Canada are provided by Henri Bourassa and Lionel Groulx. Concerns surrounding assimilation prompted Bourassa to imagine Canada with a bilingual and bicultural future; others were not so optimistic. The French language was under attack throughout English Canada as assimilation policies aimed at new immigrants also led to the loss of language rights by francophones outside Quebec. In 1912, the Ontario government introduced *Regulation 17*, which limited the use of French for instruction in schools to one hour a day. The historical events around *Regulation 17* appear in fictionalized form in historian Abbé Lionel Groulx's *L'Appel de la Race*. The 'Canada question' remained unanswered .

Continental Union

Continental Union, formed with the free consent of Canada and of her mother country, would be expansion in the true sense of the term. It would bring into the Republic a long stretch of adjoining territory inhabited by people of the same blood and trained under similar institutions. It would complete the unity of the northern continent and shut the gate on war. The natural products of Canada's forests, mines, and water-power, as well as her special farm products, are needed by the United States, while Canada needs the manufactures which the United States, having an immense market, produce on the largest scale and therefore at the cheapest rate.

[Goldwin Smith, "A Bystander," Commonwealth or Empire (Toronto: Wm. Tyrrell & Co., 1900), pp. 12-13]

The Penetration of Canada by American Civilization

The long rivalry between the French and English in Canada is ending, then, in the victory of the latter. More numerous, more wealthy, finding their strength in a form of civilization more modern than that of their adversaries, the English have distanced the French. But now a new danger threatens the victors, and fresh assaults are made upon their supremacy. By their side—nay, actually within their frontiers, in the very heart of their cities and their farmlands—there is opening out a civilization akin to their own, but more exuberant, more opulent, more modern still. Its powers of absorption are so great that one may well ask the question whether in its character and its customs the Dominion will be able always to remain British.

To begin with, let us state the problem in exact terms. In analysing the feelings of the Canadians with regard to the United States, we saw how they at present dread the idea of annexation. Save in the occurrence of unforeseen events, of some unpardonable blundering on the part of England, it is almost certain that Canada will not willingly and wittingly give herself to her mighty neighbour.

That is not the danger. The danger does not take the form either of an attempt at conquest, a treaty of alliance or a plebiscite. It lies in the imperceptible daily transformation that by a slow steady progress is Americanizing the colony, its men, its investments and its manners. It lies in the slowly changing composition of the immigration which is populating the country—immigration that contains a large British element, it is true, but is in majority American and cosmopolitan. It lies, above all, in the irresistible influence of a prestigious neighbourhood that is already making Montreal a satellite of New York and Winnipeg a little Chicago! It is thus that the individuality of Canada may be threatened. Without any positive act of disloyalty by Canadians toward the metropolitan power, without any formal divorce, Canada is in danger of finding herself one day so completely transformed, so full of Americans and of strangers formed in their image. that the title of British colony, though always true in theory, will cease practically to be applicable to her.

A first reason for anxiety is presented by the present character of the immigration into the Dominion. Formerly the great stream of European emigrants flowed into the United States. Canada, less known, less in favour, wrongly supposed to be colder and less fertile, attracted chiefly a British clientele. Its far west, wild and forlorn, remained the jealously guarded property of a great Company, and was populated chiefly by Indians, with a sprinkling here and there of French and Scots.

Presently, however, the Canadian prairies were opened out. The monopoly of the Hudson's Bay Company came to an end, and the Canadian Pacific traversed the whole Dominion with its ribbon of steel. Manitoba, the Northwest Territories, began to make rapid progress. From 1896 an energetic policy of promoting immigration was pursued by the Liberal administration. A brilliantly able propagandist system was set at work: circulars and pamphlets vaunting the wealth of western Canada were distributed in profusion; agencies were started not merely in England but in the United States and in Europe; a generous administration placed land within the reach of the poorest, every newcomer being able to count upon a grant of 160 acres. As what was wanted was to populate at any price a region needing men, new arrivals were not forced to satisfy many conditions. All that was required of them was good health. No questions were asked as to their origin or resources...

The invasion from the United States is a new feature. Ten years ago it was the Canadian for the most part who crossed the border. The remarkable prosperity of the Dominion since 1896, the boom in Manitoba and the Northwest Territories, have now induced many farmers of Minnesota, Dakota, and Kansas to sell their lands at a profit in order to buy others at a lower price on Canadian territory. An operation of this kind is quite to the taste of the speculative folk of the West. At first there was an impression that this was merely a craze of the moment, but soon it was revealed by statistics that a veritable migration was in progress. Here are the figures for five years:

American Immigration into Canada

1898	9,119 immigrants
1901	17,987 "
1902	26,388 "
1903	49,473 "
1904	45,229 "

These newcomers, moreover, are not for the most part people without means, or failures anxious for a fresh start; on the contrary, they are generally people who have put by considerable savings and who have already had a long experience of agriculture. They make excellent colonists, therefore, of a class that the Dominion is very happy to welcome...

How is the British civilization to stand up against this invasion? What attitude do the Americans take up in their new country? And what is the line adopted by the cosmopolitans? On the combination resulting from these heterogeneous elements will depend in great part the political future of the Canadian West.

The durability of the British civilization is very great, for it possesses strong trump cards. In the first place, the majority of the population is still almost everywhere Canadian or British. The census of 1901 does not, unfortunately, enable us to distinguish the Americans from among the other Anglo-Saxon actual residents in the colony—these being deliberately classed together as the same race. The census by nationality is no more useful, for most of the American immigrants become naturalized. We cannot tell, therefore, how many Americans there are now living in Canada. In spite of this lack of precise figures, however, we can safely affirm that the general character of the people of the Canadian West is still British. The English, Irish, and Scottish form a compact mass, strongly united by political or religious traditions.

It counts for something in the evolution of the customs of this region that the Dominion is an English colony. The political connection, however relaxed it may be, obliges the Canadians to look often towards the mother country, and in this way they keep up such relations with Europe as their American neighbours have long ceased to know. The Americanization of Canada, though it seems inevitable, is thus perceptibly retarded.

What retards it even more is the distinctly British complexion of Canadian Protestantism. The Americans are of course Protestants themselves, but after a fashion much more vague and often erratic as compared with the conservative Protestants of Great Britain. In the domain of religion Great Britain has exerted more influence than America on the population of Canada. Once you cross the frontier from the United States, whether you go to Victoria or Winnipeg or Toronto, you at once feel yourself in a religious environment that is purely British. Without quite knowing in what it consists, you are conscious of a moral atmosphere in the air very different from the joyous anarchy and exuberant gaiety which reigns in the neighbouring country. Winnipeg, for instance, so American in so many ways, is Scottish on Sundays; the Presbyterians exercise a sort of moral dictatorship, just as in Edinburgh, Sydney, or Melbourne, and everyone must submit to it willy nilly. From this standpoint Canada will remain a British colony for a long time to come.

It results from these observations that the Canadian West looks British to those who come to it from the United States. But to those who come to it from Eastern Canada and from Europe it looks American. The habits and customs of the people are entirely those of the States. Regina, Winnipeg, Vancouver are cities built in the American fashion—huge skyscrapers flung up alongside wooden shanties. The railways are modelled exactly on American railways. The way business is conducted, the accent with which English is spoken, the appearance of the people, their hotels and bars and theatres—everything combines to make the visitor feel that he is the guest of Uncle Sam and not of John Bull. You have to look much more closely to see under the surface the strong British current that is still flowing. Thus it is that western Canada may remain politically British, and in some respects even imperialist, while socially it is already practically American.

In this country so like their own, what happens to the immigrants from the United States? Do they become Anglicized, so to speak? No, for they continue to lead exactly the same kind of life they led before. They change neither their habits, their ideas, nor their manners of action. They do not need in truth to undergo any change at all to feel at home in this new region to the north of the purely imaginary frontier which they have crossed. They are perfectly willing to become naturalized Canadian citizens and take the oath of allegiance to King Edward VII, which is one of the conditions of naturalization. It seems clear that these matters of form and convention are to them of minimal importance. Provided they can make money, and are not forced to speak a foreign language, and can secure the kind of education they require for their children, they are satisfied. They go so far, indeed, as to declare that the Dominion is better governed than the Republic. They do not feel at heart that they are in an alien land. Doubtless many of them think that Canada will eventually be American, but this is merely a vague impression in their minds, and they do nothing, so far, to hasten the coming of this union. They must be regarded, then, as excellent Canadians. But they are not becoming British Canadians.

We still have to speak of the cosmopolitans. In America immigrants of all nationalities and races become assimilated within a few years to their new environment. This assimilation takes place in Canada more slowly. The life is not so active, and many of the newcomers remain isolated. For example, entire groups of people of the same origin get hidden away in odd corners of the prairie, where they retain their language and habits. This is the case with regard to many of the semi-Asiatic immigrants sent from Austria and Russia. Sooner or later, however, especially in the cities and along the railway lines, these foreign immigrants of all kinds become Americanized.

To whose advantage will this transformation work? To that of the French-Canadian civilization? We have seen that any such hope must be laid aside. To that of Anglo-Saxon civilization? Obviously, but in its American, not its British, form. The newcomers will learn the English language, but what will their accent be like? They will sign the oath of allegiance to King Edward, but they will become republicans. They will become loyal Canadians at the same time, it may be admitted, but that is not to say that they will ever become Britishers like their English, Scottish, and Irish fellow-citizens.

From a narrowly political point of view, it results from this analysis that the recent flood of immigration constitutes no danger to the Dominion. The new citizens are submissive and well disposed, and harbour as a rule no feeling of regret for their own countries. But as I have been at pains to show, the delicate point of the problem does not lie here. It is as to the future of Canadian civilization that one speculates. It is not a question of men merely. Ideas and customs and capital have to be taken into account.

American capital occupies a considerable place in Canadian affairs. Not that money is lacking in the Dominion, or that the British underestimate the value of their splendid colony, but the natural riches of the land are so colossal that financial aid from the outside is constantly required. The United States are always ready to furnish it. Formerly they themselves had to go to Europe for such assistance, but during the last ten years their affairs have flourished so brilliantly that they hardly know what to do now with their profits. It is only natural, therefore, that they should be willing to turn to the magnificent fields of opportunity offered them by Canada.

They began by mere investments which were warmly welcomed. Then, afterwards, they began to start industries in Canada themselves, bringing with them their plant and staff. Great American industrial houses, which had been hit by Sir John Macdonald's protectionist policy and only in a less degree by Mr. Fielding's, have not hesitated to set up branch establishments on Canadian soil. To-day a large number of industries in the Dominion are thus controlled from without. Economically speaking, the colony is as much dependent upon the United States as upon Great Britain.

It cannot be denied, therefore (though the Canadians themselves do not like to admit it), that there is an American peril for Canada. It does not take the shape of a military conquest—*that* is almost inconceivable; or of a political union—that is not desired by Washington and is sincerely dreaded by Ottawa. It manifests itself in the unceasing and irresistible permeation of one form of civilization by another. It is safe now to predict that Canada will become less and less British and more and more American. The best we can wish for—a wish that may well be realized—is that she may become quite simply Canadian.

[*André Siegfried,* The Race Question in Canada *(Toronto: McClelland and Stewart, 1966; orig. pub. 1906), pp. 187-193, translated]*

Editorial on the French-Canadian Identity

Our own brand of nationalism is French-Canadian nationalism. We have been working for the last twenty-three years toward the development of a French-Canadian national feeling: what we want to see flourish is French-Canadian patriotism; our people are the French-Canadian people; we will not say that our homeland is limited to the Province of Quebec, but it is French Canada; the nation we wish to see founded at the time appointed by Providence is the French-Canadian nation.

[La Vérité, *1 April 1904, p. 5, translated]*

The Official Languages of Canada

by Henri Bourassa

I am to address you on the two official languages of Canada. In Quebec, as in Ontario and Manitoba and New Brunswick—in every corner of Canada—there are two official languages, French and English. I am not going to prove by what statute or text of law those two languages have been made official. But taking things as they are, as a result of centuries of history of noble struggle between these two great races who have fought for the possession of Canada, who have tried on the battlefield of America to secure the possession of the northern portion of America—what do I learn as a modern man, as a man who is able to sympathise with the men who are living in the days in which I live myself? I find that the teaching of history and the will of Providence is that, after those great races have struggled for dominion, the time has come when it was found that it was better for each of them and better for the country at large that they should agree together; not for one to impose its will or language or traditions upon the other, but to combine their traditions; not to merge them into a bastard civilisation that would have left aside the best traditions in each, but to make a living combination of both, preserving to the Canadian people the best traditions, the most precious intellectual possessions of both nations; so that Canada instead of being English and French should be Canadian. The noble alliance between the two races was to preserve for the future generations their best traditions; and that includes the language and literature and all that that gives—the highest expression of their noblest thoughts and feelings.

If this is worth living for and working for, it goes without saying that the representatives of the two great races in Canada must understand each other. Now, the way to understand each other is not either to decry each other nor to flatter each other. It is to be true to each other, and the way to be true to each other is to speak freely and frankly. If there is a threat against the civilisation of Canada, if there is a threat which menaces the ideals of both English and French in Canada, it is that in public life—and by public life I mean not only the sphere of the politicians, but the broad national arena, where both races come in contact with each other, where they work together and against each other at times, where they come in rivalry, where they have their causes of agreement and disagreement—if there is anything which threatens the good understanding between the two great races in Canada, if there is anything which threatens the maintenance of the high ideal which inspired the fathers of the Federation, it is the lack of frankness and free talk between the two races. The disposition to say different things to different classes has been the curse of our country in every sphere of public life. How often have we not read of those who are supposed to lead our people, using different arguments and language when addressing an English-speaking community, from that employed when speaking to a French community? If there is one thing in which I remain British, and thoroughly British in spite of all things to the contrary, it is that in Great Britain more than in any other country, you find men who are always prepared to say what they think, and to act according to what they believe is right by their country and by themselves, whether it is profitable or popular or not. A moment or so ago I was speaking to my neighbor here of my visit to England during the dark and troublesome days of the South African War. I had been threatened with hanging and quartering, I had been characterised as a disloyal rebel because I dared say in the House of Common in Canada what was freely expressed in Great Britain.

When I came to London and was asked to express my opinion there I expressed it in exactly the same manner as in the House of Commons of Canada. That expression in Canada had caused two venerable looking ex-ministers of the Crown to leap upon their chairs and sing 'God save the Queen' to drown the disloyal expressions of a man who dared to say in Canada that the South African war was unjust and should not have been helped by the people of Canada. And yet in the London streets, and in the Colonies of the Empire, the same expression of opinion was given to the English pro-Boers of London, Manchester, Birmingham and Liverpool, Glasgow and Edinburgh as a model of moderation, which could be made use of by the English pro-Boer so as not to hurt the feelings of those who were in favor of that war! I said to myself how strange it is that in Canada, a distant colony which has nothing to do with the war, which is not responsible for the war and never has been or will be consulted as to the cause or settlement of the war, a man is not allowed to say things which when said in London are given by the daily press as models of moderation! ...And that made me come to the conclusion that the first thing was to get into a way of thinking, feeling and speaking, so that Canadians could exchange their views freely wherever they were. And so I came back more British than when I went, and more British even than many who are waving a flag, for they are lacking the first quality of British citizenship, and that is freedom of thought and perfectly fearless expression of that thought, whether it is agreeable or not. The Canadian Club can do a great deal in this matter; because whatever the future of Canada, there is one thing sure—that that future will be producing something good for all Canadians, and for Canada, *only* when we have become British and Canadian and manly enough to allow freedom of thought for all legitimate opinion in this country. The first elements of the national organization of Canada are those elements that have grown out of tradition. We cannot undo what has been done in four centuries of history. It has been said frequently that men are not made for constitutions but that constitutions are made for men. Likewise a nation is not built in theory, on the ignorance or the narrowness of any given generation a nation passes through, but builds itself, in spite of passion, in spite of blindness, through what has been accumulated by generations and generations of men and women. What is the historical fact governing the whole history of Canada? It is that Canada was first discovered by the French, and first peopled by the French; that years and years before there was one word of English spoken in Canada the French language was spoken with the utmost purity by missionaries, noble men and women who had sacrificed all that could attach them to their native land—one of the most beautiful, one of the most civilized, one of the noblest lands on earth—and came to this country with the idea of securing an Empire first for Christ and second for the King of France. It may be that in the bosom of some of the French citizens of Canada still remains the thought that it was a sad day the day that French domination disappeared from this country. It may be that in the minds of many English-speaking Canadians dwells at the present time the thought that it would be far better if this country was wholly French or wholly English and Protestant. But we have to take facts as they are—and the outstanding fact remains that the French race developed the country. Canada could not die, every true Canadian should not desire that it should die, and therefore the French, in a century and a half of occupation, planted in the soil of Canada roots of civilisation, both social, civil, individual and intellectual—that should not be disregarded...

There are today more cases of misunderstanding between the two races than there were some years ago. Some say the French Canadians have no grudge. They have a grudge, and the main grudge is that his attachment to his language is not properly understood by the English-speaking Canadians. When Canada has become a civilised country to the full extent of the word, every educated Englishman in Canada, as in London and every civilised country, will be obliged to learn and speak French—because French is today what Greek was two thousand years ago, the highest expression of the noblest thoughts of humanity— because French remains today what Greek was two thousand years ago, the means of the interchange of thought between the whole of the human race— because French, being the most complete, the most thorough and perfect of modern languages, is the means of exchange of diplomatic acts and treaties between governments. Undoubtedly the French nation is weaker than the English, but its language remains supreme, because it has been for three or four centuries perfected and worked upon. The late King Edward VII, one of the noblest sovereigns that the human race has known for the last two centuries, said that if there was one thing which he as an Englishman envied the French race it was their French Academy. Thanks to the work of those men the French language has become today what the Greek language was in the days of old. We in Canada have an enormous advantage over every other portion of the British Empire, in possessing the double inheritance of the French and the British. We have the spirit of organizing, the business spirit, the spirit of co-operation that marks the one; and we have also the enormous advantage of possessing a people who are attached to their language more than they are attached to their country, who are prepared to fight for their language more than for their dollars. Therefore instead of antagonising them and ignoring them, why don't you come and meet them and prove that you are willing to help them in maintaining that great inheritance which is not only their moral right but which is also your national asset? Thereby you will prove that you are big enough and broadminded enough not to be afraid of the fact that your fellow countrymen will maintain that language which is the expression of the highest civilization of modern times. You will show yourselves prepared to learn it, and have your children learn it just as the French Canadian understands that to be a thorough Canadian he must learn and speak your language. And all that I ask the Canadian Club of Montreal to do is to give an example and to prove that it is desirous of helping in the noble work of keeping the two great races of this country working hand in hand together, not for one to dominate the other, but for the two to co-operate in making the highest ambitions and faculties of both prevail for the benefit of the whole Dominion.

[Addresses Delivered Before the Canadian Club of Montréal, *Season 1913-1914, "Annual Banquet Speech"*]

Jules de Lantagnac's Address to the House of Commons

Lantagnac did not present, like the others before him, another historical account of the Ontario school question, or expound the rights of bilingualism. The natural elevation of his mind quickly took him to the heights. His speech was an exposé of general ideas, in which his mind soared at ease. Forcefully, reiterating his favorite ideas, he pointed out the danger of the present struggle for the peace of the country and for the continuation of Confederation:

"What object do the persecutors of the French language in Canada seek?" he exclaimed, turning towards the row of ministers. "Do they want, at any price, to rock to its very foundations the edifice so laboriously erected fifty years ago? I shall remind them then of certain obvious realities: along the extensive line separating us from our neighbours to the South, we lack natural frontiers. From one ocean to the other our territories are unified by geography. Frontiers exist only within our country, which they separate into three impenetrable zones. And this is not, alas, the only factor which makes for our division. Western Canada is for free trade; Eastern Canada is protectionist. You, the Anglo-Saxons, are imperialists; we, the sons of Canada, are above all Canadians. How great, then, is the political blindness of this country's politicians who, to all these threats of rupture, deliberately add the fearful clash of religious and national conflicts?"

"Yes," the MP for Russell went on, "the persecutors will perhaps destroy Confederation by killing the faith of my compatriots in federative institutions and by wrecking the principle of the absolute equality of associates, which was the foundation of our political alliance. For, I warn this House, we are too proud a people to consent to indefinite victimization, under a constitution which gave us all equality in this country. Likewise, I warn the ambitious men who perhaps entertain more evil designs against us, to banish fanciful hopes from their minds: we are too strong to succumb to their blows. We are no longer, thanks be to God, the handful of dispossessed that we were in 1760. We are three million strong, undisputed masters of a province of the Dominion that is four times the size of the British Isles. We are the most strongly constituted nationality on the whole North-American continent. Among the human groups established above the forty-fifth parallel, none possesses a more perfect homogeneity than ours; none has adapted better to the atmosphere of the New World; none has more traditions, or more vigorous social institutions. More than a century and a half after being conquered, Quebec remains a national entity whose language and whose soul are as French as in the far-off days of New France. And if amorphous fragments of the German nation or of the poor Polish nationality have been able to triumph over the assimilating power of our formidable neighbours, is it within the capacity of a few thousand persecutors to crush a race whose roots plunge deep into Canadian soil like the maple tree, its immortal symbol?"

Going on from there, and modifying his argument in a way which he knew would give the government and the Ontario persecutors pause for thought, the speaker appealed to the moderate elements and to the Catholic elements of other national groups. To the former, the men of orderly and conservative bent, he portrayed the old Catholic, traditionalist Quebec standing as an insurmountable rampart against antisocial propaganda; he outlined the part that all French communities, across the country, might play in maintaining the Canadian entity, because of their resistance to annexationist tendencies. To the Catholics across Canada, he pointed to the war on bilingual schools as a prologue to sectarian ventures against the Catholic separate schools. In the name of the fraternity of beliefs and misfortunes, he especially implored Irish Catholics to renounce this fratricidal struggle:

"I can well see," he said to them, "what we are both losing in this woeful battle; I do not yet see what our brothers in faith will be able to erect on the ruins of our schools."...

Lantagnac sat down amidst almost unanimous applause. Around him, his colleagues congratulated him warmly. And while the galleries were applauding in their own way, by a prolonged buzz of talk impatiently making up for a prolonged silence, Sir Wilfrid Laurier rose from his seat and came to offer the speaker his congratulations:

"My dear Lantagnac," he said to him in a flattering tone, "you are a force to reckon with. Heaven grant that I never have you against me."

[Lionel Groulx, The Iron Wedge *(Ottawa: Carleton University Press, 1986; orig. pub.* L'Appel de la Race, *1922)]*

QUESTIONS

1. What was the role of history in imperialism? What was meant by 'imperial unity?'
2. Why did Stephen Leacock conclude that it was neither 'possible or desirable that we in Canada can form an independent country?'
3. According to André Siegfried why was Canada becoming less British?
4. How did Henri Bourassa understand the relations between English and French Canadians?
5. What issues did Lionel Groulx, through the character of Jules de Lantagnac, raise in his defence of bilingual schools?

READINGS

Carl Berger, *The Sense of Power: Studies in the Ideas of Canadian Imperialism, 1867-1914* (Toronto: University of Toronto Press, 1970)

John S. Ewart, *The Kingdom Papers* (Ottawa, 1917)

John Kendle, *The Round Table Movement and Imperial Union* (Toronto, 1975)

Joseph Levitt, *Henri Bourassa and the Golden Calf: The Social Program of the Nationalists of Quebec, 1900-1914* (Ottawa: University of Ottawa Press, 1969)

Carman Miller, *Painting the Map Red: Canada and the South African War, 1899-1902* (Montreal-Kingston: McGill-Queen's University Press, 1993)

Social Reform and Moral Purity

Social reform was one of the most important political movements between 1880 and 1920. It was the result of an intersection of currents from science, religion, and gender relations, and was a response to concerns and anxieties around immigration, urbanization, and industrialization. The campaign for a moral, rational, ordering of society had parallel organizations in the United States and Great Britain, and Canadian reformers were often part of an international network for change.

Science played an important role in social reform as it complemented the religious beliefs that led many middle-class Canadians to profess the 'perfectibility' of men and women. Poverty and alcoholism were not intractable characteristics of humanity. Charles Darwin's ideas on biology were distorted and reapplied to society as a whole. The concept that societies evolved was widely adopted, and optimists believed that nations could, like humans, be improved and perfected. This betterment would not necessarily happen naturally, but with the efforts of activists educating the public and lobbying governments, nothing was impossible. For example, some Protestant social reformers strongly advocated the science of eugenics, promoting selective breeding and the segregation and sterilization of 'undesirables,' in order to weed out potential prostitutes, criminals, feeble-minded individuals, and alcoholics. This preoccupation with breeding was linked to the idea of racial degeneration, and concern about dropping birth rates among middle-class Anglo-Celtic Protestant families. If the so-called 'best' people were not having children, Canadians risked being swamped by the inferior stock of the urban working class or immigrants. The idea of eugenics was rejected by Canadian Catholics.

Science's call for intervention into society was supported by a new force in Christianity, the Social Gospel. This interpretation of Christianity was strongest in the Methodist Church, although it was present in all Protestant denominations, as well as in Catholic social activism. The Social Gospel sought to apply Christianity to the problems of modern industrial society, and saw social activism as following Jesus' model in trying to bring about the Kingdom of Heaven on earth.

The third influence on social movements was the perception of women as having familial roles and obligations. This potentially limited identity of mother, daughter, and sister was transformed by maternal or social feminists to justify women's intervention and activism in the world beyond their homes as they sought to bring about change for the good of their families. Women and women's issues therefore shaped many of the social reform campaigns.

Whether called social reformers, social gospellers, progressives, or social purity workers, these activists represented a loose, overlapping network of organizations and individuals who sought to improve morals and social conditions. Usually, they had some connection to religion, education, or medicine. Campaigns were directed at issues as varied as temperance, woman's suffrage, prostitution, juvenile delinquency, disease and public health, urban reform, the protection and training of children, Sunday observance, domestic violence, divorce, illegitimacy, and the suppression of obscene literature. With the important exceptions of temperance and woman's suffrage, the issues and campaigns were centred in urban areas. Reformers were personally motivated by a complex mixture of religious beliefs, genuine humanitarian concern, and a degree of self-interest, as public health concerns and fear of social disorder had direct ramifications on their own lives. Their actions led to an increasingly interventionist state, morality legislation, and the formation of national organizations such as the Dominion Alliance for the Total Suppression of the Liquor Traffic, and the Woman's Christian Temperance Union (WCTU).

Section A
Prostitution

Economic, demographic, and social changes led many to fear that young girls were drifting or being lured into prostitution or 'white slavery.' This problem attracted attention from a range of activists—from middle-class social reformers and church officials, to 'rescued' former prostitutes such as Maimie Pinzer, to organized labour. The issue of prostitution offers insight into the reform movement and the position of women in society, as women's expanded 'public' life was thought to make women more vulnerable to sexual exploitation.

Causes of the Social Evil

An organization formed with the object of effecting an important social reform has recently been established in Hamilton under the name of the White Cross Army. The following pledge taken by the members fully explains the purpose:

"To treat all women with respect and endeavor to protect them from wrong and degradation. To endeavor to put down all indecent language and coarse jests. To maintain the law of purity as equally binding upon men and women. To endeavor to spread the principles among companions and to try to help younger brothers. To use every possible means to fulfil the commandment 'Keep thyself pure.'"

There is no doubt great need for such an institution to check the social vices which are rampant everywhere. With the objects of the White Cross Army we cordially sympathize. We wish to point out, however, that under present industrial conditions, mere pledges and resolutions will accomplish little. They may effect a needed reformation in the lives of individuals, but they will make small impression upon the mass of society.

The great cause of female unchastity is poverty and the degradation caused by unhealthy, moral and physical surroundings. The reason why prostitution flourishes is because women are paid such miserably low wages in many departments that it is a constant struggle with them to obtain even the merest necessaries of life if they have no other resources than their own Labor. When girls receive the wretched pittance of a couple of dollars a week for continuous and exhausting Labor is it surprising that the constant temptations to a life of guilty ease and plenty should cause many to succumb? They are more sinned against than sinning. It is all very well for those who have never known the pains of hunger or the terrible mental strain of continuous anxiety for the morrow, to say that they had better starve in silence than sell themselves for bread. There are such heroines in the world. Many a poor working girl suddenly deprived of employment or prevented by ill-health from following her honest means of livelihood, has actually gone down to the grave sooner than lose the jewel of her maidenly purity. All honor to such, and we believe there are far more of them than a censorious and evil world has any idea of. But all women have not the high resolve and courage of martyr. Many are weak though well intentioned. They may struggle on for months and years in the ways of honest but ill-requited industry, and give way at last to the overmastering temptation, not of lust nor of pleasure, but simply of the rest and freedom for a while from the strain and pressure of a monotonous, weary round of Labor and penury.

Overwork, small pay and harsh treatment of female employees are the influences which more than any other tend to degrade women to subvert her naturally pure instincts, and to pave the way for the libertine and pander to rob her of maidenly virtue or wifely chastity. If the White Cross Army would strike at the root of the evil and protect women from wrong and degradation, they should seek to secure her industrial position, to abolish the evils of starvation pay and long hours. It is expecting too much of poor human nature to suppose than when the dread alternative of starvation or shame is presented as it so frequently is to the poor needlewoman or factory girl, than the majority will have fortitude enough to choose the former.

[Palladium of Labor *(Hamilton, Ontario), 21 June 1884]*

Morals According to the Report of the Royal Commission on the Relation of Labor and Capital, 1889

Grave charges of immorality have from time to time been made against female operatives in the large mills and factories. Whenever such charges have been made very serious apprehension has been felt by the public and careful enquiry has been made, in order to arrive at a correct conclusion upon this all-important subject.

In considering this matter it is necessary to look closely at the conditions of life in which—through no fault of their own—these young girls are placed. Stern necessity obliges them to earn a livelihood, and in pursuance of the avocation by which they earn their daily bread they are frequently compelled to toil for long, weary hours in close, ill-ventilated rooms. In these rooms there is a general co-mingling of the sexes, which is partly necessitated by the nature of the work in which they are engaged, and which cannot be avoided so long as the division of the task between males and females remains as at present. To this extent employers are not to blame, but when we find that in many cases the closet accommodation is lamentably insufficient, and that no attempt is made at a separation of these conveniences, grave censure is merited. It has been sufficiently demonstrated that in some factories closets are used indiscriminately by the operatives of both sexes, and where the employer is thus careless of the moral feelings of his operatives it should be the duty of the State to interfere and see that the proprieties of life are strictly observed. In further consideration of the case of these girls it must be remembered that for a considerable period after commencing work in a mill or factory they are paid such small wages that it is almost impossible for them to live respectably and clothe themselves decently out of the amount.

Given these conditions, it is not a matter for surprise that one is occasionally driven in despair to a life of sin. But it is monstrous to condemn the whole class because of the occasional sinner, as has been far too frequently done in this matter.

This subject came prominently before the Commission in Montreal and was also touched upon in other places. At Montreal one witness asserted that a condition of gross immorality prevailed in one of the mills of that City... His charges were very general in their nature, and provoked an outburst of natural indignation from the present employees of the company. A large number of these appeared before the Commission, and conclusively proved that the statements made by this witness were not warranted by the facts.

To make sweeping assertions of immorality against a whole class seems to be a comparatively small matter with some people; nevertheless, when their assertions are not consistent with the facts the cruelty and injustice involved ought not lightly to be passed over. The bare fact that a girl is willing to work hard during a long and tedious day for a very small allowance ought to be conclusive evidence that she is not inclined to a life of sin. The operatives of this mill who gave evidence before the Commission showed that though the toil is severe and long continued it is but rarely that one of the girls departs from the strict line of virtue. That occasionally one is led astray is probably true, just as it is equally true, that cases of immorality are found, from time to time, in what are termed the "higher walks of life." We need go not further than the divorce cases in the Dominion to prove that immorality is not confined to the poor, hard-working factory operatives.

[Canada, Report of the Royal Commission on the Relation of Labor and Capital *(Ottawa, 1889), pp. 90-91]*

War on the White Slave Trade
The Canadian Crusade

By Rev. J.G. Shearer, D.D., Secretary, Moral and Social Reform Council of Canada

The day has passed for proving the existence of a traffic in girls for immoral purposes. It has been demonstrated beyond a doubt. All the world has been convinced of the truth of this terrible statement. Hon. Edwin W. Sims' estimate, announced through the megaphone of the press, that 15,000 foreign girls, and 45,000 native born are the victims every year in the United States and Canada, has reached the ear of the world and aroused the indignation or terror of all who have hearts to feel. And a multitude is asking, "What can be done to suppress the cruel business; punish the heartless traffickers, and rescue their victims?"

One thing alone should satisfy us of the existence of the terrible traffic, namely, the fact that more than twenty Governments—our own being one—have signed an international treaty, in terms of which each has entered into covenant with all to co-operate in detecting and punishing the traders in innocent or foolish girlhood and in restoring their victims to their own country and friends. Even individual Governments do not, without reason, sign treaties for any purpose. Official and diplomatic inertia is proverbial. Only an unusual need, a need fully demonstrated, a most urgent need, can result in well nigh all the nations of the world binding themselves together in a great common effort such as that undertaken in the Treaty for the Suppression of the White Slave Trade.

But we Canadians, ready though we are to believe almost anything of the great cities of the United States, the Mother Land, and the rest of the world, are loath to believe that such things can by any possibility be going on in Canada. No wonder we are hard to convince. The trade is so despicable, so cruel, and one would suppose so difficult.

Everyone knows that for many years a constant stream of Canadian girls have crossed the border to earn their living as writers, nurses, teachers, stenographers, ladies' companions, seamstresses, domestic helpers, etc. Success in unusual degree has crowned their effort. Their integrity and industry and ability have been rewarded with generous remuneration. Stories of their success are widely known. This makes the work of the procurer the easier. His promises of an easy life and otherwise incredibly large wages are believed. Deceptive advertisements are answered. The innocent victims go blindly into a bondage worse than Hell. Once within the door of the house of shame, escape is well-nigh impossible. Locked doors, barred windows, withheld street garments prevent escape, while drugs and brutality do their debasing, enslaving, crushing work…

Others are first seduced, then half willingly go, this seeming to them a less evil than facing the shame at home. Still others are wooed, won and wedded in cold blood by heartless slavers, then inveigled or forced into the segregated colonies in the great American cities.

Mr. Clifford G. Roe, of Chicago, Assistant U.S. District Attorney, after investigating in Boston, Mass., says in Woman's World: "Taking the biography of one hundred girls in disreputable houses at random, it was learned that about one-third come to Boston from Canada, mainly Nova Scotia."

A scoundrel bearing a French-Canadian name is at this writing in prison in Buffalo for endeavoring to force his 21-year-old Toronto bride into a house of ill-fame, intending no doubt to be her "cadet" and live at ease on her "earnings."

Two other young villains from Ottawa were recently convicted in Ogdensburg of procuring for immoral purposes two foolish girls whom they had induced to go from the Dominion Capital "for a lark," and are now doing time in the Federal Penitentiary at Atlanta, Georgia.

These are sample instances of recent occurrence. Many others might be given.

The American authorities, with commendable energy are both legislating and enforcing the laws against procuring and prostitution. Their Federal Law directs that any alien woman found living the life of shame, within three years of the time of her entry into the States, shall be sent back to the country from which she came, as an "undesirable."

… These also are but samples of many available instances. And we may expect many more in the future. What shall we do with these, our own Canadian daughters, who went out from their homes pure, strong, hopeful, and are thus sent back as "undesirables"? We must be ready to give them refuge, and in mercy, love and patience to reclaim, and by the grace of God, to save them.

Canada is to-day the Mecca of the immigrant from all lands. Its lands are wondrous wide, its grain and sand and rock are indeed golden. Men are wanted So are women—young women—for domestics, waitresses, wives. Here then is the slaver's golden opportunity. Men and women (!) hunt and bait and ensnare them, even as the wild things of the forest are hunted, baited and ensnared. It is easy to do. The true stories of demand and opportunity and success that the mails bear back to every land make the deception of victims and immigration officials, and Moral and Social Reform agents, alike easy...

The Immigration Chaplains at Atlantic ports see many instances of foreign girls which they have reason to believe are victims of this damnable traffic, but it is extremely difficult to detect or prove this to be the case. White Slave Agents are closely watched wherever suspicion is aroused, and no such get access to the wharves. But who can guard unchaperoned girls after they leave the wharves and start on their overland journey? The Chaplains report that many such never reach their destination as declared to the Immigration officials. What happens to them? How easy for a Slave Agent of either sex who can talk their victim's native tongue, to win her confidence, a lonely stranger in a strange land, and persuade her to change her plans and go with the Agent to an inviting situation among her own country folk!

Letters from anxiously inquiring parents in the Old Lands about daughters from whom they have not heard, tell their own tale, confirming the suspicions of the Chaplains. Who can even imagine the horrible tragedies hidden, shall we say mercifully, by this mantle of mystery? Verily the "Black Slave Trade" of other days was humane by comparison with this inconceivably heartless traffic of the 20th century, with unintended satire denominated "White"!

But Canada is responsible for furnishing her share of the DEMAND for as well as of the SUPPLY of the victims of the White Slave Trade. We are not without our vice markets in the form of Red Light Colonies with or without the "red light" as the business sign. Such colonies "segregated" or "tolerated" are said to be a "necessity" for men—that is for human males—and essential to the "safety" of good women and girls, who otherwise would be assaulted by the said males. Of course if prostitution is a necessity, and must be tolerated, then a "supply" of prostitutes must be furnished. Hence on this theory the White Slave Trade is justified or at least must be "tolerated" since it simply supplies the "victims"! "Segregated" or "tolerated" colonies are an essential adjunct of the "business." Only in such colonies can the "victims" be HIDDEN and securely HELD. Anywhere else an unwilling victim can easily enough reach the eye or ear of respectable citizens who will give refuge or find it...

It is not surprising therefore that victims of the Trade are reported almost exclusively in Canada from those centers where the business of vice is permitted. The slaver baits his victims everywhere, in the rural village or town, or in the cities even where the business of vice is uniformly suppressed. But he or she invariably heads for a city where prostitution is allowed, to dispose of the victim.

The writer, after careful investigation covering two years, has found no exception to this rule. Victims are reported as ensnared in the prairie, old Ontario, rural Quebec, and the Maritime provinces. They are in every case reported as taken to such cities as Halifax, Montreal, Winnipeg, mining camps of New Ontario, or certain centers in British Columbia, in all of which are found colonies of vice more or less openly "tolerated" or more or less "segregated" by official action or inaction. In no case coming under his notice, or of which he has been able to get trace, has a slaver taken a victim to a city where "suppression" is the policy of the authorities, even if in some instances the policy is not very vigorously carried into effect...

An excellent illustration of how the purest and most innocent girls may be entrapped and enslaved is given in the following incident: A winsome young lady from a rural village that might be named, was on her way to visit a girl friend in a well-known city. She was not expecting her friends to meet her. A well dressed, respectable looking matron in the train managed to get into casual conversation with her and to learn the circumstances. She was most kind, said she lived quite near her young companion's friend, and invited her to go up with her. They took a carriage. The woman insisted on the girl going in with her, then prevailed upon her to stay for tea, invited her to stay over night. It would be such a pleasure, and her friend was not expecting her anyway. This, however, being refused, she invited the girl to make use of an upstairs room in preparing to leave, then coolly turned the key upon her. She was perplexed and alarmed, but helpless. No response met her knocks and calls. By and by the door opened and a man entered the room. He was a commercial traveler. He knew the girl by sight. He had sold goods to her father. He was not heartless. He told her she was in a house of ill-fame. She was horrified and ready to collapse of fright. He sought to devise her deliverance. This was not easy without exposing his own wrongdoing. A clever scheme enabled him to get permission of the mistress to take her out for a drive. He left her at her friend's door, after exacting a solemn promise, easily obtained, that his "beneficiary" would protect his own reputation and hers. What if almost any other patron of such a place had been the first to visit her?

Incidents like this surely demonstrate how easily the unsuspecting girl fresh from the security of the family circle may be victimized by smooth-tongued, unscrupulous wretches of either sex, and put beyond doubt the need of faithfully warning all girls of the perils threatening them when they journey unchaperoned to any large city. These dangers are many times greater when girls go to the city to remain and earn their living amid new surroundings, and are compelled to make their home in the less expensive boarding houses, and to find amusement on the streets or in the cheaper places of entertainment, as well as to be exposed to various insidious temptations from employers and work-mates.

[Ernest A. Bell, ed., Fighting the Traffic in Young Girls; or, War on the White Slave Trade: A complete and detailed account of the shameless traffic in young girls ... *(Chicago, c. 1910), pp. 333-348]*

Socialism on Prostitution. *[Western Clarion, 2 August 1913]*

Prostitution in Toronto

1. Poverty as a Cause of Prostitution

Prostitution is a social disease, i.e., it is not merely an affair between the sensual man and the depraved and avaricious woman, as individuals, but is the outcome of a complex social condition, which through artificial stimulation, multiplies both the demand and the supply. When an attempt is made to analyse the complex causes and to discover the effects of each particular contributing cause, the question of the relation of poverty to prostitution at once comes into view, because this is one condition which is everywhere present. This Commission has, therefore, been at some pains to arrive at well-grounded conclusions regarding the part played by economic pressure in keeping up the supply of recruits for the traffic of vice...

Another fact that should be borne in mind in this connection is the prevalence of what has been elsewhere in this Report described as "occasional" prostitution. Our investigators have reported to us the particulars of a surprisingly large number of interviews with girls and women actually working at various occupations, who by their own admission, make a practice of having intercourse with men for payment in money or gifts. And of the still larger number of professional prostitutes interviewed, a considerable proportion had formerly belonged to the "occasional" class, but had eventually ceased working. The causes of prostitution, therefore, whatever they are, are causes which operate to some extent among girls and women who rank with the reputable classes of society, and drives some of them into a life of vice...

As to the importance to be attached to economic pressure as a contributing cause to the social evil, the following considerations should be borne in mind:

1. It is obvious that insufficient wages is not the only nor indeed the chief cause, for if that were the case then wherever wages fall below a certain point, it would be found that practically all women whose wages are below that point would be immoral; and this is very far from the case. In spite of the severity of the pressure of such economic conditions, most girls in such positions successfully resist the pressure and retain their virtue.

2. If insufficient wages and consequent inability to procure the necessities of life were either the only or the principal cause of girls resorting to prostitution, we should expect to find domestic servants less frequently than any others among those who succumb, for the servant is less exposed than almost any other to periods of unemployment and when at work has always her board and lodging assured, and is not, therefore, driven to immorality as alternative to starvation. As a matter of fact, however, domestic service contributes quite as large a quota to the ranks of the fallen as does any other occupation. The explanation of this must evidently be something else than the pressure of want.

3. While economic pressure is not the sole cause, it is one of the important contributory causes, as is evidenced by the fact that prostitution is recruited almost entirely from one social class, the class, namely, by whom the pressure of economic conditions is most severely felt...

2. Housing and Sanitation

Undoubtedly overcrowding exists to a great extent in Toronto... Dr Hastings, the Medical Officer of Health, reports as follows:

"In regard to the influence of overcrowding on the moral conditions of our City, I might say that many cases have come under the observation of our Inspectors from time to time in which grown-up sons and daughters occupy the same sleeping apartments, and in some cases grown-up daughters occupy the same rooms with their father and mother, or with the father alone.

"In every case they have been notified to secure separate accommodation for the male and female adults in the home...

It must be apparent that conditions such as these must necessarily tend toward immorality, as they deprive young people of that sense of modesty which is one of the most valuable barriers girls possess in safeguarding them against temptations that they are exposed to, especially when they are forced to earn their own livelihood...

3. The Problem of the Foreigner

The great tide of immigration that has of late years been flowing into this country has presented serious problems to our Canadian communities, especially larger cities; and among these problems not the least is the complication of the social evil.

To begin with, it must be recognized that in some of the countries of Europe from which large numbers of immigrants are coming to us, the standards of sexual morality as well as the general standard of living, are not those of Canada. And when these immigrants, speaking little or no English, are huddled together in crowded city quarters, in squalid surroundings, without wholesome recreation facilities, vicious conditions readily arise and are difficult to cope with. And the possibilities of vice as a business are a strong temptation to some who, beside being naturally keen a business way, have come to this new country with great expectations of its opportunities for acquiring wealth. If to these conditions there is added the careless and supercilious attitude which looks upon these new citizens as "only foreigners," and upon the foreign sections of the City as regions where "you couldn't expect anything better," there will be grave danger of the great volume of immigration, of which as Canadians, we are inclined to be proud, becoming a source of moral and social infection.

That this danger is not merely an imaginary one will be seen from a consideration of certain facts disclosed by our investigations... The opportunities for the establishment of a "white slave" system are nowhere so favorable as in the foreign sections of a great city, where the inhabitants are comparatively isolated by their ignorance of English, and where the newest comers, especially, are easily victimized, on account of their lack of knowledge of the laws and customs of a new and strange country...

It is not alone the immigrant of foreign birth, however, whom this problem touches. The facts show that in connection with young women immigrants from Great Britain there is a problem for the protection both of the young women themselves and of the Canadian communities. The records of three institutions for unfortunate or delinquent women in Toronto, which are all under one management, show that fifty-one per cent of the women cared for in the year 1913 were British, and forty-three per cent Canadian, the remaining six percent being of other nationalities... As compared with other nationalities the explanation no doubt is that girls of foreign birth do not so often immigrate alone, but come for the most part, with their families. Still the fact remains a serious one that so large a proportion of this social wreckage should consist of young women who have recently come to theis country from the motherland...

4. Feeble-mindedness as Relation to Vice

The seriousness and extent of the problem of the proper care of the feeble-minded have long been keenly felt by social workers, but are still far from being understood by the public at large...

The reasons for the prevalence of immorality among the feeble-minded are various. Abnormal sensual propensities and lack of moral perception are among the forms of mental deficiency. Defectives, when not having these immoral tendencies, are usually lacking in initiative, and incapable of resisting suggestions, and hence are easily led astray. Again, the subnormal mentally are inefficient economically, and so often unable to earn a living. Further, many of the feeble-minded are children of feeble-minded parents, and have consequently lived in an unfavorable environment and lacked even such training as they were capable of receiving.

The last-named condition brings up one of the most serious phases of the problem of feeble-mindedness, viz: that feeble-mindedness is hereditary, and that feeble-minded persons are more than normally fertile, so that, in the absence of custodial care, they are continually reproducing their kind in large numbers...

As pertaining directly to its special problem, the Commission would repeat here the recommendation... that girls and young women of the delinquent class should, when convicted in Court, instead of being fined and let go, to become hardened offenders or social wrecks, be committed to institutions where their physical and mental conditions could be carefully ascertained. Reformatory treatment could then be prescribed for those capable of benefiting by it, and permanent custody for those whose condition indicated that as the proper course to be adopted.

The Commission would emphasize,...the importance of representations being made to the Department of Immigration with regard to the need of greater care to exclude mentally defective immigrants.

[Report of the Social Survey Commission *(Toronto, 1915), pp. 34-50]*

A Former Prostitute as Reformer

Montreal, Canada
September 21, 1915
Mrs M.A. DeWolfe 0Howe has asked me to write to you about the mission to be conducted in Montreal... "The Montreal Mission for Friendless Girls."

I know the girls very well. Their ambitions, hopes, lives, etc., and when I try to do anything to better their condition, I bring to mind my own experiences and try to supply—as much as possible—that which the girls lack to make their lives (away from sin) interesting and happy.

In my own life, I am sure I lacked love... Many girls, before they give themselves over to the sinful life, have the love of their parents, but people of the sort they spring from—as were my people—are singularily undemonstrative and often it isn't for lack of love, that the girls go astray, as much as for the evidence of it, which in the sinful life, they get in abundance... While there are many places in the larger cities where a girl would be treated kindly by people..., yet the average girl of any mental power shuns them. This I know from my own experience and from what girls have told me. I was many times sorely in need of a friend and knew they were to be had in "missions" and "settlements," but I was never the sort that belongs to the "beggar" class and I believed that places of the above sort were conducted to help any self confessed incompetents, who applied for help.

If I had ever—through some circumstance—come in contact with any of the fine women, that I realize, now, work so unselfishly and hard in the "missions" and "settlements," I am sure I would have been spared worlds of misery and some awful experiences. This then is what I hope to do. Supply the love—i.e.—really show love for every foolish little girl that I find on the downward path...

My attitude towards the girls has always been that of a comrade. I let them know right at the start that I have lived their lives and understand. Because I am not much older than they are, they know I can enter into their plans, plays, etc., without taking an old lady's viewpoint and frowning upon everything which it is natural for youth to enjoy...

I have taken a flat right in the beaten path frequented by these girls who are just starting out.

One bedroom will be my own and I hope to be able to occupy it alone but if the bed space is needed, I will be glad to share it with another girl.

In the other room, I will always keep a girl—or two, if later that is financially possible...

It is a theory of mine that anything done to help or better a girl has it value even if not perceptible at the time. In the case of these girls, even though they are but children—for I find it is with the younger ones that I am most successful—their experiences in the evil life makes them wiser than their years, and one must bear this in mind to cope successfully with their various problems.

If at the end of three months in my care, with love and every kindness shown to her, a girl will not try to live by her own efforts honestly and decently, I am of the opinion that she had better make way for the next girl, who is also a victim of circumstances and needs the life I can give her.

In selecting this one girl, to stay with me, from the many who will come to visit thru the day, I will take the one who seems most in need of that help which I can give her. Love, attentions of all sorts, training, etc., and I feel reasonably sure that in three months time, this girl will have benefitted and will be willing to go out to work and keep the good work up by giving her place up to the next girl...

Aside from this one girl—who will stay will me for the period of three months—I will take in for a night or two any girl in need of a bed. I could put to bed three more girls beside myself and my "three months" girl—i.e.,—each of us take a girl in our beds and one other could occupy the couch.

This business of being "locked out" is a serious one and is often the beginning of a girl's career in brothels.

Living at home a girl's parents lose patience with her and after repeated threats to "lock you out," if she persists in coming home later than the prescribed hour, she is finally "locked out." The girl is not prepared to go anywhere and the hour being late, she casts about in her mind as to the place where she would be welcome at such an hour, and the only place she can think of is a brothel.

Often when I hear from a girl's mother that she "stopped out all night," and I speak to the girl she tells me she either was "locked out" or being in company and the hour growing late before she realized it, knew if she went home, she'd only find herself "locked out," so she stayed with the "fellows" all night.

It is such times that I would want her to feel at home and come to me for the night, no matter how late and I would put her to bed somewhere. In the morning I would hope to effect a reconciliation between the girl and her parent. This I have been able to do several times already.

So much for my place as a refuge.

Aside from the sleeping at my mission I will keep the living room open to the girls who care to come. They will find attractions which I know they will enjoy and which I hope will tempt them to come to me rather than to the places where they went formerly.

I have for their entertainment, a phonograph, with some good records and some lively ones to suit their tastes. Also some books such as they can enjoy to read... They prefer the racy stories found in the 10 cent magazines but if several chapters of a good book are read to them, they will actually fight among themselves for the privilege of finishing it first. In this way, many of the girls read good books here for the time... I hope also to be able to offer the girls a cup of tea at any time when they come in...

Above all else, I will urge every girl to agree to work, if I find her a place and that I am sure I can do. I am fairly well acquainted now in all the larger factories and in a few of them—though I tell them frankly about the girls—they are willing to give them a chance. At housework, it is not so easy, for "madam" is generally most decided in her desire to secure a "respectable girl." Their chances are slim at housework though occasionally I find a woman willing to give a girl a chance to prove herself.

Aside from the material help, I will hope to direct them spiritually, as far as my ability permits me...

If you, or any friends are interested in helping on the "mission" I have planned,... I will be most grateful for even the smallest assistance. Yours sincerely,
Maimie Pinzer

[Ruth Rosen and Sue Davison, eds., Maimie Pinzer, The Maimie Papers (New York, 1977), pp. 333-337]

Section B
Temperance

The debate over the prohibition of alcohol divided Canadian society along almost every conceivable fault line, and ensured that it would be a perennial reform issue from the 1850s to the 1920s. The *Canada Temperance Act* of 1878, commonly referred to as the *Scott Act*, gave municipal or county councils the authority to prohibit the sale—but not the consumption—of liquor within their jurisdiction after the matter had been decided by a local plebiscite. The result was a 'local option' patchwork, where sales were legal or illegal according to various local boundaries. Temperance organizations such as the Dominion Alliance for the Total Suppression of the Liquor Traffic, the Order of the Sons of Temperance, and the Woman's Christian Temperance Union were successful at applying constant pressure on all levels of government. In 1893, the Conservatives attempted to resolve the issue with the establishment of the Royal Commission on the Liquor Traffic. Wilfrid Laurier's government fulfilled an election promise in September 1898 when it held a national plebiscite. While prohibitionist forces won by a slight majority in every province except Quebec, the Federal government concluded that the results were indecisive.

Mrs. Letitia Youmans, Founder of the Canadian Woman's Christian Temperance Union Remembers Her First Public Address

Cobourg was always a conservative town, adhering tenaciously to time-honoured rules. What was popularly known as woman's rights was in this town at a discount. Strong-minded women and blue stockings were below par. Still, I believe the good people felt they had some vested rights in me, and were prepared to receive me graciously.

We hear sometimes of stage fright which is said to seize the speaker when first appearing before the public. My trouble on that occasion was a choking sensation, which threatened to obstruct utterance. However, some benign influence came to my help, and the impediment was removed. It seemed imperative that I should define my position; accordingly I assured the audience that I had not come there to advocate woman's rights, but that I had come to remonstrate against women's and children's wrongs. But there is one form of woman's rights in which I firmly believe, and that is, the right of every woman to have a comfortable home, of every wife to have a sober husband, of every mother to have sober sons.

These inalienable rights had been wrested from us by the liquor traffic, and I have come here to appeal for protection for our homes and our children. This assertion seemed to strike the key-note of the meeting, and received a hearty response by way of general applause.

The term prohibition is obnoxious to many, but the idea of protection is congenial to everyone. The term protection has its political aspect, and hence is adverse to the sentiment of one of the parties; but home protection is a platform on which all parties and creeds can stand together. And thus I talked for one hour at least, without a written note, the memories of years coming to my rescue.

The meeting was pronounced a grand success. The audience numbered some thirteen hundred.

[Mrs. Letitia Youmans, Campaign Echoes: The Autobiography of Mrs. Letitia Youmans *(Toronto: William Briggs, 1893), pp. 128-129]*

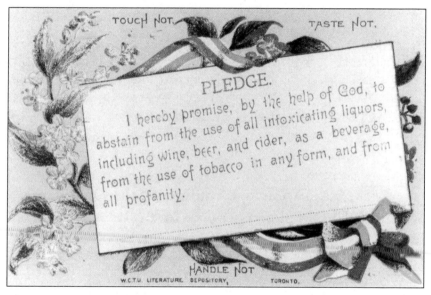

TOUCH NOT.   TASTE NOT.

PLEDGE.

I hereby promise, by the help of God, to abstain from the use of all intoxicating liquors, including wine, beer, and cider, as a beverage, from the use of tobacco in any form, and from all profanity.

HANDLE NOT

W.C.T.U. LITERATURE DEPOSITORY,   TORONTO.

The Woman's Christian Temperance Union's "Triple Pledge". *[Archives of Ontario, MU 8397-3]*

Victoria Chief of Police Is Examined by the Royal Commission on Liquor Traffic

Henry William Sheppard, Victoria Superintendent of Police Questioned by Commission Wellington J Dowler

Q: Do you find the people, as a whole, sober and law-abiding people?—Yes, compared with almost any part of the world. I have been all over the world nearly, and I think this is one of the quietest places I have ever been in.

Q: You have here quite a seafaring population?—Yes, when the sealing fleet comes in we have quite a few.

Q: Then you have here quite a large Chinese population?—Yes.

Q: So far as they are concerned, are they sober?—Yes. I do not think in our whole history we have had more than three Chinamen arrested for being drunk.

Q: You have, of course, people brought up frequently for drunkenness?—Yes.

Q: Are they sent to jail?—Yes, they serve a term.

Q: How long is the term?—It ranges from ten days to two months.

Q: From your experience with such people, do you think the present system of sending these men to prison for short terms is better than sending them for long periods to inebriate institutions with a view to their reformation?—I think the latter would be the better way.

Q: They have lost all control of themselves?—Yes, they appear to have done so.

Q: Taking your knowledge of the people, and living amongst them, and taking those who use intoxicating drinks as beverages, would the number of those who drink to excess be large or small?—It would not be very large.

Q: Would it only be a small percentage of the whole?—Yes.

Q: Then of that small percentage, some drink to excess more than others?—Yes.

Q: Have you considered at all the advisability of enacting a general prohibitory law?—Yes, and I do not think it would be advisable.

Q: If enacted, could it be enforced, taking this country as it is?—I do not think it is needed.

Q: Do you think it could be enforced if passed?—Yes.

Q: And the authorities would be able to prevent liquor being brought in?—No doubt, smuggling would go on. In this island you could smuggle almost anything.

[Canada, Royal Commission on the Liquor Traffic, *Minutes of Evidence, Part Three, Manitoba, North-West Territories and British Columbia (Ottawa 1893), pp. 478-479]*

What It Costs

DIRECT COST.

The report of the Royal Commission on the Liquor Traffic estimates the annual expenditure for strong drink in Canada in the following paragraphs:

Taking an average of the quantities of wines, spirits and malt liquors entered for consumption in the five years ending 1893, but excluding cider and native wines, and taking an average of the retail prices, the calculation shows the sum of **$39,879,854**, to be paid for liquor by consumers. As more than one-half of this amount is paid for spirits to which, it is well understood, a large addition of water is made before they are vended to the public, the total amount paid is probably considerably in excess of the sum just mentioned.

The money thus paid may be fairly said to represent so much diminution of wealth, as the liquor when consumed, leaves the community in no way advantaged. When money is paid for clothing, food, or other commodities, the purchaser is supposed to have value for his outlay. Both buyer and seller, respectively, possess wealth formerly held by the other, usually slightly increased by the exchange. The liquor seller possesses the wealth formerly held by his customer, but the customer-consumer has nothing. The community is poorer at least to the amount of money spent for the liquor. We have a right therefore to state that the country is impoverished annually by direct expenditure on liquor to the amount of $39,879,854.

The country is also impoverished by the waste of grain used in the manufacture of this liquor. Part of it was Canadian grain which, had it not been used in liquor making, would have been available for export or other use. Part of it was imported grain for which the money had to go out of the country. All the grain destroyed in the liquor manufacture has a right to a place in the calculation of loss. The Commission's estimate of the value of the material used is $1,188,765.

INDIRECT COSTS

The sums mentioned represent what may be called the direct loss which the liquor traffic imposes upon the community. That traffic also causes other and far greater losses which are not so easily ascertained. The Minority Report, however, deals with them fully and forcibly, making a careful estimate which may be summarised as follows:

Cost of Jails, Asylums, Alms-Houses, etc. By a very careful calculation it is shown that the total amount expended by the Dominion of Canada in the admin istration of justice and for the maintaining of penitentiaries, jails, asylums, reformatories, alms-houses, and like institutions, amounts to a total of $6,028,195. Assuming that one-half of this expenditure is fairly chargeable to the liquor habit and the liquor traffic, we get the cost to the country, thus caused, the sum $3,014,097

Loss of Labor.—The country loses a great deal because of the prevention of production of wealth on account of persons being in jails, hospitals, asylums, or in any way idle through intemperance. The working of a gang of men in a factory or any set of persons who work together, is interfered with by the absence of one or more in the same way. Much of our most highly organized manufacturing industry is thus seriously hampered. Not only do those who drink lose time and possibly earnings; their fellow employees are also losers. The industry which employs them suffers loss. An English parliamentary report estimates over sixteen per cent of the productive labor of the country as lost in this way. Assuming that in Canada the loss is only eight per cent, it amounts to $76,288,000.

Shortened Lives. Careful calculation shows that 3,000 lives are annually cut short in Canada by intemperance, each such death robbing the country of at least an average of ten years of productive power. It is estimated in this way we sustain an annual loss of $14,304,000.

Misdirected Work. A similar calculation shows that the country loses by having about 13,000 men engaged in making and selling liquor, not actually adding anything to the wealth of the country, but creating conditions which increase public burdens. If rightly employed these men would add to the country the amount of wealth which we now have to do without, estimated at $7,748,000.

A SUMMING UP

In this connection the fact must be noted that a proportion of the national, provincial and municipal revenues is derived from the liquor traffic. The total amount thus contributed is calculated by the Commission at $8,473,316.22, the details of which are given in the table below.

This is the amount which the liquor traffic pays for the privileges granted it. It is right that this amount should be set over against the items of loss, and the various expenditures caused by the traffic, hereinbefore considered.

This may be done as follows

Cost of the Liquor Traffic

Amount paid for liquor by consumers	$39,879,854
Value of grain, etc., destroyed	1,888,765
Cost of proportion of pauperism, disease, insanity & crime chargeable to the liquor traffic	3,014,097
Loss of productive labor	76,288,000
Loss through mortality caused by drink	14,304,000
Misdirected labor	7,748,000
TOTAL	$143,122,716

Revenue from the Liquor Traffic

Dominion Government	$7,101,557	
Provincial Governments	924,358	
Municipalities	429,107	$8,455,022
NET LOSS		$134,667,694

This startling calculation does not include, as a charge against the liquor traffic, the great amount of money spent in watching it and collecting the revenue for it...

WILL IT NOT BE WISDOM TO PROHIBIT THE WORSE THAN USELESS LIQUOR TRAFFIC, AND STOP THIS TERRIBLE WASTE?

[Dominion Alliance for the Suppression of Liquor Traffic]

An Argument Against Prohibition

Halifax has a population of not less than 45,000. She has among her own people very many of all classes of society who use liquor and who will not give it up, certainly not on compulsion without struggle, and who will not respect any law which seeks to coerce them into so doing. It is a seaport, a naval and military station; a more unlikely spot for prohibition to succeed could not possibly be discovered. The vested interests at stake are very large, so large in fact that they are of interest to the city as a whole. It is worth while to see how great they are, and how much the city would lose, supposing prohibition to be possible. A carefully compiled statement was handed to the commission at the time of their visit to Halifax, which, so far as I am aware, has never been questioned, and so far as can be judged, appears to be a moderate estimate. According to this, the capital invested in the liquor business or in businesses inseparably connected with liquor in Halifax is as follows: —

Real Estate	
Hotels	$698,100
Shops	366,760
Wholesale houses	375,000
Soda factories	25,000
Total	$1,873,360

In the opinion of the owners of these properties they would in the event of prohibition be depreciated in value to an extent exceeding one third. Of course, I am aware that the ardent prohibitionists will say such an increase of prosperity would follow upon the law so that not depreciation, but the reverse, would follow. That is a matter of opinion on which I am content to take what I believe to be the judgement of the great majority of the people of Halifax, namely, that an effective enforcement of the prohibitory law, supposing such a thing possible, would leave most of the properties now engaged in the trade empty and profitless. Then as to employment, the number of persons employed in and about establishments in which liquor is sold was, in 1882, 692, receiving wages amounting to $305,232, of whom a very considerable number at any rate would be thrown out of employment in the event of an effective measure of prohibition. In addition to these, the trade gave a large amount of employment to people not directly connected with the places in which it was carried on—freight by land and water, teamsters, insurance and the like. The taxes paid the city in respect of properties engaged in the trade amounted in 1892 to $16,628, which, when added to the $11,000 derived from licenses, made up over $27,000 of revenue which the city stands a chance of losing in good part, and which would have to be made up from the other properties. [...]

[Letters on Prohibition by "Temperance" (Halifax: Halifax Printing Co., 1897), pp. 32-36]

The Plebiscite

To the Work! To the Work!!
ORGANIZE! AGITATE!! EDUCATE!!!
Here is the Ballot and the Question asked you:

	YES	NO
Are you in favor of the passing of an Act pro-hibiting the importation, manufacture or sale of spirits, wine, ale, beer, cider and all other alcoholic liquors for use as beverage?		

God's clock has struck the hour of opportunity. Now for God, and home, and native land. Let your act of voting be an act of worship. We have done well in previous campaigns. Look at the record:

On July 23rd, 1892, Manitoba gave prohibition a
    majority of..12,522
On December 14th 1893, P.E. Island, gave pro-
    hibition a majority of 7,226
On January 1st, 1894, Ontario gave prohibition a
    majority of..81,769
On March 15th, 1894, Nova Scotia gave prohibi-
    tion a majority of 31,401

Total majority so far for Prohibition. 132,918

On April 7th, 1893, New Brunswick, by a unanimous vote of her Legislature, asked the Dominion Parliament to pass prohibition.

Never let it be said that the Prohibitionists of Canada have played a retreat. Let no consideration of blood money, called revenue, chloroform your conscience. Every cent spent for liquor is one less to be spent for boots, clothes, food, furniture, books, pictures, music, and all the other products of useful industry and art. On the question of revenue alone we claim the vote of every clear-sighted, level-headed citizen in the land.

THIS IS THE SUPREME ISSUE

Probably never before have we exercised the franchise in more solemn circumstances. Our responsibilities are grave. Our opportunities are great. The situation is full of important and far-reaching results. There is no question before the people of this Dominion to-day that is comparable in importance with that of the suppression of the drunkard-making business. Questions of tariff reform and of national schools have their importance, and may wisely be considered, but they are secondary to the liquor problem. The drink traffic is by far the greatest evil that afflicts our land, financially, politically, socially, morally and religiously. Its suppression is therefore the greatest of all the issues before the Canadian people. Remove this evil and other questions may be left to be settled as they come to the front for solution. Let the issues be presented frequently and forcibly to the people, and we may assume that the mass of voters—many of whom are at present indifferent—will side against the traffic: the people of Canada committing themselves, after full deliberation, to the support of grog shops is hardly conceivable.

[Rev. W. A. MacKay BA, DD, The Plebiscite: How Shall I Vote? An Appeal to the Electors of Canada on the Present Crisis in the Temperance Reform (Woodstock, Ontario, 1896)]

McClung on Prohibition

But moralists tell us that prohibition of any evil is not the right method to pursue; far better to leave the evil and train mankind to shun it. If the evil be removed entirely mankind will be forced to abstain and therefore will not grow in strength. In other words, the life of virtue will be made too easy. We would gently remind the moralists who reason in this way that there will still be a few hundred ways left, whereby a man may make shipwreck of his life. They must not worry about that—there will still be plenty of opportunities to go wrong!

The object of all laws should be to make the path of virtue as easy as possible, to build fences in front of all precipices, to cover the wells and put the poison out of reach. The theory of teaching children to leave the poison alone sounds well, but most of us feel we haven't any children to experiment on, and so we will lock the medicine-chest and carry the key...

Under prohibition, a drunken man is a marked man—he is branded at once as a law breaker, and the attitude of the public is that of indignation. Under license, a drunken man is part of the system—and passes without comment. For this reason a small amount of drunkenness in a prohibition territory is so noticeable that many people are deceived into believing that there is more drunkenness under prohibition than under license. Prohibition does not produce drunkenness, but it reveals it, underlines it. Drunkenness in prohibition territory is like a black mark on a white page, a dirty spot on a clean dress; the same spot on a dirty dress would not be noticed.

There was a licensed house in one of the small prairie towns, which complied with all the regulations; it had the required number of bedrooms; its windows were unscreened; the license fee was paid; the bartender was a total abstainer, and a member of the union; also said to be a man of good moral character; the proprietor regularly gave twenty-five dollars a year to the Children's Aid, and put up a cup to be competed for by the district hockey clubs. Nothing could be more regular or respectable, and yet, when men drank the liquor there it had appalling results. There was one Irishman who came frequently to the bar and drank like a gentleman, treating every person and never looking for change from his dollar bill. One Christmas Eve, the drinking went on all night and well into Christmas Day. Then the Irishman, who was the life of the party, went home, remembering what day it was. It all came out in the evidence that he had taken home with him presents for his wife and children, so that his intention toward them was the kindest. His wife's intention was kind, too. She waited dinner for him, and the parcels she had prepared for Christmas presents were beside the plates on the table. For him she had knitted a pair of gray stockings with green rings around them. They were also shown as evidence at the inquest!

It is often claimed that prohibition will produce a lot of sneaking drunkards, but, of course, this man had done his drinking under license, and was of the open and above-board type of drinker. There was nothing underhand or sneaking about him. He drank openly, and he went home, and his wife asked him why he had stayed away so long, he killed her—not in any underhand or sneaking way. Not at all. Right in the presence of the four little children who had been watching for him all morning at the window, he killed her. When he came to himself, he remembered nothing about it, he said, and those who knew him believed him. A blind pig could not have done much worse for that family! Now, could it?

Years after, when the eldest girl had grown to be a woman, she took sick with typhoid fever and the doctor told her she would die, and she turned her face to the wall and said: 'I am glad.' A friend who stood beside her bed spoke of heaven and the blessed rest that there remains, and the joy of the life everlasting. The girl roused herself and said, bitterly: 'I ask only one thing of heaven and that is, that I may forget the look in my mother's face when she saw he intended to kill her. I do not want to live again. I only want to forget!' The respectability of the house and the legality of the sale did not seem to be any help to her.

But there are people who cry out against prohibition that you cannot make men moral, or sober, by law. But that is exactly what you can do. The greatest value a law has is its moral value. It is the silent pressure of the law on public opinion which gives it its greatest value. The punishment for the infringement of the law is not its only way of impressing itself on the people. It is the moral impact of a law that changes public sentiment, and to say that you cannot make men sober by law is as foolish as to say you cannot keep cattle from destroying the wheat by building a fence between them and it, or to claim you cannot make a crooked twig grow straight by tying it straight. Humanity can do anything it wants to do. There is no limit to human achievement. Whoever declares that things cannot be done which are for the betterment of the race, insults the Creator of us all, who is not willing that any should perish, but that all should live and live abundantly.

[Nellie McClung, In Times Like These *(Toronto: University of Toronto Press, 1972; orig. pub. 1915), pp. 102-105]*

QUESTIONS

1. How did the authors of these documents explain the causes of young women entering prostitution? What solutions did they propose?
2. How was female sexuality characterized?
3. What arguments did Letitia Youmans and Nellie McClung put forward that appealed specifically to women?
4. How was the economic debate around prohibition presented by each side?
5. What interest groups can be identified as opposing prohibition?

READINGS

Richard Allen, *The Social Passion: Religion and Social Reform in Canada, 1914-1928* (Toronto: University of Toronto Press, 1971)

Christopher Armstrong and H.V. Nelles, *The Revenge of the Methodist Bicycle Company: Sunday Streetcars and Municipal Reform in Toronto, 1888-1897* (Toronto: Peter Martin Associates, 1977)

Jay Cassel, *'The Secret Plague': Venereal Disease in Canada, 1838-1939* (Toronto: University of Toronto Press, 1987)

Ramsay Cook, *The Regenerators: Social Criticism in Late Victorian English Canada* (Toronto: University of Toronto Press, 1985)

Sharon Anne Cook, *'Through Sunshine and Shadow: The Woman's Christian Temperance Union, Evangelicalism, and Reform in Ontario, 1874-1930* (Montreal: McGill-Queen's University Press, 1995)

Judith Fingard, *The Dark Side of Life in Victorian Halifax* (Porter's Lake, NS: Pottersfield Press, 1989)

Gerald A Hallowell, *Prohibition in Ontario, 1919-1923* (Toronto: Ontario Historical Society, 1972)

Andrée Lévesque, *Making and Breaking the Rules: Women in Quebéc, 1919-1939* (Toronto: McClelland and Stewart, 1994)

Angus McLaren, *Our Own Master Race: Eugenics in Canada, 1885-1945* (Toronto: McClelland and Stewart, 1990)

J.H. Morrison and James Moreira, eds., *Tempered by Rum: Rum in the History of the Maritime Provinces* (Porter's Lake, NS: Pottersfield Press, 1988)

Janice Newton, *The Feminist Challenge to the Canadian Left, 1900-1918* (Montreal: McGill-Queen's University Press, 1995)

Carolyn Strange, *Toronto's Girl Problem: The Perils and Pleasures of the City, 1880-1930* (Toronto: University of Toronto Press, 1995)

Mariana Valverde, *The Age of Light, Soap and Water: Moral Reform in English Canada, 1885-1925* (Toronto: McClelland and Stewart, 1991)

Cheryl Krasnick Warsh, ed., *Drink in Canada: Historical Essays* (Montreal: McGill-Queen's University Press, 1993)

Jan Noel, *Canada Dry: Temperance Crusades Before Confederation* (Toronto: University of Toronto Press, 1995)

Massive numbers of Canadians responded with jingoistic fervour to the declaration of hostilities in Europe in August 1914. Young men flocked to recruiting booths, determined to prove their manhood before the excitement overseas ended. Of course, the war dragged on far longer and proved far bloodier than anyone had anticipated. Yet, countless Canadians, stirred by Imperialist sentiments, and convinced that theirs was a fight for liberty against autocracy, continued to rally to the flag. As well, Canadians responded en masse to pleas for food and fuel control and, during the final year of hostilities, more than 1.5 million citizens lent Ottawa approximately $1.2 billion through Victory Bond purchases.

Attempts to produce a supreme war effort also generated coercion and repression. Rough justice was often applied against those who protested against the conflict, or whose ethnic background suggested empathy for the enemy—such as Canada's Galician population, Ukrainians who had recently migrated from an area taken over forcibly by Austria prior to World War I. Freedom of the press in wartime Canada fell by the wayside. Throughout the conflict, 253 publications considered as being pro-German, anti-British, Bolshevist, or as undermining the war effort by providing gory depictions of combat, were banned in Canada.

Typically, civilians read of stupendous victories by Canadian soldiers, and that each man stood ready to sacrifice all for liberty and the Empire. The letters that soldiers wrote home often painted the same picture—there were unit and battalion censors, and many soldiers also wanted to spare their loved ones worry as well as uphold their own manly image.

With Canada's accomplishments in battle so celebrated, the Great War went a long way toward enhancing Canadian nationalism. Yet, as well as promoting pride in large parts of the country, the conflict also generated internal division—particularly over the issue of conscription. By 1916, recruitment had slowed, and pressure quickly built for the introduction of compulsory service. This was particularly true within English Canada, where many wanted to force greater participation from Quebec—a province whose French majority regarded the conflict as Britain's struggle, and who felt little kinship toward the 'atheistic' Republic of France. French-Canadian leaders such as Henri Bourassa predicted violence in Quebec if the *Military Service Act* of May 1917 was enforced; five people were killed in anti-draft riots in Montreal and Quebec City over the 1918 Easter weekend.

Bitterness from the war years carried over into peacetime; in Quebec there emerged the quasi-separatist nationalism of Abbé Lionel Groulx and his *Action Française*. Friction also became evident between civilians and veterans. For instance, propaganda released by the Military Hospitals Commission and the Department of Soldiers' Civil Re-establishment promised a smooth transition into civilian life for Canada's returned heroes. Certainly, compared to any previous welfare package, the one created for Canada's Great War veterans was impressive—it came to include medical care, pensions, retraining for the disabled, a land settlement program, and gratuities that provided numerous veterans with several hundred dollars. Nevertheless, for many soldiers other less positive experiences stood out. Such men saw themselves as returning to a society that failed to understand the scope of their suffering, and from which there emerged post-war support programs that, despite their relative generosity, still seemed to be managed with cost control being too prominent a concern.

Section A

The Home Front

Patriotic sentiment deluged Canadian civilians, and tremendous pressure was placed upon young men to don khaki. Many could not wait to get overseas as they remained naive about the true nature of the combat. Some letters to Canada from the front revealed disillusionment; far more, however, remained upbeat and 'sanitized.' Naiveté was also encouraged by coercion—namely through the *War Measures Act*, and the rigorous application of censorship rules by Lieutenant-Colonel Ernest J. Chambers who, in June 1915, was appointed Canada's Chief Censor. The *War Measures Act* was also used to deal with those suspected of subversion. For example, although the Galicians had been promised fair treatment by the federal government at the beginning of the war, it did not take long for questionable comments made by a few Galicians to be transformed into widespread suspicion of treason. This resulted in the internment of 6 000 of this ethnic group, and the requirement that some 80 000 others report on their whereabouts monthly.

Rallying to the Cause. *[National Archives of Canada, C93228]*

The Appeal to Manhood

WAR IS AWFUL

BUT TO LIVE IN HUMILIATION IS TERRIBLE.

THE DEFEAT OF OUR ARMIES MEANS HUMILIATION
THE SPIRIT OF PROGRESS BROKEN
THE FREEDOM OF OUR GOVERNMENT IMPAIRED
THE LOSS OF SELF-RESPECT

The sooner you do your turn the quicker will come victory. Canada's future is what **WE DO TODAY.**

Our children will either bless or condemn us in the years to come.

Their heritage is wrapped up in the pluck and energy every able man brings into play now.

ARE YOU COMING?   **ENLIST NOW**

ENLIST
98TH OVERSEAS BATTALION

[Archives of Ontario, MU 22052, 1915, #40, Recruiting Circulars]

To the Women of Canada

127th York Rangers
Overseas Battalion

Extracts from letter which appeared in the *Evening Telegram*, December 3rd, over the name of G. G. Starr:—

To the Women of Canada

In addressing these few remarks exclusively to the women of the country, it is to be understood that we have arrived at that period in the struggle where we realize the utter futility of recruiting meetings.

The men who have as yet failed to join the colors will not be influenced by any eloquence from any platform.

The reason? The man we are trying to reach is the man who will never listen and the man who never for a moment considers the remarks as applicable to himself.

And so now we appeal to the women—the women who are the mainspring of all masculine action.

In the First Division of the C.E.F. we swept up the young manhood of the country in the first enthusiasm—we secured the cream of the country in the men who flocked to the colors taking thought of neither yesterday or to-morrow.

At the second call men were stopping to calculate and hesitate. Since then the hesitation has developed into stagnation. Men who see a desperate winter ahead are joining the colors, and a few others; the remainder are deadwood.

The reason? Firstly, the man who prefers to allow others to fight for him so that he may pursue a comfortable occupation, preserve his youth, be safe from danger, and explain to his friends that he would gladly join the colors could he obtain a commission—and yet take no steps towards that end.

Second. The man who is influenced by the selfish maternal appeal either from mother or wife.

Third. The man who claims his business would go to pieces without him, but is satisfied to let others throw away life and youth to sustain that business.

Fourth. The others—call them what you may.

And now my Appeal to Women

You entertain these wretched apologies in your home. You accept their donations, their theatre tickets, their flowers, their cars. You go with them to watch the troops parade.

You foully wrong their manhood by encouraging them to perform their parlor tricks while Europe is burning up.

While Canada is in imminent danger of suffering the same were it not for the millions who are cheerfully enduring the horrors and privations of bloody warfare for the millions who stay at home watching the war pictures and drinking tea.

Bar them out, you women. Refuse their invitations, scorn their attentions. For the love of Heaven, if they won't be men, then you be women. Tell them to come in uniform, no matter how soiled or misfitting—bar out the able-bodied man who has no obligations, show that you despise him. Tell him to join the colors while he can do so with honor. And the day is not far off when he will have to go. The old mother has issued the last call to her sons.

Make your son, your husband, your lover, your brother, join now while he yet retains the remnants of honor. Compulsory training is in the offing.

Get the apologist, the weakling, the mother's pet, into the service. Weed out all, and we will find out who are the cowards. Analyze your friends—you women—refuse their attentions, and tell them why. Make them wake up.

GOD BLESS HIM, THE KING CALLS!
ENLIST WITH
127th "YORK RANGERS" OVERSEAS BATTALION
Recruiting Officers all through the County
Headquarters, 860 Yonge St.

[Archives of Ontario, MU 2052, 1915, #40, Recruiting Circulars]

Recruiting Soldiers for God's War

...Germany had this war in view for years and was thoroughly equipped for European conquest. She had diligently gathered together and trained the largest army of any nation in the world—a mighty force of disciplined soldiers full of fierce zeal and lust of blood—who like hounds strained at the leash waiting for *the day* and the hour when the Prussian dogs of war should be let loose to destroy the land and slay with merciless hate all who opposed them. And that day came unexpectedly a year ago.

Moreover, these Germans entered upon this war with their minds carefully *trained out* of the idea of every moral sense and obligation—private—public—or international. The hellish cruelties practised on non-combatants in obedience to orders for the purpose of establishing frightfulness show the hideous fact that our foes boldly flout the existence of any laws, Divine or human, except what they make themselves—that they respect not age or sex—and spare not man, woman or child.

In ancient times the world was divided into two great races, Jews and Gentiles—to-day the racial division is between Human Beings and Germans. Thank GOD we are on the side of humanity, justice and honor, and with a clear conscience can lift the prayer of faith and hope "The LORD our GOD be with us."

LET US PLAINLY UNDERSTAND THIS WITHOUT ANY MISTAKE.

So long as Germany exists unbroken, unconquered, so long will humanity be enslaved and outraged. The world bears witness to-day that there is no crime, nor brutality, nor any abomination of desolation conceivable which the German has not perpetrated already, and is ready to repeat when the opportunity is given. This is the foe we are fighting to-day—the foul thing, the Imperial beast, the modern Nero—which has to be crushed.

WHAT ARE WE GOING TO DO ABOUT IT?

Recruiting has been going on vigorously for a year—but our Canadian manhood is by no means aroused yet to its full capacity. We have nearly 200,000 troops under arms—but double that number would not be too many. It is said that only one out of every twenty available single men in Canada has enlisted—and of those enrolled *one out of every three is a married man.* Ah, yes, there is the heroism of the young wife, the devoted mother in the desolate home, as well as the heroism of our men in the shell-stormed trench and the lonely bivouac that must be considered in our prayers and intercessions.

WHAT ARE OUR STALWART YOUNG MEN DOING FOR THEIR COUNTRY AND THEIR HOME!

Holding down their jobs and business propositions and adopting the phrase "Safety First" will not defeat the intention and determination of the Hun o smash us. Is it always to be Safety First? No, in a time like this it is Honour First, or Justice First, or Freedom First. In the early days of the war it was thought a wise thing to raise the cry "Business as usual," and to keep things going as before. But, brethren, that is not going to save the country. We have got to be up and doing as never before. Canadians are not merely called upon to assist the Motherland in this desperate conflict. No, we are called upon to fight for our own lives and the lives of our women and children, to secure freedom from the mailed fist of Prussian militarism—to defend our fair Canadian homes from the fate of Belgium and Flanders. We are taking part, a prominent part, a noble part in this *holy war* (as the Bishop of London calls it), and we are called upon to *energize, mobilize, sacrifice*— to bring out the best of our strength, moral and physical, the

PRIDE OF OUR CANADIAN MANHOOD,

and dedicate it with prayer and sacrament to the cause of King and Country...

[Archives of Ontario, MU 2052, 1915, #1, The Battle is the Lord's. The Substance of a Recruiting Sermon Preached by Canon Alex W. Macnab, A Vice-President of the Canadian Defence League in the Cathedral of St. Alban-The Martyr, Toronto, 4 August 1915, the Anniversary of the Outbreak of the War and the National Day of Intercession and Prayer on Behalf of our Allied Armies"]

Oh, What a Lovely War

When Jack Comes Back

By Gordon V. Thompson

When Jack comes back
There'll be a mighty welcome for our soldier boy!
And he will be the idol of his country
for he fought for liberty
Hurrah! Hurrah!
    He's home once more!
    Hurrah! Hurrah!
    The war is o'er!
When Jack comes back
There'll be a mighty welcome for our soldier boy!

*[Gordon V. Thompson, When Jack Comes Back (Toronto: Thompson
Publishing Company, 1917)] Copyright assigned 1991 to Warner Chappell
Music Canada Ltd.*

Reports from the Front: Private Frank "Mayo" Lind, Royal Newfoundland Regiment Provides Copy for the St. John's *Daily News*[1]

France, June 29th, 1916

We are out to billets again for a short rest, returning to trenches tomorrow, and then ——, but never mind that now.

Again our boys have brought honor to themselves and Newfoundland, but I have no doubt Newfoundland is ringing from one end to the other with the news of the great success of our raiding party, which under Captain Bert. Butler, Lieut. C. Strong, and Lieut. Greene, DCM, played havoc with the Huns. About fifty of our men made an attack on the Germans, and although we have to regret the loss of several of our brave fellows killed and missing, also several wounded, yet the casualties on the enemy's side amounted to about 400—score another for the Newfoundlanders. Our chaps are the talk of the whole line; every man held his life in his hands, and none knew if they would ever return alive; all heroes as brave as any that ever went over the parapet. You ought to have heard the praise given them by the Colonel, also by General Cayley.

Fred O'Neill covered himself with glory, and as a result he is in hospital with a shattered hand received from a bomb which was thrown by the enemy and landed amongst them. Fred without the least hesitation, seized the bomb and threw it

---

[1] Three days later, Lind perished at the battle of Beaumont Hamel—a clash where the Royal Newfoundland Regiment suffered a 90 per cent casualty rate.

back, but it exploded as it left his hand, although himself receiving a nasty wound. His prompt action saved many of his comrades. Jim Murphy also received a nasty wound; also Chas Butler, Lieut. Strong and Capt. Butler. They say Lieut. Greene's wounds are the worst. We all hope he will pull through, for Greene is a splendid man, a brave man, and has won honors for himself in every undertaking. No doubt you have the official list of wounded and killed, so I had better not comment on it now. Some are missing, we hope they may turn up O.K. Some of them did not turn up until 24 hours after the raid. George Phillips of A Company got back next day, "tattered and torn," but what a hero, for George slept in a German dug-out the night before, (cool), and as far as we can learn the Germans are wondering yet what struck them. Our fellows charged right into their trenches carrying all before them and in word played "hide and seek" with the Huns, chasing them in and out through the traverses, and dropping bombs on them everywhere. Fully 400 Germans were knocked out by our 50 brave fellows. The Germans never want to have another visit from the "White Indians," as they call us; for one day they put up a notice in their trenches, "When are the White Indians from Newfoundland coming over." They know now that some of them have been over, and likely will know more later...

Did I tell you about the mud here yet? Well just a word; it is mud and slush from head to toe. We are quite used to it now, and would you believe it, we enjoy it. Yes, it is great fun, for believe me, a man can get used to anything, and when this bunch gets back they will be the hardiest lot of men in the world. Here we face danger, awful danger, every hour, looking over the parapet sometimes during a beautiful clear sky, gazing across "No Man's Land" to the enemy's lines, perhaps at just before dawn. It is wonderful how our boys have hardened to this life—shot and sheels,—and some sheels you bet—flying all around them, yet not a flinch. Ah, I wish I could just, in imagination, take you into the trenches. I wish I could illustrate to you just what it is like, but I Cannot. No pen could describe what it is like, how calmly one stands and faces death, jokes and laughs; everything is just an every day occurrence. You are mud covered, dry and caked, perhaps, but you look at the chap next you and laugh at the state he is in; then you look down at your own clothes and then the other fellow laughs. Then a whizz bang comes across and misses both of you, and both laugh together...

[*Joan Horwood,* Massacre at Beaumont Hamel *(St. John's: Avalon Publications, 1975), pp. 38–40]*

The War Measures Act (excerpt)

6. The Governor in Council shall have power to do and authorize such acts and things, and to make from time to time such orders and regulations, as he may by reason of the existence of real or apprehended war, invasion or insurrection deem necessary or advisable for the security, defence, peace, order and welfare of

Canada; and for greater certainty, but not so as to restrict the generality of the foregoing terms, it is hereby declared that the powers of the Governor in Council shall extend to all matters coming within the class of subjects hereinafter enumerated, that is to say:—

(a) censorship and the control and suppression of publications, writings, maps, plans, photographs, communications and means of communication;

(b) arrest, detention, exclusion and deportation;

(c) control of the harbours, ports and territorial waters of Canada and the movements of vessels;

(d) transportation by land, air, or water and the control of the transport of persons and things;

(e) trading, exportation, importation, production and manufacture;

(f) appropriation, control, forfeiture and disposition of property and of the use thereof.

2. All orders and regulations made under this section shall have the force of law, and shall be enforced in such manner and by such courts, officers and authorities as the Governor in Council may prescribe, and may be varied, extended or revoked by any subsequent order or regulation; but if any order or regulation is varied, extended or revoked, neither the previous operation thereof nor anything duly done thereunder, shall be affected thereby, nor shall any right, privilege, obligation or liability acquired, accrued, accruing or incurred thereunder be affected by such variation, extension or revocation...

10. The Governor in Council may prescribe the penalties that may be imposed for violations of orders and regulations under this Act, but no such penalty shall exceed a fine of five thousand dollars or imprisonment for any term not exceeding five years, or both fine and imprisonment, and may also prescribe whether such penalty be imposed upon summary conviction or upon indictment...

[Statutes of Canada, 5 George V, chapter 2, 22 August 1914]

A Promise to Respect Freedom

It has come to the attention of the Government that many persons of German and Austro-Hungarian nationality who are residents of Canada are apprehensive for their safety at the present time. In particular the suggestion seems to be that they fear some action on the part of the Government which might deprive them of their freedom to hold property or to carry on business. These apprehensions, if they exist, are quite unfounded.

The policy of the Government is embodied in a Proclamation published in *The Canada Gazette* on 15th August. In accordance with this Proclamation restrictive measures will be taken only in cases where officers, soldiers or reservists of the German Empire or of the Austro-Hungarian Monarchy attempt to leave Canada or where subjects of such nationalities engage or attempt to engage in espionage or acts of a hostile nature or to give information to or otherwise assist the King's enemies. Even where persons are arrested or detained on the grounds indicated they may be released on signing an undertaking to abstain from acts injurious to the Dominion or the Empire.

The Proclamation after stating that "there are many persons of German and Austro-Hungarian nationality quietly pursuing their usual avocations in various parts of Canada and that it is desirable that such persons should be allowed to continue in such avocations without interruption," directs as follows:-

> "That all persons in Canada of German or Austro-Hungarian nationality, so long as they quietly pursue their ordinary avocations be allowed to continue to enjoy the protection of the law and be accorded the respect and consideration due to peaceful and law-abiding citizens; and that they be not arrested, detained or interfered with, unless there is reasonable ground to believe that they are engaged in espionage or engaging or attempting to engage in acts of a hostile nature, or are giving or attempting to give information to the enemy, or unless they otherwise contravene any law, order in council or proclamation."

Thus all such persons so long as they respect the law are entitled to its protection and have nothing to fear.

[Canada, Order in Council, 2 September 1914]

Pastoral Letters Issued by Nykyta Budka, Bishop of the Ruthenian Greek Catholic Church in Canada

27 July 1914

TO THE REVEREND CLERGY AND ALL THE FAITHFUL OF CANADIAN RUS'-UKRAINE

For a number of years great misfortune have oppressed our old Fatherland. It is not only a matter of that distress which has driven thousands of our brothers into the wide world, and which in the last few years, as the result of flooding, has been transformed into widespread famine, but also moral distress, namely, the demoralization of our brothers in Galicia and in Hungary by a legion of spies, agents, pamphlets and newspapers, paid for by the rubles of our Russian neighbour, either directly from Russia or through Serbia, America and Canada.

Looming over this sad state of affairs for several years now has been the spectre of war, a war, however, which the peace-loving emperor Franz Josef I has ever striven to avert and postpone.

And then an incident occurred which would try the patience of even the most peace-loving of men. On 28 June of this year, in Sarajevo, Franz Ferdinand, heir to the Austrian throne and a man of great hope at this difficult moment for Austria, perished, along with his wife, from the bullet of a Serbian student. The loss of an experienced heir to the throne was very painful to our aged monarch, Franz Josef I, and to all the peoples of Austria, especially to us Ruthenians, who placed great and justified hope in him. The enemies of Austria, especially the enemies of the Ruthenian-Ukrainians, do not disguise their joy at this tragic loss.

Canadian Ruthenian-Ukrainians, sympathizing with the misfortune of our old Fatherland, gave expression to their feelings in church services for the slain and prayers for the fate of their native land.

Now misfortune is at its height, for to all our other misfortunes has been added the greatest of them all, namely, war, at present with Serbia but possibly in a short time also with Russia, a war of inestimable consequences which could change not only the face of Austria but of all Europe, and which could touch us Ruthenians especially closely...

An official summons has reached Canada, calling all Austrian subjects who are under military obligation to return to Austria, there to be ready to defend the state.

God knows what the outcome will be. Perhaps we shall have to defend Galicia against seizure by Russia with her greedy appetite for Ruthenians; perhaps we shall have to defend our parents, wives, children, brothers and native land before an insatiable enemy. Perhaps after the war we shall remain in Austria, as it is or strengthened by millions of our brothers from abroad. It is also possible, however, that we shall find ourselves under the heavy hand of the Muscovite despot. All is in the hands of God and we cannot foresee what will happen. In any event, all Austrian subjects have to be at home, in position and ready to defend our native home, our dear brothers and sisters, our people. Whoever is called should go to defend the threatened Fatherland. All who have not been called up and are unregistered, but who are subject to military service, and all deserters have been granted amnesty by the emperor—that is, freedom from punishment if only they immediately report to the consulate and depart for the old country to defend the Fatherland.

It is also fitting that those who have decided to remain for the rest of their lives in the new Fatherland, Canada, being bound merely by a part of their lives to the old country, should also participate in this great adventure of Austria and our native brethren—for indeed, the fate of our people too is being decided over there.

Our participation should not be limited to reading the newspapers to find out about the events of the war, but we should help our old Fatherland however we can...

6 August 1914

TO THE REVEREND CLERGY AND THE FAITHFUL CANADIAN RUTHENIAN-UKRAINIANS

Not long ago the news that Austria was at war with Serbia stirred the entire world. All other states adopted a wait-and-see position, and England especially strove with all its might to localize the war and restore peace.

At that moment, when no state except Austria and Serbia was threatened by war, and England was not calling its subjects to defend their state, we published our pastoral letter in which we indicated that Austria through the I[mperial] and R[oyal] Consulate in Canada was calling upon its subjects to join the Austrian colours; and we said that all Ruthenians who had come to Canada for a short time only should obey Austria's call and go to defend their families and property. And now in the course of a few days political relations have changed completely. Today all Europe is enveloped by war; today England and the entire British state are threatened by enemies; today our new fatherland, Canada, calls its faithful subjects to rally around the English flag ready to give up their property and lives for the good of the British state.

Today all peoples who live under the flag of the British state are sending their sons to defend it.

And so at this moment when England is turning to us, its faithful subjects, with a call to join the colours, when the British state needs our help also, now, as its loyal sons, we Canadian Ukrainians have a great and holy obligation to join the colours of our new fatherland, under those of the British state, and, if necessary, to sacrifice our property and blood for it.

Ruthenians, citizens of Canada! It is our great duty to come to the defence of Canada, for this is the country which has taken us to its bosom and given us protection under the banner of liberty of the British Empire, where we have found not only bread but the possibility of spiritual development.

It is our sacred duty to be ready to sacrifice our property and blood for the good of Canada, for this is the new fatherland to which we have sworn loyalty and bound ourselves by oath to sacrifice all our property and lives if ever required of us.

This is our beloved fatherland, for here are our families, our children, our property, our hearts and our entire future...

In view of the fact that our earlier letter of 27 July referred to a time when the war was exclusively a war between Austria and Serbia, when few believed that it would spread to other states and England was at peace and not summoning its subjects to the defence of their state, we emphatically declare that in light of the changed political situation our previous letter of 27 July of this year no longer serves any purpose and must not be read publicly in the churches. Instead, we order all priests to read this pastoral letter during Divine Service in their parishes and to instruct the Ruthenians, in accordance with this letter, in their obligations toward the British State...

[Frances Swyripa and John Herd Thompson, eds., Loyalties in Conflict: Ukrainians in Canada During the Great War *(Edmonton: Canadian Institute of Ukrainian Studies, 1983), pp. 161-162, 164-165]*

Dealing with the Unemployed Enemy Alien
T.G. Shaughnessy, President of the Canadian Pacific Railway, to the Hon. Martin Burrell, Minister of Agriculture, 26 August 1914

There are a good many Germans and Austrians in the four Western Provinces. Probably a majority of the Germans are on farms or in employment which they can retain, but practically all the Austrians [Galicians] are of the labouring class, who will be out of work very soon, owing to the shutting down of operations by the Government, Corporations and Municipalities. If these men be permitted to reach a starving condition they will be dangerous, and, beyond doubt, some steps should be taken to deal with the problem. They are practically prisoners of war, and cannot leave Canada.

In these circumstances, might it not be desirable for the Government to select a suitable site, or two or three suitable sites in each of the Provinces, where a Detention Camp could be located, and properly equipped, so that any German or Austrian who applies for relief or is out of employment and cannot take care of himself, may be removed there and held under military supervision until the war is over, or employment offers.

If the war extends through the Winter there is little doubt that there will be several thousand of these men who will have to be detained and provided for. If anything is to be done, the Government should give notice in the Press, and a special officer[1] should be detailed to look after the matter.

A View from the Solicitor-General—Hon. Arthur Meighen to Prime Minister Borden, 28 August 1914

Answering your letter of yesterday enclosing a copy of letter of Sir Thomas Shaughnessy to the Honourable Mr. Burrell, my view is as follows:

There will be undoubtedly a great many Austrians in the West out of work, and doubtless many of them in distress. These Austrians I have come in contact with a great deal and I would be very much surprised if they showed any very general ill feeling or gave us much trouble. However, distress always carries with it danger and my idea would be to take advantage of the circumstances to try a general movement to get these men on small pieces of land. I think it would be unwise to follow Sir Thomas' suggestion to simply have them idly interned in the three [Prairie] Provinces. Such a camp would be looked upon as a lazy man's haven and men of all nationalities would be fruitful of expedience to get there. It would affect the quality of labour of those who remain and that is bad enough already. Some large scheme of policy should be thought out including the setting

---

[1] In October 1914, General William Otter was appointed as Canada's Director of Internment Operations.

aside of areas of land in various parts—some plan which would open up to each individual the chance to procure say forty acres of land or even less. Public assistance would be necessary for a time and thorough government supervision. The plan might include provision for a lien on each holding for assistance rendered.

These Austrians are workers as a rule and those I know would jump at the chance to acquire a small piece of land. They can live on very little.

I realize that there are big difficulties in the way. The necessities are great and the goal is the correct one.

[NAC, MG26 H, Robert Borden papers, Vol. 191, pp. 10593, 105951-105952]

Compulsory Service

TERRITORIAL ENLISTMENT
The following record of the enlistment
in each province up to May 31, 1918....

Alberta	42,538
British Columbia and Yukon	49,628
Manitoba	63,408
New Brunswick	22,622
Nova Scotia and P.E.I	28,516
Ontario	231,274
Quebec	62,761
Saskatchewan	32,521
	533,268

[Reconstruction, November 1918, p. 5]

Dealing with the Conscientious Objector

Memorandum of the Judge Advocate General, 10 October 1918

1. Under Section 11 (1) (f) of the Military Service Act, 1917, exemption from military service may be granted to every applicant on the ground that he conscientiously objects to the undertaking of combatant service and is prohibited from so doing by the tenets and articles of faith, in effect on the sixth day of July, 1917, of any organized religious denomination existing in Canada at such date, and to which in good faith he belongs.

2. Under this provision the Central Appeal Judge has given decisions establishing the existence and recognition in Canada on the sixth of July, 1917, of sev-

eral religious denominations, and the fact that the tenets and articles of faith of such denominations did then prohibit undertaking combatant service. The question of whether an individual of such denomination has a conscientious objection bringing him within the statute is one for decision in each case, and exemption is not granted to all members of denominations which satisfy the conditions.

3. There are individuals who have a conscientious objection to military service but do not belong to a denomination which comes within the statute. To them no exemption can be granted by a tribunal, their conscientious objection not being such as the law can recognize, and they require to be dealt with by the military authorities, as do some members of recognized denominations to whom exemption is refused.

4. It has been found necessary to punish some 130 alleged conscientious objectors. Until recently the practice has been to try them by district court martial and to punish them by sentences of imprisonment up to a limit of two years... Such sentences were not found to constitute a sufficient deterrent against the setting up of conscientious objections which were not, in truth, *bona fide* entertained, many men preferring a short sentence of imprisonment...to military duty.

5. Instructions were, accordingly, given to the general effect that the Officers Commanding units to which were ordered to report men who, on their arrival, set up conscientious objection, were to endeavour by enquiry to determine whether or not the man's objection was *bona fide*. If the Commanding Officer was of the opinion that the conscientious objection alleged was *bona fide* held by the man concerned, he was instructed to transfer him to a non-combatant unit, provided the man expressed himself ready to do non-combatant duty. If, however, the objection did not seem *bona fide* held, or refused to perform military duty of any kind, a general court martial was to be applied for.

6. ....Such general court martials have been applied for in some twenty-five cases and the sentences imposed have ranged from five years penal servitude to penal servitude for life. Speaking generally, the larger sentences have been mitigated to ten years penal servitude. The imposition of these sentences has been found very effective in preventing conscientious objections being set up unless they were very strongly held....

[NAC RG24, Department of National Defence Records, Vol. 5953, File HQ 1064-30-67 (part 3)]

Objections from Quebec

We are opposed to further enlistments for the war in Europe, whether by conscription or otherwise, for the following reasons: (1) Canada has already made a military display, in men and money, proportionately superior to that of any nation engaged in the war; (2) any further weakening of the man-power of the country would seriously handicap agricultural production and other essential industries;

(3) an increase in the war budget of Canada spells national bankruptcy; (4) it threatens the economic life of the nation and, eventually, its political independence; (5) conscription means national disunion and strife, and would thereby hurt the cause of the Allies to a much greater extent than the addition of a few thousand soldiers to their fighting forces could bring them help and comfort....

Conscription is sure to bring serious troubles in the labour circles. Indiscriminate enlistment has already disorganized labour conditions. Rightly or wrongly, labour leaders apprehend that conscription is sought for not so much for military purposes as with the object of controlling wages and work. The enforcement of conscription will certainly be resisted by the organized labour in Canada.

There is also in Canada a large foreign enlistment to which conscription is distasteful to the extreme. Most of these foreigners were invited to come. The government paid premiums to secure them. They [such as Mennonites] were assured that Canada was free from military service. They have therefore against conscription a case much stronger than that of the so called "hyphenated" Americans [such as Hutterites who migrated to Canada in 1917-18 to escape the U.S. draft].

The situation and sentiments of the French Canadians, who form between one-third and one-fourth of the population of Canada, have also to be reckoned with. Such silly things have appeared about them in some of the English-Canadian papers, and occasionally in the American press, that elementary truths have to be recalled.

In spite of all the statements to the contrary, the French-Canadians are loyal to Great Britain and friendly to France; but they do not acknowledge to either country what, in every land, is considered as the most exclusive national duty: the obligation to bear arms and to fight.

Much has been said about the small number of French Canadians who have enlisted for the war; but very little about the large number of European-born volunteers in the so-called "Canadian" force. The truth is, that the over-proportion of British-born volunteers, as compared with Canadian-born volunteers of English or Scottish attraction, is as great as between English-speaking and French-speaking "Canadians." The fact is that the proportion of enlistments, among Canadians, of various extractions, has been in inverse ratio to their enrootment in the soil.

The only trouble with French Canadians is that they remain the only true "unhyphenated" Canadians. Under the sway of British Imperialism, Canadians of British origin have become quite unsettled as to their allegiance: they have not yet made up their mind whether they are more British than Canadian, or more Canadian than British; whether they are the citizens of a world-scattered empire, or members of an American community. The French-Canadians have remained, and want to remain, exclusively Canadian and American...

Without any previous declaration of war, Canada has thrown herself into the conflict as a mere satellite of Great Britain. She was not forced to do so, either by constitution or previous understandings. On the contrary, a well-defined agreement with Great Britain made it clear that, in case of war, Canada had no other duty to perform than that of defending her own territory, if attacked.

When war broke out, it was specified that military service was and would remain voluntary. Under that pledge, the number of men to be enlisted for overseas service was gradually raised from 20,000 to 50,0000. When, in January 1916, parliament, at the request of the government, decided to allow the latter increase, the prime minister, Sir Robert Borden, made the following declaration:

"In speaking in the first two or three months in the war, I made it clear to the people of Canada that we did not propose any conscription. I repeat that announcement, with emphasis today."...

That pledge has been repeatedly given by every representative of Quebec in the government...

So that, in the eyes of all French-Canadians, the adoption of conscription would not only result in an economic collapse of the country: it would also shake their faith in the honour and truthfulness of their public men.

Finally, the economic readjustment of the country is sure to bring dispute between the rural provinces of the West and the industrial provinces of the East.

In short, apart from the menace to the economic equilibrium of the country, the inevitable outcome of conscription and of any overstrained effort for the war in Europe is three-fold: (1) labour troubles and class hatred; (2) racial strife; (3) a deep cleavage between East and West...

Opposition to conscription and war-madness in Canada is not anti-patriotic; it is essentially patriotic and clear-sighted.

[Henri Bourassa, Win the War and Lose Canada *(Montreal: Quebec Daily Telegraph, 1917), pp. 3, 11-14]*

Section B
Soldiers in Action

Soon after arriving at the front, young men, who had once waxed enthusiastic about getting overseas before the excitement ended, often came to speak with despair about a war typified by mud, rats, lice, incompetent commanders, and massive, gruesome casualties. The dash and thrill expressed in newspaper columns was, from the soldier's perspective, replaced by a mole-like existence in trenches, and a bloody, stalemated war of attrition. Upon returning to Canada, countless men, like Pierre Van Paasen, were unable to find the words to explain to naive civilians the horrors they had witnessed. It took a decade for Charles Yale Harrison, a former machine-gunner with Canada's 14th Battalion, to convey his perceptions of combat. For countless veterans, frayed nerves did not permit an easy return to civilian life—especially into a society that had lived the war through sanitized news copy, and which could not comprehend the psychological difficulty soldiers had in separating themselves from the battlefield.

Heroic Combat: The "Worm's Eye" Perspective

12 Oct 1915

At this stage it may be well to mention what the ordinary infantryman in the firing line has to go through and what his nerves have to stand. Old No Man's Land had an average width of 150 to 250 yds.; in many parts of the line it would come as close as 35 to 75 yds. As a rule, the narrower No Man's Land, the weaker the wire. The distance between is so little that fixing up wire is impossible. Ready made wiring obstacles have to be thrown over and, of course, they cannot be expected to be very effective. In fact, later on, Fritz had the audacity to fix on one of our wiring obstacles and pulled it on to his own side. Anyway, besides being liable to be shelled at any moment, the man in the firing line is liable to have bombs, grenades and trench mortar [bombs] thrown at him. Machine-guns may open up and rip the sand bags at pleasure. Clamped rifles go off every now and then, trained at likely spots the infantryman has to pass. Any moment a swarm of Huns may rush him. He is liable to be blown up by a mine tunnelled underneath [the trench]. On dark nights the enemy could crawl into his trench without being seen. It is the same when it is foggy. He exists under these conditions, wet or dry, often in mud and slush over the knees and almost frozen with the cold. Sometimes he sleeps on the firing step or in the bottom of the trench with practically no covering or protection. When he gets wet, his clothes have to dry on him—at times he is worked off his feet digging, draining, making dugouts, carrying timber, corrugated iron, etc. and has to run the gauntlet of being sniped on many occasions. Knowing that any moment he may be hurled into oblivion, his nerves are keyed to a certain pitch and his existence is one of suspense. No wonder the average man's stay in the trenches is a few months. Unfortunately these men who brave such dangers daily, hourly, have nothing to show for it. A Canadian in England gets service stripes the same as he does, not so the British Tommy. A Brigade runner, who once in a while reaches the line, stands a better chance of a decoration. Hangers-on who are seldom within the fighting area and who sleep comfortably and soundly at night and can do their own cooking, get all the medals or clasps they are entitled to. It is high time some distinction was made between the actual fighting man and his numerous knockers in khaki who take practically no risk at all.

January 20, 1916

I have noticed in orders that two of the 27th Battalion and two of the 29th Battalion have received the D.C.M.[1] Sometime ago a 28th man received the same honour. He helped to dig out several of the men who were buried when Heiny exploded the mine beneath the 28th in the "Glory Hole." The military medal had not come into being yet. There are many anomalies in this war. The public still conceive the old fashioned idea that, because a soldier receives commissioned rank when in the field, he has done exceptional work and the advancement is an award for his gallantry. This is a fallacy that needs exposing. The facts are: the ambitious soldier merely puts in his application, which being earmarked by his colonel or someone of like authority, receives in due course, in nineteen times out of twenty, official sanction. In ninety per cent of decorations a similar anomaly exists. It has been often remarked that officers spend a considerable time recommending each other for honours. There is no question of doubt but D.S.O.s and M.C.s[2] have been sprinkled around like water, the vast majority of recipients doing absolutely nothing out of the common to earn these awards…

This indiscriminate trafficking in decorations is a crying disgrace. It is a pity these honours were not retained solely for men who have done deeds of bravery. Amongst the crowd it is difficult to pick out the real man. One has to enquire through his fellow men in his unit to ascertain if he earned the honour or not. Any eulogy from them can be taken as a sure sign that he deserved the award and full credit should be accorded him. Decorations have become so much of a joke that the recipient, conscious that he has done nothing, often remarks when questioned by his "pals" what did he do: "Oh, I guess I was first at the rations!" as if to signify that the Quartermaster dealt them out. Failing which he may answer quizzically, after pondering the matter over, "Blest if I know." There have been many jests made over the "Iron Cross" owing to their lavish distribution, but our Military Cross and Military Medal could stand as much banter. Comment is unnecessary when in 1916 the Prince of Wales had the Military Cross conferred upon him.

[Reginald H. Roy, ed., The Journal of Private Fraser, 1914-1918: Canadian Expeditionary Force *(Victoria: Sono Nis Press, 1985), pp. 43-44, 84-85]*
Reprinted by permission of C.E.F. Books.

---

[1] D.C.M.—Distinguished Conduct Medal, an award for bravery given to those who did not hold an officer's commission. The Military Medal (M.M.), somewhat less prestigious, was later awarded "for bravery in the field."

[2] D.S.O. and M.C.—the Distinguished Service Order and the Military Cross were awarded only to officers.

The Artist's Landscape: "German Prisoners" by Frederic Horsman Varley. *[Canadian War Museum, #8961] Copyright Canadian War Museum.*

The Camera's Eye: Remnants of War. *[Archives of Ontario, #3920]*

Memories of War

There is a call for volunteers for a brigade raid. A hundred men are to go over. Some of our section offer themselves, I among them.

There is a rumour that the volunteers will receive ten days' leave either in Paris or London...

We stand in the dugout which is battalion headquarters. We feel quite important. The colonel is giving us last instructions. We are to destroy the enemy's trenches and we are to bring back prisoners. We are to have a two-minute preliminary bombardment in order to smash the enemy wire and to keep the sentries' heads down. We are to rush the trenches as soon as the fire lifts and drop depth charges into dugouts. At the end of five minutes red flares will be lit on our parapets. This will be the signal that it is time to return and will show us the direction.

The raid is to take place shortly after midnight.

We are each given a sizeable shot of rum and sent back to company headquarters.

At midnight we start on the way up to the front line. We carry a pocketful of ammunition, a few Mills grenades and our rifles.

All our letters, paybooks and other means of identification are left behind.

I have left my papers with Cleary...

I run down the trench looking for prisoners. Each man is for himself.

I am alone.

I turn the corner of a bay. My bayonet points forward—on guard.

I proceed cautiously.

Something moves in the corner of the bay. It is a German. I recognize the pot-shaped helmet. In that second he twists and reaches for his revolver.

I lunge forward, aiming at his stomach. It is a lightning, instinctive movement.

The thrust jerks my body. Something heavy collides with the point of my weapon.

I become insane.

I want to strike again and again. But I cannot. My bayonet does not come clear. I pull, tug, jerk. It does not come out.

I have caught him between his ribs. The bones grip my blade. I cannot withdraw.

Of a sudden I hear him shriek. It sounds far-off as though heard in the moment of walking from a dream.

I have a man at the end of my bayonet, I say to myself.

His shrieks become louder and louder.

We are facing each other—four feet of space separates us.

His eyes are distended; they seem all whites, and look as though they will leap out of their sockets.

There is a froth in the corners of his mouth which opens and shuts like that of a fish out of water.

His hands grasp the barrel of my rifle and he joins me in the effort to withdraw. I do not know what to do.

He looks at me piteously.

I put my foot up against his body and try to kick him off. He shrieks into my face.

He will not come off.

I kick him again and again. No use.

His howling unnerves me. I feel I will go insane if I stay in this hole much longer...

It is too much for me. Suddenly I drop the butt of my rifle. He collapses into the corner of the bay. His hands grip the barrel. I start to run down the bay.

A few steps and I turn the corner.

I am in the next bay. I am glad I cannot see him. I am bewildered.

Out of the roar of the bombardment I think I hear voices. In a flash I remember that I am unarmed. My rifle—it stands between me and death—is in the body of him who lies there trying to pull it out.

I am terrified.

If they come here and find me they will stab me just as I stabbed him—and maybe in the ribs too.

I run back a few paces but I cannot bring myself to turn the corner of the bay in which he lies. I hear his calls for help. The other voices sound nearer.

I am back in the bay.

He is propped up against the parados. The rifle is in such a position that he cannot move. His neck is limp and he rolls his head over his chest until he sees me.

Behind our lines the guns light the sky with monster dull red flashes. In this flickering light this German and I enact our tragedy.

I move to seize the butt of my rifle. Once more we are face to face. He grabs the barrel with a childish movement which seems to say: You may not take it, it is mine. I push his hands away. I pull again.

My tugging and pulling works the blade in his insides.

Again those horrible shrieks!

I place the butt of the rifle under my arm and turn away, trying to drag the blade out. It will not come.

I think I can get it out if I unfasten the bayonet from the rifle. But I cannot go through with the plan, for the blade is in up to the hilt and the wound which I have been clumsily mauling is now a gaping hole. I cannot put my hand there.

Suddenly I remember what I must do.

I turn around and pull my breech-block back. The click sounds sharp and clear.

He stops his screaming. He looks at me, silently now.

He knows what I am going to do.

A white light soars over our heads. His helmet has fallen from his head. I see his boyish face. He looks like a Saxon; he is fair and under the light I see white down against green cheeks.

I pull my trigger. There is a loud report. The blade at the end of my rifle snaps in two. He falls into the corner of the bay and rolls over. He is still.

I am free.

[Charles Yale Harrison, Generals Die in Bed *(New York: Morrow, 1930),*
pp. 105-106, 110-114]

The Homecoming

...I was going to forget the nightmare, burn my uniform as soon as I would be finally discharged, throw my badges and tokens into Lake Ontario, and erase every trace of my shame and humiliation. The thought of returning to my theological studies [at the University of Toronto], interrupted three years earlier, flitted through my mind occasionally. The idea plunged me into a most sober mood. No doubt it would provide a tranquil existence after the tumult, but the war had implanted a restlessness in my spirit which filled me with an inescapable contempt for the uneventful drudgery of everyday life. I did not crave adventure, but subconsciously, I suppose, I had expected something phenomenal to happen upon the return home, some great change, a new start. There had been a thunderstorm and the atmosphere had failed to clear. It was the same petty, monotonous, joyless, suffocating world of three years before, only now I was more intensely aware of it. Faces and voices of old acquaintances looked and sounded familiar, and yet we did not understand each other. Something had come between us. Friends wanted to hear stories of the battlefield, experiences, heroism, and you felt like vomiting when the subject was mentioned. There were still individuals who would get excited about the Kaiser, urging that he be hanged and the Crown Prince be brought to trial. But their ravings only produced a snicker among the majority of the returned men. Why the Kaiser? Why Hindenburg? Those war lords had been victims of circumstances as much as the humble privates in the ranks. The war had not been started because the Kaiser had decreed it. Germany had been manoeuvred into a position where there was no other way out but war. The cause lay much deeper. There was something in the nature of the constituted order which produced wars as naturally as toadstools come to the surface after a spell of rain in the forest. Vaguely men had begun to feel that there was nothing gained in attributing the guilt of the war to certain individuals.

The Dean of Theology tapped me on the shoulder in a friendly way when I met him on the street one day. He said that everything was ready to pick up where I had let off. "Nothing has changed," he said. "It will be an honour to have you back with us."

An honour? An honour to take back an apostate. How could one like me—whose hands were stained with blood—ever approach the Lord's table...?

[Pierre Van Paasen, Days of Our Years *(New York: Hillman-Curl, 1939),*
pp. 91-92]

QUESTIONS

1. What sentiments were used in wartime propaganda in order to rally Canadians?
2. Was the internment of the Ukrainians justified? Were there economic considerations behind the internment order?
3. In what other areas was coercion applied by the state? Was this justified in wartime?
4. What do Private Fraser, Charles Yale, and Pierre Van Paassen tell us about conditions at the front? Which of their accounts appears most accurate, and why?
5. What feelings are conveyed in Frank Varley's painting of German prisoners?

READINGS

Pierre Berton, *Vimy* (Toronto: McClelland and Stewart, 1986)

Robert Craig Brown, *Robert Laird Borden: A Biography* (2 Vols) (Toronto: University of Toronto Press, 1975, 1980)

John English, *The Decline of Politics: The Conservatives and the Party System, 1901-1920* (Toronto: University of Toronto Press, 1977)

J.L. Granatstein and J.M. Hitsman, *Broken Promises: A History of Conscription in Canada* (Toronto: Oxford University Press, 1977)

Sandra Gwyn, *Tapestry of War: A Private View of Canadians in the Great War* (Toronto: HarperCollins, 1992)

Stephen J. Harris, *Canadian Brass: The Making of a Professional Army* (Toronto: University of Toronto Press, 1988)

Jeffrey A. Keshen, *Propaganda and Censorship During Canada's Great War* (Edmonton: University of Alberta Press, 1996)

Desmond Morton, *When Your Number's Up: The Canadian Soldier in the First World War* (Toronto: Random House, 1993)

Desmond Morton and Glenn Wright, *Winning the Second Battle: Canadian Veterans and the Return to Civilian Life* (Toronto: University of Toronto Press, 1987)

Desmond Morton and J.L. Granatstein, *Marching to Armageddon: Canadians and the Great War, 1914-1919* (Toronto: Lester & Orpen Dennys, 1989)

Bill Rawling, *Surviving Trench Warfare: Technology and the Canadian Corps, 1914-1918* (Toronto: University of Toronto Press, 1992)

Reginald Roy, ed., *The Journal of Private Fraser* (Victoria: Sono Nis Press, 1985)

John Herd Thompson, *The Harvests of War: The Prairie West, 1914-1918* (Toronto: McClelland and Stewart, 1978)

Barbara Wilson, *Ontario and the First World War* (Toronto: Champlain Society, 1977)

New challenges to convention emerged in Canada after the Great War. The desire of many people to 'let loose' following years of tension and privation, and their disillusionment over the fact that a notably improved society had not resulted from the sacrifices of war, helped usher in a 'live-for-the-day' attitude epitomized by flappers, flaming youth, and speakeasies. But many Canadians showed little tolerance for this lifestyle. Calls for censorship greeted authors whose work tended toward the risqué; many castigated flaming youth as the product of parental delinquency; and numerous Canadians desperately tried to retain prohibition.

Canadians also demonstrated anxiety about, and practically no tolerance toward, political radicalism. In Winnipeg, long-standing complaints from metal trade workers over the refusal of iron masters to accept unionization, along with demands for better pay from those in the building trades, triggered a May 1919 city-wide general strike that ultimately included some 30 000 workers. Strikers insisted that they were not pursuing revolutionary aims, but newspapers, government authorities, self-classified 'respectable' citizens, and eventually the courts, concluded differently.

Despite social strains, Canadians emerged from the Great War more confident in their country's ability to participate on the world stage. Canada pushed successfully for recognition of its wartime contributions and achievements in the form of separate representation at the Paris Peace Conference, and at the new League of Nations. The 1920s saw quick progress for Canada toward independence in foreign affairs: Prime Minister King in 1922 refused to send troops to Chanak to help Britain against Turkey before consulting Canada's parliament; Canada's first independently signed treaty came in 1923 (with the United States, concerning halibut); the 1926 Balfour Declaration reconstituted the Empire into a Commonwealth of independent nations; and the 1931 Statute of Westminster formally recognized Canadian control over all aspects of its foreign policy.

But how would Canada utilize its new independence? Some worried that the country was moving too far from Britain and into the arms of Uncle Sam. During the 1920s, several commentators noted with concern that Canadians flocked in ever-expanding numbers to Hollywood productions, chose American magazines over home-grown products, and only listened to American radio shows. Also by the early 1920s, Canadian trade with the United States surpassed that with Great Britain. But World War I had left Britain economically strained, and had created fear among many Canadians about being dragged into another imperial struggle. For Canadians, the costs of the war had been substantial: 60 000 dead, 180 000 wounded, a national debt of $1.3 billion, and a country almost torn in two along French-English lines.

It was not just binding imperial commitments that Canada tried to avoid during the interwar years. At the League of Nations, Canadian representatives attempted to repeal Article 10—the 'collective security' provision—from the League's Covenant, claiming that it was unacceptable to hand over the decision on Canadian military participation to European statesmen. Although Canada did not follow the American example of rejecting membership in the League of Nations, Canadian foreign policy clearly tilted toward isolationism—toward withdrawing into what many considered as the 'fireproof house' of North America. Many contended that by pulling back from European affairs and focusing upon North America, Canada adopted a foreign policy reflecting its internal interests, namely: to preserve national unity, protect Canadian lives, and promote economic growth. But among others, especially in light of Canada's meagre response to the rise of European and Far Eastern militarism during the 1930s, such conduct generated anger and shame as they considered the thousands of Canadians who had died in the Great War to defend democracy.

Section A

Protecting Canada from 'Outsiders'

Disillusionment and militancy within Canada's labour movement peaked in the years immediately following World War I. Wartime conscription and hyper-inflation, combined with rising post-war unemployment, incensed many workers. Some, such as numerous members of the Western Canadian

Canadianize Our Alien Workers

The Grasping Hand of the I.W.W.

It is antagonistic to the ideals of honest labor

Bolshevism offers no possibility of advance for labor. It is an imported theory fomented by foreigners, which is impracticable and incompetent. Men that never knew how to get money will never know how to keep it.

Bolshevism, though doomed to extinction, may not die before several nations of the earth have had a big dose of it. Russian industry is turning somersaults and breaking its neck by turning the factories over to workmen without any directing boss or head. The equable distribution is of little value if little is produced.

In Russia, Bolshevism must be left to burn itself out. In Canada, it must be fought with the ancient weapons of a free people—the applied principles of law and order under a government of the people by the people.

The average normal man believes that the toilers will see ultimately that there is nothing in the false doctrines of Bolshevism.

The war has revealed that everything depends on the loyal and continuous support of labor. Employer and employee came together on one plane of common interest and common effort. The good spirit then developed should never be lost.

Democracy does not always get the best, but it always gets what it wants. It reserves for people the right to make their own mistakes. We do not believe in the class idea, but that one man is as good as another.

The Canadian laborer does not hate millionaires. He may be a millionaire himself some day. Most men of success have labored with their hands and have begun small and raised themselves above the other fellow

The Man Promoted Is The Coming Business Man

One of a Series of Articles Published by The Canada First Publicity Association

Canadianize Our Alien Workers. *[Calgary Herald, 17 June 1919]*

based Industrial Workers of the World whose leaders espoused socialist rhetoric and advocated the use of general strikes to defeat capital, spoke about being inspired by the 1917 Russian Revolution. Behind its power, claimed many Anglo-Canadians, lay the foreigners, particularly Slavs and Finns, who were cast as being inclined toward disloyal and violent behaviour. This behaviour included the May 1919 Winnipeg General Strike that, after six weeks, was crushed by authorities through the use of force. To ensure that such an event would not reoccur, new provisions were added to Canada's Immigration Act in July 1919, allowing for the easier deportation of those considered as radical. As well, section 98 of the Criminal Code was amended and, until its repeal in 1936, established wide definitions for, and extraordinary penalties against, those who advocated or defended political or economic change through force.

Anti-foreign sentiment remained strong in Canada during the 1920s. Emily Murphy, the first woman magistrate in the British Empire and a tireless campaigner for women's rights, clearly was not moved to extend similar empathy to Canada's Oriental and Black populations whom she cast as largely responsible for the scourge of narcotics. Also fuelling anti-foreign sentiment was a 1925 agreement between the federal government and Canada's railway companies to bring over more newcomers to the still sparsely populated prairies. The end of the decade brought the Great Depression—during which immigrants were accused of stealing work from Canadians, as suggested by the University of Toronto historian, A.R.M. Lower.

Bolshevism in Winnipeg?

This newspaper is issued because of the unquestionable necessity for placing before the great body of the citizens of Winnipeg the actual facts of the strike situation from the standpoint of the citizens themselves and in order adequately to inform them of the issue that faces Winnipeg in this, the most serious hour of her history.

It must be stated at the outset that this publication is not issued on behalf of the workers, nor on behalf of the employers, nor in opposition to either of them as such, but simply and solely in the interests of the hundred and fifty thousand or more non-participants in the issues which served the cause of the strike—or as the excuse for it. It is issued only on behalf of the great mass of the public which is suffering from the strike's effects.

It is to the general public of Winnipeg that we speak, in stating without equivocation that this is not a strike at all, in the ordinary sense of the term—it is Revolution.

It is a serious attempt to overturn British institutions in this Western country and to supplant them with the Russian Bolshevik system of Soviet rule.

Winnipeg, as a matter of plain fact, is governed by the Central Strike Committee of the Trades and Labor Council...

To those who think that the mere dickering of trades unions for schedules is in issue and that the strike is a strike for higher wages, for shorter hours, for better working conditions, for the "closed shop" or even for the principle of collective bargaining, we say it is no longer that.

It ceased to be anything of the sort from the very moment that the first Trade Union struck work in sympathy with the previous strikers on Thursday, May 15, at 11 a.m. From that hour the dictum of the Central Strike Committee became effective, viz., that no one union would return to work until all the current demands and disputes of every union were conceded by all employers.

Let us take that at face value: Who, for one moment, imagines that this condition would end if the strike were settled at this moment by all demands of all unions being granted in full? Does anybody think that such a course would prevent a repetition of this dictatorship?

Or would it not strengthen the "Reds" and enable them to do the same thing over and over again whenever they felt like it...

Let us repeat—this is not a strike; it is just plain, ugly revolution. Two-thirds of the unions now on strike have struck in defiance of their Internationals, knowing that they sacrifice strike pay and that they lose all the benefits they have been paying for thirty or forty years. They have burned their bridges behind them; the railroad unions have been expelled from their Internationals. What do they hope to gain by this? They knew, that is the Reds among them knew, quite definitely, what they hoped to gain—the destruction of the present industrial system and the present system of government, so let nobody for one moment imagine that any degree of famine or starvation will drive them back to work. Instead, it will drive them to excesses, if the lessons of history are any guidance...

The only way to defeat Bolshevism is for the people, the injured, the sufferers, those who are put to hardship, through this strike, those who stand in the posi-

Replacing Constituted Authority? *[Norman Penner, ed.,* Winnipeg 1919: The Strikers' Own History of the Winnipeg General Strike, *2nd edition. (Toronto: James Lorimer & Company Limited, 1975), p. 50]*

tion of the proverbial 'innocent bystander' who always gets shot in a riot, to organize. They must consolidate and stand solidly behind those public-spirited bands
of citizens who are protecting the city from fire, who are helping the constituted
authorities in every possible manner—and they must be prepared to answer the
call at any time when necessary to defend and uphold the free institutions under
which we live...

Certain work is being carried on—by permission of the Strike Committee.
The government of this city is out of the hands of the constituted authorities. The
Strike Committee rules. You can see the printed signs everywhere—"Permitted—
by the Central Strike Committee." The police force is only at work by order of the
Strike Committee.

The theatres and motion picture establishments are operating—"By permission of the Strike Committee." The water is kept at 30 pounds pressure—"By permission of the Strike Committee." A few restaurants are open to feed the public—
"By permission of the Strike Committee."

How long must Winnipeg submit to such outrage as this defiance of constituted authority—yes, of law and order?...

There is but one way out—the Strike Committee has pronounced in print for
"A Fight to the Finish"; the sway of the Strike Committee and the rule of the
Bolshevik must be decisively ended.

All true citizens must unite to defeat the Revolution...

[Winnipeg Citizen, 19 May 1919, p. 1]

The Strikers' Defence

For the benefit of those who fear the strike had some ulterior purpose, such as the
overthrowing of the present system, the establishing of a Soviet form of
Government, and the calling of a revolution, let us say calmly and with conviction that the workers of Winnipeg would respond to no such call. Even supposing
a few hot-heads made such an appeal, the mass of the workers would defeat it by
their votes as overwhelmingly as they supported the strike.

No, the workers are dissatisfied, but they are not revolutionists. They want
the control of industry in their own hands as soon as possible so that they can get
the full product of their toil and eliminate production for profit. But they will wait
until this is accomplished by constitutional processes. Some of the leaders who
are most maligned and suspected at this juncture are members of the Labor Party,
whose platform is that of gradual change from the present system to that of a
more equitable one. Were they revolutionists they would form some revolutionary society of their own or link up with some already in existence wherever they
were found.

It was this fact that the workers were prepared to carry on the process of education so that reform could be achieved by peaceful means, that was behind the

general strike, for the amelioration of their position. Their demands were for the recognition of the right to organize and the establishment of a living wage and there were no other demands...

It was eventually decided to ask the bakers, teamsters, etc. directly concerned, to resume their labors, which they were willing to do, provided they had something to show their fellow-workers and the general public that they were not scabbing—which sentiment was fully concurred in by the sub-committee of the City Council and by the managers of the particular firms concerned; in fact two of the aforesaid managers, distinctly instructed their employees not to take out their delivery rigs without first securing the cards agreed upon by the Joint Committee of representation from the Strike Committee and City Council, which cards were to be obtainable at the Labor Temple. These cards, about 12 × 16 inches in size, bore the inscription: **"Permitted by Authority of the Strike Committee."** Employers of labor, from the firms involved, voluntarily went to the Labor Temple to secure these cards, knowing what was printed thereon, and themselves placed these cards upon their own property...

[Norman Penner, ed., Winnipeg 1919: The Strikers' Own History of the Winnipeg General Strike, *2nd edition. (Toronto: James Lorimer & Company, 1975), pp. 45, 51-52]*

Findings of a Provincial Royal Commission

SPECIFIC CAUSE OF GENERAL STRIKE

The specific and immediate cause of the general strike was the refusal by the employers in the Iron Contract shops to recognize the demands of the workers for agreement by those employers on the method of collective bargaining indicated by the Metal Trades Council on behalf of the employees. The general concurrence of labor therein and the determination upon a general strike was due to the mood in which workers of all classes were at that particular time...

AGGRESSIVE SOCIALISM

There has for a long time past existed in Winnipeg an element which strongly advocated socialistic views. The group of men who have forced themselves to the front in that way directed their energies towards the conversion of their ideas of the working classes of Winnipeg. They were particularly successful with the foreign element and, since the revolutions in Europe gave point to socialistic propaganda, Europeans of the Russian and Austrian type in this country were most willing disciples of these leaders. The Russian revolutions were represented as indicative of the realization of a bright day for the workers and the accomplishments at last of the predominance of Labour over Capital. The idea also made some headway among original British subjects, but the matter should be treated as though it was purely the work of pronounced Socialistic agitators and that their chief following was the Russian and Austrian, who thought he was merely following the steps of his European brother. There had been open declarations of these people in Winnipeg, particularly in January this year. The Socialistic leaders were not in the true sense labour leaders. It was unfortunate that, from different causes, genuine labour was given the appearance of being linked up with the movements of these men. The ordinary trades union labour leader found himself on the same committee as the extreme socialistic leader and naturally there was a general conclusion that the principles of all were the same...

It is not hard to understand how the foreign element in the workers followed this leadership immediately when the Strike was declared, but it is impossible to believe that the great mass of workers, intelligent and loyal to British institutions, and who accepted the existing order of things, no matter how discontented they were, acquiesced in all that was said and done. It was clear to them that the motive of the radicals was not that of obtaining the right to a mode of collective bargaining for a group of workers, but that the purpose was to elevate Labour into a state of dictatorship. The undersigned cannot think that these workers of British and Canadian origin ever intended to go to that extent. The strikers included men of education whose very occupation assumed high intelligence and fidelity. The great majority of them were brought up in accordance with and reliance upon British and Canadian institutions. It is impossible to assume that such would ever endorse the course which would lead to the Russian condition...

THE PROSECUTIONS

The undersigned is aware that there are now pending certain prosecutions in which facts connected with the General Strike will be involved. It was at one time thought that the question of the cause of the Strike and the issues in the prosecutions were the same and, therefore, that the Commission could not report until the prosecutions had terminated and the facts there elicited could be made a basis, in part at least, of this report. Whether or not, the facts in question will be elements in the prosecution seems to the undersigned not to affect or necessitate any further delay in this report, as the undersigned finds that the general widespread Strike was the result of the determination to support by mass action the demand for the type of collective bargaining in question. The condition described by Winning and the general unrest above set forth were contributory. Certain leaders no doubt perceived this condition, but it is too much for me to say that the vast number of intelligent residents who went on Strike were seditious or that they were either dull enough or weak enough to allow themselves to be led by seditionaries. The men referred to may have dangerously inflamed certain minds, but the cause of the Strike, or of the exercise of mass action, was the specific grievance above referred to and the dissatisfied and unsettled condition of Labour at and long before the beginning of the Strike. It is to be clearly understood that the undersigned refrains from expressing any opinion upon the question of the guilt or innocence of the individuals now committed for trial at the forthcoming assizes upon charges of seditious conspiracy...

CONDUCT OF STRIKE

On the question of the method of conducting the Strike, very little need be said. The relentless determination of labour is evident from the facts already recited. The Union leaders suited the action to the word and even those who were not making use of revolutionary language, were nevertheless persistent in their drastic methods and regardless of the consequences of a complete cessation of labour in every avenue of life. Evidently it was of no consequence to them that there might be great suffering from want of medical aid or want of food and milk deliveries or in many other ways. That there was in fact loss of life, other than that caused by riots, cannot be doubted. Labour leaders frankly say that even this had to be suffered, if necessary, to bring the community to a realization of labour's predicament, and that the damage that would result from the General Strike was slight compared with the ordinary sufferings of labour...

This report now returns to consideration of the alleged causes of the dissatisfaction...

HIGH COST OF FOOD PRODUCTS

But, as everyone knows, the one main cause of the great increase in prices since the beginning of the war was the tremendous demand made upon all food products and upon all clothing and wearing apparel, the enormous destruction thereof that took place, and the fact that so many millions of men were taken away from production into destructive employment. That is the one great fact to be considered, and we are probably fortunate in this country that the condition has not been actually worse than it has been and is at the present time. The extraordinary demand immediately forced prices upward, and the increased consumption and destruction brought about a shortage. The enormous demand during the war has not wholly abated. The foreign demand for all Canadian products, whether of native origin or results of manufacture of imported raw materials, is still very great, and has the inevitable effect of causing high prices at home.

ECONOMIC INEQUALITY

This may also have the wider interpretation of a deplorable class distinction. The question of proportion of reward might well be treated by adjustment methods. But the grievance of class distinction is deeply rooted. Only a radical change of attitude on all sides can overcome that. Such a radical change is necessary to reach a stable and satisfied condition. Labour has seen manufacturers and the merchandising class prosperous during the war, and in too many cases self indulgent, whereas the condition of the very labour essential to the prosperity, instead of improving, grew worse...

UNEMPLOYMENT

While the foregoing is of immediate importance and far-reaching in its effect, it must be remembered that before the community at the present time is the question of probable unemployment. This may be due to dismissal due to the loss of engagement by men who went on strike, or to the fact that, owing to the Strike, business became so reduced that labour demand is less and therefore unemployment exists. There is a further fact that the labouring population has been largely increased by the return of men who went as soldiers. The undersigned does not think that in the conditions and circumstances the matter of present unemployment of men who went out on strike should be treated with indifference or that these men and their families should be made to suffer out of any punitive idea that the want of employment was their own fault...

MEDICAL SERVICE

Another contribution to the conservation of the human asset and to the contentment of the people involved is brought out by the disclosure during the hearings of the Commission of the impossibility at times of manual labourers to secure for their wives and families medical assistance and the necessary provision of medicines. It is not to be thought for a moment that there was any forgetfulness of the great amount of devoted and gratuitous work which the medical profession renders to the community in question, neither can there be for a moment overlooked the philanthropic services of, and sacrifice of individuals and of organizations of men and women in Winnipeg, who in various ways spontaneously provide for many of the wants of that community, but in this connection, as also in the matter of unemployment, there comes up the fact that Labour looks upon charitable relief, no matter how tactfully bestowed, as nevertheless charity, and has a feeling of discomfort thereat. This is very much pronounced in some cases, and tends to set class against class probably as much as any other circumstance...

The undersigned respectfully submits that it is only by application in concrete form of the good intentions of Government and of the employer that Labour will develop a contented spirit. Volumes are written, and there are conferences innumerable, with the object of removing what are called Labour troubles. Unless these are followed by immediate application of something that Labour can see and realize, and that has its immediate and direct benefit upon the individual at his work and in his home they will be fruitless.

There should be no difficulty in deriving the means for the carrying out of the specific objects above mentioned. It is submitted that there should be a scheme of taxation of those who can afford it and application of wealth to the reasonable needs of the others in the community whose lot in life has not been favored.

[Manitoba, Report of H. A. Robinson, K.C., Royal Commission to Enquire into and Report Upon the Causes and Effects of the General Strike Which Recently Existed in the City of Winnipeg for a Period of Six Weeks, Including the Methods of Calling and Carrying on Such Strike, *1919,* pp. 9-10, 13, 17, 24-25, 27-29]

A Legislative Response to the Strike

98.   Any association, organization, society or corporation, whose professed purpose or one of whose purposes is to bring about any governmental, industrial or economic change within Canada by use of force, violence or physical injury to person or property, or by threats of such injury, or which teaches, advocates, advises or defends the use of force, violence, terrorism, or physical injury to person or property, or threats of such injury, in order to accomplish such change, or for any other purpose, or which shall by any means prosecute or pursue such purpose or professed purpose, or shall so teach, advocate, advise or defend, shall be an unlawful association...

3. Any person who acts or professes to act as an officer of any such unlawful association, and who shall sell, speak, write or publish anything as the representative or professed representative of any such unlawful association, or become and continue to be a member thereof, or wear, carry or cause to be displayed upon or about his person or elsewhere, any badge, insignia, emblem, banner, motto, pennant, card, button or other device whatsoever, indicating or intended to show or suggest that he is a member of or in anyway associated with any such unlawful association, or who shall contribute anything as dues or otherwise, to it or to any one for it, or who shall solicit subscriptions or contributions for it, shall be guilty of an offence and liable to imprisonment for not more than twenty years.

4. In any prosecution under this section, if it be proved that the person charged has

(a) attended meetings of an unlawful association; or

(b) spoken publicly in advocacy of an unlawful association; or

(c) distributed literature of an unlawful association by circulation through the Post Office mails of Canada, or otherwise;

it shall be presumed, in the absence of proof to the contrary, that he is a member of such unlawful association.

5.   Any owner, lessee, agent or superintendent of any building, room, premises or place, who knowingly permits therein any meeting of an unlawful association or any subsidiary association or branch or committee thereof, or any assemblage of persons who teach, advocate, advise or defend the use, without authority of the law, of force, violence or physical injury to person or property, or threats of such injury shall be guilty of an offence under this section and shall be liable to a fine of not more than five thousand dollars or to imprisonment for not more than five years, or to both fine and imprisonment...

8.   Any person who prints, publishes, edits, issues, circulates, sells, or offers for sale or distribution any book, newspaper, periodical, pamphlet, picture, paper, circular, card, letter, writing, print, publication or document of any kind, in which is taught, advocated, advised or defended, or who shall in any manner teach, advocate, or advise or defend the use, without authority of law, of force, violence, terrorism, or physical injury to person or property, or threats of such injury, as a means of accomplishing any governmental, industrial or economic change, or

otherwise, shall be guilty of an offence and liable to imprisonment for not more than twenty years.

9. Any person who circulates or attempts to circulate or distribute any book, newspaper, periodical, pamphlet, picture, paper, circular, card, letter, writing, print, publication, or document of any kind, as described in this section by mailing the same or causing the same to be mailed or posted in any post office, letter box, or other mail receptacle in Canada, shall be guilty of an offence, and shall be liable to imprisonment for not more than twenty years.

10. Any person who imports into Canada from any other country, or attempts to import by or through any means whatsoever, any book, newspaper, periodical, pamphlet, picture, paper, circular, card, letter, writing, print, publication or document of any kind as described in this section, shall be guilty of an offence and shall be liable to imprisonment for not more than twenty years.

[Revised Statutes of Canada, 1927, chapter 36, part II, section 98]

Keeping Foreigners Out

…Two deductions regarding the growth of population in Canada may therefore be set forth.

1. Our population grows rapidly when there are large areas of fertile land available for settlement.

2. Otherwise, it will grow in proportion to the demand of the rest of the world for our products.

These are the laws of Canadian growth.

It is now desirable, as an aid in formulating a definite policy, to make some inquiry into the rate at which the country is likely to grow in the future. From 1861 to 1881 the annual growth was 1.7 per cent; from 1881 to 1901, it was 1.15 per cent; from 1901 to 1911 it was 3.7 per cent; from 1911 to 1921 it was 2.1 per cent; an average for the sixty years of 1.91 per cent, an average rendered unduly high by the great influx after 1900, and which cannot be repeated. We have no Dominion figures for the period since 1921 but our three western provinces during the first half of this period increased by about one per cent per annum, slightly less than the worst previous experience of the Dominion as a whole. We shall probably do a little better than that during the present five years, 1926 to 1931, but even providing we do very well we shall probably not grow at the rate of two per cent per annum for the ten years 1921 to 1931. The annual rate of increase in the United States at present is between one and one and a half per cent and I do not think we can hope to grow at a much faster rate than they are doing, more particularly as our chief market, Great Britain, is fast approaching a stationary population. It would, therefore, seem that if Canada continues to grow at the rate of one and a half per cent per annum, adding about 135,000 persons to its total every year, it will be doing very well.

Where are we to get the people who will provide an increase at this rate of growth. It happens that at present our natural increase, that is the surplus of births over deaths, is approximately 135,000, or one and a half per cent per annum. Obviously, then, we do not need to go outside our own borders for the population that we shall need for our future growth. The conclusion, therefore, is justified that we have no need of immigration to increase our population and if immigrants in large numbers continue to come to us there can be only one result. Our own people, those who are born in the country, will have to go away. The presence or absence of immigration will not affect in the slightest degree the rate at which the country will grow, for this is dependent upon natural causes which we cannot influence much more than we can influence the weather...

So will it be with Canada. It is very easy to get the cart of population before the horse of production and this, unfortunately, is frequently done. People do not make jobs but jobs make people and if the number of jobs in this country increases rapidly in the future, we do not need to worry about there being plenty of people on hand to fill them. We have been curiously blind to this rather obvious fact in the past, and Canadians seem to have been oppressed by a fear that if they did not import people constantly and in large numbers, the country would not be adequately peopled.

Strange as it may seem, had we never had a single immigrant come within our borders since Confederation, 63 years ago, it is probable that our population to-day would not be materially different from what it is. Save under exceptional and limited circumstances, immigration does not increase population. This seeming paradox is capable of proof and the proof lies in the fact that, except when we had large areas of vacant land to be filled up very quickly, our immigrant population simply displaced the native born. This is a process that has been happening for years in Canada and is happening to-day. During the decade of the 'eighties the natural increase of our population was between 800,000 and 900,000. We received therefore from both sources roughly one and three-quarter millions of people. Of these we retained about one-half million. As we must have retained some of the immigrants who came to us as well as some of our natural increase it is obvious that among those who left us were a great many of our native born. Probably as many as sixty or seventy per cent of the people born in Canada in the decade of the 'eighties left the country. The immigration of the 'eighties, therefore, was not an accession to the population; it was simply the exchange of one set of persons for another.

In the opening decade of the nineteenth century, there was an immigration of one million eight hundred thousand and a natural increase of eight hundred and fifty thousand. Yet there was an increase in total population of only one million eight hundred thousand. During this decade, therefore, we had eight hundred and fifty thousand people more than we could accommodate. Fortunately for ourselves we managed to export them. Since there was a substantial increase in the immigrant-born population of the country during that decade, it follows that the exports must have consisted very largely of native born...

The country, in short, may be likened to a ship which can carry only a fixed number of people, crew and passengers. If she takes on a number of passengers in excess of her complement, there is only one way of compensating for it, some of the crew must be left behind. We in Canada for sixty years past have been taking on so many passengers, that is immigrants, that we have had to keep leaving many of the crew behind. To provide room in the ship of state for immigrants we have had to embark a large proportion of our own children for the voyage of life in another vessel, the good ship *United States*...

In the days of good Queen Bess, Sir Thomas Gresham, founder of the Royal Exchange, formulated the important monetary law which has since borne his name. "Cheap money will drive out dear money," said Sir Thomas, by which he meant that in times when the currency system is not satisfactory a depreciated currency will circulate and people will keep in their possession the sound money that comes their way. If he had directed his thought to immigration Sir Thomas might have stated his law thus: "Cheap men will drive out dear."

Everyone is familiar with this "Gresham's Law of Immigration", in its application to Orientals. The white labourer cannot compete with the Oriental and the only way to prevent the country being swamped by Asiatics is to limit their migration to our country. We are willing to admit the principle as applied to Asiatics because of a difference in colour. It is more difficult to grasp the application of the law to persons whose skin is the same colour as our own. But whether they be of different race or not, "cheap" men will always drive out "dear" men. The man with the higher standard of living cannot compete with the man with the lower. In this sense, virtually all immigrants are 'cheap' men for on arriving in this country they are not in a position to bargain for the sale of their labour. They must get a livelihood on what terms they can. In this respect, people from the Mother Country differ from other immigrants only in degree. Their standard of living is higher than that of foreigners but it is not as high as that of the native born. If it were they would not emigrate. Thus they compete with the Canadian and innocently displace him in many walks of life. The result is that the people born in this country, because of competition with the immigrant, whether that immigrant be English-speaking or not, tend to go over the border in greater numbers than if there were no immigration.

The enormous magnet to the south will always draw away some of our children but the only way in which we can resist its attractions will be by creating a drawing power of our own. It is possible that if our standard of living were not being continuously depressed by the arrival of the immigrant, opportunities would be relatively equal on both sides of the line. A continental rather than a national standard of living would then obtain and we would be more likely to retain all the population which our natural resources justify our having...

It seems plain that since we do not need immigration we should discontinue all the various attempts now being made to secure it. There should not be one cent of public money spent on securing immigrants of any type. Steamship transportation should be made not easier but more difficult. No one should be allowed to come here who does not come on his own initiative and even the immigration of this class of person should be selective.

[A.R.M. Lower, "The Case Against Immigration," Queen's Quarterly, Vol. 37 (Summer 1930), pp. 565-574]

Nativism and the Drug Problem

Concerning the operations of Drug Rings in Asia especially in relation to opium…the opium traffic in Asia has grown to immense proportions and has become one of the greatest industries in the world, being organized with Standard Oil efficiency. In Persia, Turkey and India, immense plantations are operated by powerful interests, while great banking institutions for financing the drug traffic are well established.

Among the pedlars who are the agents of the Ring, the traffic is chiefly in the hands of Americans, Canadians, Chinese, Negroes, Russians and Italians, although the Assyrians and Greeks are running closely in the race.

It is claimed also, but with what truth we cannot say, that there is a well-defined propaganda among the aliens of color to bring about the degeneration of the white race.

We have no very great sympathy with the baiting of the yellow races, or with the belief that these exist only to serve the Caucasian, or to be exploited by us.

Such a belief was exemplified in a film once shown at a five-cent theatre in Chicago, and was reported by Jane Addams.[1]

In the pictures, a poor woman is surrounded by her several children, all of whom are desperately hungry, and hold out pleading hands for food. The mother sends one of the boys on the streets to beg but he steals a revolver instead, kills a Chinaman, robs him of several hundred dollars, and rushes home with the money to his mother.

The last scene portrays the woman and children on their knees in prayer thanking God for His care and timely rescue of them.

The Chinese, as a rule are a friendly people and have a fine sense of humor that puts them on an easy footing with our folk, as compared with the Hindu and others we might mention.

Ah Duck, or whatever we choose to call him, is patient, polite, and persevering. Also he inhales deeply. He has other peculiarities such as paying his debts and refraining from profanity…

Still, it behooves the people in Canada and the United States, to consider the desirability of these visitors—for they *are* visitors—and to say whether or not we shall be "*at home*" to them for the future.

---

[1] A well-known social worker, who established Hull House in Chicago to help the poor and immigrants.

A visitor may be polite, patient, persevering, as above delineated, but if he carries poisoned lollypops in his pocket and feeds them to our children, it might seem wise to put him out.

It is hardly credible that the average Chinese pedlar has any definite idea in his mind of bringing about the downfall of the white race, his swaying motive being probably that of greed, but in the hands of his superiors, he may become a powerful instrument to this very end.

In discussing this subject, Major Crehan of British Columbia has pointed out that whatever their motive, the traffic always comes with the Oriental, and that one would, therefore be justified in assuming that it was their desire to injure the bright-browed races of the world.

Naturally, the aliens are silent on the subject, but an addict who died this year in British Columbia told how he was frequently jeered at as "a white man accounted for." This man belonged to a prominent family and, in 1917, was drawing a salary of six thousand dollars a year. He fell a victim to a drug "booster" till, ultimately, he became a ragged wreck living in the noisome alleys of Chinatown, "lost to use, and name and fame."

This man used to relate how the Chinese pedlars taunted him with their superiority at being able to sell the dope without using it, and by telling him how the yellow race would rule the world. They were too wise, they urged, to attempt to win in battle but would win by wits; would strike at the white race through "dope" and when the time was ripe would command the world.

"It may sound like a fantastic dream," writes the reporter, "but this was the story he told in one of the brief periods when he was free from the drug curse, and he told it in all sincerity."

Some of the Negroes coming into Canada—and they are no fiddle-faddle fellows either—have similar ideas, and one of their greatest writers has boasted how ultimately they will control the white men.

Many of these Negroes are law-abiding and altogether estimable, but contrariwise, many are obstinately wicked persons, earning their livelihood as free-ranging pedlars of poisonous drugs. Even when deported, they make their way back to Canada carrying on their operations in a different part of the country.

[Emily Murphy, The Black Candle *(Toronto: Coles, 1973; orig. pub. Thomas Allen, 1922), pp. 186-189]*

Section B
Internationalism Versus Isolationism

At the 1923 Imperial Conference, the Winnipeg newspaperman and Liberal party supporter, J.W. Dafoe, recorded in his journal that Prime Minister King proved a formidable opponent to those seeking to promote a common defence force for the Empire. Moreover, though Canada was a member of the League of Nations, its leaders recoiled from the principle of collective security. There were critics of this cautious approach; Vincent Massey, a member of an important industrial and philanthropic family in Toronto, portrayed Canada's withdrawal into isolationism as a shameful legacy to the sacrifices made during the Great War. However, it was precisely because of the horrific costs of the war that the Women's International League for Peace and Freedom was able to gather 500 000 signatures in Canada on a petition to support a conference promoting disarmament, at Geneva in 1932. Pacifist associations—such as that under Richard Roberts, the moderator of the United Church of Canada—flourished in interwar years. Mackenzie King, in reading the political mood, soon lent his support to the appeasement of aggressive European dictators. In 1935, King, fearing hostile public opinion at home, fired Dr. Walter Riddell, Canada's representative at the League of Nations, for sponsoring a resolution favouring oil sanctions against Benito Mussolini's Italy following its brutal invasion of Abyssinia.

Prime Minister King Battles Against Empire Solidarity
Observations from the 1923 Imperial Conference by J.W. Dafoe of the Winnipeg Free Press

Tuesday, November 6—Returned from Paris last night. Early this morning Skelton[1] telephoned me to go over as important matters had developed.

When I got over he told me that a Prime Minister's conference had been called for the previous afternoon...

The business before the Conference was to agree to a statement about the Conference and Empire foreign policy which Curzon[2] had prepared. Skelton showed me this report. It was a remarkable document. Not only did it represent the Conference as giving its general approval to the conduct of joint common

[1] Oscar Douglas Skelton—Queen's University professor, special advisor to the Canadian government at the 1923 Imperial Conference, and later appointed Canadian Under-Secretary of State for External Affairs
[2] Lord Curzon, British Foreign Secretary

affairs since the last Conference, but it announced that the Conference had laid down policies for the future which the Foreign Office would be authorized to carry out. It meant the acceptance in its most unqualified form of the doctrine of the joint foreign policy with joint responsibility. Its general purport is indicated by the statement in it that "The British Government is not merely anxious to proceed upon the principle of mutual co-operation and responsibility laid down at the last meeting in 1921, but it is also conscious that in all international affairs here G.B was conducting negotiations affecting the British Empire so she would speak with more powerful effect if it were known that her voice was not that of herself alone but of the entire body of states affecting the Empire. This principle does not contravene but is on the contrary in strict harmony with the practise by which individual Dominions negotiate directly with foreign governments in matters especially affecting their responsibilities."...

According to Skelton King rather went up into the air upon the conclusion of this statement and gave Curzon a piece of his mind. He said that he thought that he had made it quite clear that Canada did not subscribe to the theory of joint policy and joint responsibility in foreign affairs and would take no part except in matters of direct concern to her. He also insisted upon the conference being regarded as a conference between governments not having power to bind governments and commit them even to moral obligations. Yet at the close of the Conference he was asked to agree to a statement which ignored these Canadian declarations of Canadian policy and committed Canada definitely to courses which she objected. He intimated that this was an illustration of tactics which made these conferences not very pleasant prospects for Canadian governments. The repeated attempts by resolutions or statements commit them to policies to which they had expressed disagreement. He said flatly that unless there was an acceptance of the fact that these Conferences were only conferences Canada would in future decline to take part in them...

I suggested the right place for this report was the waste paper basket or the fire place because it did not seem to me that it could be amended and that another attempt at a report be made. But King was opposed to this. He said that it was plain to him that Curzon and the other Prime Ministers were set on having a report of some kind; the wisest course for him, he said, was to make it as unobjectionable as possible and then to insist upon the incorporation in it of what he called a "caveat" which would reserve to the various countries freedom to dissent. He was obviously alarmed at the possibility that it might go on record that on this matter he was in formal disagreement with all the other parties to the agreement. Skelton and he had been working over the suggested "caveat". Though this was the most critical moment of the Conference for him, King was obliged at this moment to go off to Oxford to get an honourary degree.

I stayed around for another hour working with Skelton over the reservation to be suggested. As drafted it consisted of four paragraphs—the first two by Skelton, the others by King. Skelton's contribution was a perfectly clear declaration that it was desirable and necessary that the Dominions should attend to their own foreign affairs recognizing their powers to confer together for the formulation of common policies where this was in their interests. King's paragraph was a jumble of words from which it was hard to derive any clear meaning. They seemed to suggest that the report of the Imperial Conference was an attempt only to indicate what it was thought might prove to be a consensus of opinion among the various peoples upon certain large matters of general interest; and affirming that this was only a conference of governments...

[Ramsay Cook, "J.W. Dafoe at the Imperial Conference of 1923,"
Canadian Historical Review, *Vol. XLI, No. 1 (March, 1960), pp. 35-36.]*
Reprinted by permission of University of Toronto Press Incorporated.

Canada's Moral High Ground

...Samuel de Champlain, the founder of Canada, was a son of France. For a century and a half Canada was a French dominion. In more than a century and a half Canada has been a British dominion, the descendants of the two races who fought on the Plains of Abraham have lived side by side, enjoying a like measure of freedom in their personal and social life, and in the development of their political institutions—forgetful of the enmities of the past and rejoicing in the vastness of their common inheritance. The only monument commemorating the event which occasioned the great transition is the simple shaft erected at Quebec and dedicated to the memory alike of Wolfe and Montcalm, the two generals who led the opposing forces. Our country is a land of reconciliation. In achieving racial concord within our borders, we have for more than a century successfully exemplified the fulfilment of at least one fundamental principle of the League [of Nations].

In another particular, namely, in achieving international peace with our great neighbour, we have fulfilled for more than a century another fundamental principle of the League...

For a distance of over three thousand miles, stretching from the waters of the Atlantic Ocean on the east to those of the Pacific Ocean on the west, the frontier of Canada is divided from that of the United States by a boundary which is undefended from coast to coast. The undefended frontier is a symbol as remarkable in its way as the shaft erected at Quebec to the memory of Wolfe and Montcalm. It is a joint possession not made with hands, but is the creation and expression of the minds and hearts of the peoples of the respective countries...

It is not to be assumed that in the period of more than a century no differences have arisen between the two countries. There have been differences, some of them might have conceivably led to war. Ceasing to rely upon force, we have looked to reason as the method of solving our differences, and reason has supplied us from time to time with conference, conciliation, or arbitration in a form all sufficient to settle our various differences as they have arisen...

[Canada, House of Commons, Debates, 13 December 1926, pp. 44-46.
Statement by Prime Minister William Lyon Mackenzie King]

Shameful Isolationism

...But for all our cloistered life, we have learned that an obscure Balkan quarrel can cost us thousands of lives and millions of money, and it would seem that the Great War should have shaken us out of our habitual provincialism, not only through the repercussion of world events in Canada, but also through the personal experience of hundreds of thousands of Canadians overseas...

But with the crisis over, we relapsed into our traditional indifference to events beyond our shores, and, instead of stemming the full current, we have slipped into a back-water of provincial aloofness. The other day I was counting up the number of days that had been spent on the subject of external affairs in the Canadian House of Commons in the last five years. By "external affairs" I mean everything outside our own internal affairs—trade treaties, the estimates of the Department of External Affairs, Trade Commissioners, in fact everything that is not "our own show." Out of the 548 days of the last 5 sessions, 13 1/2 days were devoted altogether to external affairs. I do not suppose that a smaller proportion of time has been spent on foreign business in the legislature of any country in the world.

There are, I suppose, three schools of thought in Canada on the subject of foreign affairs, or to be more accurate, two schools of thought and one given to mental inertia. In the first place there are persons with the "colonial mind", those, fewer now than before the war, who still regard the Empire as being in conflict with the Dominion nationality, who sentimentalize over the one to the disparagent [sic] of the other. They give us not sentiment, which is a good thing, but sentimentality, which is not.

Then there are the "continentalists," men who believe that in North American life there is something inherently superior to the European, that the Almighty has established a larger reservoir of virtue for this continent, to preserve which we should keep entirely detached from Europe—"the plague spot of the world." They believe, too, that is the more profitable. I came across a letter in a Toronto paper, on the occasion of the Chanak incident, which represents this point of view. May I quote a sentence: "It is time to decide, once for all, that, hereafter, European nations shall be left to settle their own quarrels and that America, all America, shall attend strictly to human business at home."

Then, thirdly, there are those of us whom, for lack of a better term, I shall call the "ostriches" who, metaphorically speaking, keep their heads in the sand and think that by so doing they will avoid a knowledge of what is going on in the world and so escape all worry over the matter. Someone must attend to these things, but they are content to "let George do it" (George in this case presumably meaning George V). This is the prevailing attitude of indifference to the issue of external affairs of which most of us are guilty. They seem too remote from us to attract attention...

This attitude of negation is, of course, inconsistent with the status which we achieved in 1919, and its persistence will not only threaten imperial unity but will be injurious to our own nationality...

We in Canada, apparently, have a decision to make. It remains [for us] to make a conscious choice between two alternatives. Either we accept the implications of the status which we have half-unconsciously received, or we reject the implications and the status too. We have for the last ten years quite rightly been insisting upon the rights of Dominions. Now that they have been fully granted our attention might appropriately be directed to our obligations...

With all its faults and lapses and occasional insincerities, as one looks abroad to-day and to the part which the British Empire is playing, one cannot escape the conclusion that this strange, misshapen, illogical, creaking old structure is the one agency which has an active sense of responsibility in the world at large, and is capable of giving effective application to those principles of international decency in which it believes. But the choice is not between the Empire and something else. There are few of us who want that "something else." The choice is rather that between, on the one hand, an isolation from the world—an isolation far from "splendid"—and, on the other, within the limits of our slender powers, the continued self-respecting discharge of our obligations.

[Vincent Massey, "Canada and External Affairs," Journal of the Canadian Bankers' Association, *April 1925, pp. 381, 384-385, 388-390]*

Support for Disarmament

A Radio Broadcast by Miss. M. Winnifred Kidd, President of the National Council Women of Canada and Delegate of the International Women's League for Peace and Freedom to the 1932 Geneva Conference on International Disarmament

...For the past three weeks, the leaders of the delegations in turn have stated the positions of their countries, and all their speeches have reflected the aspirations of the peoples of the world for secured peace. There are of course some vital differences in the points of view, but it is abundantly evident here that every country in the world is anxious to make real progress towards disarmament.

We now approach the more specific and technical aspects of the question, which we have come here to discuss. In a word, we are expected to find, during the coming weeks, practical ways and means whereby the prayer of many millions of thinking men and women throughout the world may be answered...the prayer that future wars may be prevented...

You will notice that I have several times referred to world opinion, and I have done this because of the profound impression which was made on all of us by the session which was devoted to the reception of the petitions [for disarmament] from all the countries signed by millions of men and women. When we came to Geneva there was a general feeling of doubt regarding the outcome of the Conference, but now, although no one expects to realize immediately all that we had hoped for, it seems to me, that some really practical steps will be taken towards the goal which we all so much desire. I am convinced that you, who have laboured so devotedly to have these petitions signed and placed before the Conference, are largely responsible for this more friendly atmosphere in which our work is proceeding. I appeal to you not to relax your efforts.

Here women may play an important role. Our organizations exist both nationally and internationally and are well fitted to undertake and carry on this important educational work, which must continue in the future.

You in the United States and Canada sent your delegates here with a clearcut impression that we were representatives of nations to whom the ideal underlying this Conference was of the utmost importance—the ideal of permanent peace.

Let us maintain our faith in this ideal and steadily work toward its practical realization.

[NAC, MG28 I 25, National Council Women of Canada papers, Vol. 69, File 4]

The Church Joins the Crusade for Peace

Reverend Richard Roberts to the Rt. Hon. R.B. Bennett, 12 December 1933

It is clear, even from the inadequate press reports, that your [Bennett's] speech at London on world pacification calls for the gratitude of every lover of peace. I am emboldened by it to pass on to you a "concern" (as the Quakers say) that has been exercising my mind for some time—and before I do so, I may perhaps premise that I am not a person who writes long letters to public men offering infallible panaceas for this, that and the other trouble.

There can, I believe, be no serious doubt that the introduction of "poison gas" into warfare and the development of the bombing aeroplane, especially since the War, have revolutionized the whole theory and practice of war. You are yourself too well versed in what has actually come to pass in relation to the "improvement" of the quality and the mass production of poison gas, and of the capacity and the manufacture of bombing planes, to require my saying anything about that aspect of the question. But what is not generally understood is how far this new development puts out of action the former types, both of strategy and of arms. One thing has been made abundantly evident—especially by the air manoeuvres in London—that *there is no means of defending a city from a night attack by air.*

...The only possible defence is retaliation—which is poor comfort for the non-combatant victims of air attacks, and is in no case a defense. The strategy, therefore, will concentrate upon the element of surprise—in which case such a formality as a declaration of war will hardly be considered, since the whole effort of the parties engaged will be, each to strike its blow first. Such a beginning makes it certain that none of the mitigating conventions of war will be repeated at all; and of such a situation the consequences are easier to imagine than to describe. And it is difficult to see what relevancy arms of the traditional type, and the strategy and tactics that are appropriate to them can possibly have in circumstances of this kind.

The upshot of all this is the question whether it would be possible for the Government of this Dominion to instruct its representatives to the next assembly of the League of Nations to move for the appointment of a committee, constituted very much like a Disarmament Conference, *for the single purpose of getting the nations to look frankly at the actual facts bearing upon the production and development of arms and materials for aerial warfare, and in that light to endeavour to envisage the situation which would immediately be created in the event of an outbreak of war.* When it has (as it has) become certain that the brunt of the next war will fall upon the non-combatant populations, and in particular upon the dwellers in cities, it is not just to the common people, whatever nation they may be of, to allow the further discussion of disarmament to proceed without first of all endeavouring honestly to envisage...the fate that awaits them in a future war and especially since the discussion on its present basis is far too much occupied with questions that are hardly more than academic in view of the new and awful possibilities opened up by the resources available today for aerial war.

Inasmuch as here in Canada we are only very lightly implicated in warlike preparations of any kind, it is easier for us than for most peoples to plead for such a step...

[United Church Archives, Richard Robert papers, R62, Box 2, File 47]

King's Cautious Approach Toward Aggression

....Two conditions are essential to the working of any such plan of universal compulsion [Collective Security]. In the first place, there must be an overwhelming preponderance of power, economic and military, in the League [of Nations] as against any possible aggressor or combination of aggressors. Even economic pressure, if it is to be strangling enough to be effective enough against a strong nation, must be backed by a definite readiness, in the last resort, to have recourse towards armed force. That is surely clear. That condition does not now exist. For one thing, the League is not the universal association anticipated by its founders when they dreamed of its imposing peace throughout the world. The United States, Germany, Japan, Brazil are outside the fold. A league facing the abstention of some and the hostility of others of such powers clearly cannot operate as it might in other circumstances. In the second place, there must be the certainty that the members of this body will be ready to exercise that force when the occasion arises, regardless of where it arises or whether they have any direct interest in the quarrel. That condition again does not exist. There are a few countries which have evidenced some measure of idealism in their approach to the question, but in most cases action has depended on a calculation of immediate interest. That was shown beyond doubt in the Manchurian and Chaco incidents. The

League did not apply military or even economic sanctions in the Manchurian affair; its action was confined to a recommendation not to recognize the state of Manchukuo[1]. In the Chaco war, between Bolivia and Paraguay, it did even less. That was not a minor conflict. It was a long and bloody war, dragging out for nearly three years, costing the lives of a hundred thousand men, bleeding and bankrupting both countries, and leading lately to the establishment of military dictatorships...

Under such conditions it is clearly impossible for a country like Canada to make blinding commitments to use economic force or military force. The League cannot operate as a one-way road. European states cannot throw overboard all obligation to action in Asia or America and expect other members of the League to accept obligations in European disputes. Occasions may arise where military action may become advisable or essential, but, so far as Canada is concerned, that would be for the Parliament of Canada to decide in light of all the circumstances at the time...

But that does not mean that there is not a great part for the League to play. If it cannot become the international war office, neither need it become a mere debating society. It can emphasize the constructive side of its task. It is of great value to have at Geneva a world-wide organization where the machinery for conference and conciliation is always available, not having to be improvised in the midst of a crisis; where representatives of fifty countries meet periodically and come to have some appreciation of the difficulties and the mentality of other lands, and slowly develop the habit of working together on small tasks leading to greater...

It can press on to its task of disarmament, or at least to the halting of armaments. It can develop and apply the instruments of conciliation and of arbitration in settling specific disputes before they lead to open challenges and entrenched positions...

*[Canada, House of Commons, Debates, 18 June 1936, pp. 3868-3873.
Statement by Prime Minister William Lyon Mackenzie King]*

Public Reaction to Appeasement

...We French-Canadians are determined to remain faithful to our policy of "Canada First". May all Canadians realize that for us patriotism has no other meaning...

Of course, if our country is attacked...we shall defend our territory...

Charity begins at home, and our internal problems are quite enough for us.

---

[1] In 1931, Japan forcibly took over the Chinese territory of Manchuria and created the puppet state of Manchukuo.

The Covenant of the League of Nations will have to be modified. Useful organizations like the Permanent Court of International Justice will be retained, provisions for arbitration will be retained, etc. But Canada cannot undertake to preserve Peace for the whole world...

*[L.M. Gouin {former federal Minister of Justice and Premier of Quebec},
"The French-Canadians, their Part, and their Aspirations," in V. Anderson,
ed., World Currents and the Canadian Course (Toronto: Thomas Nelson and
Sons, 1937)]*

Mr. Mackenzie King's speech to the League of Nations at Geneva was admirable in form and matter... And Mr. King spoke, we think, for the vast majority of Canadians when he said emphasis in the League's policies should be placed upon "conciliation rather than coercion"... And Canada does not propose to be dragged into a war in which she has no interest, and over the origin of which she has no responsibility or control, through any automatic obligation. This is simple doctrine and sensible...

[Ottawa Journal (Independent Conservative), 30 September 1936]

This is the last in a long series of acts by successive Canadian governments intended to circumscribe the League's powers; and it is the most discreditable of them all because it amounts to the rejection by Canada of the League...Mr. King in his speech to the Assembly sought to commit Canada to the acceptance of certain propositions:

That the League should be permitted to continue in existence provided it agrees not to recognize or act upon the principle that is its reason for existence.

That Canada will continue to subscribe to the obligations of the Covenant provided it is understood that she can repudiate them without moral obliquity. These propositions are unworthy of Mr. King and if adopted as governing principles of policy would be discreditable to Canada and, in the long run, ruinous to the peace and prosperity of this country... If the League ever acts in keeping with the spirit which called it into being... Canada will reject the suggestion that she should deny her obligations and stand aside...

[Winnipeg Free Press (Liberal), 1 October 1936]

QUESTIONS

1. Did authorities over-react to the Winnipeg General Strike? What reasons did the 1919 provincial royal commission under H.A. Robson cite as responsible for the strike?
2. Assess the logic of A.R.M. Lower's argument about immigration.
3. Why was Vincent Massey critical of Canadian foreign policy? Were his criticisms valid?
4. What was the 'North American example' that Mackenzie King espoused to Europeans?
5. Was Mackenzie King's foreign policy a good one? Did it serve Canadian interests?

READINGS

David Jay Bercuson, *Fools and Wise Men: The Rise and Fall of the One Big Union* (Toronto: McGraw-Hill Ryerson, 1978)

James Eayrs, *In Defence of Canada* (vol. 1 and 2) (Toronto: University of Toronto Press, 1963)

E.R. Forbes, *The Maritime Rights Movement, 1919-27: A Study in Canadian Regionalism* (Montreal/Kingston: McGill-Queen's University Press, 1979)

James Gray, *The Roar of the Twenties* (Toronto: Macmillan, 1975)

Gerald Hallowell, *Prohibition in Ontario, 1919-1923* (Toronto: Ontario Historical Society, 1972)

John Hilliker, *Canada's Department of External Affairs: The Formative Years, 1909-1946* (Montreal/Kingston: McGill-Queen's University Press, 1989)

Charles M. Johnson, *E.C. Drury* (Toronto: University of Toronto Press, 1986)

David Laycock, *Populism and Democratic Thought in the Canadian Prairies, 1910-1945* (Toronto: University of Toronto Press, 1990)

Andrée Lévesque, *Making and Breaking the Rules: Women in Quebec, 1919-1939* (Toronto: McClelland and Stewart, 1994)

Peter G. Oliver, *Howard Ferguson: Ontario Tory* (Toronto: University of Toronto Press, 1977)

C.P. Stacey, *Canada and the Age of Conflict, 1921-1948: The Mackenzie King Era* (Toronto: University of Toronto Press, 1981)

Veronica Strong-Boag, *The New Day Recalled: Lives of Girls and Women in English-Canada, 1919-1939* (Toronto: Copp Clark Pitman, 1988)

Tom Traves, *The State and Enterprise: Canadian Manufacturers and the Federal Government, 1917-31* (Toronto: University of Toronto Press, 1979)

Susan Mann Trofimenkoff, *Action Française: French-Canadian Nationalism in the Twenties* (Toronto: University of Toronto Press, 1975)

Mary Vipond, *Listening In: The First Decade of Canadian Broadcasting, 1922-1932* (Montreal/Kingston: McGill-Queen's University Press, 1992)

The Great Depression

Historians still debate the causes of the Great Depression; few, however, dispute its far-reaching effects. The 1929 Wall Street crash, which was replicated on stock exchanges in Toronto and Montreal, touched off a decade-long economic crisis. By 1933, Canada's unemployment rate hovered around 30 percent. Hardest hit were the prairie provinces, especially Saskatchewan, where, between 1929 and 1932, the gross provincial product plummeted by nearly 75 percent—the result of declining crop prices, followed by drought and high winds that created 'dustbowl' conditions.

Public support for Prime Minister Mackenzie King, who initially cast the economic collapse as a temporary glitch in the business cycle, quickly dissipated. But King was operating under the long-standing assumptions that it was wrong for governments to assume large debts, and that the widespread distribution of welfare would create mass dependence upon the state. Ottawa provided grants-in-aid to the provinces, reaching up to 33 percent of what was clearly inadequate expenditures upon social welfare—a situation that led to the virtual bankruptcy of provincial governments in Western Canada and of scores of municipalities.

Sometimes the federal government addressed the problem of surplus labour with extreme measures—such as deporting thousands who were not yet naturalized but who had become a public charge. The deportation policy, which affected more than 8 000 people during the first three years of the Depression, also related to the perception that widespread suffering was establishing a fertile ground for political extremism—something with which certain immigrant groups, such as Russians and Finns, were linked to in the popular mindset.

Most Canadians were not inclined toward extremism; but an increasing number also were not wedded to old-line political parties whose rather traditional approaches to economic problems seemed to accomplish little. More Canadians began turning their attention to the unorthodox agendas put forward by new political movements, and dynamic or revolutionary figures. Emerging at both the federal and provincial levels was the Co-operative Commonwealth Federation (C.C.F.), a coalition of farm and labour groups formed in 1932 that, in its Regina Manifesto, advocated the replacement of capitalism with a system under which the 'common good' would supersede the drive for private profit. Although failing to obtain power, the C.C.F. gathered some 400 000 votes in the 1935 federal election.

Charismatic figures—including Liberals Mitchell Hepburn in Ontario and Duff Pattullo in British Columbia, as well as Maurice Duplessis of Quebec's new *Union nationale*—were successful at the provincial level. In Alberta, there was the Social Credit phenomenon led William Aberhart. Simplifying the economic theories of the Scottish engineer, C.H. Douglas, Aberhart offered Albertans $25 a month to increase their purchasing power, and thus close a gap that Social Crediters identified as existing between total wages and the total cost of goods.

As the 1935 election approached, these patterns made clear to Canada's Conservative Prime Minister, Richard Bedford Bennett, that he too would have to demonstrate a willingness to initiate significant reform if he wanted to survive politically. Countless Canadians noted that in the United States, President Franklin Roosevelt, who had assumed office in 1933, initiated a New Deal that included massive expenditures on public works and, ultimately, an unemployment insurance scheme. Despite drawing criticism from some quarters for driving up America's public debt, and for not significantly decreasing unemployment, Roosevelt was still admired by most people for trying to do something concrete and for providing hope. This message was conveyed to Bennett by his brother-in law, W.D. Herridge, the head of Canada's legation in Washington. In fact, since 1933, Bennett had consulted with key advisors on creating an unemployment insurance scheme, as well as legislating a minimum wage and maximum hours of work, but hesitated because such measures fell under the provinces' constitutional control. However, in January 1935, shortly before Bennett was obliged to call an election, he went on the radio to announce, in a series of five talks, his intent to create a New Deal. But to many Canadians, the initiative was seen as a desperate and insincere gesture—a conviction confirmed to countless voters after Mackenzie King in parliament managed to expose that much of Bennet's proposed legislation had not been prepared.

Returning to office in 1935, King talked about balancing the budget, and soon reduced federal grants to the provinces. In 1937, the Judicial Committee of the Privy Council declared the unemployment insurance and labour standards legislation proposed by the Bennett government as beyond Ottawa's powers. To many Canadians, however, the idea of constitutional legalese getting in the way of action to alleviate suffering was unacceptable. Pressure built upon King to assume a more activist approach, especially as 1937 produced another economic downturn. Having already lost power once because of inaction, King—who was also facing threats of resignation from progressive members of his Cabinet—had the federal government assume an extra $40 million in debt in its 1938 budget, in order to increase social welfare. In 1937, the King government created a royal commission to examine a possible redistribution of dominion-provincial powers. Three years later, in 1940, what became known as the Rowell-Sirois Commission recommended that Ottawa assume responsibility for the unemployed, take over provincial debts, and pay the provinces a subsidy in exchange for gaining exclusive control over income, corporate, and inheritance taxes. With World War II underway by the time the report was released, and the federal government needing to raise money fast, these recommendations were used to create a more interventionist and paternalistic central government.

Section A

A Nation Suffers

Innumerable sources point to widespread despair in Canada during the Depression. Poetry from Dorothy Livesay evokes the pain of transients arriving in Toronto; Irene Baird's fiction conveys the anger of Vancouver's unemployed that, in 1938, resulted in the occupation of government buildings and clashes with police; ordinary Canadians inundated Prime Minister Bennett with desperate letters . Photographs, statistics, and reminiscences, such as memories of the 'dustbowl' prairies from the Winnipeg newspaperman, John Gray, also tell of devastated lives. As well, other documents reveal that Canadians still coped with a rudimentary and penurious system of public welfare.

A Poet's Lament

We in a struggling train. Its raw cry rips the air.
The country stubble and the tattered fence flash by
And settle into memory. On rails unseen
We splash into the clouded city's rim, its long
Bare bones stretched out directionless: suburban houses
Spread like playing cards between garages, hencoops—
Children stiff as splinters saluting the unknown
Waving at these our faces, too far off to put
The fear and strangeness in them—impersonal salute.
Now there are coalyards, runways of smudgy steel, and next
The squat and rounded oil tanks with their vacant eyes.
Here funnels fat with smoke from soot-grimed factories
That stare beyond the bridge, beyond the muddy Don
Down to the blue lake water guarded by the cranes
And churned by tugs, commercial steamers, fishing boats,
Oil-manned tankers, flat red barges dull as freight-trains
—O this the expected city, this the dream!
We see a self-important ferry harried by
The flash of life, the wings of diving gulls, cry shrill
And nose in air for refuse and the cast-off things men stuff
Into a pail and clamp down quick the lid.

Take off the lid, scatter the refuse far,
Tear down the "WELCOME" from the city-hall.
For you're not welcome, vagabond, nor you
Old man, nor you, farmlabourer, with sun
Still burning in your face. Burn now with shame
Take to yourself the bread ticket, the bed
On John Street—fifteen cents, GOOD CLEAN
And pluck out all the hungers from your brain...

It's good food for the birds, the old man said
Rifling a garbage can behind the Royal Bank.
His round eyes gleaming under a battered hat
He peered at dried out sandwiches, half-bitten crusts,
And nervous twitches cut across his mouth.
It's good food (where's the cop). Please lady, see
I'm such a benefactor, though I'm poor
(That can't be hid)—But see how kind I am!
Believe, believe! It's good food for the birds...

[Dorothy Livesay, "Queen City" in Collected Poems: The Two Seasons
(Toronto: McGraw-Hill Ryerson, 1972), pp. 81, 84]

Fiction and the Depression

Matt Striker rolled the door of the box car open a crack, waited for his eyes to grow used to the strong light, then slid the door wider and dropped down onto the hot, sharp flints of the roadbed. For an instant his narrowed eyes combed the long lines of standing cars for yard police, then he reached back for his pack, slung it up onto his shoulder and moved quickly up the tracks towards town. He walked the length of the empty nine-thirty Trans-Canada and when he came out from the shelter of the last cars he headed up towards the Capper Street grade crossing. Two things were noticeable about the way he moved; he moved with experience yet like a stranger to the Aschelon yards. Any city bum could have told him the things he did wrong and given him a shorter route into town. He thought it funny that he did not see any bums around. He did not see anyone except the crew of his own train. Just the glare on the tracks, the high rear walls of waterfront buildings, the tiered uptown skyline...

On the first street corner he stopped and fished up a crumpled scrap of paper from the back pocket of his jeans, spreading it open so that the pencilled words came clear. Then he glanced up at the street name lettered in black on a yellow sign half way up the light standard. He frowned at the sign, looked down at the paper again, then shoved it back in his jeans and moved on. He did the same on the next corner and the next. He did not seem to know the names of any of the streets except the one written on the paper.

Half-way up Capper Street there was a small lunchroom with the door standing open, called Harry's Place. That is, the inner door was open. The screen door was closed and had holes in it, where the wire had rusted and gone into little jagged tears. Harry's name was lettered in white across the window. A grease-marked card with Saturday supper specials, a cup of synthetic coffee and a cut of the same kind of pie, shared window space with a handful of dusty paper flowers and a well-diluted bottle of ketchup. Harry, himself, was leaning out among them swatting bluebottles with a rolled newspaper. A sprinkling of dried-up corpses lay among the flowers.

When Matt saw Harry there he stopped and went inside and pulled out a piece of paper. He asked, "Can you tell me how I get to 111 East Third?" He pushed the paper across the counter...

Matt repeated the address. "Yeah," Harry said, ruminating, "I heard you the first time." He pulled a toothpick out of the jug on the counter, pushed it in one corner of his mouth. His jaws began to grind up and down. He eyed Matt steadily. Then, "Better wait," he remarked at last, "better wait until things quiet down around there. You won't want to go bustin' into a hot spot like that. They got enough boys like you there awready and plenty of 'em has their heads broke."

Matt's body stiffened. "What d'ya mean? What's all the mystery?"

"You mean you ain't heard?" Harry's voice was incredulous.

"Heard what? I just got in town fifteen minutes ago."

"You didn't hear yet about the big sit-down in the Dominion Building an' the public library being broke up?"

Matt's eyes lost their cold deadpan look. He dropped his pack and swung up onto a counter stool. "What d'ya mean, 'broke up'?"

Harry said, "I mean the single unemployed boys staged a sit-down in them two places and sat there for nineteen days an' nights because they couldn't think of no other way to force the authorities to provide 'em with a program of work an' wages, an' this morning early the cops chase 'em out with tear gas an' riot sticks. Don't tell me you didn't hear nothing about all that yet?"

Matt's face grew taut with interest. He leaned forward. "I never had the chance to hear anything yet, I tell you I just got in town."

Harry gave a low rumbling laugh. He said, "You didn't come riding the cushions, I seen too many not to know the signs." He turned away and spat out the pick. His little eyes surveyed Matt shrewdly. "Are you one of them transients the authorities is raisin' such a stink about?"

Matt nodded. "Sure, I'm a transient," he said quietly, "I was born back in the province of Saskatchewan but that province don't own me no more. Six years now I bummed around trying to rustle up some kind of steady job. I bummed around so long even the country don't own me no more."

Harry's voice broke in softly, "You an' who else?"

Matt smiled coldly. "Sure...me an' who else? A hundred thousand other boys. Every place we go the authorities as good as tell us, 'You boys get th' hell out of here, see?' There's no work an' no prospect of any. 'Now you boys get the hell out before we citizens has to call the police to protect ourselves.'"

Harry's heavy head swung up and down... His voice grew satirical. "Tell me something new, somethin' I ain't been listenin' to for the past eight years, then maybe you'd stand a chance of makin' a hit with me." He scratched his stump and his face grew serious. "Seems like the country's waitin' to get a real scrap on its hands so all you guys can be heroes overnight."

[Irene Baird, Waste Heritage *(Toronto: Macmillan, 1974), pp. 3-6]*

Children Write to the Prime Minister

Passman Sask,
Oct 16th/33

Dear Sir,—I am a girl thirteen years old, and I have to go to school every day its very cold now already and I haven't got a coat to put on. My parents can't afford to buy me anything for this winter. I have to walk to school four and a half mile every morning and night and I'm awfully cold every day. Would you be so kind to send me enough money... so that I could get one.

My name is

Edwina Abbott

[Reply: $5.00]

Chichester, Que.
March 13 1935

Dear Mr. Bennett.
I am a little boy 11 years old I live in a very back wood place and I am very poor
there is a big bunch of us I am going to school My little Sister and I we have three
miles to go and break our own path but we dont mind that if we were only able
to buy our books, the Quebec books are very expensive so I just thought I would
write you maybe you would give us enough to buy our books if you dont I Guess
We will have to stop and try and earn a little money to help out our father please
excuse paper and pencil as I have no better Hoping to hear from you real soon I
am

      Yours loving Friend
      Albert Drummond

Please answer soon soon soon

[Reply: $2.00]

[L. M. Grayson and Michael Bliss, eds., The Wretched of Canada
(Toronto: University of Toronto Press, 1971), pp. 56, 128]

Local Relief:
Memories of Larry Frezell, North Bay, Ontario

Locally, the city fathers did what they could to help. They would put men to work
doing some kind of menial task and then give them a voucher which they could
cash at any local food store.

The vacant lot on the corner of Main and Timmins Streets, where the
Canadian Longyear plant now stands, the city used as a wood storage lot. They
had men go out around the surrounding area and cut wood to earn their food
vouchers. The wood was then piled on this lot, there was a veritable mountain of
it, and it was given to people a cord at a time for winter fuel. This corner lot, now
vacant, had previously been a lumber storage lot for the Standard Planing Mill.
Of course, the mill suffered the ravishes of the Depression and had closed down,
throwing all their employees out of work.

[Larry Frezell, Survivors: The Great Depression, 1929-1939 *ed., Elizabeth
St Jacques, (Sault Ste. Marie: Maplebud Press, 1991), p. 84]*

The Prairie Dustbowl

By the time we got back onto the road, it was late afternoon. Scott decided he had
seen enough of south-east Saskatchewan, and we decided to head for Regina by
following the C.P.R. north-west from Stoughton. Nature stepped in and changed

our plans. Just before we got to Stoughton, we were hit by the thickest clouds of grasshoppers either of us had ever seen. They blew out of the south and west in numbers beyond computation. The swarm was upon us so suddenly that our windshield was solidly encrusted with splattered insects in a matter of seconds. We pulled over and stopped. Scott, who was experienced in such things, said so dense a swarm would pass over and the thing to do was wait until it did. It would descend some place, eat everything in sight, and take off again.

He was right, of course, but our car was a ghastly mess. The crashing grasshoppers had given it a sickly, stinking green coating. The windshield wipers only created a gooey smear, so we rummaged around in the trunk for something we could use as a scraper. There was nothing. We searched the ditches for a couple of hundred yards. Then I recalled that I had a Rolls razor in my bag. This was a razor with a sword-shaped blade that came in a patented case with a hone and a strap. I turned the blade into a scraper and it worked perfectly.

We almost had the windshield clean when a farmer came by in a truck and stopped to see if he could help. He had a wide putty knife, which he put to work for us. After the grasshopper grease was off, we washed the windows with water from our can and took off once more. The grasshopper smell in the car, on top of the heat and the dust we had already inhaled, was too much and I became bilious. We decided to detour to Weyburn and drive to Regina the next day.

The Prairie Dustbowl. *[Prairie Farm Rehabilitation Administration, Regina, Saskatchewan]*

In Weyburn we made a deal with the son of a garageman to clean the grasshoppers off our car for a dollar. It took him almost two hours and a gallon of coal-oil. We hung around the garage for an hour, talking to farmers who drifted in and out, and then invited a couple to join us for a glass of beer. We spent the evening converting lukewarm beer into perspiration as we eased in and out of a dozen conversations.

[James Gray, The Winter Years: The Depression on the Prairies, (Toronto: Macmillan Canada, 1966), pp. 179, 164] Reprinted by permission of Macmillan Canada.

> FOR SALE: 800 acres highly improved stock farm, located on Pelletier Creek. Would sell on cash instalment basis. If interested write Fred Hearsey, Duncairn, Sask. N.B.: I might he tempted to trade this farm for something really useful, say some white mice or goldfish, or even a playful little monkey. F.H.

Section B

Challenges to Political Orthodoxy

In 1935, William Aberhart, a former Baptist preacher whose weekly religious broadcasts on radio attracted some 350 000 listeners, swept to power in Alberta, winning 56 of 63 seats. There were many who were sceptical of Social Credit theory, and in 1937, Canada's Supreme Court declared as unconstitutional attempts by Aberhart's government to control banks and the money supply. But when Aberhart ran for office in 1935, desperate Albertans were uninterested in the words of 'nay-sayers.' Also in 1935, in a federal election, Prime Minister Bennett preached the politics of reform; however, too many voters considered this an insincere gesture from someone who had run a far more conservative government during the previous five years. Following Bennett's defeat, the Judicial Committee of the Privy Council rejected Bennett's New Deal legislation, and concluded that Canada's signature on treaties to uphold the goals of the International Labour Organization did not entitle the federal government to intrude upon provincial control over labour policy. However, a royal commission to address such constitutional obstacles was struck by the King government in 1937 and, three years later, its findings drastically altered the nature of Canadian federalism.

William 'Bible Bill' Aberhart Rallies Albertans

Tonight I am picking up the gauntlet that was thrown at my feet...May I remind you that there are 40,000 voters in Calgary that have been fighting for their God-given rights for the past five years. The people know that I have been battling to make life more worth living. So let them roll out their barrels of money, these big shots... Throw it away like water if they like to beat Aberhart and keep inefficient government. I say let them begin at once their double-dealing, gossip-mongering, whispering campaigns, to their own destruction... Let them go ahead and put their malicious, revolting, insulting cartoons in their financially-servile muckraking press...Because the people, the people whose hearts are right, the people who know such scaremongers for what they are, the people who place happiness and human values above money...the people who know that this old system of scarcity, poverty, and squalor must go—these people are not going to be misled, cajoled, cheated and robbed...simply because these...financial henchmen sit back like jackasses, cowtowing and praying to the stars the one phrase, "lick Aberhart."...Let them lie to their hearts content...these henchmen of financial bondage. Let them spring every nefarious trick they know to try and belittle these representatives of the people, the men and women who are giving the best days of their lives to bring economic security into the homes of this city [Calgary] and of this province. I'm persuaded that they can never sway a solitary decision of any sane loyal man or woman whose conscience knows what is best for them and best for Alberta. Yes my friends, this is your friend Aberhart...This is Aberhart telling the enemies of the people...listen you money-grabbers...the people of this province are not going to be hoodwinked by...turncoats of [your] type...

[NAC, Audio-Visual Section, Excerpt from Radio Broadcast by William Aberhart on CFCN (Calgary), 21 August 1935, ISN# 164693]

Funny Money

...The [Social Credit] dividends will not be paid in money, but they will be issued in the form of credit much the same way as banks issue many of their loans at the present time.

The citizen will be given a dividend book of blank, non-negotiable certificates. Each month he will be required to present his dividend book at the branch State Credit House, when a credit entry of $25 will be made. If he earns wages, these will also be entered on the credit side.

When the citizen desires to purchase goods or services, he merely fills out a blank non-negotiable certificate for the amount of the goods or services secured by him and, after signing it, passes it over to the party with whom he is dealing.

The non-negotiable certificate is non-transferable by the creditor to anyone else and must be deposited in the State Credit House Branch.

There will be no new money issued.

Where will all the credit come from to pay the basic dividends?

ANSWER—The credit issued will be a charge against the Natural Resources of the Province much in the same way as the present Government Bonds are.

Will not the issuance of the Basic Dividends rapidly sink the province into an enormous debt?

ANSWER—The scientific system of recovery through the cycle of credit will have to be introduced at the same time that the Basic Dividends are issued. This must not be a giant scheme of taxation. It has been called to the attention of the public that there is an enormous spread in the price between the producer's cost and the consumer's price. It is the intention under the Social Credit system to reduce this spread, increasing the producer's cost so that he may have a fair turn-over if it is at present adequate, or reducing it if it is too high. The same procedure will be followed all the way through in the marketing or processing of the goods. On account of the increased turnover that will be produced by the augmented purchasing power through dividends, salaries, commissions and so forth, it is felt that the producer and distributor will be able to carry on their business with a closer margin of profit or commission on turnover. Thus the province will be able to collect a levy that will provide the basic dividends to distribute to the various citizens. To illustrate this let us take a bushel of wheat say at a just price of sixty cents. Fifty-five cents of this is to go to the farmer and will provide a fair commission on his turnover. Five cents will be set aside for the Government levy. The wheat is sold to the miller who grinds it into flour. The cost of grinding will be covered by the shorts and bran and other by-products of the process. This will produce about forty pounds of flour. We will suppose that the flour sells for $1.10, ten cents of which is again given to the Government as its levy. The flour is next turned to the baker who makes it into bread which he sells at seven cents a loaf. The forty pounds of flour with the water and other ingredients would make fifty loaves of bread. Suppose the Government Levy on this bread was a cent a loaf.

```
$..............................                                      ................................ 198 ..............
        100

                        STATE CREDIT HOUSE BRANCH


                        ..................................................
                                      Address

        This is to certify that I am in debt to ........................................... for the sum of

        ................................................................................................... ——— Dollars
                                                                          100

        for.....................................................................................................
              Please credit him and charge to my account.

        No. ......................................          ...................................................
```

Sample of Non-Negotiating Certificate

That would give an additional fifty-cents levy. Thus from a bushel of wheat, processing it to flour, the Government would be able to collect possibly sixty-five cents...

[Social Credit Manual as Applied to the Province of Alberta (Calgary, 1935), pp. 9-12]

What Is Wrong with Social Credit?

...The Social Credit programme would make good the deficiency in income by creating new credit, which means essentially creating new money, and giving it away to the people to spend. Aberhart proposes to do this by paying all citizens a free dole of $25 a month... Now such a measure would certainly increase the demand for goods if they could be carried out. The trouble is simply that they would increase it much too much. Eventually if prices were not controlled, they would rise rapidly as soon as production reached its limit. If prices were controlled as Social Crediters usually propose, the people would be left with a lot of money which they could not spend and they would waste much time trying to buy things of which there would not be enough to go around. The system of rationing and price control would entail endless trouble and mistakes, endless arbitrary decisions on the part of the price fixing board, and would mean the abandonment of the system of pricing on which the capitalist system is based. Ultimately the whole exchange mechanism would probably break down. Thus the continued issue of social credit would lead to chaos either by way of inflation of prices or the breakdown of the pricing system under rationing and control...

The rise of such a political force during severe depression is only to be expected. Disgusted with the existing economic situation and the helplessness of traditional policies in the face of it, confused and bewildered by the paradox of poverty in the midst of plenty, the ordinary man is ripe for the easy solution offered by the monetary heretics... It has something in common with the general nature of ordinary liberal or progressive programs but is more positive and sure of itself. Its professed enemies are the bankers and financial powers—popular bogey-men, particularly in times of depression. In the hands of able and imaginative demagogues it can be made a most attractive doctrine. But it is rotten at the core, for it is based upon faulty economic analysis.

Underlying Social Credit theory is the fundamental principle that there is a chronic lack of purchasing power in our economic system which arises because business always pays out less as income than it takes in as payment for its products. Income paid out by business then proves to be less than enough to buy the products created. This shortage of income paid out is attributed to various factors by the different schools of social credit theory... It is this...which makes the theory so difficult to attack. The original and simplest form of the theory contended that income paid out, in the form of wages, interest, rent and dividends was only part of the expenditure of any firm out of its sales revenues, the rest going to pay for supplies, bank services and reserves. But it was easily seen that payments made to other firms for supplies or services sold to this firm went to create income in those other firms and so on. However the Social Credit theorists were clever enough to use more and more subtle fallacies as the basis for their doctrine as the more obvious ones were exposed. The result is that to see the mistake in some of the latter forms of the theories requires a good training in monetary theory, and to point out such mistakes would take much more space than we have here...

The basic contention that business somehow always absorbs income and does not pay out as much as it receives is...wrong. When we allow for profits or losses...then total income must equal the value of what is produced, including both capital and what is consumed, and there is no discrepancy, no gap which swallows up money or credit...

[R.B. Bryce {future federal Deputy Minister of Finance}, "What Is Wrong with Social Credit?" Public Affairs, Vol. 1, no. 2 (December 1937), pp. 47-49.]

A 'New Deal' Radio Broadcast by Prime Minister Bennett

I believe there should be a uniform minimum wage and a uniform maximum working week. I hold the view that if we are to have equality of social and political conditions throughout this land, we must have equality in economic conditions as well. Labour in one part of Canada must not be at a disadvantage with labour in another part. That is wrong socially and it is foolish in a business sense, for clearly it creates a disequilibrium in the nation's industrial life.

Then there is another phase of the worker's life upon which we must have a more definite agreement and arrangement. When, because of fluctuations in industrial conditions, the worker is thrown out of employment, he should not be punished when the fault is that of the machine. For whatever is the cause of these depressions, whoever is to blame for them (if anyone is to blame), assuredly it is not the workman. If he is able and willing to work, but can get no work, provision must be made for his security in a decent way. By this I do not mean the dole. The dole is a rotten thing. It is alike an insult to the worker and to those who profess to have control of our industrial system...

However few or many unemployed we normally may have, no man must be left to the uncertainties of private charity or to the humiliation of government gratuity. He must not be unemployed in the old, hateful sense of the word. As a member of our economic society, he should have security—provided always that he is willing to work. That is a condition precedent. For our reformed economic system is designed to encourage industry, not idleness. Therefore, the worker, when unemployed, must, with the help of the state, be provided with the means to effect his own security against unemployment. This security will be provided by means of unemployment insurance. For this reason, I believe in unemployment insurance, not as a means of bolstering up a faulty system, but as an element in establishing a sound modern one...

[NAC, MG27 III F18, Miss Muriel E. Black papers, "Text of the Radio Broadcast delivered by the Right Honourable R.B. Bennett," 4 January 1935]

Emotional *Volte Face*

...The apparent *volte face* that has been performed by Mr. Bennett in the past few weeks has been so astounding that many of us have been looking for evidences by which we can judge of its genuineness. It is accompanied by much emotional fervor that carries conviction to many hearers.

But in his broadcast we thought we detected a flaw in the metal. He intimated that all his life he had been applying his mind to this subject of reform. If ever he became head of the Government he had it all planned out what he was going to do.

That does not go down. If these reforms had been so dear to his heart all these years one would have expected him to let people know about it. He has been in Parliament for many years. He has had ample opportunity, both as oppositionist and as minister, to state his views.

He said himself it is the duty of oppositions to have policies alternative to those of the government and to expound them.

How does it come then, that in his opposition days he never advocated minimum wages and six-hour days, and regimentation of industry?

No, we think a humble confession of former error, a frank admission that he has been "converted" to a new faith would have carried more conviction of sincerity.

Mr. Bennett has had a sufficiently harrowing experience in the past five years to bring about a change of heart in anybody. It would have been in no way derogatory to his intelligence to admit that his former ideas were wrong and that he has at last seen a new light.

But that is not the way he will have it. He says he has not changed. These are the reforms that he has believed in for a lifetime, he insists.

****

There was a lot of the old Bennett in the last broadcast: much of the need for patience and courage and fortitude, much of meeting our contractual obligations, of preserving the integrity of our institutions.

Those phrases rang true. We have heard them before. So when he says he has always believed in these new reforms as much as he does today, perhaps some of his hearers may be excused for transposing his words and taking it that he believes today in these reforms no more than he did in all the preceding 25 years of his public life when he said nothing about them and did nothing to advance them.

[NAC, MG26 K, R.B. Bennett papers, Vol. 1266, Press Clipping Service, the Vancouver Sun, 17 January 1935, n.p.] Reprinted by permission of The Vancouver Sun.

A Case for Constitutional Change

Between 1867 and 1934 over 136 constitutional cases have faced the Privy Council with the task of saying what the Canadian constitution means. Despite those cases, or because of them, it is still quite certain that unless legislation falls clearly within one of the specific heads of s. 91 or s. 92 of the B.N.A. Act, it is virtually impossible to guess where legislative authority over any question will finally be found to reside. In practice this depends not only on the Act and the cases but in part on the way the issue is raised and presented and in part on each judge's personal inclination towards federal or provincial authority. The further circumstances that the form of the proposed reform legislation has not been finally settled at the time of writing increases the difficulty of even describing fairly the constitutional issues raised by the government's social legislation which is the subject of this paper. It is like guessing what attitude the Privy Council in England will take to a series of constitutional earth quakes that have not yet happened.

In all this uncertainty one thing at least appeared to be certain. This was that everything proposed in Mr. Bennett's policy of social reform was beyond the powers of the Dominion. Out of all those who considered the question before the current session of Parliament, only four authorities seem to have thought it possible that the Dominion might have jurisdiction. The situation was recognized by Mr. Bennett last August when he wrote to the provinces indicating his intention to call a Conference to discuss, among other matters, the question: "Are the provinces prepared to surrender their exclusive jurisdiction over legislation dealing with such social problems as old-age pensions, unemployment and social insurance, hours and conditions for work, minimum wages, etc., to the Dominion Parliament? If so, on what terms and conditions?" But the Provinces' cool response to this letter led to the proposed Conference being abandoned, and in January Mr. Bennett in five radio speeches broadcast the policy of reform. In introducing the Employment and Social Insurance Act on January 29, 1935, Mr Bennett set under way the...drive through current conceptions of the constitution, if not through the constitution itself. It might almost seem that his reading of the speeches of the Fathers of Confederation led him into the error of thinking that the constitution was what they intended it to be.

When Mr. Bennett claimed jurisdiction to establish an Employment and Social Insurance Commission, Mr. King asked if the prime minister had thought of submitting the question of constitutionality to the Supreme Court, and Mr. Lapointe [Minister of Justice] inquired if it would not be better to try to come to an agreement first with the provinces...

Everything that has been said here, everything that has happened since Confederation—the cost and waste of effort in constant constitutional litigation, the uncertainty to business and governments alike, the spirit of antagonism engendered, the uncertainty as to whether the Dominion Parliament may secure an amendment by joint resolution even against the opposition of the provinces, point to the wisdom of proceeding by way of cooperation with the provinces, and prove the necessity of securing the power to amend the constitution. Far more important than the constitution itself or the cases interpreting it is "the case of millions of Canadian people who are to-day looking for remedial measures". A situation cannot be allowed indefinitely to continue where these measures and the very right of business to exist may depend on the ability of one set of counsel acting for us as citizens of Canada to beat another set of counsel acting for us as inhabitants of a province...

1. There is an immediate need of arriving at some method of amending the B.N.A. Act.

2. The method chosen should make it unnecessary to have recourse to the British Parliament, subject in certain cases to the assent of the provinces.

3. While safeguarding the rights of minorities and the provinces, the method of amendment should provide for the greatest possible flexibility. Except upon "reserved" subjects, the Dominion Parliament should have power to amend the constitution by an Act passed by an absolute majority of both Houses in joint session...

4. To avoid delay, a province not dissenting within a year should be presumed to have given its assent to an amendment.

5. The vote of the provinces, like that of the Dominion Parliament, should be given by resolutions of the Legislatures, not by referendum.

The question which presents the greatest difficulty, is how to deal with amendments affecting Property and Civil Rights in the province. It will be seen that the Civil Code of Quebec has been put on the "reserved" list. Apart from this the Dominion should be able to add specific subjects to the heads of s. 91—either without consulting the provinces or perhaps with the assent of a majority of them. Otherwise, we would have the most rigid constitution in the world at a time when every country is finding it necessary to meet rapidly changing conditions....

6. The Dominion Parliament shall be able to add to the enumerated heads of s. 91 subjects not within the reserved class with the assent of a majority of the provinces...

While we were at it, we might repeal s.7 (1) and (3) of the Statute of Westminster and thus obtain, like South Africa, the legal power to provide ourselves with the kind of constitution we think we need and the machinery to change it. Such a step could be taken only if all the people of Canada were willing to trust each other, but the recognition of that trust would of itself produce a new feeling of loyalty to each other and respect for ourselves. As Mr. [Henri] Bourassa said: "We shall not develop in this country a true national spirit, superior to all provincial, religious and racial prejudices, until we are capable of administering our own laws." Moreover the B.N.A. Act with textual changes to bring it up to date should be re-enacted as a Canadian statute and as a living document... More important, the divisions of the fields of taxation and the provisions for subsidies are hopelessly out of date and should be completely overhauled, in the light of the vastly changed conditions between 1867 and to-day...

[F.R. Scott, "Social Reform and the Constitution," Canadian Journal of Economics and Political Science, Vol. 1, no. 3 (1935), pp. 409-411, 430-433]

The Rowell-Sirois Commission

...A detailed account of various relief measures is here unnecessary. It will be sufficient for our purposes to note the principal characteristics of the system, or lack of system, which developed for handling the relief problem.

At the outset the problem was regarded as a municipal responsibility, and this assumption has coloured the whole system ever since. The burden was first undertaken by the ancient municipal machinery of poor relief, assisted by private charity. But unemployment relief and agricultural relief in Western Canada were quite different problems both in origin and in magnitude from municipal poor relief, and the machinery quickly broke down. Senior governments came to the aid of municipal and local governments by a system of short-term grants-in-aid but the municipalities were left the responsibility of administration, including costs. All governments, however, regarded the situation as an emergency, and financial and administrative arrangements were hastily made on this assumption. Makeshift arrangements expected to be temporary have tended in the course of a decade to become permanent...

Without Dominion aid probably no province could have financed relief. Dominion aid, however, was apportioned largely on the basis of a percentage of costs, and substantial though Dominion contributions were, this system could not prevent great differences in the relief burden as between provinces and violent fluctuations of provincial costs from year to year...

Efforts were made by all provinces in...expenditures and most noticeable in the case of the Western Provinces where other services such as education, road maintenance and conservation suffered seriously. All provinces made vigorous efforts to maintain and increase revenues by new or increased rates of taxation. Some provinces resorted to wage taxes...some to disguised forms of retail sales taxes, all increased gasoline taxes and all increased taxes on corporations. But it was not until 1935 that total provincial tax revenues reached the level of those of 1929. Thus the provincial burden of relief during the worst years of the depression had to be met out of depleted revenues. The inevitable result was to compel the provinces to resort to deficit financing on a scale unparalleled in the history of the Dominion. During the years 1930-37 total provincial deficits on current accounts exceeded $300 million. The provincial share of relief during this period excluding charges to capital account of $200 million for provincial relief works, colonization and land settlement schemes, and relief advances to municipalities amounted to more than $250 million or approximately 92 per cent of total provincial deficits on current accounts. The portion of provincial debt directly chargeable to relief mounted rapidly.

The combined pressure of relief and depleted revenues destroyed, temporarily at least, the credit of the four Western provinces and they were all unable for a time to meet their respective shares of the relief burden either out of current revenues or by borrowing. In consequence loans had to be extended by the Dominion

to the provinces concerned. In certain instances the provinces also were compelled to borrow from the Dominion the municipal share of relief and re-loan to
the municipalities. This was particularly so in the case of Saskatchewan.
Substantial loans and bank guarantees were also made from time to time to the
Prairie Provinces to finance seed grain advances. The total of Dominion loans for
relief purposes to the four Western Provinces from 1931-1937 was $125 million.
Large inter-governmental loans of this sort can scarcely be conducive to sound
public finance whether on the part of the Dominion or of the provinces concerned, however necessary they may have been under the circumstances.
Repayment of inter-governmental loans in a federal system is always liable to
give rise to political difficulties and serious friction and especially so if prior collection from electors or subordinate bodies such as municipalities has to be made
by the borrowing government...

The Dominion is the only government which can meet in an equitable and
efficient manner, the large fluctuating expenditures due to unemployment. Its
unlimited powers of taxation give it access to all the incomes which are produced
on a national basis regardless of where they may happen to appear, and it can
obtain the needed revenues therefore in a manner which is the least harmful to
welfare and productive enterprises. With its control over the monetary system the
Dominion is able to finance the temporary deficits that may arise from sudden
increases in expenditure without suffering such a drastic weakening of credit as
occurs when the budgets of local governments are seriously out of balance. The
monetary and taxation powers of the Dominion would enable it to follow a
planned budgetary policy of deficits during depressions and surpluses and debt
repayment during prosperity—a policy which is generally impracticable for
provinces and municipalities...

The planning of public works and developmental expenditures, an intelligent
and co-ordinated use of credit, foreign exchange, trade, transportation and taxation policies are powerful instruments with which to combat unemployment and
to reduce fluctuations in income. The Dominion is the only government which
can use these instruments effectively. So long as the responsibility for unemployment rests with the nine provinces (and their creatures the municipalities) which
may follow different and conflicting budgetary, taxation, development, and public works policies Canada will be unable to eliminate the avoidable economic
wastes and social consequences of mass unemployment...

SUMMARY OF PLAN 1
1. Relief to the Provinces
The Dominions would relieve the provinces (and the municipalities) of the
whole burden of relief for the employable unemployed and their dependants.

The Dominion would assume the whole of the provincial (but not the municipal) debts, and would in effect bear the deadweight cost of this debt, as it would
collect from the provinces no more than the return which they receive today from

their revenue producing assets. The provinces would thus have no further provisions to make for sinking funds.

In the case of Quebec, where the provincial debt is an unusually low proportion of combined provincial and municipal debt, the Dominion would assume 40 per cent of the net, or deadweight, cost of combined provincial and municipal debt service.

2. Withdrawal by the Provinces from certain Tax Fields.

The provinces would cease to use the following forms of taxation: the provincial income tax; taxes on corporations or corporate income which would not be imposed on individuals or partnerships; and succession duties.

3. Surrender of Subsidies

The provinces would surrender all existing subsidies.

4. Remaining Provincial Revenue Sources

The Dominion, while retaining its unlimited taxing powers, would recognize an obligation to respect the remaining revenue sources of the provinces.

In addition the Dominion would pay annually to each province a sum equal to the tax which that province would have received had it collected from mining and oil producing companies 10 percent of the net income which was derived from mining, smelting, and refining of ores and oils produced in the province.

5. New Provincial Revenue Sources

The Dominion would pay annually a National Adjustment Grant to certain provinces. The amount of the grant...would be such as to enable each province (including its municipalities), without resort to heavier taxation than the Canadian average, to provide adequate social, educational and developmental services. The weight of taxation is estimated by comparing the provincial and municipal taxation with the total income of the province. The test of adequacy of social and educational services is found in the Canadian average for these services. The adequacy of developmental services is tested by what the province itself has done in years which may be considered normal.

The original adjustment grants would be irreducible. Increases would be granted (on the advice of the proposed Finance Commission) at appropriate intervals if they were needed, in order to enable a province to perform its functions adequately without exceptionally heavy taxation.

In addition to the National Adjustment Grants payable to some provinces the Dominion would pay an Emergency Grant to a province in which abnormally bad conditions prevailed. Such a grant would be made for a year at a time, reduced as soon as possible, and eliminated as soon as possible.

6. Future Borrowing

Future provincial and municipal borrowing would have to be in lawful money of Canada.

Future provincial borrowing might be either (a) as today on the sole credit of the province, in which cases the debt charges could not be counted as part of the financial need of the province if it is applied for a National Adjustment Grant (if it were not receiving one) or for an increase in its grant; or (b) on the credit of Canada, if the proposed Finance Commission is asked to approve it, and after reviewing all the circumstances does so.

7. Freedom of Provinces.

No control of provincial expenditures is contemplated. Every province would be quite free to improve its services, by specially heavy taxation, or to have specially light taxation by reducing its services, or to develop some services in excess of the Canadian average at the expense of others which would remain below it.

[Privy Council Office, Canada, Report of the Royal Commission on Dominion-Provincial Relations, *Vol. 2 (Ottawa, 1940), pp. 18-20, 23-24, 86]*
Reproduced with the permission of the Minister of Public Works and Government Services Canada, 1997.

QUESTIONS

1. What does the work of Dorothy Livesay and Irene Baird reveal about attitudes toward and within the ranks of the unemployed?
2. Assess the potential benefits and pitfalls of using letters from ordinary Canadians to R.B. Bennett as evidence.
3. What do the documents reveal about government welfare policies during the Depression?
4. What was the appeal of William Aberhart and the Social Credit party? Did Social Credit have a logical approach to economic analysis?
5. Why did many Canadians during the Depression believe it necessary to change the British North America Act?

READINGS

Pierre Berton, *The Great Depression, 1929-1939* (Toronto: McClelland and Stewart, 1990)

R.D. Francis and H. Ganzevoort, eds., *The Dirty Thirties in Prairie Canada* (Vancouver: Tantalus Research, 1980)

Larry A. Glassford, *Reaction and Reform: The Politics of the Conservative Party under R.B. Bennett, 1927-1938* (Toronto: University of Toronto Press, 1992)

Michiel Horn, *The League for Social Reconstruction: Intellectual Origins of the Democratic Left in Canada, 1931-1942* (Toronto: University of Toronto Press, 1980)

___, ed., *The Depression in Canada: Responses to Economic Crisis* (Toronto: Copp Clark Pitman, 1988)

Allen Mills, *Fool for Christ: The Political Thought of J.S. Woodsworth* (Toronto: University of Toronto Press, 1991)

H. Blair Neatby, *The Politics of Chaos: Canada in the Thirties* (Toronto: Macmillan, 1972)

Doug Owram, *The Government Generation: Canadian Intellectuals and the State, 1900-1945* (Toronto: University of Toronto Press, 1987)

H.F. Quinn, *The Union Nationale*, rev. ed. (Toronto: University of Toronto Press, 1979)

A.E. Safarian, *The Canadian Economy in the Great Depression* (Toronto: University of Toronto Press, 1959)

John T. Saywell, *"Just Call Me Mitch": The Life of Mitchell F. Hepburn* (Toronto: University of Toronto Press, 1992)

James Struthers, *No Fault of Their Own: Unemployment and the Canadian Welfare State, 1914-1941* (Toronto: University of Toronto Press, 1983)

___, *The Limits of Affluence: Welfare in Ontario, 1920-1970* (Toronto: University of Toronto Press, 1994)

John Herd Thompson and Allen Seager, *Canada, 1922-1939: Decades of Discord* (Toronto: McClelland and Stewart, 1985)

Richard Wilbur, *The Bennett Administration, 1930-1935* (Ottawa: Canadian Historical Association, 1969)

World War II

Worl War II accelerated the pace of change in Canada in several ways. The need to raise money quickly helped the federal government achieve an agreement with the provinces in 1941, based upon the Rowell-Sirois Commission report. Under the terms of this agreement, Ottawa assumed exclusive control over income, corporate, and inheritance taxes. Soon, levies upon Canadians rose to record levels, but most citizens remained solid in their support for the federal government—not only out of patriotism, but also because Ottawa was seen as mobilizing the country effectively. Under the direction of C.D. Howe, officials within the Department of Munitions and Supply skilfully guided private industry in retooling for wartime production and started a number of Crown Corporations that transformed Canada into a major supplier of arms for the Allies.

Over the course of the war, an increasing number of Canadians expressed support for the concept that a planned economy as well as better social welfare should become permanent features in post-war Canada. In the minds of many, the *laissez-faire* approach to economic affairs was responsible for the Great Depression. By contrast, the highly regulated wartime economy witnessed full employment and, with the creation of the Wartime Prices and Trade Board, low inflation. Such feelings provided growing popularity for the Co-operative Commonwealth Federation (C.C.F.), which advocated large-scale state intervention. In 1942, the C.C.F. stunned both major political parties when its candidate defeated the Conservative leader, Arthur Meighen, in a Toronto by-election. The next year, the C.C.F. finished within three seats of obtaining power in Ontario; a public opinion poll released in September 1943 placed them at 29 percent support compared to 28 percent for the Liberals and Tories; and in 1944, the C.C.F., under Tommy Douglas, swept to power in Saskatchewan.

Prime Minister King had long fancied himself as a social reformer— one who, in his 1918 book, *Industry and Humanity*, stressed the need for government to promote Christian conduct and social harmony. But King was also a careful politician, determined to keep himself at the centre of public opinion. In 1941, as part of the deal transferring taxation powers to Ottawa, King's government created an unemployment insurance plan; soon, however, political trends compelled him to go much farther. In 1944, based upon recommendations made the previous year in *The Report on Social Security* (drawn up by McGill University social scientist, Dr. Leonard Marsh), King's government announced its intention to introduce a family allowance. Also helping King undercut support for the C.C.F. was a 1944 *National Housing Act*, which promised to make it easier to buy a home; a new Department of Veterans' Affairs, which administered a more generous benefits package than that introduced after World War I; and a Department of Reconstruction (under C.D. Howe) to guide the country back to peacetime prosperity. Finally, in 1945, an election year, the Liberal government adopted recommendations made in a White Paper it had commissioned by declaring its intention to use state powers actively to retain 'high levels of income and employment.'

Section A

The Limits of Patriotism

In order to control inflation, the federal government organized production, and created a Wartime Prices and Trade Board. In November 1941, it froze both wages and prices and, the following year, helped administer the rationing of alcohol, beef, sugar, coffee, butter, cloth, tires, and gas. Government statistics pointed to tremendous success; between late 1941 and the end of the war, total inflation amounted to just under 3 percent. Countless Canadians rigorously followed rationing ordinances; salvaged scarce items; grew victory gardens to save food; and cheerfully coped with housing shortages. However, a number of citizens remained determined to place their own needs first, even to the point of gouging their countrymen to obtain windfall profits.

The Housing Crisis

Between the Fall of 1939 and May 1942 more than 23,000 people had moved into the Halifax district, increasing the population by about one-third...

By the Autumn of 1940 a marked shortage of living shelter was evident; landlords were exploiting the situation. Halifax and immediately around was declared a designated area and rent control was introduced...

The tenants were conscious of the shortage of shelter and they were more anxious to retain possession of the space they occupied than to argue about the rate of rental asked. Experience showed that this class of tenant was afraid to complain about rates of rental lest the landlord be annoyed and their possession endangered.

> *[NAC, RG64, Records of the Wartime Prices and Trade Board, Vol. 29,*
> *Undated report, "Canadian Rental and Eviction Control."]*

Suites Wanted

RELIABLE party desires 6-room house
or apartment close in by February.
Excellent references. Ph. 28014 between
8:30 and 5:30.

$5 Reward offered for information leading
to rental of 3- or 4-room furnished suite.
Couple, no children. Room 412, Corona Hotel.

> *[Edmonton Journal, 23 December 1942, pp. 2, 15]*
> *Reprinted by permission of the Edmonton Journal.*

Consumer Goods and Food

...I believe that nearly every merchant is making a small black market of his own, with regular customers. Whatever goods are in short supply, he will put aside some for these regular customers and charge them a higher price for that service. I am quite positive that this situation exists all throughout Canada, except maybe in stores of importance, where all sales are made on a cash basis. I am afraid, however, that there is very little that we can do about that...

> *[NAC, MG26 J2, William Lyon Mackenzie King papers, Vol. 372, File W-*
> *130-1, G. Woodery (private citizen) to Prime Minister King, 6 January*
> *1943]*

...Rumours have also been going around that there are Jewish stores selling tea, coffee and sugar at high prices with no ration coupons required.

Again it has been heard that there are travellers from Jewish manufacturers and jobbers in the East offering merchandise to certain selective retailers who in turn are ready to buy and sell at their own price to the consumer...

[NAC, RG64, Records of the Wartime Prices and Trade Board, Vol. 690, File 23-30, George J.A. Young (Prices and Supply Representative in Winnipeg for the Wartime Prices and Trade Board) to Donald Gordon (Director of the Wartime Prices and Trade Board), 23 July 1943]

Automobiles Run by Black Markets

Windsor, Nov. 3—(CP)—A Royal Canadian Mounted Police officer testified in police court here today that he and another member of the force took over operation of a service station in Windsor for two hours recently and that during that time 30 cars drove up for service and only four presented proper credentials for purchases...

Hamilton, Feb. 10—(CP)—Police said today loose gasoline ration coupons were stolen from the Sun Oil Co., here, last night by a thief who left a note saying: "Ha, I dood [*sic*] it again." It was signed the Lone Wolf. Two weeks ago the same office was entered and a note left by the "wolf" ridiculed police for their inability to catch him...

[NAC, RG64, Records of the Wartime Prices and Trade Board, Vol. 690, File 23-30, Clippings from the Ottawa Citizen, *17 April 1944, n.p.]*
Reprinted by permission of The Canadian Press.

Section B
The International Dimension

Nationalism and collective pride grew with Canada's substantial contributions to the war effort. As such, in 1942, Canada sought to use the 'functional principal,' recently developed by officials within its Department of External Affairs, to obtain separate membership on several Combined Boards established by the Allies. These were in areas (such as food production) where Canada considered itself as a significant power. Ottawa proved so determined to obtain this representation that it threatened to curtail, or even cut off, war loans to Great Britain if that country did not drop its opposition to Canada's presence on these boards.

Some, however, were concerned that strides made by Canada toward greater autonomy were being compromised by a growing collaboration with the United States. By 1940, many wondered if Britain would survive the Battle of Britain—if not, it could leave Canada as a prime target for Germany. To meet this threat, the 1940 Ogdensburg Agreement between Canada and the United States established a Permanent Joint Board of Defence that treated North America as a single defensive unit. The same pattern was evident in Canada's northwest, with the apparent threat posed by Japan. During the early part of the war, Japanese forces conquered large parts of Southeast Asia and the South Pacific, attacked U.S. naval forces at Pearl Harbor and, in 1942, briefly occupied two outer Aleutian Islands off Alaska. Thousands of American troops poured into Canada to build the Alaska Highway—a project that most Canadians endorsed for security reasons, and that brought several communities economic benefits. Still, concerns were voiced over sovereignty, as well as over the impact of the highway on several northern Indian tribes.

Moving from the Crown?

Which of these would you like to see Canada do after the war: 1. Decide for herself how she will deal with other countries in the world, or 2. Join with the other dominions and Britain in deciding one foreign policy for the whole empire? (*Canadian Institute of Public Opinion*, 25 March 1944)

	Decide for herself (%)	Join with dominions (%)	Undecided (%)
Total	47	46	7
Quebec	70	21	9
Rest of Canada	39	55	6
By age:			
21-29 years	58	37	5
30-49 years	48	45	7
50 years and over	39	54	7

[J.L. Granatstein and Peter Neary, eds., The Good Fight: Canadians and World War Two (Toronto: Copp Clark, 1995), p. 449]
Reprinted by permission of the University of Chicago Press.

The Functional Principle

...The time is approaching, however, when even before victory is won the concept of the united nations will have to be embodied in some form of international organization. On the one hand, authority in international affairs must not be concentrated exclusively in the largest powers. On the other, authority cannot be divided equally among all the thirty or more sovereign states that comprise the united nations, or all effective authority will disappear. A number of new international institutions are likely to be set up as a result of the war. In view of the government, effective representations on these bodies should neither be restricted to the largest states nor necessarily extended to all states. Representation should be determined on a functional basis which will admit to full membership those countries, large or small, which have the greatest contribution to make to the particular object in question. In the world there are over sixty sovereign states. If they all have nominally equal voice in international decisions, no effective decisions are likely to be taken. Some compromise must be found between the theoretical equality of states and the practical necessity of limiting representation on international bodies to a workable number. That compromise can be discovered, especially in economic matters, by the adoption of the functional principle of representation. That principle, in turn, is likely to find many new expressions in the gigantic task of liberation, restoration and reconstruction.

[Canada, House of Commons, Debates, 9 July 1943, p. 4558, Statement by Prime Minister William Lyon Mackenzie King]

Protecting the North

...At the present time Alaska is the most exposed area on this continent. This does not necessarily mean that if Japan attacks North America her first blow will inevitably fall on this northern outpost, but it is generally accepted by the intelligence services that there is more likelihood of an attack on Alaska than on any other part of America except the Panama Canal Zone. It is in recognition of this fact that the recent steps have been taken to strengthen Alaska defences...

Notes approving the construction of a highway from Fort St. John, British Columbia, to Alaska as a defence measure and at the expense of the United States, were exchanged on March 17 and 18, 1942. United States Army Engineers have established a base at the Dawson Creek, British Columbia, railhead and under the direction of Brigadier General Hoge work on the location and construction of the pioneer road is well started...

The construction and equipment of Canadian airports between Edmonton and Fairbanks which was undertaken by Canada as a result of a recommendation made by the Permanent Joint Board of Defence[1] a little over one year ago has been one of the most spectacularly efficient jobs of construction ever undertaken on this continent. The airway is now in constant and effective operation. The facilities provided are adequate to take care of every type of plane except the largest and heaviest of the bombers and transports. Discussions are now under way with the object of extending the runways, building additional emergency strips, and providing supplementary radio and other equipment. It has been indicated that the United States may be prepared to pay for this extension of facilities along the route but the Canadian Government may wish in light of possible present and post-war complications, to keep full control in its own hands in spite of additional cost. (With the exception of the Alaska Highway the Canadian Government has always adhered to the policy of itself supplying any facilities required in Canada by the United States forces engaged on joint defence projects)...

> *[NAC, MG26 J4, William Lyon Mackenzie King papers, Vol. 348, File "Defence of Alaska," Memorandum for the Prime Minister, 13 April 1942, pp. 239920, 239923]*

The Impact on Northern Aboriginal Peoples

...There is no question but what the impact of all the construction activities in Southern Yukon and its consequent influx of white people is having a very harmful effect upon the natives, and it is noticeable that the degree of this harm is in direct proportion to the closeness of the association that the natives have with the whites. The new era is here to stay and is and will continue to present many new problems to the administration. One of these problems is how to soften the blow upon the natives and ameliorate conditions so as to prevent their complete decimation.

The Indians in the Yukon are divided into bands, not tribes and each band centres on some trading post. Furthermore, each band speaks a separate language from the others. Thus in Southern Yukon, we have bands centering on Burwash, Champagne, Whitehorse, Teslin and Lower Post; the latter from an administrative point of view might be considered as being in Yukon territory.

The bands at Burwash and Champagne have to a considerable extent or to a greater extent than others, continued their normal nomadic life and have been least harmfully affected by contacts with white people. Thus, while at

---

[1] Agreement signed in August 1940 between the United States and Canada to provide for the defence of North America

Champagne, two weeks ago, I found that all the Indians were out salmon fishing in the Dezadeash River. The Indians in Whitehorse have been so long associated with white people that the surviving members may be considered to have built up an immunity against the diseases of white people.

The Indians of the Teslin and Lower Post bands until the advent of this new era, have been almost completely isolated from contacts with white people and, have had the least opportunity of creating an immunity to white peoples' diseases. Consequently they have been distressingly affected by the new contacts. No doubt a contributing factor has been the fact that to a considerable extent the adult males have abandoned their normal nomadic pursuits and have accepted work on various construction projects, both American and Canadian.

The band at Teslin suffered epidemics of measles and whooping cough, which in some cases developed into pneumonia, last year, and now are plagued with an epidemic of meningitis and have suffered three deaths so far from the latter. The band at Lower Post were devastated last Spring with an epidemic of influenza which caused 15 deaths among a total population of about 150 of all ages. There is no doubt in my mind that if events are allowed to drift along at will, that the Indian bands at Teslin and Lower Post will become completely decimated within the next few years...

Technically, I believe the Indians are free agents and should be permitted the same opportunities of obtaining lucrative employment as white people and of associating with them. In practice this will be to their detriment if the majority of them die of disease within the next few years. Consequently, I think every endeavour should be made to influence or persuade them to continue their ancestral and nomadic life of hunting and trapping with white people.

Whatever policy is followed, it will be impossible to avoid all harmful effects upon the health of the Indians. The necessity of providing greater medical care than has been necessary in the past, will thereby become an obligation upon the Department. It is realized that with a large proportion of the medical and nursing professions in the Armed Services and the civilian members all overworked, the provision of medical or nursing care is an almost insuperable problem...

However, U.S. Army doctors have co-operated in a wonderful manner in providing medical care and assistance wherever possible. They have given and are continuing to give greater assistance in caring for the health of the Indians at Lower Post, Watson Lake and Teslin and, have provided anti-typhoid serum for an epidemic now or recently raging among the Moosehide band of Indians near Dawson, Y.T...

[NAC, RG85, Northern Affairs Records, Vol. 1872, pt.1, C.K. LeCapelain (Liaison Officer) to R.A. Gibson (Director of Lands, Parks and Forests Branch, Department of Mines and Resources), 17 July 1943]

Section C
New Roles for Women

More than 300 000 Canadian women entered the wartime workforce. And, in order to release more men for military service and to entice women into the labour market, between 1942 and 1946 the federal government provided state-supported daycare, as well as tax breaks for working wives. However, from many newspapers and other barometers of public opinion, there emanated considerable concern over the migration of women, especially mothers, into the job market. Canadians were assured that women sought only to 'back the attack' temporarily for patriotic reasons; that they would return to the hearth at the first opportunity; and that they would not become masculine, morally com-promised, nor permanently distanced from family life by their new roles. Such themes were also applied to the more than 40 000 women who joined new aux-iliary services within the Canadian military and who, as far as possible, were assigned jobs, such as administrative work, that connected to female stereo-types. Yet, in several publications there also appeared articles emphasizing the competence of women in traditionally male jobs, and suggesting that more women believed that they had earned equal access to and treatment within the workplace—a conviction that many women reiterated in later years when asked about how the war changed their lives.

A Basis for Social Change?

If women take the place of men in industry, should they be paid the same wages as men? (*Canadian Institute of Public Opinion*, 16 February 1942)

Yes   — 78%
No   — 14%
Undecided— 8%
By sex:

	Men(%)	Women (%)
Yes	71	85
No	20	7
Undecided	9	8

After the War, do you think women should be given equal opportunity with men to compete for jobs in industry, or do you think employers should give men the first chance? (*Canadian Institute of Public Opinion*, 21 April 1943)

	Total (%)	Men (%)	Women (%)
Equal chance	24	21	27
Give men first chance	72	75	68
Undecided	4	4	5

[J.L. Granatstein and Peter Neary, eds., The Good Fight: Canadians and World War Two *(Toronto: Copp Clark, 1995), pp. 448-449]*
Reprinted by permission of the University of Chicago Press.

Hopes for Equality

You can tell your great granddaughter some day that this was the time and the place it really started; the honest-to-goodness equality of Canadian women and men in all the work of this country that is to be done; and the pay and the kudos and the rights and the problems.

And you can say that it wasn't done by club women at luncheons; or orators on soap boxes; or legislators in parliaments.

It began to happen that hour when Canadian girls left desks and kitchens, elevators and switchboards, stepped into overalls and took their places in the lines of workers at lathes and drills, cranes and power machines, tables and benches in the munition plants of Canada...

As you leaf through the recent pages, you will find one of the most exciting stories of our generation. It is the story of women who today form as high as 60 percent of the payroll at some of our larger war plants and who will, according to officials close to the labour situation, make up 80 percent of the war workers of this country before the fight is won...

So Canada, occupied with the greatest war in history, which her men must fight, is gradually handing over the carrying on of industry to the sex which even five years ago was occupied mainly in tending house.

How are they doing the job, these women war workers? What is happening to them in the world of overalls and wrenches; union meetings and graveyard shifts; dirty hands and oil-soaked shoes; time clocks and blasting machinery; secret methods and formulaes.

No one can say exactly. But as in any other great social evolution, you can feel the trend and the swing of events in a hundred little things. In the changing attitude of public men toward women and their capacities; in the education (which sometimes amounts to conversion) of foremen and bosses and factory heads, as they watch women quietly fitting into the gaps in their plants, taking on the most difficult work, with little fuss and no feathers...

You can sense it in the decreasing layoffs and absenteeism, and in the swelling turnout of material that comes off their machines and benches for the People's War.

For the People's War has become, in a sense never previously known, the woman's war. Canadian women are stretching to a new stature to fight it...

There is no picking of "soft" jobs or shifts for women. It is the best person for the job with the foreman of today.

"It is like this," said a grizzled supervisor as he watched a slip of a girl swinging a great crane to lower a gun barrel, "she does the job as well as he does (pointing to a man at the same operation) and with less fuss and swearing.

Women in the Workforce: Servicing Aircraft at the No. 2 Air Observer School in Edmonton.
[Provincial Archives of Alberta, BI. 529/3]

"I don't see why she shouldn't keep at it, after the war. We'll be using cranes for other things than this."

Then he scratched his head thoughtfully.

"Darned if I don't think she's going to—and I'd hate to be the one to try and stop her."

[Lotta Dempsey, "Women in War Plants," Mayfair, May 1943, pp. 92-93]

Worries over Children

An increase in juvenile delinquency is an inevitable consequence of total war. It appeared after the first world war and it is in this. While we are fighting for our very existence, we are also fighting for a certain way of life. It will be a great pity, if because of this war, children are needlessly doomed to a life of slavery— slavery to crime, with anti-social habits as the great dictator of their lives.

The war will inevitably bring its toll in crippled bodies, but if we can save some of our children from crippled minds and impaired characters, surely it is wisdom to do it.

The International Police Chiefs' Association sounded a warning that Juvenile Delinquency was on the increase. J. Edgar Hoover, chief of the [American] Federal Bureau of Investigation, reported, "Delinquency is mounting rapidly, and unless we all do our jobs better we can expect an era of lawlessness..." The Toronto Juvenile Court reported a 50% increase in delinquency in the year 1941, but the 8 to 12 year-olds showed an increase of 100%. Toronto's Chief of Police, General D.C. Draper, stated in his annual report that burglary, house and shop-breaking among adults has declined but the rise in Juvenile Delinquency "merits serious consideration."...

In war time you have an overhanging atmosphere of anxiety and uncertainty. Such ideas as aggressiveness, attack, and the like are in the air, and since children do not live in a vacuum, they seek to emulate the ideas around them. Their heroes are airmen, soldiers, sailors, hard tough fighters. Even the comics, which are carefully read by children, have turned to supermen and spy plots. It is little wonder that children are now playing 'commando' and go on wild raids.

War is the great scatterer of families and destroyer of adequate family life. Broken homes in peace time contributed more than their fair share of children who fell foul of the law, and in war time, with the father away in the army, mother finds the added strain too difficult for her. Even if the father did not play an active part as disciplinarian, he was always in the background as a court of final appeal. Many mothers are now in war industries and the children fend for themselves as best they can with the aid of relatives, neighbors or social agencies...

[Saturday Night, 14 November 1942, p. 26. Written by Scott Young]

Liberation Differed

Look Ladies; it's reconversion time. Tanks and tail guns have vacated the priority list in favour of new refrigerators and nail scissors. We've written two V-Days into the record, and re-establishment, rather than re-armament, is the order.

So how about coming out from behind those welder's masks and swapping your overalls for aprons? The menfolk are returning from overseas; they will take a very dim view of the situation if they find that you have permanently muscled in on their toiling territory...

He's sick of whipcord. He wants a clinging vine.

It will be quite a shock to him to discover that instead of staying home and crocheting borders for the hand towels, his better half is driving a streetcar...

In England it was commonplace to see a gal step up to a packing case almost as big as herself, fluff out her back curls, and casually toss the load onto a lorry. Another gal would be standing by, ready to drive the load away.

The spectacle was successively astonishing, amusing, and boring. In due course a woman porter became just a porter. She literally worked herself sexless...

Refrain from any act which would even suggest your ability to lift anything heavier than a dry mop. Make like a lady, not like a lady wrestler...

Let a repatriated fighter pilot illustrate our position in the matter:

"I got the car out the other evening and went out for a spin in the country. The machine hadn't been used for over three years, so I wasn't really surprised when it conked. I pulled off the road and lifted the hood.

"Well, I was standing there, giving the job the once over, when another car stopped beside me, and out stepped a babe in something green. 'Having some trouble?' she asks, giving me a nice smile. 'Maybe I can help.'

"The next thing I know, I'm elbowed right out of the play. This doll fiddled around with a couple of wires, then stepped away and turned the smile back on. 'That should do it.' And before I could even ask her name, much less her phone number, she was away. What makes it really bad, my bus has been running like a rocket ever since."

"So," the pilot concluded. "I've decided to find me a girl who doesn't know a basket from a grease gun. I'm going to give her a vehicle maintenance test. If she flunks, I'll lay my heart in her lap. But if she passes—so will I."

Which will it be, ladies? Matrimony or a monkey wrench?"

[Mayfair, December 1945, pp. 40-41]

"Rub your eyes, honey—it's a brand-new Singer!"

Yes! Christmas is coming—and
so are the new Singers!

LOOK—and blink—and look again!
Yes—those are *new* Singer Sewing Machines. Real, not a dream!
They're beginning to roll off the
assembly lines again—cabinets, port-
ables, consoles, electric models and treadle models—the
best in more than 90 years of Singer history.

We know that many of you have been *needing* a new
Singer—*needing* it to make your family dollars go
further.

Now you can carry out those plans
of yours. Make lovely new clothes. Fix
up old ones. Freshen the house with
curtains and slip covers!

So speak to Santa Claus and your Singer Sewing Cen-

ter* about your new Singer today.
Order your new Singer *right now* if
you want it in time for Christmas.
We can arrange easy terms for you
so you may use your new Singer—
and enjoy it—and pay for it as
you go along. Ask us about our budget plan.

SINGER
SEWING MACHINE COMPANY

*FOR YOUR PROTECTION: Singer Sewing Machine Co. continues its long-time
policy of selling its machines only through
Sewing Centers identified by the famous Red
"S" trade-mark on the window—never
through department stores or other sewing
machine dealers.

SEWING CENTERS
EVERYWHERE

[National Home Monthly, *December 1945, p. 63*]

**Wind or no wind, you must stand erect and
salute, Miss.**

Belittling Female Soldiers. *[W. Hugh Conrod,* Athene, Goddess of War: The Canadian
Women's Army Corps, Their Story *(Ottawa: Consumer and Corporate Affairs, 1983), p. 28A]*

Military Responsibilities. *[National Archives of Canada, PA129075]*

The Whispering Campaign

"Spreading of harmful and irresponsible rumors is undoubtedly one of the factors most damaging in Canada's war effort. There are rumors of all kinds and descriptions and unfortunately many people seem to take an unthinking, inane and even mischievous delight in passing them on. Naturally the farther such stories go, the more fanciful and exaggerated they become. We may not believe them ourselves, but inevitably they stick persistently in the minds of some, exerting an insidiously disruptive effect.

"Most inexcusable of the current crop of rumors are certain reports concerning women serving in the Army Corps and in the Women's Division

R.C.A.F. Comparatively harmless, but utterly ridiculous is the story that these girls live a soft and easy life, doing practically no work at all. Their officers as well as the girls themselves brand this rumor as a stupid lie. Girls are kept plenty busy in the various army centres throughout the country, training, and performing a wide variety of essential tasks.

"It should not be necessary to labour the point that these girls are preparing for, and doing, jobs that would otherwise have to be done by men, and that they are thus releasing many of the latter for more strenuous service.

"As a high ranking officer put it recently: 'The more women we get into the Army, the more jobs and types of work we find for them, the more men will be released for work which for obvious reasons, cannot be performed by women.'

"Much more vicious is the charge, covertly made and freely passed from mouth to mouth, that once in uniform girls tend frequently to fall into habits of loose living. This is an ugly rumor, most decidedly not substantiated by the facts. Unfortunately this slander has been bandied about so widely that it is having an adverse effect on recruiting in both the C.W.A.C. and the R.C.A.F.(WD).

"Girls are being deterred from joining up by this scandalous whispering campaign, most certainly fifth columnist in origin.

"The C.W.A.C., the R.C.A.F. and the Navy insist that girl applicants must be perfectly fit when they join up and that they must maintain this condition. There is medical supervision of the strictest sort. Instruction in hygiene, physical training, and adequate recreational facilities are a part of the military health program. Talks on sex matters are given to the girls and they are warned against various vices to be avoided.

"Discipline in respect to their relationship with male members of the service is strict. Every effort is made to supply the members of mixed military camps with normal recreation and amusement. For instance, the girls at Dundurn Camp attend dances sponsored by the service clubs.

"A high ranking army officer, mentioning that there have been many opponents and detractors of the policy of employing women in the Canadian forces, had this to say. 'I do not hesitate to state that these critics have been thoroughly confounded, and no one who has had the opportunity of seeing our Canadian Women's Army Corps at work can fail to be impressed by their zeal, their efficiency or their 'esprit de corps.'

"It would be well for the disseminators of these injurious rumors to remember that by far the greatest majority of these girls have joined the services from the very highest and most patriotic motives, and that while there will be occasional lapses from grace, just as there are in civilian life, most of them remain as fine, clean-living and straight-thinking as they were in normal life. It is far too easy for a few idle rumormongers and gossips to destroy the reputation of the men or women who wear the King's uniform. One disorderly soldier should not blacken the name of an entire unit, nor should the unfortunate actions of a mere handful of girls in the services be held as typical of the thousands of very splendid young women who ask nothing more than that they be permitted to do what they can for Canada, in this time of urgent need. People who deliberately slander these fine forces are 'not worthy to polish the shoes of Canada's women in uniform."

[*W. Hugh Conrod*, Athene, Goddess of War: The Canadian Women's Army Corps, Their Story *(Ottawa: Consumer and Corporate Affairs, 1983)*, *pp. 112-113]*

To My Laundress

(The following poem was dedicated to the CWAC Division of No.1, S.B.L. from the "men" of the Ordnance Reinforcements Unit.)

"Ah! lovely young Venus, the maid of the tubs,
Combatant in chemical warfare with suds,
The witch of the woolens, distiller of grime,
So adept with the washboard and chloride of lime
Who left all the joys and comforts of home
To envelope herself in a billow of foam.
Your part in this war we have lively concern in,
You keep the troops clean, free from B.O. and vermin,
But is it your plan, in removal of dirt
To return with my laundry a buttonless shirt?
Must the sox that I send, which were once size eleven
Return to my feet a diminutive seven?
I grant I am lucky to see them at all
But my toes are so cramped when I wear them so small.
I regard all my comrades with dubious air
Wondering which one is wearing my best underwear.
The heather-toned sox in exchange for the blues
Are pretty—admitted—but don't match my shoes.
Enough of these groans—in these troublesome days
Your efforts earn nothing but national praise.
Keep up your good work and practice your scrub,
Some day you'll find Hitler adrift in your tub!"
(Anonymous)

[*W. Hugh Conrod*, Athene, Goddess of War: The Canadian Women's Army Corps, Their Story *(Ottawa: Consumer and Corporate Affairs, 1983)*, *p. 146]*

Women in the Military. *[W. Hugh Conrod,* Athene, Goddess of War: The Canadian Women's Army Corps, Their Story *(Ottawa: Consumer and Corporate Affairs, 1983), p. 320]*

The Sense of Accomplishment

Our first route march came after we had been in training for three weeks; we were the first to act as escort for the graduating base squadron. It was a blazing hot day, but our ardour was dampened only by perspiration...When we got under way, we felt that we were squirting like street-sprinkler units. We fell in, feeling very important.

In front of us was the band; behind us was a station wagon to pick up the fallen. The corporal told us later that she held it against us that none of us fainted so that she could get a ride back in the wagon with the casualty.

The streets were crowded in spots with people who cheered or made sassy remarks. There were spatters of applause, but the most touching thing was the sight of old soldiers standing at rigid attention.

Former member, RCAF (WD)

The experience of having been in uniform was very rewarding for a lot of people. They ended up doing all sorts of things that they probably would never have dreamed of before the war... I remember one girl on our station who was an airframe mechanic—one of the very few women in that trade. She passed all her trade tests with flying colours, which irritated some of the men, because they had to try theirs several times before making it... I think her Air Force experience expanded her life in a way that it wouldn't have been otherwise.

Former member, RCAF (WD)

[Carolyn Gossage, Greatcoats and Glamour Boots: Canadian Women at War (1939-1945) *(Toronto: Dundurn Press, 1991), pp. 101, 204)*

Back to Civvy Street

During the war we did everything a man could do except fight, and after it was all over there was a lot of unrest as well as happiness and sadness, all mixed in together. Some women were saying to themselves, "I don't really want to have children. I don't have to be a housewife. I want my own freedom, now, because I've proved that I'm smart as any other person..."

Former member, RCAF (WD)

During the war I felt like I was somebody, I was recognized, and then it was all over and I was nobody again. My family didn't seem to care what I'd done. I was just supposed to forget all that and fit in. It wasn't quite that simple.

Former member, RCAF (WD)

Having shared that experience was like having a language of your own that all of you could understand. I was most conscious of it, I think, just after the war, when I got out of uniform and went to university. It was really hard to connect with my fellow students, who hadn't been through what I had. They were living in a totally different world. I only survived because I was able to spend all my free time with friends from the service...I thought about things differently and reacted to things differently. It's hard to say exactly why this was. All I know is that it was very different. I guess you could call it part of the postwar letdown. Things would never be the same again.

Former member, RCAF (WD)

[Carolyn Gossage, Greatcoats and Glamour Boots: Canadian Women at War (1939-1945) *(Toronto: Dundurn Press, 1991), pp. 197, 204-205]*

1. What type of black markets existed in wartime Canada? What do the reactions to black marketeering reveal about Canadian society?

2. Explain the 'functional principle' and why it was useful for countries like Canada.

3. What were the advantages and disadvantages of Canada's wartime collaboration with the United States?

4. To what extent did World War II alter the status of women?

5. What are the advantages and pitfalls in using oral testimony to assess the ways in which the war affected women's lives?

READINGS

Donald Creighton, *The Forked Road: Canada, 1939-1957* (Toronto: McClelland and Stewart, 1976)

W.A.B. Douglas and Brereton Greenhous, *Out of the Shadows: Canada in the Second World War* (Toronto: Oxford University Press, 1993)

John A. English, *The Canadian Army and the Normandy Campaign: A Study of Failure in High Command* (New York: Praeger, 1991)

J.L. Granatstein, *Canada's War: The Politics of the Mackenzie King Government, 1939-1945* (Toronto: Oxford University Press, 1975)

_____, *The Generals: The Canadian Army's Senior Commanders in the Second World War* (Toronto: Stoddart, 1993)

J.L. Granatstein and Desmond Morton, *A Nation Forged in Fire: Canadians and the Second World War, 1939-1945* (Toronto: Lester & Orpen Dennys, 1989)

Brereton Greenhous et. al., *The Crucible of War, 1939-1945: The Official History of the Royal Canadian Air Force* (Vol. III) (Toronto: University of Toronto Press, 1994)

Norman Hillmer et. al., eds., *On Guard for Thee: War, Ethnicity, and the Canadian State, 1939-1945* (Ottawa: Canadian Committee for the History of the Second World War, 1989)

Laura Sefton MacDowell, *"Remember Kirkland Lake": The History and Effects of the Kirkland Lake Gold Miners' Strike, 1941-42* (Toronto: University of Toronto Press, 1983)

Desmond Morton and J.L. Granatstein, *Victory 1945: Canadians from War to Peace* (Toronto: HarperCollins, 1995)

Ruth Roach Pierson, *"They're Still Women After All": The Second World War and Canadian Womanhood* (Toronto: McClelland and Stewart, 1986)

Patricia Roy et. al., *Mutual Hostages: Canadians and Japanese During the Second World War* (Toronto: University of Toronto Press, 1990)

C.P. Stacey, *Arms, Men and Governments: The War Policies of Canada, 1939-45* (Ottawa: Queen's Printer, 1970)

Ann Gomer Sunahara, *The Politics of Racism: The Uprooting of Japanese Canadians During the Second World War* (Toronto: James Lorimer, 1981)

Brian Loring Villa, *Unauthorized Action: Mountbatten and the Dieppe Raid* (Toronto: Oxford University Press, 1994)

Canada's Postwar Consensus

Following victory over the Axis powers in 1945, and with the economic and political upheavals of the Great Depression and the war fresh in Canada's collective consciousness, most citizens yearned for a sense of security. The initial postwar period provided the basis for optimism, and encouraged a number of shared assumptions that impacted upon politics and society. A spending spree created by the release of pent-up wartime savings, combined with hefty tax breaks to industries to speed up their peacetime reconversion process, produced record output and employment levels. Home construction and purchases boomed; according to popular imagery, practically everyone was moving to suburbia and a coveted middle-class lifestyle. Federal Liberal governments enjoyed considerable popularity as their policies were credited for bringing the 'good life' to most Canadians; until 1957, unemployment remained below 5 percent. Outsiders as well, it seemed, recognized Canada's postwar success story. Referenda in 1948 and 1949 saw a majority of Newfoundlanders leave behind their isolationist tendencies, and seek out the economic benefits and social programs that awaited within the Canadian federation.

Consensus in postwar Canada was built not only upon optimism, but also on the fear and intolerance of Communism—a system seen by most Canadians as being geared toward destroying the liberty and prosperity they connected with capitalism. Thus, Canada's strongly anti-communist foreign policy did not generate significant internal division. Support remained high—including within Catholic Quebec where Communism was loathed because of its official atheism—for Canadian membership in the North Atlantic Treaty Organization (NATO), and for Canadian participation in the 1950-1953 Korean 'police action.' The official line from Ottawa was that through such initiatives, Canada was helping to defend freedom, giving the principle of 'Collective Security' concrete meaning, serving its own economic interests (such as through defence production agreements with the United States), and gaining access to and some influence within important decision-making circles.

As the 1950s wore on, however, dissent was heard. Some Canadians wondered if their country had exchanged colonial status to Great Britain with being a satellite of the United States. In 1951, the federal government, perhaps in part to address such concerns, established a Royal Commission on the Arts, Letters, and Sciences to explore the need of supporting the cultural endeavours of Canadians—an initiative that, six years later, resulted in the creation of the Canada Council. Also, in 1956, the government of Louis St. Laurent found itself under fire for siding with the United States against Britain during the Suez Crisis, and for imposing closure upon parliamentary debate to ensure the speedy passage of additional loans to the American-owned Trans-Canada Pipeline Corporation. The next year, a Royal Commission on Canada's Economic Prospects warned against too much American ownership in Canada; and in part by adopting nationalism as his rallying cry, John Diefenbaker became Canada's first Conservative prime minister in nearly 25 years.

Section A
Anti-Communism in Canada

Canada emerged from World War II having shed isolationism; its leaders talked with considerable confidence about the ability of this new 'middle power' to contribute meaningfully within the international community. However, from the perspective of those such as Reverend James Endicott, head of the Canadian Peace Council, unthinking anti-Communism trapped Canadian foreign policy—a view that, along with Endicott's sympathy for Communist forces in China, resulted in his severance from the United Church. Meanwhile, in Quebec, the government of Maurice Duplessis, with the support of conservative clerics, sought to cleanse universities of 'leftist' professors, as well as to decertify unions that had any communist affiliation. Canada's labour movement, perhaps to prove its loyalty, expelled scores of officials, as well as some unions viewed as too left wing. In this atmosphere, an increasing number of Canadians took political views into account when choosing their friends. As well, many homosexuals moulded their behaviour to reflect so-called heterosexual norms because, if discovered, the politics of the Cold War era often cost them their jobs.

Minister of External Affairs, Louis St. Laurent, on the United Nations

...We must realise also that the effectiveness of the United Nations is at the moment greatly reduced by the divisions which have grown up between the countries of western Europe and the countries of the rest of the world. Until there has been some measure of settlement of the issues that appear to divide the world, we should not expect too much from the United Nations in its present form and organization. No one should expect, for instance, the machinery of the United Nations to produce a solution for problems on which the two most powerful nations of the world may have diametrically opposed views that cannot be reconciled.

During the last two years our faith in the United Nations as an effective organization for peace and security has been pretty shaken. What is unshaken is our determination to make of it, or within it, an effective organization for these purposes. Unshaken also is our faith that this can be achieved. It is therefore important that the United Nations be kept in existence, and that we make every possible use of the very high degree of vitality which, in spite of these divergent opinions, it has shown. There are, for example, subjects such as the dispute in Kashmir...and the difficulties which have arisen in Indonesia, which are not directly within the area of conflict between the eastern European states and the rest of the world, and where the machinery of the United Nations has been used very effectively.

Our willingness to stand for, and our ability to secure, election to the Security Council last September was an earnest expression of our desire to play our full part in the United Nations. That part involves us in discussions and decisions on matters which may have seemed to be remote from our interests. Although we know, as I have already said, that this remoteness is illusory, nevertheless this does not alter the fact that during the next year and a half Canada, as a member of the Security Council, will, at times, have to declare its position publicly on certain matters which previously might not have come to the attention of the government at all, or might have been dealt with confidentially through diplomatic channels.

The position of a power of the middle rank on the Security Council is under any circumstances a difficult one. A small power is in a sense by its very smallness relieved from much of the responsibility which participation in decisions involves, and which the implementation of such decisions requires. At the other extreme the great powers can protect their positions with the veto. A "middle power" such as Canada, however, is in a different position. Its economic strength and political influence are of importance, and its prestige is high. The material and moral contribution which Canada can make to collective action, as the last two wars have shown, is significant. The judgements which the Canadian government express on United Nations matters must therefore be made with care and a sense of responsibility, especially since Canada is a country the views of which are taken seriously and which has the reputation of conscientiously carrying out the commitments into which it has entered.

Canada's position on the Security Council, as a middle power, would be an important one in any circumstance. The special nature of our relationship to the United Kingdom and the United States complicates our responsibilities, though it also enlarges our opportunities for influencing developments. Canada will be expected by some to follow the lead of the United Kingdom; by others to follow the lead of the United States. The fact that these two states are now in general agreement on fundamental questions eases but does not remove our particular difficulties. Unfriendly observers will write us off as a satellite of both, hoping in this way to minimize the effect of our independent action. More objective observers will tend to assume that it will be hard for Canada to follow a policy of its own. The fact that Canadian interests will often naturally be identical with those of the United Kingdom and the United States, without any suggestion or influence from these states, in a sense makes Canada's position more ambiguous. It will not be easy to secure credit for independence and honesty of argument and decision. Nevertheless we will continue to make our decisions objectively, in the light of our obligations to our own people and their interest in the welfare of the international community...

[Canada, House of Commons, Debates, 29 April 1948, pp. 3444-3445]

Minister of External Affairs, Louis St. Laurent, Explains the Basis for the North Atlantic Treaty Organization

...Six weeks ago, speaking in the House of Commons, I said that the free nations, or some of them, might soon find it necessary to consult together on how best to establish a new collective security league under Article 51 of the [U.N.] Charter. I said that Canada should be willing to enter such a league...

Why was it that the proposal met with unanimous support in the House of Commons from members of all political parties? I suggest it is because we, in Canada, are agreed upon the essential bases of our foreign policy.

We are agreed, to begin with, that totalitarian communist aggression constitutes a direct and immediate threat to every democratic country, including Canada. It endangers our freedom and our peace. It puts in jeopardy the values and virtues of the civilization of western Christendom of which we are heirs and defenders.

Secondly, we have come to a common realization of what communist totalitarianism means to the people subjected to its tyranny. We have seen the Bolshevists create in Russia the most omnipotent and pervasive state in history.

We have seen them take over what was the worst feature of the Czarist regime, the secret police, and expand it. The Soviet Government, though proclaimed by communist parties to be the champion of the oppressed, is itself an oppressor on a scale surpassing even Nazi Germany. It has already, in ten countries of Eastern Europe as well as in the Soviet Union itself, suppressed the freedom of millions of men and imposed a police regime upon them. It has demonstrated that the division today is not, as the communists vainly assert, between the forces of reaction with the Fascists on the extreme right and the forces for progress with the Communists on the extreme left. The reactionary parties are those which advocate a police state; and they are reactionary whether they call themselves Nazi, Fascist, or Communist. The parties of progress are those which advocate a free society. The police state, by coercion and regimentation, ultimately makes progress impossible. Only in a free society can there exist a firm foundation for social and spiritual progress. Therefore, the things that divide the democratic parties of the free nations, by whatever names they call themselves, are as nothing compared with the gulf that separates them all from the communists and the regimenting totalitarians.

It is, I suggest, because virtually all the people of Canada have come to realize these things that there are today no fundamental differences between them on questions of foreign policy...

In the interests of the peoples of both worlds—the Communist and the Free—we believe that it must be made clear to the rulers of the totalitarian Communist states that if they attempt by direct or indirect aggression to extend their police states beyond their present bounds by subduing any more free nations, they will not succeed unless they can overcome us all.

The best guarantee of peace today is the creation and preservation by the nations of the Free World, under the leadership of Great Britain, the United States and France, of an overwhelming preponderance of force over any adversary or possible combination of adversaries. This force must not be only military; it must be economic; it must be moral. Just as in the last war, so also today, we are engaged in a "struggle for the control of men's minds and men's souls."

Victory in war requires a pooling of risks and a pooling of resources. Victory over war requires a similar pooling by the Free Nations. Such a pooling cannot take place unless we realize that the giving of aid to an ally is not charity but self-help...

[External Affairs Bulletin, July 1948, p.7]

Dissent from the Toronto Peace Conference: The Words of James G. Endicott

... Just two days ago a Toronto paper carried a huge black headline which said Canada had entered into a "war pledge," whatever that may mean. How does it come about that we have wandered so far from the paths of peace?...

During the [Second World] War we made statements of faith and purpose which were an elaboration of the commonly held ethical values of men. A necessary part of every man's religion has been a desire for a more brotherly spirit and a better social integration of our common life. During the war this religious spirit was given expression in the Atlantic Charter, the declaration of the Four Freedoms, the United Nations Relief and Rehabilitation Association, and finally in the United Nations Organization which had as its purpose the gradual working out of such international cooperation as would not only take care of serious disputes, but would also bring about a state of cooperation so that no disputes could lead to war...

We pledged ourselves to freedom from want for everyone, which, translated into world terms, means economic understandings which will secure to every nation a healthy peacetime life for its inhabitants, everywhere in the world.

Freedom from fear, which means a world-wide reduction of armaments to such a point and in such a thorough fashion that no nation will be in a position to commit an act of physical aggression against any neighbour, anywhere in the world...

There is no room here for wars against ideologies... When we recall these statements, and a host of other documents of similar content, we are justified in saying that the people expected of their government that it would take all measures for peace based on the principle of collaboration and the settlement of all disputes by negotiation...

It would be folly, however, to shut our eyes to the fact that the chances for maintaining peace have deteriorated since 1945, when we were supposed to get on with the job of building the peace. All signs point to preparations for conflict. The Canadian people are being taught that between the Western powers and Russia there is no opportunity for peaceful settlements of disputes. The desire of the ordinary citizen for peace at home and no interference in the affairs of other people is being sapped by a tremendous press propaganda which is sustained by half truths, innuendos, distortions and scarcely hidden ulterior motives...

Last year when the U.S. Navy was wanting a greatly increased grant of money, a rumour about Russian submarines was floated. Nearly every large newspaper in the U.S. carried big scare headlines. A more disgustingly untruthful exhibition has scarcely ever been offered the public. It was so gross that the *Christian Science Monitor* rebuked the press with a full page reproduction of the various headlines.

Reaction to Endicott. *[Canadian Forum, June 1952, p. 53]*

But the public was left with the idea of war and with the residue of fright. Last week the Chinese democratic revolutionary forces were coming near to the final kicking out of Chiang-Kai-shek and his oppressive and corrupt military dictatorship. Government of the people, by the people and for the people is coming to China. Immediately a red scare is conjured up and big headlines appear about a survey to defend the British Columbia coast from Chinese attack...

It is being charged in high places that those who advocate peace as we are doing are subversive. It may well be that history will prove that those at this critical stage [who] fought for peace were the real lovers of the people of Canada. I do not know of any reasonable military man who thinks Canada is in danger of being attacked, either soon or in the foreseeable future. There is a danger, however, that Canadian boys may be sent to Asia to suppress legitimate movements of the people for reform...

The most patriotic citizen today is he who tries to make his country play an honourable and useful part in the United Nations and within the frame-work of the United Nations and the Atlantic Charter. Let us boldly proclaim that advocating peace, today, on this basis, is the highest form of patriotic activity...

It is because of the ruin that will be visited on us that we should now refuse to commit ourselves without reservations to any attempt by the United States to settle differences by preventative wars instead of by debate and compromise in the United Nations. But we are already committed by our government, perhaps even by secret order in council...whether we like it or not. We should seek to change this condition...

It cannot be denied that there are powerful groups who deliberately foster war scares in order to get armament orders for the purpose of keeping up high profits. Last week's *U.S. News* stated quite frankly,

> All apparently is not well with business at the moment. The boom is losing some of its zip... Armaments might easily be increased by $20,000,000...

It is a fact of much significance to me that none of the big businessmen of Canada are out campaigning for peace at this time. They are open to the charge that we are now so subservient to American foreign policy that we have become dependent on war scares, deliberately fostered, to keep up our prosperity. In that case, what we are enjoying is a false prosperity and it will lead us to disaster...

[United Church Archives, James G. Endicott papers, 3807, Box 1, File 3, Address, 3 December 1948]

Internal Purges by Labour
65ᵗʰ Convention Liquidates Communism

Montreal is a unique city in our own country, and in the world. It is bi-lingual, and, I might say, bi-focal. You look out from this great port along the water-borne trade lane of the St. Lawrence eastward to a world full of vast possibilities, yet gripped with troubles and threatened with aggression. To the west you look towards a tremendous continent teeming with resources and almost unlimited opportunities, yet forced to turn its energies from normal pursuits to the preparation of defensive works against the possibility of attack from a new and unprincipled totalitarianism all too obviously intent upon dominating the world and the destruction of our free institutions.

It is in this atmosphere, and with these unfortunate facts before it, that this Convention—this Parliament of Labor—will face the issues before it during the next five and a half days. We are well situated here in Montreal to make up our minds and render our decisions with due caution and yet with complete confidence and determination.

It is the job of this Parliament of Labor—a job which it cannot gloss over, shirk, or evade—to resolve the problems in which we and the whole free world finds itself. We want peace. Working people everywhere want peace. But we shall not accept peace at any price. We will not accept peace at the price of domination and enslavement.

If we are to have peace—enduring peace—we must create a basis on which peace is possible. If we are to stop Communism, we must encourage people in our country and in other countries to believe our tried and proven ways of governing, living and working are better. I have no hesitation in saying that we can do that. We know that our free trade unions are better than a union dominated by the state, in the same way, as we know from experience that our free unions are better than a union dominated by the employer. It is not possible to have a free trade union when the state becomes the only employer. We know that the social and economic improvements gained in Canada are the result of our direct efforts, or, in some cases at least, of our inspiration. We know that we can do more along those lines.

As a result of efforts made after we last met in Convention, we are to-day joined with free trade unionists in fifty-two other countries in a great organization, the International Confederation of Free Trade Unions, comprising a membership of more than fifty millions. We have been associated with the International Labor Organization since its inception over thirty years ago. Both of these great organizations, which serve our working people throughout the world, have direct and consultative relations with the United Nations. As trade unionists we are thus in a good position to influence the trend of world affairs. As trade unionists we can make constructive efforts towards building a political, social and economic framework in this old world upon which enduring peace can grow and flourish.

However, we shall have to do more than improve the living and working standards of people throughout the world. We shall have at the present time, due to the prevailing international situation, to increase our defence preparations both at home and abroad. As working people these defensive measures that must he taken in accordance with our commitments to the United Nations and under the North Atlantic Treaty will weigh in double measure upon us. We shall have, as usual, to put up the lion's share of the money to pay for them, and we shall have to do the work of producing them. But we shall go about this task with light hearts and calm, cool heads, knowing that it is our living and working standards, the social and economic objectives we have set for ourselves, that we are protecting.

To say, to-day, that we are opposed to Communism, is by itself, not enough. We must be active and effective in our opposition. We must recognize—and this is most important within our own trade union ranks—that the government of Soviet Russia grew out of the Communist Party. That is true. But any control over that government by the Communist Party has been destroyed. Russia is ruled by a dictatorship. The satellite countries are under the domination of that dictatorship. The government of North Korea is a puppet of that dictatorship. The people in our unions who follow what is still called the 'Communist Line' are but the dupes of that dictatorship. They are the dupes of a dictatorship more deceitful, yet better organized, better trained, and better armed than any other in all history.

Our Navy and Air Force are fighting with the United Nations against the attacking North Korean armies in South Korea. Let us not mince words any longer. We are fighting Stalin's puppet government of North Korea. We are fighting Stalin's Russian Soviet dictatorship in South Korea. We must fight its willing dupes right here at home, and most particularly, it is our job to expose them and destroy their influence inside our own trade unions...

Amendments to Constitution

... the Committee on Constitution and Law, under the Chairmanship of Brother Marcel Francq, introduced Constitutional amendments which provided that "no organization officered or controlled by Communists or members of the Labor-Progressive Party or any person espousing Communism or advocating the violent overthrow of our institutions shall be allowed representation or recognition in this Congress or any organization chartered by it." Another amendment provided that any person who is a member of the Communist Party or Labor-Progressive Party or any other named subversive organization would be ineligible as a delegate to Conventions of Congress. These amendments carried with but few dissenting votes.

[Trades and Labor Congress Journal, October 1950, pp. 11-12, 15]

Proposed Labour Legislation in Quebec

Section 16. Notwithstanding any legislative provisions to the contrary, no person can be an officer or representative of an association of employers or of employees,

a. If he is a member of a communist or marxist organization or movement, or of a party recognized as such, whatever be its title or name;

b. If he supports such organization, movement or party, or cooperates, in any manner whatsoever, with them in the pursuit of their ends.

Section 17. Any association of employees or of employers which counts among its officers or representatives one or more of the persons who come under article 16, or which is affiliated with an association which counts among its officers or representatives one or more of the persons who come under article 16, or which is affiliated with a syndicate organization which is notoriously under the direction or influence of followers of the communist or marxist doctrine, cannot be certified by the Labour Relations Board as the collective representative of employees or of employers with respect to a collective agreement, a conciliation, an arbitration, a dispute, or for any other purpose mentioned in this Code.

If such an association has been certified, through error or for any other cause, contrary to the provisions of this article, such association must expel from its ranks any officer or representative who comes under article 16, and in default of its doing so, the Labour Relations Board shall cancel its certification.

[Trades and Labor Congress Journal, February 1949, p. 5]

Guilt by Association

Writer sees danger of a Communist witch-hunt in Canada. Will an old boyhood friendship take on a new sinister light? Should he—and other Canadians—denounce such friendships now?

About the time I finished high school in Winnipeg I met a boy three months younger than I who became my best friend of that time. When my family left Winnipeg, his mother, a widow, took me in and treated me as if I were her son. We shared a room. We both wanted to be writers. He had his father's typewriter and I bought one…and we sat on the edges of our twin beds at night and wrote.

One time when we had a double date for a Saturday night, but no money, he wrote four poems and sold them to the Winnipeg *Free Press* for $1.50 each and the $6 paid the freight for both of us. No friendship can last into manhood with quite that boyish intensity, but if I had to name my five best friends over the last fifteen years, he would be one of them.

But the question I would like to put to the Government of Canada is this: How should I treat my friend next time that he has become a Communist?…

In the U.S., people like me have been dragged into public investigations, smeared, ruined, for friendships, acts, and associations in the past which were reasonably popular and certainly legal at the time. At a certain stage in each country's anti-Communist purges it seems there is no defence against past association with Communists. I think it is normal to consider the possibility that it could happen to us too…

Because I'm worried for all of us, I ask the government… 'What should I do? What should we do?'…I think that there is a way in which our Government could allay permanently the fears of people like me who wish freedom but feel that by clinging to our conception of full freedom, we may be making ourselves candidates for treason…This would be for the Government to advise the people of Canada that, as of a certain time, associating with Communists might some time in the future require an explanation.

Such advice would have the effect of telling us that the past is the past and that if we gave money to the Spanish Republicans in 1936, or were too vigorous in support of Aid to Russia in 1944, or went fishing with a Communist in 1950, we are forgiven our trespasses. The Government would say to us: 'The line is drawn as of November 15, 1951. From now on, although associating with Communists is still legal enough you will have to give good reason for such association after this date if we ever go to war with a Communist country'…

Naturally there is sadness in this, as there must be in any suspension of freedom. But it would be easier to be a little sad now than very sad later. And once the Government spoke, any man who ignored the advice, and later had to answer for his actions, at least would have no reason to cry out that he was merely the victim of his old-fashioned belief in freedom. The people who have chosen to treat the difference between Communism and the West as the same sort of conflict which exists between the CCF and the Conservatives would be obliged to stop kidding themselves. And those of us who have tried to convince ourselves that the Communist-West conflict can be kept outside of personal friendships would have to recognize the reality that we are obsolete.

By writing this, I have in effect made my own choice to sever relations with my Communist friend. He can read, and he'll read this, and that will be the end of my own particular problem...

[Saturday Night, *10 November 1951, pp. 11, 22-24. Written by Scott Young*]

Searching for Security Risks: The Case of Canadian Homosexuals

This paper has reference to Security Panel document SP-199 dated May 12, 1959, particularly to the conclusion wherein it is recognized that homosexuality constitutes a security threat, that certain homosexual characteristics—instability, willing self-deceit, defiance towards society and a tendency to surround himself with other homosexuals—do not inspire confidence, and that information obtained on homosexuals is often limited. Its purpose is to provide information on homosexuality obtained through recent investigations, to set out some of the problems encountered and anticipated in our investigations and to make certain recommendations regarding future investigations...

Investigation over the past year has brought certain results and problems which, it is felt, could not have been fully anticipated when the subject of homosexuality was discussed by the members of the Security Panel and Security Panel Directive #199 was drawn up. Firstly, our investigation to date which was limited because of its selectivity has revealed the names of over 700 proven, suspected or alleged homosexuals across Canada. More than 300 of these are, or were recently, residing in the Ottawa area where the investigation was concentrated. Of the 700 more than half are, or were recently, employed in federal government service. The investigation of necessity went beyond the government service in order that the most complete picture possible might be obtained. However, it is apparent that only a portion of the total number has come to light thus far.

While we have no concrete evidence upon which to estimate the total number of homosexuals who are employed by the government in relation to the total number in the Ottawa area we have found that each new source of information has revealed additional names. One source, a self-confessed homosexual residing in Ottawa has suggested there are at least 3000 homosexuals in this area alone. We have no way of confirming this figure, or of saying it is not in line with the facts.

In order that the meaning of our figures not be misinterpreted it must be explained that because a person has come to attention in this connection it does not mean that he is, in fact, a homosexual. It does mean, however, that further investigation is required if the matter is to be satisfactorily resolved.

The second point for consideration concerns our sources of information. Our files reflect fairly conclusively that general security screening enquiries, carried out in accordance with existing policies rarely uncover evidence of homosexuality. The investigation of charges or suspicions of homosexuality usually develops on opinions or knowledge expressed by friends and acquaintances, usually homosexual, of the person concerned.

The information is sometimes based on an intimate relationship but more often on mannerisms, appearance, conversation, association and, to a lesser extent from an evidence standpoint, a frequenting of places where these people gather ranging from taverns to resort areas. Because the information is usually not conclusive, corroboration is imperative lest an injustice be done either through an error in judgment or through motivation by spite or jealousy. In nearly all cases on record the information and corroboration was obtained from homosexuals...

Considered from the investigation viewpoint, the characteristics of the problem under investigation are such that we have to rely on the information or evidence of the homosexuals themselves. In fact, their individual co-operation is essential to the success of this investigation. To illustrate, if an allegation is made that a person is a homosexual, in the absence of an admission by the person so alleged corroboration must be obtained from a homosexual who knows the person concerned if any credence is to be placed in the allegation...

In addition to the reasons mentioned in the preceding paragraphs there are other grounds which we feel support this recommendation. There is no better way to dispose of an accusation of homosexuality than to interview the person accused. In the absence of an interview, particularly in doubtful cases, there is no alternative but to keep the information on file and thereby maintain the doubt. If interviewed however, in addition to allowing the person concerned an opportunity to deny the allegation or admit its truth it also makes him aware that the weakness is known to the security authorities which, in itself, serves a useful purpose by reducing the danger of compromise by blackmail, even though it may disclose the reason for departmental action at a later date...

Although there are divergent views on the degree of risk involved, it is generally accepted that homosexuality within the government service is a security risk because of the potential for compromise by a foreign intelligence service through the threat of exposure. While the risk is most acute when a homosexual is employed on duties requiring access to classified material there is a reduced danger represented by those homosexuals who may not in the course of their present duties have access to classified material but who, through normal advancement, may be expected to require access at some future date. Additionally, since neither the bonds of friendship nor of homosexual liaison are dependent on employment there is a danger present in the normal, friendly relationship between two government employees when one is a homosexual and in a homosexual relationship between a government employee and a non-government employee. An instance of the latter came to light recently where a homosexual government employee, with access to classified material, displayed a considerable lack of security concerning his work during the course of his close association with his homosexual friend who was not a government employee.

There is evidence at hand that the Soviet Intelligence Service, through threat of exposure of homosexual practices, compromised a Canadian government employee...Their plan failed only because the person concerned was imbued with a strong sense of loyalty to his country and immediately confessed to his superiors. This was most fortunate, as otherwise the Soviets would have been successful in obtaining a well-placed source of information within a Canadian service at an important level in terms of access to highly classified material. There may have been other similar attempts that have been successful and about which nothing is known...

[NAC, RG 73, Solicitor General Records, Vol. 13, File 117-92-8, Report to the Royal Canadian Mounted Police Commissioner on Homosexuality Within the Federal Government Service, 29 April 1960]

Detecting Homosexuality

...Although serious efforts continue to be made toward understanding the homosexual in Western society, progress is impeded by the recurring stereotypes of the homosexual. He is thought to be 'unstable', 'abnormal', 'incurable', 'a seducer of children', and the possessor of many other undesirable traits. While one or all of these descriptions do apply to some homosexuals, like all stereotypes they tend to reduce a complexity to a vague, inaccurate simplicity. There is a large and growing body of respectable opinion, based on scientific research, which holds that the development of homosexuality is not a matter of heredity or of the individual's perverse choice, but in the great majority of cases is rather the result of a combination of environmental circumstances during the years of childhood or early youth...

For reasons that are not clear, the general populace has assumed, and scientists have pursued, the myth that there is a 'type', a 'personality' called homosexual. Pragmatically, if homosexuals were discovered to fit such a pigeonhole, it would be possible to recognize them easily and deal with them uniformly. If it were desirable, they could be set apart in some fashion from those with heterosexual interests.

Currently, social scientists, the medical profession and others are adopting the view that there is as much variety of personality within homosexuals as within heterosexuals. Further, there is a continuous shading from the most extreme homosexual through lesser degrees to bisexuals to the most confirmed heterosexuals...

A great deal of research has been pursued, particularly by mental health scientists, to find a way (or ways) of detecting homosexuality so that patients, job applicants, and so on, may be handled more adequately. While no single test or combination of tests yet has proven entirely successful...some show considerable promise and one, when used in a special way, appears very valuable indeed...

Hess and Polt (1960), University of Chicago, reported an experiment where different interest patterns were uncovered by use of a machine which simultaneously projected a visual stimulus and photographed the pupil of the subject's eye...

The experiment was as follows: The subject placed his eye at the level of an opening in a box. The opening was surrounded by foam rubber...The subject first saw a slide consisting of a grey background with five white numbered dots...

The subject was instructed to look at the slide, follow the numbers in order and finally focus on 5 [situated in the middle of the screen]...The subject was then shown a series of five pictures (mother and child, pastoral scene, animals, Greek athlete, female near-nude from *Playboy* magazine), each stimulus lasting for 10 seconds during which a movie camera took a picture of the subject's pupil at 1/2 second intervals (20 exposures).

Adult males and females were used as subjects and it was found that the pupils of the female subjects (as a group) enlarged at the pictures of mother-and-child and athlete, decreasing at the pastoral scene and *Playboy* picture. Male respondents were roughly the reverse.

The results strongly suggest that the interest patterns of individuals can be detected by means of a response that cannot be controlled by the subject...

Here, then, is a most promising instrument for detection, not only of homosexuals but of homosexual potentiality. Conceivably, with suitable changes in stimuli, it could also be used to detect alcoholism and other 'frailties'...

[NAC, RG 73, Solicitor General Records, Vol. 13, File 117-92-8, Report on the Special Project by Dr. F.R. Wake, 19 December 1962]

Section B
Social Conformity

The dominant view of the initial postwar period is that, following years of strain and commotion, life quickly settled down into a more conservative order—based in large part upon widespread confidence in a buoyant economy and an acceptance of strictly defined gender roles. Reflecting this was Canada's baby boom. Between 1940 and 1960, fertility rates for women aged 20 to 24 increased by some 80 percent to 233.5 children per 1000. Popular imagery projected the happy stay-at-home suburban housewife with time for

Suburban Toronto in the Late 1950s. *[National Archives of Canada, PA129292]*

her children. Mass, and relatively uniform, home construction on cheaper suburban land provided affordable accommodation. But there were many women who desired more than the supposed paradise of suburbia. Despite images of pervasive postwar domesticity, many women took paid employment. Certainly, gender-based barriers persisted in the postwar employment market; and job ghettoes remained prevalent—as did unequal pay between the sexes for performing the same job. Even Ellen Fairclough, Canada's first female federal cabinet minister, stressed that gender stereotypes impacted significantly upon her career.

Life in a Suburban Toronto Community

...At about the time when the male is ready to launch his career, he seeks a life partner, a woman who will assume the traditional responsibilities of helpmate, *confidante*, companion, and mother of his children. He marries a girl who occupies about the same position in the class structure as himself. She is about as well educated as he is. Even when prosperous economic conditions make an early marriage a not too imprudent venture, the girl will he old enough and well enough educated to have a job, or be capable of securing one. However, marriages are more often prudently delayed until sufficient capital has been accumulated to make the establishment of a household a substantial venture, and a safe one for both contracting parties. Upon marriage, the woman takes charge of the home. When children come, they are her main responsibility. It was exceedingly difficult to find women in Crestwood Heights who had continued their vocations past motherhood. After marriage, the claims of the husband and, later, of the children on the woman's time and energy are so dominant that she must abandon her aspirations towards a career; often she may do this with reluctance, hoping to return to them later, only to find, in the fullness of time, that this is not to be. The role of wife and mother in these circumstances lacks many of the satisfactions commonly associated with it in a more stable rural type of society, even though the biological and emotional fulfilments it provides are still powerful.

Many a mother in Crestwood Heights stated somewhat ruefully that motherhood had "cut short" her career. She was unlikely to think of motherhood itself as a career, even though she felt that she was doing a good job as wife and mother. If questioned directly, she would aver that motherhood *was* a career, but she would omit mention of housekeeping, unless closely questioned as to her attitude towards it. Then, although she might not dismiss housekeeping as plain drudgery and lament the lack of domestic help, she would nevertheless qualify her acceptance of housekeeping by linking it to other ends: child-rearing, making her husband happy, or her interest in entertaining...

[John R. Seeley, R. Alexander Sim, and Elizabeth W. Loosley, Crestwood Heights: A Study of the Culture of Suburban Life, *(New York: Basic Books, 1956), pp. 139-140]*

Marital Status of Females with Jobs, 1946 to 1960

(thousands)

Year	Total	Single	Married	Other
1960	1,590	703	716	171
1959	1,491	661	671	159
1958	1,434	661	616	157
1957	1,398	681	569	148
1956	1,301	657	509	135
1955	1,227	648	451	128
1954	1,181	640	426	115
1953	1,174	667	392	115
1952	1,180	684	385	111
1951	1,162	684	370	108
1950	1,112	676	328	108
1949	1,099	672	321	106
1948	1,074	655	317	102
1947	1,069	670	299	100
1946	1,089	687	314	88

[K.A.H. Buckley and M.C. Urquhart, Historical Statistics on Canada *(Toronto: Macmillan, 1965), series C191-194]*

Women in Politics

Since I was a woman—the only woman in an all male House in 1950 —my path had special hurdles. Parliamentary reporter James Roe captured something of the flavour of the day for me when he filed this story which appeared in the *Ottawa Citizen*:

The ceremony started in an impressive manner. Mrs. Fairclough, dressed in a trim suit decorated with three red carnations, waited in the gloom outside the oaken doors of the House where she was met by Opposition leader George Drew and Frank Lennard (PC-Wentworth).

The two men then escorted her slowly up the floor of the House, and paused at the foot of the House table before the Speaker. The only woman member was claiming the right to take her seat—granted affably by Speaker [Ross] Macdonald.

After a moment of confusion, Mrs. Fairclough took her seat, vacated by Mr. Lennard and the House rang with applause. Mr. Lennard gallantly retired to the back bench.

But over the clatter of hands and desks came the raucous tones of Kissing George's [Cruikshank] voice: 'Boy! I could kiss that!' The member for Fraser

Valley rushed to the lady's side and planted a decorous but genial kiss on her left cheek.

When Mrs. Fairclough regained her composure, she was welcomed by the Prime Minister who crossed the floor. Then came George Drew and the CCF leader M.J. Coldwell and Labor Minister Humphrey Mitchell, an old Hamiltonian himself.

Mrs. Fairclough will have a single office, the privilege of a lady MP.

In the House she will add a dash of color to the business suits and quiet Conservative ties of her Parliamentary neighbors.

Especially warm will be the new member's welcome by Senator Iva Fallis, who until today had no Progressive Conservative feminine support in the PC caucus this session...

From the moment I entered the House most media gurus were more interested in my personal life and what I wore than in my political views. I made it clear to anyone who asked that both Gordon and Howard [her husband and son] were supportive of my activities and, with the help of a housekeeper, were able to look after themselves. They were, after all, adults. During my campaigns they worked tirelessly on my behalf. Gordon and Howard both did door-to-door canvasses and worked the bars and clubs where a woman's presence was forbidden. Fairclough Printing produced most of my campaign posters and literature. Whenever I needed a pianist to help with campaign rallies, Howard was invariably on hand.

As for my wardrobe, I stuck to business suits and hats for my daily activities, but I chose bright colours (often red or blue) and soft lines to minimize the jarring effect of being the only woman in so many gatherings. Many men became twitchy in the presence of women, so I felt obliged to put them at their ease by looking as feminine as possible. Above all, I wanted to be comfortable. As I told reporter Helen Allen shortly after entering the House, 'You can never do your best work if you don't feel comfortable in your clothes'...

Early in my career as a cabinet minister, the top brass of Toronto-Dominion Bank, as was their custom, hosted a luncheon for the cabinet at the Rideau Club in Ottawa. Since there had never been a woman in the cabinet, the fact that the Rideau Club was closed to women had posed no problems for earlier celebrations. I did not, as has sometimes been claimed, even try to get into the luncheon. I just wrote a little note thanking them for the invitation but saying that, for obvious reasons, I would be unable to attend. When our hosts realized the implications of their choice of venue, they sent enough flowers to my room in the Château Laurier to dignify a state funeral.

Only once did the fact that I was a woman cause me to be excluded from cabinet deliberations. The death penalty was still occasionally imposed, and appeals were made directly to cabinet. As it turned out, the last such case was that of Stephen Truscott, who had been convicted of a murderous sexual assault. When the case came before cabinet, the documents included a number of graphic photographs of the deceased. Diefenbaker turned to me and said, 'Now Ellen, this is a matter we have to discuss and I suggest you leave.' I did so willingly—not in tears, as some have claimed—because I was requested to do so by the Prime Minister of Canada. However, I could see no reason, other than the discomfort of the men, as to why I should be excluded. The incident was more amusing than annoying and revealed a rather old-fashioned side to Diefenbaker's personality...

[Ellen Louks Fairclough, Saturday's Child: Memoirs of Canada's First Female Cabinet Minister *(Toronto: University of Toronto Press, 1995), pp. 73-74, 85, 158-159]*

QUESTIONS

1. Why did Canada come to criticize the United Nations and opt for membership in NATO?
2. How did anti-Communism affect Canada's union movement?
3. Why were homosexuals targeted by the government during the Cold War? How were they detected?
4. What feelings were expressed by women in Crestwood Heights?
5. In what ways did gender stereotyping effect Ellen Fairclough?

READINGS

Irving Abella, *Nationalism, Communism and Canadian Labour: The CIO, the Communist Party and Canadian Labour* (Toronto: University of Toronto Press, 1973)

Robert Bothwell, Ian Drummond, and John English, *Canada Since 1945: Politics, Power, and Provincialism* 2nd edition (Toronto: University of Toronto Press, 1989)

J.L. Granatstein and Robert Cuff, *American Dollars/ Canadian Prosperity: Canadian-American Economic Relations, 1945-50* (Toronto: Samuel Stevens Hakkert, 1978)

J.L. Granatstein and David Stafford, *Spy Wars: Espionage in Canada from Gouzenko to Glasnost* (Toronto: Key Porter, 1990)

John Holmes, *The Shaping of Peace: Canada and the Search for World Order, 1943-1957* 2 vols. (Toronto: University of Toronto Press, 1979, 1982)

Paul Litt, *The Muses, the Masses, and the Massey Commission* (Toronto: University of Toronto Press, 1992)

B.W. Muirhead, *The Development of Postwar Canadian Trade Policy: The Failure of the Anglo-European Option* (Montreal/Kingston: McGill-Queen's University Press, 1992)

Daniel J. Robinson and David Kimmel, "The Queer Career of Homosexual Security Vetting in Cold War Canada," in *Canadian Historical Review* Vol. 75, No. 3 (September, 1994), pp. 319-345

Joan Sangster, *Dreams of Equality: Women on the Canadian Left, 1920-1950* (Toronto: McClelland and Stewart, 1989)

Denis Smith, *Diplomacy of Fear: Canada and the Cold War, 1941-1948* (Toronto: University of Toronto Press, 1988)

Denis Stairs, *The Diplomacy of Constraint: Canada, the Korean War, and the United States* (Toronto: University of Toronto Press, 1974)

Veronica Strong-Boag, "Home Dreams and the Suburban Experiment in Canada, 1945-60," in *Canadian Historical Review* Vol. 72, No. 4 (December, 1991), pp. 471-504

—————————, "Canada's Wage-earning Wives and the Construction of the Middle-Class, 1945-60," in *Journal of Canadian Studies* Vol. 29, No. 3 (Fall, 1994), pp. 5-25

Shirley Tillotson, "Human Rights Law as Prism: Women's Organizations, Unions, and Ontario's Female Employees Fair Remuneration Act, 1951," in *Canadian Historical Review* Vol. 72, No. 4 (December, 1991), pp. 532-557

Immigration and the adoption of a formal policy of multiculturalism have shaped contemporary Canada. The issues they raise touch upon
every aspect of Canadian society—from cultural and social issues, to current economic and political debates. Immigration and multiculturalism are
also at the heart of the questions that surround Canadian 'identity,' as they
have challenged notions of a Canada based on two founding peoples.

In 1945, Canada had not experienced significant levels of immigration
since the 1920s, as population movement was interrupted by both the Great
Depression and World War II. The issue of renewed postwar immigration
was a contentious one, as Canadians feared a return to pre-war depressed
economic conditions. The first postwar immigrants to arrive in Canada
were war brides who had married Canadian soldiers overseas, and displaced persons, commonly referred to as DPs (deepees), whom we would
now recognize as refugees. By 1947, and continuing in dramatically
increasing numbers during the 1950s, the push of economic privation in
postwar Europe and the pull of North American prosperity encouraged
massive immigration. Between 1947 and 1960, over 2 million 'New
Canadians' made their homes in Canada, becoming part of a total population that rose from 12.5 to 17.8 million. The numbers in any given year did
not reach the heights of pre-World War I immigration, but the immigrants
of the 1950s represented a wider variety of ethnic origins than those of earlier years. Yet immigrants remained primarily British, and almost completely European. Immigration reforms in the 1960s removed the most
restrictive barriers to non-Europeans, and by 1987, Europeans accounted
for only 25 percent of all immigrants.

Immigrants to Canada since 1945 have not been equally dispersed
across the country. Most have chosen to live in an urban environment, and
entire regions—such as Atlantic Canada and Quebec outside of Montreal—
have seen few immigrants. By 1991, 31 percent of all Canadians claimed

no connection to either French or British origins, and 16 percent of all Canadians were born outside the country. In multi-ethnic cities such as Toronto and Vancouver, this number composes nearly 40 percent of the population.

Section A

Postwar Immigration Policy

Postwar immigration policy was based on Prime Minister W. L. M. King's phrase of 'absorptive capacity,' a concept which referred to the Canadian economy's ability to incorporate the labour of 'New Canadians,' and to their ability to adapt and assimilate into life in Canada. Cold War policies were reflected in the support the Canadian government offered Hungarian immigrants after the failed 1956 revolution, and the suspicion which greeted many East European Jews because of possible leftist politics. Despite an increased awareness of human rights concerns—proved by Canada's signature on the 1948 United Nations Declaration of Human Rights—and the slow evolution of Canadians into a more tolerant society, immigration policy virtually excluded all non-European immigrants before 1967.

The 1960s brought about important shifts in government policy as the *Immigration Act*, which had generally restricted entry to white Europeans, was revised to become non-discriminatory. The expansion of the pool of potential immigrants to include Asians, Africans, Latin Americans, and people from the Caribbean was reflected almost immediately in immigration patterns. Government policy continued to be driven by economic goals and to favour educated and skilled workers.

In 1963, the Royal Commission on Bilingualism and Biculturalism (Laurendeau-Dunton Commission) was appointed to investigate the status of Canada's two founding peoples. Its findings resulted in the adoption of bilingualism, in the *Official Languages Act* of 1969, and recognition that many Canadians did not belong to a model of society based on only French and English. In 1972, Prime Minister Pierre Trudeau introduced an official policy of multiculturalism. This policy was, and continues to be, contentious in many parts of Canada such as Quebec, where bringing new immigrants into a francophone environment is seen as essential to preserving the French language. In 1982, multiculturalism was enshrined in the Constitution, and its significance was further elaborated upon in the 1988 *Canadian Multiculturalism Act*.

Prime Minister King and 'Absorptive Capacity'

Because of the limitations of transport, the government decided that, as respects immigration from Europe, the emphasis for the present should be on the admission of the relatives of persons who are already in Canada, and on assisting in the resettlement of displaced persons and refugees.

Up until the end of the war and since—under order in council P.C. 695 of March 21, 1931— four broad categories of persons were admissible to Canada. These were:

1. British subjects from the United Kingdom, Ireland, Newfoundland, New Zealand, Australia or the Union of South Africa, who possessed sufficient means to maintain themselves until employment was secured.

2. United States citizens, similarly possessed of means of maintenance.

3. Wives, unmarried children under 18, or fiancees of men resident in Canada.

4. Agriculturists with sufficient means to farm in Canada.

During the 1930s, due to the adverse economic conditions of the period, these provisions were necessarily interpreted in a restrictive manner. Because of improved economic conditions, it is now possible to interpret them broadly...

Canada is not obliged, as a result of membership in the United Nations or under the constitution of the International Refugee Organization, to accept any specific number of refugees or displaced persons. We have, nevertheless, a moral obligation to assist in meeting the problem, and this obligation we are prepared to recognize.

The government is sending immigration officers to examine the situation among the refugee groups, and to take steps looking towards the early admission of some thousands of their number. In developing this group movement, the Immigration Branch and the Department of Labour will determine jointly the approximate number of persons who can be readily placed in employment and absorbed into various industries and occupations. Selection officers will then consider applicants for entry into Canada, examine them on a basis of suitability and physical fitness, and make arrangements for their orderly movement and placement. Persons so admitted will, of course, be included in whatever quota Canada finally accepts as its share in meeting the general problem...

Let me now speak of the government's long term programme. It is based on the conviction that Canada needs population...

The population of Canada at present is about 12,000,000. By 1951, in the absence of immigration, it is estimated that our population would be less than 13,000,000 and that by 1971 without immigration, the population would be approximately 14,600,000. Apart from all else, in a world of shrinking distances and international insecurity, we cannot ignore the danger that lies in a small population attempting to hold so great a heritage as ours.

The fear has been expressed that immigration would lead to a reduction in the standard of living. This need not be the case. If immigration is properly planned, the result will be the reverse. A larger population will help to develop our resources. By providing a larger number of consumers, in other words a larger domestic market, it will reduce the present dependence of Canada on the export of primary products.

It is of the utmost importance to relate immigration to absorptive capacity. In the past, Canada has received many millions of immigrants, but at the same time many millions of people have emigrated. Of the latter, a large proportion were young people born Canada, and others who had benefited by education or training received in Canada. The objective of the government is to secure what new population we can absorb, but not to exceed that number. The figure that represents our absorptive capacity will clearly vary from year to year in response to economic conditions...

With regard to the selection of immigrants, much has been said about discrimination. I wish to make it quite clear that Canada is perfectly within her rights in selecting the persons whom we regard as desirable future citizens. It is not a "fundamental human right" of any alien to enter Canada. It is a privilege. It is a matter of domestic policy. Immigration is subject to the control of the parliament of Canada. This does not mean, however, that we should not seek to remove from our legislation what may appear to be objectionable discrimination.

One of the features of our legislation to which strong objection has been taken on the ground of discrimination is the Chinese Immigration Act. This act seems to place persons from one particular country in an inferior category. The government has already initiated action for the repeal of that statute. Chinese residents of Canada who are not already Canadian citizens may now be naturalized. Once naturalized, they are permitted to bring their wives and unmarried children under 18 to join them in this country.

The East Indians legally resident in Canada are British subjects who have resided here for many years. They are therefore Canadian citizens. As such, their wives and unmarried children under 18 are admissible.

With regard to the Japanese, I stated, on August 4, 1944, at which time we were at war with Japan, that the government felt that in the years after the war the immigration of Japanese should not be permitted. This is the present view and policy of the government. It will be for future parliaments to consider what change, if any, should be made in this policy.

There will, I am sure, be general agreement with the view that the people of Canada do not wish, as a result of mass immigration, to make a fundamental alteration in the character of our population. Large-scale immigration from the Orient would change the fundamental composition of the Canadian population. Any considerable Oriental immigration would, moreover, be certain to give rise to social and economic problems of a character that might lead to serious difficulties in the field of international relations...

[Canada, Debates, 1 May 1947, Statement by Prime Minister William Lyon MacKenzie King, pp. 2644-2646]

Britain Puts the Pressure on Canada

Ordinarily, the restrictive aspects of Canadian immigration policy pass un-noticed in the mumbo-jumbo of departmental statements designed to bemuse the casually curious and deter the suspicious.

But, this year, an exodus from the West Indies is casting Britain in the role of inquisitor showing up the inadequacies of current Canadian immigration practices.

All the elements of the dispute are equally rooted in self interest. The West Indians, cut off from any significant entry into Canada and the United States, are fleeing to Britain by the thousands to escape their islands' economic underdevelopment and stagnation.

The British, traditional providers of an open door policy to all Commonwealth and colonial nationals, are seeking to avoid serious inundation by persuading other Commonwealth nations (Canada in particular) to follow suit. And Canada, bedevilled by her domestic economic crisis and long-established immigration policies based on skilled white admissions only, is trying to keep the door shut without losing newly-won prestige among the Afro-Asians.

Numbers are bringing the situation to a head. After percolating along at reasonably acceptable levels for 10 years (total net immigration was an estimated 300,000), arrivals into Britain from the West Indies spurted during the last year to the 60,000 mark. And they show no signs of abating, despite intensive "information" campaigns on the islands, warning of unemployment, climatic pitfalls and a growing sense of racial prejudice.

So, what to do? Up to this year, informal agreements did the job. With India and Pakistan, for instance, a gentleman's agreement was possible, mainly because these nationalistic-minded Asian countries both favor policies designed to discourage net emigration.

In each case, Britain got off the hook by persuading the respective governments to pass legislation at the source that discourages mass departures with requirements of substantial cash sureties to underwrite a passport application. As a result no one becomes angry at Britain, simply because the British government has never been openly involved.

But with the West Indies, this back-door approach just won't work. For one thing, the passport dodge doesn't apply as long as full independence remains to be granted.

In effect, something else has to be done. Some alternative to Britain has to be found to take a share of the émigrés.

And that, at the moment, means Canada.

Already, in his brief talks in Ottawa in April, Britain's Prime Minister Macmillan has made some first, tentative enquiries. To follow now, it's certain that official channels at every level will be pressing the suit wherever possible.

Is there a case to be made? Macmillan and his aides say yes. They base their argument on these main points:

—Political realism demands special attention now to keep open all possible channels between the white races and the emergent and belligerent Afro-Asians. The Commonwealth, especially since South Africa's enforced withdrawal, is one of the most important vehicles for maintaining contact and co-operation. But this will fail if, even by appearance alone, the white members erect racially-based barriers. Alternatively, token co-operation may well mean salvation in the future.

—The economies of the "white" nations are ripe for a gradual, absorbable influx of non-white labor. Both in Britain and Canada the rising standards of living mean that a whole range of low-productivity, menial jobs are either unfilled or inadequately filled.

—Longer term adaptability is on a par with any other racial group. Once settled and given equal education, the sons and daughters of the first generation prove to be wholly competent at all levels in society. Even now, you find West Indian doctors, lawyers, engineers, draughtsmen, and skilled workmen living fully within a British context.

—The myths of unsuitable temperament and climatic susceptibility are wholly unfounded. In term of every vagary of unhealthy weather, Britain can claim greater extremes than Canada, yet medical records show no discernible evidence that West Indians or any other non-whites wax any more sickly than their British counterparts.

If anything, the cruel process of the selectivity of survival tends to give the newcomers a slight edge in strength and resilience. Temperamentally, it's generally agreed that West Indians prove in practice to have a greater degree of family responsibility, to be more law-abiding and more interested in community affairs than other comparable groups. In rough, tough Brixton for example—one of the hard-core working class districts of London—welfare workers report "the closest and most harmonious integration possible."

These are the basic British arguments being put to Ottawa right now—an appeal to political common sense, to economic opportunism and, in a resignedly muted way, to basic humanity.

Now, suppose it were taken up and it was announced that West Indians would be allowed into Canada in numbers rather greater than the present bare token allotment.

West Indian Commission workers here in London predict two main results: (1) About 30% of the present emigres to Britain would choose Canada instead; (2) The majority who would choose Canada would come from the top echelons of emigrating West Indian society.

"You should remember that most West Indians are hard working and ambitious," explained (Miss) Patsy Pyne of the Commission's London office. "The ones that would choose Canada would be mainly from that group attracted by the possibility of good (in comparison to island rates) salaries and education for their families.

"A lot of them would he the sort that wouldn't ordinarily go to Britain at all—the middle class of person earning around £1,000 a year in professional or skilled work.

"And you know, to be blunt about it, we West Indians really are rather a better bet for Canada than some of your present immigrants. We think far more in North American terms than Europeans do, we are well accustomed to North American customs and values. For us, there's little real change involved in moving from one English-speaking Commonwealth area to another in the same hemisphere.

"All we ask is the chance to prove this to you in practice."

Will the chance be given? British officials say privately that they're going to do their damndest to persuade Canada during the next year, but concede that they really aren't too optimistic.

"It's up to your Mr. Diefenbaker," summed up one carefully anonymous official. "If he really is building common policy with the Afro-Asians—as he seemed to be doing here at the Prime Ministers' Conference—he may fly in the face of domestic economic realities. But we will be rather surprised if he does."

[Saturday Night, *13 May 1961, pp. 37-38]*

The 1966 White Paper

HOUSE OF COMMONS
Friday, October 14, 1966
(11:10 am.)
(English)
TABLING OF WHITE PAPER ON GOVERNMENT POLICY

Hon. Jean Marchand (Minister of Manpower and Immigration): Mr. Speaker, it is my pleasure to table today a white paper on Canadian immigration policy. It is bilingual and probably multicultural. In doing so I would like to express my sincere appreciation to those who have worked on the preparation of this document; some have done so not only this year but also during 1965 under two of my predecessors.

No one who understands the immigration problem will be surprised that this white paper could not be produced quickly and easily. Immigration policy depends on a complex interrelationship of economic, social, humanitarian, legal and international considerations. There are few issues, indeed, that bring into play so comprehensively all the delicate balances and tensions of our Canadian society.

Our problem is to avoid the ill consequences of these inevitable complexities. Immigration policy and procedures have to adjust to changing circumstances. The natural tendency, when the issues are so difficult, is to make the adjustment by small, partial, ad hoc modifications. And as these accumulate, immigration procedures tend to become complicated, confused, uncertain, even contradictory.

I hope we can all recognize this problem without partisanship. The difficulties I am talking about have been at work under all governments, irrespective of party label.

We will cure them only if we are prepared from time to time to take stock, to reassess our policy and sort out our procedures, to develop a new synthesis as the basis for an immigration policy suited to contemporary needs.

The white paper is an attempt to do that. I do not expect it to be accepted without criticism. Immigration touches too many emotional issues to be clarified without dispute. I believe, nevertheless, that most people will find that the synthesis we have developed in this white paper meets the main needs of Canada today while taking reasonable account of all legitimate special interests.

I would like at this stage merely to draw attention to three main features of the policy I propose. First, it is expansionist. It seeks to establish the basis for a steadily active immigration policy adapted to our manpower needs, a policy that will assist Canada's growth by bringing here every year a good number of people able to adapt to our society and qualified to contribute to our economy.

Second, it is non-discriminatory. It establishes principles and procedures that can and will operate entirely without regard to race, colour or creed. I do not mean that it is in our power to ensure that geography will make no difference at all to people's chances of coming to Canada. We have to take account of the differing attitudes to emigration among other governments and peoples. There are practical limitations on our side. We cannot afford to establish the same facilities to assist immigrants in countries where the facilities will be little used as we have in countries where they are in heavy demand

These, however, are practical problems, to be treated as such, to be overcome as much as possible. There will be no discrimination by principle and no practical differences that are within my department's power to remove.

Third, the white paper policy establishes, for the future, a new balance between the claims of family relationship and the economic interest of Canadians as a whole, which is that immigrants should generally be the well qualified people for whom employment opportunities are increasing.

[Translation]

Where there are at present some anomalies in the range of relatives who may be sponsored, these will be corrected by broadening the range. Canadian citizens, and other people who are already here as landed immigrants, will be able to sponsor everyone they now can, and a few additional classes of relatives, with the one reservation that those who are going to be entering the labour force must have either some needed skill or the equivalent of an elementary school education.

The effect of this limitation will not be to reduce the number of sponsored immigrants entering Canada. Its purpose is only to remove from the sponsorship system its present potential for explosive growth. If that were not done, we would face the danger of admitting to Canada an ever-increasing number of people for whom our economy will offer not more but fewer employment opportunities.

The sponsorship rights of Canadian citizens will for the first time have full legal recognition, with an appeal board that can over-rule the Minister's decisions. And, of course, the new immigrant will be able to bring to Canada, without waiting for his citizenship, the members of his immediate family who are or become dependent on him.

I am sure, Mr. Speaker, that the house will wish to explore these proposals with care and consideration. I would therefore say that I intend to propose that the white paper be referred for study to a special joint parliamentary committee which would be able to examine the issues in the depth that their importance requires.

[Canada, House of Commons, Debates, 14 October 1966]

A 'Third Force': The Other Ethnic Groups

In the last few years, attempts have been made to emphasize the importance of the non-British, non-French cultural groups by using the terms "third force" or "third element" to embrace all such groups. Since, in 1961, 26 percent of the Canadian population was of neither French nor British ethnic origin, these terms have been used by some to distinguish this section of the population from the Anglophone and Francophone sections. This concept is too simplistic to reflect adequately the Canadian reality for it encompasses vast numbers of people whose only common feature is not being of either British or French ethnic origin. Can the aspirations of those of Chinese origin in Vancouver be amalgamated with the aspirations of those of Ukrainian origin in Winnipeg? What are the tendencies among people of Dutch or German origin to integrate? How extensive is assimilation among those of Scandinavian origin? How strong, in fact, is the will to exist on the part of certain apparently well-organized groups? The other cultural groups are scattered all across the country, and not one of them—even the biggest and most active—represents as much as 20 percent of the population of any of the ten provinces. While some cultural groups are concentrated in considerable numbers in Montreal, Toronto, Winnipeg, and Vancouver, and account for as much as 10 percent of the population in certain western cities, they are not sufficiently concentrated to contemplate the institution of other official languages, or the expansion of the concept of two societies to include four or five. It is clear that this "third force" does not exist in Canada in any political sense, and is simply based on statistical compilations. All the available evidence indicates that those of other languages and cultures are more or less integrated with the Francophone and

Anglophone communities, where they should find opportunities for self-fulfilment and equality of status It is within these two societies that their cultural distinctiveness should find a climate of respect and encouragement to survive.

[Privy Council Office, Canada, Report of the Royal Commission on Bilingualism and Biculturalism, Vol. IV, (Ottawa, 1970), p. 10] Reproduced with the permission of the Minister of Public Works and Government Services Canada, 1997.

The Premier of Quebec's 'Objections to Multiculturalism'

In a letter dated October 7, 1971, you informed me that you intended to put forward a policy based on multiculturalism. At the same time, you sent me a document in response to Vol. IV of the Report of the Royal Commission on Bilingualism and Biculturalism, setting forth the objectives of this policy and the programs to be implemented by your Government and its various organizations. There are two aspects to this policy, the one being a statement of principle defining multiculturalism as understood by you, and the other the assistance you propose to provide to ethnic groups who express a wish for help to promote their culture.

The following comments relate to these two aspects.

I have serious misgivings about the principle of the multicultural policy. The multicultural policy which, to quote your words, you "intend to pursue" clearly contradicts the mandate of the Royal Commission on Bilingualism and Biculturalism as defined by the Government of Canada. From the 43 pages of the General Introduction and from Articles 81 and 92 in particular, it seems clear that the guiding principle of the Laurendeau-Dunton Commission was the equality of the two founding peoples of the Canadian Confederation, which confederation was to take the form of a bilingual and bicultural society, with due regard for the contribution of the other ethnic groups and for the steps to be taken to safeguard this contribution.

Furthermore, the document tabled in the House of Commons dissociates culture from language, which seems to me to be a questionable basis on which to found a policy.

You will have gathered that Quebec does not accept your government's approach to the principle of multiculturalism. Actually, the concept seems scarcely compatible with the facts of Quebec, where the predominant population group is linguistically and culturally French, where a large minority is linguistically and culturally English, and where there are many minorities having other linguistic and cultural origins. In a word, with the federal government assuming responsibility for all the cultures which are to be found in Canada, Quebec must take on within its own territory the role of prime defender of the French language and culture. The Government of Quebec feels that it has a special responsibility for spreading the French culture in North America and it proposes to do this with all the means at its disposal. This does not mean that there will be the slightest discrimination against other cultures.

With regard to the programs to be decided upon jointly with the various groups concerned, the government of Quebec, through its Department of Immigration, has for some years been implementing similar types of programs by providing subsidies to ethnic groups and for language courses. I feel that it is imperative that we should reach some understanding, in order to avoid duplication between your new programs and ours and to safeguard Quebec's jurisdictional rights which are involved in most of the projects you are putting forward.

[*Robert Bourassa, Letter to Prime Minister Trudeau*, Le Devoir, *17 November 1971, translated*]

Section B
Responses to a Multicultural Society

The transformation of Canada into a more multicultural society was not easy. The dominant host society voiced its unease regarding new population balances, and 'New Canadians' who looked and acted differently. Of course, the ethnic and racial diversity of Canada was not the only result of new immigration. Established communities of visible minorities, together with newcomers, used formal ethnic or racially based organizations such as the Negro Citizenship Association of Toronto, and the Canadian Jewish Congress, to fight racial or religious discrimination.

How Can We Keep Our British Racial Balance?

A successful conclusion to the war being reasonably within sight and increasing attention being paid to the post-war order, the immigration question is showing signs of vigorous life after lying dormant for nearly a decade and a half. Economists are visioning an eventual Dominion population of some thirty millions, the inference being that this is to be largely built up by an influx of people from elsewhere. Views on a post-war movement to these shores are casually aired as if immigration were a tap of fix and uniform flow to be turned off and on at will. As a matter of fact immigration is one of the most complex of Canadian problems, involving a host of factors.

It is only proposed to consider one—but one of the most important—phases here—the bearing of immigration upon the constituency of population. The nature of any post-war immigration movement to Canada may have a very pronounced effect upon the character of the Dominion population of the future, and is a fact to be borne in mind. With some serious publicists have already forecast a time when French-Canadians will be in a majority in this country, foreign-born stock occupy a proportionately stronger position than they do today, and those of the Anglo-Saxon races drop to a correspondingly lower place.

This is a logical and reasonable view granted a continuance of the present trend and with population accretion dependent on natural increase. There is no need to give columns of statistics to acquaint the average intelligent citizen with the fact that the birth rate and rate of natural increase among French Canadians and the foreign-born are higher than among those of Anglo-Saxon stock. Left entirely to itself the Canadian people would become steadily less Anglo-Saxon in content. The only fact which under present circumstances can offset this trend is appropriate immigration.

The effect of the manner of population growth during the past four centuries of Canadian history has been to achieve a certain racial ratio which in general is regarded as satisfactory and desirable, and any serious disturbance to which would be deplored. Canada's population today, in spite of the many nationalities which have contributed to it, is approximately half British. Those of English, Irish, Scottish and other British extraction account for 49.67 percent of the total people. Those of French origin in Canada make up 30.28 percent of the aggregate. Thus the two great races which founded Canada and accounted for its early development constitute nearly 80 percent of the total population. Those of other racial origins in Canada comprise only 20.05 percent of the total, with the highest individual proportion being under 5 percent.

British Stock Declining

Going further into the matter, however, a trend is revealed provoking uneasiness and of special concern as Canada deliberated over the framing of a post-war immigration policy. This is the fact that ever since the modern history of the Dominion began with Confederation, with immigration becoming the most influential factor in population building, the proportion of British stock in the Canadian people has steadily and almost consistently declined. When the first Dominion census was taken in 1871 the proportion of people of British extraction to total population was 60.65 percent; made up of English 20.26 percent, Irish 24.28 percent, Scottish 15.78 percent and other British 0.23 percent...

It is pretty safe to say that after the war there will be legions of people from many countries desirous of coming to Canada to make homes. Canada, when she decides to open her doors, should largely be able to pick and choose. But every national impulse, both of sentiment and practicability, will be, as in the period following the last war, to induce and encourage a British movement by every means.

This being so, what appear to be the prospects for a sustained volume of British immigration to maintain the existing ratio of population and offset the trend of decline of British stock?

Few adequately appreciated the extent to which Britain has in the past century and a quarter sent her sons and daughters abroad to lend their leaven to the development of new peoples. In 125 years approximately 28,000,000 left the Homeland for the British Dominions, the colonies and the United States. The greatest number of these, over 16,000,000 or roughly 57.9 percent landed at United States ports, Canada being host to the next highest total, or more than 5,000,000 representing about 18.3 percent of the total...

Social Security Needed

This gives some rough idea of the difficulties Canada is going to be faced with at the war's end when she sets about devising a post-war immigration policy, the cardinal consideration in which must be to keep the British content in the population dominant. It will be a new era in many respects, with free land, so powerful a lure in the past, practically gone, with the mechanization of agriculture virtually closing the popular avenue of farm labor as leading to farm ownership, and with, on the other hand, the unfavorable experience with paternalized British immigration in the last post-war period. It will tax the best brains of Canada to solve this...

One thing seems to become increasingly clear. To attract and maintain any volume of British immigration this country must be made as attractive as Britain from the standpoint of social security. A people that has experienced a depression and a devastating war cannot be expected to possess such enterprise and initiative as would result in the surrendering of those measures which cushion them against the material vicissitudes of life.

And there is some evidence that the authorities recognize this. The suggestion has emanated from England, prompted by the almost simultaneous publication of social security reports in Britain, the United States and Canada, that a plan may be evolved of international security, which would allow people to move from one country to another without losing the benefits they enjoyed in the homeland. To induce people to leave Britain, Canada must offer them at least as much as they have at home.

[Saturday Night, *11 December 1943, pp. 6-7]*

Editorial on Immigration

In the past, we have failed to distinguish between the immigration policy of the Canadian Government and the people that it has brought us. To the same degree that it is necessary that we should combat mass immigration and that immigration should be supervised when it is more or less effective, selective, so, to the same degree, we should display understanding towards immigrants and help them to integrate themselves in Canadian life. We have in the past, been far too prone to take the idea for granted that these new Canadians would inevitably become Anglicized, while, on the contrary, it is necessary to encourage them to keep their own culture and to acquaint and familiarize themselves with the French-Canadian background and environment under the best possible light. It has taken us a very long time to become aware that the community of faith creates a very strong bond between the majority of these new Canadians and ourselves and that they have been familiar with and appreciated French culture. We have been too slow in realizing that the choices which are presented to the immigrant who enters Canada can often be exercised in favour of French culture if we wish to take the trouble to make efforts in that direction.

[Le Devoir, *20 October 1949, translated*]

Toronto Negro Citizenship Association Protests Discrimination

Ottawa, Ont.—A group of twenty-five delegates, representing the Negro Citizenship Association of Toronto, met with the Honourable Walter Harris, Q.C., Minister of Citizenship and Immigration, in his office, on April 27th, to present a brief protesting the present discrimination against Negroes in Canada's immigration policy.

The delegation was headed by Donald Moore, President of the Toronto Negro Citizenship Association, and Stanley G. Grizzle, President, Toronto Division, Brotherhood of Sleeping Car Porters. Brother Norman S. Dowd, Executive Secretary, accompanied the delegation on behalf of the Congress.

The Association's brief made the five following requests:

(1) That the definition of "British subject" be amended in the Canadian Immigration Act, so as to include all those who are, for all other purposes, regarded as "British subjects and citizens of the United Kingdom and Commonwealth."

(2) That provision be made in the Act for the entry of a British West Indian, without regard to racial origin, who has sufficient means to maintain himself until he has secured employment.

(3) That the word "orphan" be deleted from the regulation which provides for the entry of nephews and nieces under 21.

(4) That the term, "persons of exceptional merit" be defined specifically.

(5) That an Immigration Office be set up in a centrally located area of the British West Indies for the handling of prospective immigrants.

The Association claimed that the Immigration Act denies equal status to those areas of the Commonwealth where coloured peoples constitute a large part of the population, by creating a rigid definition of "British subject" which excludes those who come from such areas as the British West Indies, Bermuda, British Guiana, Ceylon, India, Pakistan, Africa, etc. The brief asserted that such a definition of "British subject" is discriminatory and dangerous, creating two classes of Her Majesty's subjects, and raising animosity between persons born in different geographical areas. The delegation stated that it did not believe that Canada, as a democratic nation committed to promote world peace, should countenance anything which may lead to sowing the seed of race hatred.

The brief called particular attention to the situation of West Indian Negroes. It said that one of the official reasons given by the Government for refusing West Indians as immigrants is that people from tropical areas will have difficulty in adjusting themselves to the Canadian climate. However, the Government has itself admitted that it has no statistics available to support this claim. Another reason for refusal is the claim of the Government that West Indians do not readily become integrated in the life of the Canadian community. The delegation pointed out that customs, habits, modes of life, and methods of holding property in the West Indies are essentially the same as in Canada, and these people would have no difficulty in adjusting to the Canadian way of life.

The policy of the Government regarding immigration from the West Indies is that only close relatives and "cases of exceptional merit" are admissible. Yet considering the few who have been admitted to Canada since 1922, it is evident that there are not many persons in the West Indies with close relatives in Canada, who could take advantage of this provision. With reference to the term "cases of exceptional merit," the brief claimed that it was difficult to determine exactly what cases the Government considered to be "of exceptional merit," since persons have been rejected whose skills would seem to be most desirable, such as nurses, draughtsmen, stenographers, and graduates of Canada's leading educational institutions. Even students have been refused admission or denied extensions to complete their studies.

Later in the day, the group visited the Honourable Milton F. Gregg, V.C., Minister of Labour, to discuss the Federal Government's Fair Employment Practices Act and similar legislation.

[Canadian Unionist, *28 May 1954, p. 181*]

I Felt Like a Stranger in My Own Home Town

Speechless but Hospitable

I remember the first time I began to realize a change was taking place. It was in the spring of 1946, I was driving along a country road about three miles from town and as so often happens in this season, the car hit a soft spot and refused to budge. I walked to the nearest farm to call a garage. I knew he wouldn't mind my using his phone. Most likely he would invite me to stay for supper, or a cup of coffee for sure. Then came the surprise.

I rapped on the door. After a long delay it opened, and I looked in amazement at the man who greeted me. It was someone I had never seen before. He looked half scared, as if he thought I was the police come to question him. Behind him in a dimly-lit room was his wife, dressed in a multicolored floor-length skirt, a dark blouse, and with a black scarf over her head. Along with two small children she was leaning over an antiquated victrola and listening to records that sounded like German polkas. All of the family had a definite foreign look. A large pile of household goods in one corner of the room showed they had just moved in.

"May I use your phone?" I stuttered to the man who faced me. After a hesitant pause he said a few words I couldn't understand, but which I took meant he could not speak English. Finally, with a series of gestures I managed to show him what I wanted and he let me in. As I was about to leave he took a bottle of wine from the cupboard and offered me some. (I was to learn later that wine is as common to them as coffee is to us.) I refused, but thanked him and hurried back to the car to wait for the wrecker.

I didn't think much of the incident afterwards, because after all, there had always been a few immigrants in the area. In the months that followed, however, I noticed that more and more European families were moving into the farming district...

Finally I stopped one of the older Scottish farmers in town and asked him why so many native families were moving away and selling their farms to immigrants.

"I'm thinking of doing the same thing," he answered. "My three boys have gone to the city to get the big wages. I'm getting along in years—the prices they offer for my farms are just too good to resist."

"But a lot of immigrants came here on little more than a shoestring. Many of them lost practically everything in the war. How are they able to buy farms now?" I inquired.

"I've never seen anything like it," he said. "Their determination and stamina are amazing. Why I believe they can actually live on nothing. And they work almost twenty-four hours a day.

"Do you see that new Buick over there?" he asked, pointing across the street. "The fellow who owns that now, and a farm along with it, slept in a pigpen when he first came here."...

The New Look

In the years following the initial wave of immigrants, still great numbers came into the Rodney area. Soon not only the surrounding country but my home town itself began to take on a foreign look, as scores of new Canadians moved into town.

Almost overnight my next-door neighbor moved, to be replaced by a total stranger. He spoke a different language, he wore different clothes; he associated with his own people, he lived a different kind of life. There was no more borrowing sugar or coffee when our family unexpectedly ran out, no more friendly chats over the back fence.

Village streets became frequented by New Canadians in native dress. The women with their colorful skirts and head scarves and the men with their single-breasted dark suits were the rule, not the exception, on the main street. As I walked down town, particularly on a busy Saturday night, I passed groups of strangers, speaking any one of 14 different languages or dialects. I felt out of place—out of place in a town I had called home for over 20 years.

The newcomers built their own churches. They built their own meeting places. The modern swing of Canadian dances I was used to in the town hall changed into German or Lithuanian polkas. The orchestra of accordions, guitars, saxophone and drums was new to me. The dances lasted to nearly four o'clock in the morning, by which time the New Canadians were pretty well polka'd out. In contrast to the sedate weddings of Anglo-Saxon residents, were the weddings of immigrants. The celebrations lasted all night with a banquet table set for guests about every hour. Gentlemen paying to dance with the bride often contributed hundreds of dollars.

I grew to dislike the mass intrusion into the routine of life I had been brought up in. I could not understand the majority of the immigrants, and they could not understand me. I resented their "taking over" in my home town. Some of them seemed to be trying to remain as un-Canadian as possible. Many New Canadians, it appeared to me, even refused to try to learn English, while most of those who did were quick to revert back to their former tongues when talking with their own group. Very few attended languages classes held in the local school

Business, too, began to come within the orbit of the New Canadians. Many of them bought stores with money they had made in tobacco...

The stores run by immigrants were of three kinds. First, there were those in direct competition with older businesses—grocery stores, garages, dry good stores, appliance shops. Second, the immigrants took over many former businesses—like the shoe store or tailor shop—that had no similar opposition in town. Third, the immigrants started a few lines of business the town had never had before—such as a bowling alley...

The First Link

Perhaps the most important factor in the change was the influence of the young people who went to school with Canadian children. Language had been the great barrier, but when immigrant children played and laughed with Canadians, almost overnight they were talking English as well as their schoolmates. Parents, who hadn't taken much advantage of language classes, learned English from their children and association with older residents.

Goodwill between the young people spread to make goodwill between parents... One day two New Canadians joined our hard ball team. They were good—they played hard—we were part of a team. Baseball has always been a big thing in Rodney. When hundreds of local fans began cheering for Kovacs or Schneider, prejudices vanished. We were all one race, one people, one nationality...

Old Canadians learned the polka; we taught our new neighbors the foxtrot. Marriages between the two groups, once rare, are now common. The change in attitude was hastened when both groups began to realize that each was benefitting from the other, and that each owed the other a debt of thanks...

A Two-Sided Problem

Greatest benefit received, however, not only for the community but for the nation, is the fact that most of the immigrants have become excellent Canadian citizens. Many of them have joined the local Businessmen's Association. the Kiwanis club, the Odd Fellows fraternity, and various other committees. They have run in local politics. Many of their sons and daughters, both those born in Canada and those who came over with their parents, are going to university to become doctors, lawyers and teachers. The first immigrants have long since become citizens and are so Canadian in their ways, that it is hard to tell that their ancestors have not lived in Canada for decades.

As I got to know them better I found the New Canadians had some beefs and resentments against us.

"Canadians aren't very friendly," a Hungarian said to me.

"We are not made to feel at home," a Belgian exclaimed...

When we realized we too had shortcomings we made more effort to get to know our neighbors. I began to think that maybe I had forgotten about the principles of democracy and brotherhood I had been brought up on; to wonder whether the feeling of strangeness was not chiefly my own fault. I discovered that the New Canadians were grateful for their new home. At a Latvian meeting I attended, the speaker, in broken English, summed up his feelings like this: "Canada has been good to us. We live like civilized people once more, in peace and security. Let's keep our national ties, but give our whole-hearted support to our new country—Canada."

"What do you think of Canada?" I asked a Czechoslovakian one day.

"It's wonderful land," he answered. "We get chance to live in freedom. We build for future. My children get good schooling. They laugh and are happy."

A Broader View

Another thing that made for better feelings between us was when we learned to pay no attention to radicals on either side, who are frequently ready to make trouble. Friendships now well-established between hundreds of us are far too great to be shaken by these few...

Today as I walk down the main street I often stop to talk to dozens of New Canadians. They are the guys who bowl on the same team as I do; the ones who try just as hard for me as I do for them. They are the guys I share the latest stories with ... laugh with. Many of them worship with me in our church. They sing hymns—they share our faith, in "our" country, in "our" God.

I'm rather proud of Rodney today; where people in some 15 nationalities work, live and laugh together; where liberty and brotherhood are not just talk or theories but fact. I no longer feel like a stranger in my own home town.

[Canadian Business, December 1954, pp. 28-30, 70-74. Written by Cal Mistele]

How We Cover Up Our Racial Abuses

Last fall, as Canadians boiled with righteous indignation over the race riots in Little Rock, Arkansas, a small crowd gathered on a quiet Vancouver street.

A real estate salesman had just shown a Chinese-Canadian family through a house which was for sale. The crowd outside, in cultured loud tones, told the salesman, "We don't want any Orientals, Jews or Italians on the street."

There was no violence, no stones were thrown; but the salesman and the family got the idea. They moved on.

About the same time the Sault Ste. Marie *Daily Star* published an editorial defending Northern Ontario resort owners who were refusing Negro guests. The *Star* reasoned the resort people couldn't afford to antagonize American tourists who didn't happen to like Negroes.

It called the Ontario Fair Accommodation Practice Act, which specifically forbids such discrimination, "foolish" and "restrictive."

Similar arguments were used by several of 38 Toronto apartment house owners asked if they would rent to Negro people. (50 percent indicated they would not).

"There are white South Africans in that block," said one landlord apologetically, "and—well, you know how *they* feel..."

Small incidents, all of these. Thousands of them occur every year. Canada's race problems are so polite and pallid compared with those of the United States that they rate few headlines. Many well-intentioned people feel the incidents should be ignored completely as publicity intensifies the trouble...

The pattern of prejudice varies across the country. In the Maritimes, Negroes are partly segregated and have difficulty finding white-collar jobs; in Central Canada, Jews and New Canadians as well as Negroes meet prejudice in jobs and accommodation; on the Prairies, Indians who leave the reserves are the big problem and on the West Coast, the Orientals.

Race feeling seldom flares up in Canada. The most dramatic recent example was the Dresden case, which lasted two years and received wide publicity. Millions of Canadians were shocked to learn there was an Ontario town of 1,700 people, 300 of whom where not permitted a shave in a barbershop, a game of pool or a meal in a restaurant because they were Negroes.

Two years ago I returned from covering the Autherine Lucy riots and the rebirth of the Ku Klux Klan in Alabama to attend another in the long series of court hearings which finally broke the Dresden color bar.

I heard the very same arguments—"Education, not legislation is the answer," "These people are pushing us too hard, too fast", "The trouble is all caused by outsiders"—that the Southern segregationists had given me.

At last after a judicial inquiry, two court cases and two appeals, a cafe owner paid a $50 fine for race discrimination. He served cups of coffee to the next two colored people to enter his cafe—and peace returned to Dresden.

The color bar which has been in force more than a century—since "Uncle Tom" Henson led the first runaway slaves to Ontario from the South—was ended through publicity and legal action.

It was not stopped by "education" or sermons on the brotherhood of man—the local clergy, with one exception, tried to dodge the issue; so did the teachers.

Since the war, Canada has introduced an impressive number of laws designed to stamp out discrimination in employment and housing.

There are Fair Employment Practices (FEP) Acts: the Dominion Act (1953) Nova Scotia (1955) New Brunswick (1956) Ontario (1951) Manitoba (1953) Saskatchewan (1956) and British Columbia (1956).

Ontario was first in the accommodation field with its Fair Accommodation Practices (FAP) Act (1954). Saskatchewan followed with a similar act in 1956. Premier Leslie Frost called the Ontario FAP the proudest piece of legislation of his career. Later it proved to have a large hole in it: it could not be applied to housing.

Other human rights measures include Saskatchewan's Bill of Rights (1947) Federal anti-discrimination provision in the fair wages policy and National Employment Service; measures outlawing restrictive covenants in property (Ontario and Manitoba) and insurance (Ontario) and anti-discrimination by-laws in several cities. One of these, in Windsor, forces builders to sell without discrimination any housing built on land bought from the city.

Quebec, Alberta, Prince Edward Island and Newfoundland have no human rights laws.

The record of trade union human rights committees are filled with sad little tales of racial and religious slights.

A Negro sleeping porter saved up and bought a house in a new Montreal suburb. For the first few days he and his family were too busy moving in to notice anything amiss. Then one evening he saw a group of neighbors gathering in a house across the street, casting cold stares at his front window.

The next day he learned the meeting had been planning ways of getting him out of his house—raising a petition, making things uncomfortable for him, buying him out. The plot failed when two friendly families refused to go along with it and threatened to expose it.

A Winnipeg bank manager sent a letter to high school principals outlining job prospects in banks but suggesting Jewish children should not bother to apply...

The worst victim of discrimination is always the Negro. Stamped by his skin, he faces more and higher barriers than members of other minority groups.

If Canada's Negro discrimination problem is relatively small it is not because Canadians are noticeably more tolerant than anybody else but because the Department of Citizenship and Immigration has done its best to keep Negroes out.

As Premier Grantley Adames of Barbados pointed out at a recent Couchiching conference: "Your immigration laws are worse than the McCarran Act in the United States. It at least allows 100 nationals from each territory in the West Indies to enter the U.S. each year."

So most of Canada's 24,000 Negroes are third and fourth generation citizens. They live in the southern tip of Ontario around Chatham, Dresden and Wallaceburg (about 5,000) in the Maritimes (about 9,000) and in Toronto and Montreal (5,000 each).

Ontario's last segregated school for colored children closed in Chatham in 1891, but the law still provides for separate Negro schools.

Some restaurants in Halifax and New Glasgow bar Negroes. Until recently, Truro public schools provided separate toilet facilities for Negro children and New Glasgow theatres restricted Negro people to the balcony.

One Negro woman was refused service in a Nova Scotian Chinese restaurant. "How dare you!" she fumed at the Oriental owner. "We are both in the same boat."

The rate of advancement of the 5,000 Negroes in the Halifax area can be judged from the numbers of Negro professional men—no doctors, one lawyer and two ordained ministers.

How can the new FEP and FAP laws help these people?

Experience in the courts has shown that race or religious discrimination is extremely hard to prove, but that it can be done.

In July 1956 Judge Douglas C. Thomas drew the "logical and irresistible inference" that Sid Forbes, a Negro sales organizer, was refused a Toronto apartment because of his color.

But the judge ruled that an apartment house was not a "public" place so the owner could not be guilty of an offence under the Ontario FAP Act. An attempt to mend this hole in the act was made at the last session of the Ontario Legislature but the motion did not get a second reading.

FEP Acts in five provinces forbid employers to ask the race, religion or place of birth of a job applicant, or to publish advertisements restricting applications in this way.

The Federal act extends this to cover federal jobs and firms with federal contracts.

Habit dies hard, however, and the illegal questions are still being asked. A survey of application forms issued by Vancouver firms showed 63% of them asked about nationality, 70% place of birth, 18% religion and 14% racial origin.

In Toronto, 30% of firms surveyed, including a Crown corporation, four insurance companies, two banks, an oil company and a government employment service, had illegal questions on their forms.

Laws against discrimination are still new in Canada. So far they have been more effective as a threat than when actually applied in court.

Prime Minister Diefenbaker has promised a Bill of Rights for all Canadians.

Whether this will increase the freedom of the people as a whole or, as some fear, limit it, remains to be seen. However general its terms, it should offer some hope to those of us who are less free than the rest.

[Saturday Night, 15 February 1958, pp. 11-12, 46. Written by Gordon Donaldson]

In Search of Tolerance

Raminder Singh was on his way to a Christmas party in late 1987 when he suffered what he calls "the ultimate humiliation." He was denied admission to Edmonton's Jasper Place Royal Canadian Legion hall because he refused to remove his turban. Legion policy prohibits guests from wearing hats inside the premises, except on special occasions, such as Remembrance Day. Almost two years later, the baptized Sikh is still bitter about the incident. "I realized then that we Sikhs are at the bottom of the social hierarchy here in Canada," he says. "I feel like how the Jews must have felt during the Second World War."

Mr. Singh's complaint, which he presented before an Alberta Human Rights Commission tribunal in Edmonton last week, has a familiar ring. The same issue is at the heart of the ongoing controversy over allowing Sikh RCMP officers to wear turbans and other religious accoutrements while in uniform. But it is becoming increasingly apparent that the debate over turbans is merely a symptom of a larger societal conflict. It is a clash of cultures, as the multiplicity of Canadian eth nic communities seeks ways to reconcile their competing interests and conflicting beliefs. Observes Pali Pawa, president of the Council of Sikh Organizations of Calgary: "That is the question of Alberta's multicultural landscape. How can so many different cultures and races get along with one another?"

Over the last two decades, Canada has developed a legal, political and bureaucratic framework which presumes that the best way to guarantee minority rights and ensure racial and cultural harmony is to create a "multicultural mosaic" in which distinctive cultural characteristics are celebrated and promoted. But the bitter turban debate and other signs of disharmony suggest the laws, policies and programs based on the principals of multiculturalism may not be working. Indeed, there is a growing body of opinion which argues that greater ethnocultural conflict is an inevitable by-product of government-imposed multicultural policy. Moreover, it has been suggested that the appearance of ethnic and racial tension in Alberta today may be greater than the reality, thanks to the overzealous efforts of the multicultural and human rights bureaucracies to unearth evidence of discrimination.

Both the Alberta and federal governments have multicultural legislation in place which is designed to protect the rights of ethnic minorities. The Alberta Cultural Heritage Act, passed in 1984, vows to "encourage in all Albertans an awareness of and appreciation of the cultural heritage of Alberta and a pride in their unity and diversity." The Canadian Multiculturalism Act, passed by the Mulroney government in 1988, aims to "preserve and enhance the multicultural heritage of Canadians while working to achieve the equality of all Canadians in the economic, social, cultural and political life of Canada."

Ethnic diversity is further encouraged and protected by the Canadian Charter of Rights and Freedoms, particularly subsection 15.2, which authorizes programs and policies dedicated to "the amelioration of conditions of disadvantaged individuals or groups including those that are disadvantaged because of race, national or ethnic origin, colour, religion, sex, age or mental or physical disability." Constitutional experts sometimes refer to 15.2 as the "affirmative action clause," because it can be used to sanction laws which impose hiring quotas on the public or private sectors. Canadian political scientist Alan Cairns, in his book *The Embedded State*, observed that the clause is "an invitation to...government to engage in micro social engineering to readjust the status order produced by history...[It] illustrates the recurring tendency of the Canadian state...[to single] out particular groups or categories for individualized treatment."

Some critics of multicultural law and policy believe governments should go even further to ensure ethnic minority rights. "Unless there are some tough legal measures to ensure minorities are treated equally," says Yvonne Hebert, a multilingualism expert at the University of Calgary, "these policies have no teeth."

The Getty government is often maligned for its alleged lack of enthusiasm for multiculturalism. A recently-released report by the Alberta Multicultural Commission was vigorously attacked by ethnic lobbyists on the grounds that its numerous recommendations for improving public awareness and expanding services and programs failed to include a call for new legislation promoting, among other things, affirmative action employment programs.

Doug Main, Alberta's Minister of Culture and Multiculturalism, says he's "nervous about creating laws which force people to accept the principles of multiculturalism. You can force people to change their behaviour, but it won't change their attitudes. And I think attitudes must change first." That may be best achieved, he says, by helping develop "our national culture. And that culture is a diverse multitude of cultures. To foster its growth, it requires government programs. We are trying to create a global society."

Unlike more zealous proponents of multicultural diversity, Mr. Main is cautious of enacting laws that impose his vision of a "national culture" or "global society" on Albertans. Similarly, University of Calgary political scientist Thomas Flanagan rejects the notion that governments should act as "social engineers. Our governments are there to protect individual rights," he says, "they have no business trying to work on social attitudes." Any attempt to do so, adds Prof.

Flanagan, is likely to divide rather than unite Canada's diverse cultural groups. "The government's multicultural policies have only encouraged immigrants to become departmentalized and distinct. It hasn't helped them integrate into society at large. Nor have [multicultural policies] helped mainstream society accept ethnic minorities."

Despite the continuing controversy over turbans, and a recently-released report by the Alberta Human Rights Commission which said that complaints to the commission are up 74% in the first seven months of 1989, Prof. Flanagan thinks there is a decided lack of hard evidence to indicate that Alberta faces a racial crisis. "Why should I assume there's anything above the normal conflict, just because the [commission] says complaints of discrimination are up? The commission does every thing it can to drum up business for itself. It encourages people to complain. The numbers of complaints it reports are in my mind totally meaningless."

Even the AHRC's chief commissioner, Fil Fraser, admits he isn't sure if there is more discrimination in the province than usual. "I can't really say that," admits Mr. Fraser. "People are just speaking out more. We are open to all sorts of complaints. We'll look at almost anything." But Mr. Fraser insists tough human rights legislation is necessary to "create a level playing surface for all Albertans, regardless of race or ethnic background."

The question remains, can ethnic harmony be assured through legislation which protects individual rights alone, or is it necessary to also protect group rights, as set out in the Charter? In the United States, where there is less emphasis on pluralism, individual rights take precedence over group rights. In the Canadian context, attitudes on this issue appear partly influenced by regional factors. Multiculturalism holds little appeal in Quebec, for example, where governments are primarily concerned with enacting laws specifically designed to protect the French language and culture. And Alberta was settled by a disproportionate number of Americans, who imported that country's so-called "melting-pot" philosophy for assimilating ethnic minorities into a homogeneous culture.

"Too a great degree," says University of Alberta sociologist Baha Abu-Laban, "we have never achieved that ideal of a mosaic in Alberta. Our society is much more like the American melting-pot." Prof. Abu-Laban points out that although the ethnic background of Alberta's population has changed over the years, our institutions have not. "The traditional British systems of justice and politics remain in place. Everyone must work within specific guidelines."

Prof. Abu-Laban emphasizes the importance of ensuring fair and equitable treatment for all minority groups, and he champions ethnics' rights to maintain their cultural heritage. But, he adds, "there's a point where implementing enough special privileges for everyone becomes a real problem, if not impossible."

Reform Party of Canada leader Preston Manning argues that current multicultural policies are a sure-fire recipe for social disharmony. "There is a rising amount of racism in Albertan society," says Mr. Manning. "I think it's encouraged when we define ourselves in racial terms." The Reform leader opposes multicultural policies which "put group rights before those of the individual."

At the RPC annual convention in October, delegates passed a resolution rejecting Ottawa's funding of multicultural programs. The resolution was developed Dr. Rais Khan, chairman of the University of Winnipeg's political science department. Dr. Khan opposes the idea of multiculturalism as defining Canadian society. "A mosaic by its very definition is fragmented," says Dr. Khan. "And funding multicultural programs does nothing to stop further fragmentation of our society. It encourages newcomers to cling to their culture, and makes Canadian a vast assortment of special groups. It can only lead to hostility." Dr. Khan understands the desire to preserve one's cultural heritage, "but that is a private matter. It isn't up to governments to fund."

Both Dr. Khan and Mr. Manning suspect government funding of multicultural programs and groups may have less to do with politicians' belief in the mosaic than with their greed for garnering the ethnic vote. "I think there's always the potential for political corruption in multicultural grants," says Mr. Manning. "Politicians hand out money to groups under the label of cultural funding, on the assurance his party will get their vote." Allegations of ethnic vote-buying were rampant during last year's Liberal and Tory nomination races preceding the federal election. "The ethnic vote is becoming more and more important," says Dr. Khan. "Throwing money at minority groups, or at least promising to distribute grants, is an easy way of winning ethnic support."

It would be unfair to suggest all ethnic minorities manipulate multicultural laws and policies in an effort to recreate their own societies within Canada. Many immigrants are clearly satisfied to escape poverty or persecution elsewhere for relative peace and prosperity in Canada, with or without cultural grants. Generally speaking, it appears the longer an ethnic community has been established in Canada, the less use it has for modern multicultural policies and programs. "Real multiculturalism didn't come by an act of the legislature," says Marian Strezlecki, past president of the Canadian Polish Congress' Edmonton chapter. "It is a result of ethnic groups organizing themselves a long time ago. I think Polish groups in Alberta recognize we have the opportunity to enjoy our cultural heritage, but that we are a part of Canadian society first."

Many members of Canada's founding ethnic culture also oppose official multiculturalism. "It's a very touchy subject with a lot of Indians," says Dennis Francis, president of the Calgary Native Friendship Centre. "Some see multiculturalism as an attempt on government's behalf to assimilate the aboriginal population." Mr. Francis points out that native groups throughout the province—and across the nation—have been struggling for years to win a measure of autonomous self-government. "Joining the multicultural pattern lumps us in with immigrants when we'd rather be recognized on our own," says Mr. Francis. He says native cultural aspirations contrast sharply with those of immigrants, simply because natives are the original inhabitants of Canada.

Immigration patterns in recent years have had a profound affect on the demography of Canada. Visible minorities from countries with radically different linguistic, social, cultural and religious traditions have replaced white Christian Europeans as the predominant immigrant population. The trend is likely to continue for the foreseeable future. Laws, policies and programs that foster fragmentation rather than accommodation might provide work for the human rights police, but they may also foster intolerance and disharmony. As Mr. Strezlecki observes, it is in the best interests of all concerned to consider themselves Canadians first, ethnics second. The opposite view, he concludes, "has lost the sense of true democracy."

[*Alberta Report, 4 December 1989, pp. 8-10.*
Written by Brian Hutchinson and Paul Bunner]

Faces from Far Shores

Immigrants Are Testing Canada's Self-Image of Racial Tolerance

Throughout Canadian history, immigration has been a source of change—and of conflict. And for Employment and Immigration Minister Barbara McDougall and contemporary Canadians, the issue remains contentious. Fuelling the current debate is the fact that the pattern of immigration to Canada has changed dramatically. In 1957, 95 percent of the 282,164 immigrants were Europeans or Americans. But of the 152,098 immigrants to Canada 30 years later, the percentage of Europeans and Americans had dropped to 24 percent. The remainder in 1987 came mostly from the Third World, a shift that is changing Canadian society—and severely testing the country's self-image of racial tolerance. In fact, as the results of the sixth annual *Maclean's*/Decima poll show, Canadians have yet to come to terms with the influx of visible minorities—expressing their support for the concept of multiculturalism, but also showing a marked hostility towards ethnic distinctiveness.

Despite that situation, the majority of respondents—53 percent—said that increased immigration from the Third World was "just a fact of life," as opposed to 27 percent who called it a "bad thing" and the 19 percent who said that it was good. As well, when asked to assess the benefits of Canada's diverse multicultural makeup, only 30 percent of respondents expressed agreement with the poll statement "We would be better off if we were more the same"—compared with 68 percent who chose the response that being "made up of people from different ethnic backgrounds makes Canada a more interesting and even better country." But when asked if new immigrants should he encouraged to maintain their distinct cultures and ways, 57 percent of respondents said that new immigrants should "blend with the larger society," compared with only 40 percent who said that new arrivals should maintain their ethnic identities.

That result is much the same as the finding of a special *Maclean's*/Decima poll done last summer, in which 61 percent of respondents said that immigrants should change their culture. And other recent polls have also shown that Canadians, although prepared to support and often praise Canada's multicultural identity, are less likely to tolerate the underlying essence of multiculturalism—that ethnic groups he encouraged to retain their respective identities. "We are revelling in our multi-cultural identity," said Allan Gregg, chairman of Decima Research Ltd. "But Canadians demand, in the end, stability. And anything that threatens to upset that stability, they eschew."

In fact, intolerance of cultural distinctiveness proved higher than average in provinces where immigration-related issues are paramount. In British Columbia, which in recent years has attracted large numbers of Asian immigrants, 62 percent of respondents said that new arrivals should adapt to the larger culture. That figure was matched in Alberta, where the backlash to RCMP Commissioner Norman Inkster's proposal to change the RCMP uniform and allow Sikh officers to wear their distinctive turbans has been especially virulent.

Antipathy towards ethnic distinctiveness also ran high in Quebec, where 58 percent of respondents said that immigrants should he encouraged to assimilate. In Quebec, increased immigration has become a vital concern for the government because of the rapidly declining provincial birthrate—which now stands at a record low of 1.4 children per woman, compared with 1.7 nationally. At the same time, the majority of new immigrants to Quebec resist assimilation into francophone culture—at a time when Quebecers are becoming increasingly concerned over the future of the French language in North America.

But in spite of the underlying intolerance among respondents towards new immigrants and ethnic diversity, younger Canadians were more willing than older respondents to accommodate cultural differences. In the 18-to-24 age group, 61 percent of respondents said that new immigrants should maintain their distinctiveness—as opposed to only 30 percent in the 55-to-64 age group. Those results, said Gregg, "hold out some optimism for the future"—and the hope that the Canadian ideal of tolerance will prove to be more than a myth.

[Macleans, 1 January 1990, p. 40. Written by Peeter Kopvillem]

Hijab Banned in Montreal School

A 13-year-old girl who was sent home to change after she wore traditional Muslim clothing to school will be changing schools, a Montreal Catholic School Commission officer said yesterday.

But the dress code that kept 13-year-old Emilie Ouimet from wearing her hijab at Louis Riel Secondary school remains. And so does a growing debate about the place of religious expression in Quebec's schools.

Ouimet, whose mother recently converted to Islam, wore a traditional head covering and long tunic to the east-end Montreal school on Wednesday. School officials told her she had to go home and wear something more in line with the school's dress code.

Clothing which would "marginalize" students at Louis Riel isn't allowed, principal Normand Doré said in an article published yesterday in La Presse. "Distinctive clothing like a hijab or neo-Nazi regalia could polarize aggression among young people."

Doré wasn't taking calls from journalists today. But Michel Charron, the MCSC's director of intercultural relations, said Ouimet's parents had decided to send her to another school without Louis Riel's strict dress requirements. He didn't know which school.

Charron insisted that the decision to send Ouimet home had nothing to do with religious discrimination. "That's not at all the way this affair should be considered," he said.

"Every MCSC school has its own educational project. Louis Riel's places enormous importance on matters of dress."

'Profound dismay'

Anti-racism activists weren't buying that explanation.

The Canadian Jewish Congress, in a news release, expressed its "profound dismay" at the school's behavior.

"Respect for religious and cultural diversity is not a matter that should have lower priority than the desire of school administrators, however laudable, to avoid marginalizing students," the CJC's Max Bernard said.

The group SOS Racisme called the decision to send Ouimet home "deplorable" and called for a review of the MCSC's policy on dress codes.

The Louis Riel incident is only one sign that the debate over religion's place in Quebec's schools is heating up, Université de Montréal education professor Jean-Pierre Proulx said.

The increasing ethnic diversity of the Montreal region is pushing the matter onto the public agenda, Proulx said.

But so is Bill 107, the law designed to replace most Protestant and Catholic school boards with English and French boards.

Some of the strongest supporters of non-denominational instruction find Bill 107 a frustrating law because it protects the rights of Catholics, Protestants and other religious groups to religious education under some circumstances.

Quebec's largest federation of teachers' unions, the Centrale de L'Enseignement du Québec, voted in June to call for the complete absence of religious instruction in public schools.

The CEQ motion "made waves within the Centrale itself," Proulx said, "and spurred a debate that is growing outside its ranks."

It is a debate both of Quebec's major political parties would rather avoid, Proulx said.

Parti Québécois chief Jacques Parizeau has said that a promised commission on the future of Quebec education won't touch on the role of religion.

But even if the debate were settled and Quebec decided to take religious instruction out of its schools, incidents like Wednesday's could repeat themselves, another Université de Montréal professor said.

Marie McAndrew, a specialist in the integration of immigrant students, said dress codes that infringe on religious expression clearly violate Quebec and Canadian human-rights charters. But mistrust of other cultures keeps leading educators to implement such codes.

"It's a basic issue, and the issue is: Do we want everybody to be exactly the same?" McAndrew said.

[The Gazette (Montreal), 10 September 1994, p. A13. Written by Paul Wells]

1. What were the main points of Prime Minister King's 1947 statement in Parliament?
2. Why was Britain putting pressure on Canada to increase immigration?
3. What were the ideas behind the 1972 policy on multiculturalism? How was it received by the other parties in the House of Commons? What was the reaction of French Quebec?
4. Identify the demographic assumptions behind the 1943 argument by E. L. Chicanot.
5. Attitudes changed with both education and legislation. What were the arguments put forward on both sides? What examples can you provide of the continuing emphasis placed upon 'absorption'?

READINGS

Neil Bissoondath, *Selling Illusions: The Cult of Multiculturalism in Canada* (Toronto: Penguin, 1994)

Milda Danys, *DP: Lithuanian Immigration to Canada After the Second World War* (Toronto: Multicultural History Society of Ontario, 1986)

Robert A. Harney, *If One Were to Write a History: Selected Writings* (Toronto: Multicultural History Society of Ontario, 1991)

Freda Hawkins, *Canada and Immigration: Public Policy and Public Concern* (Montreal: McGill-Queen's University Press, 1988)

Franca Iacovetta, *Such Hardworking People: Italian Immigrants in Post-war Toronto* (Montreal: McGill-Queen's University Press, 1992)

Howard Palmer, *Immigration and the Rise of Multiculturalism* (Toronto: Copp Clark, 1975)

Frances Swyripa, *Wedded to the Cause: Ukrainian-Canadian Women and Ethnic Identity, 1891-1991* (Toronto: University of Toronto Press, 1993)

Reg Whitaker, *Double Standard: The Secret History of Canadian Immigration* (Toronto: University of Toronto, 1987)

The Country in Question

Changes in Quebec, brought about in part by the Quiet Revolution, soon reverberated throughout the rest of Canada. These reforms, which aspired to create an expanded role of the state and the *francaisation* of Quebec society, also questioned the *status quo* of Canadian federalism. The federal Liberal party, which had dominated postwar national politics, had overseen an increasingly centralized and powerful government in Ottawa.

During the summer of 1967, while many Canadians celebrated the hundredth anniversary of Confederation and the birth of their country, others sought to change it. General Charles De Gaulle, then President of France, offered words of encouragement to Quebec separatists with his cry of "Vive le Québec libre!" On 18 September that year, Liberal cabinet minister René Lévesque made a more important speech, when he publicly announced his new position of political independence for Quebec while maintaining an economic union with Canada.

The victory of the Parti Québécois in 1976 put the issue of competing visions of Canada at the centre of political life. Countless government reports, commissions, meetings, constitutional amendments, and two Quebec referenda have not resolved the question. During the 1980 referendum, federalists campaigning on the *non* side held out the promise that a rejection of sovereignty was not a vote for the *status quo*, but a signal for constitutional renewal.

Prime Minister Pierre Trudeau believed he fulfilled his commitment to constitutional renewal with the repatriation of the Constitution in 1982, and the introduction of the Charter of Rights and Freedoms. He did so, however, over the objections of Quebec. New federal and provincial leaders restarted talks in 1986, as Prime Minister Brian Mulroney sought his place in Canadian constitutional history by sponsoring the 'Québec Round'—a second set of negotiations which were intended to recognize the distinct character of Quebec, and bring it into the 1982 constitution. The result was the 1987 Meech Lake Accord. This agreement, however, failed to be ratified by every province before the deadline of 30 June 1990, when Cree Manitoba MLA Elijah Harper refused to co-operate in special legislation which would hasten its passage in the Manitoba legislature. The accord was also opposed by the government of Newfoundland. The failure of Meech Lake reinvigorated the Quebec separatist movement, and motivated other attempts at constitutional compromise, such as the 1992 Charlottetown Accord. The Charlottetown Accord was unsuccessfully put before the Canadian people in the first national plebiscite since the debates around conscription in World War II. In October 1995, Quebec had its second referendum with the sovereigntists losing by a tiny minority.

The decline in support for the Meech Lake Accord between 1987 and 1990 coincided with major economic changes in Canadian society. The 1985 report of the Royal Commission on the Economic Union and Development Prospects for Canada (the Macdonald Commission), urged Canadians to take a 'leap of faith' and change economic policies to meet the challenges of globalization. It took federal economic policy away from the direction originally established by the 1879 National Policy. Tariff-protected domestic industry and a subsidized transportation policy would be replaced by the principles of free trade and a reduced role for government in the economy. This policy direction reflected the current economic orthodoxy of neo-liberalism, and was embodied in the introduction of the Free Trade Agreement with the United States in 1989, and the 1993 North America Free Trade Agreement (NAFTA) which extended this arrangement to include Mexico.

Section A
The Place of Quebec in Canada

Quebec author Solange Chaput Rolland pondered the place of Quebec within Canada in her writings of the early 1960s. A conclusion similar to that she reached was drawn by René Lévesque, a member of the provincial Liberal cabinet, who left his party in 1967 to form the *Mouvement Souveraineté-Association*, and, in 1968, the *Parti Québécois*. While the *Parti Québécois* and its followers pursued democratic means, other groups such as the revolutionary *Front de libération du Québec* (FLQ), were influenced by international liberation movements associated with decolonization, and adopted violent, direct action. The democratic strategy of the *Parti Québécois* was successful in 1976 when it formed the government. The following year it introduced language legislation to entrench the status of French as the only official language of Quebec; francophones outside Quebec feared for their future.

Solange Chaput Rolland's 1966 Canadian Travel Diary

I shall end this diary by noting the similarities between French and English societies both subjected to cultural, economic, and political pressures. *Vis-à-vis* the U.S.A., English Canada does not exist politically; economically it offers to the Americans some good possibilities for investment which allow them to reaffirm their strength on this continent.

Vis-à-vis English Canada, French Canada has no political power either, but the economic development of our province rests on English and American capital. Thus, French and English Canadians are satellites of the Americans and we are both in danger of becoming more and more Americanized. The only difference between our two nations is that we in Quebec hold desperately to our identity, while English Canada does not yet fully understand the meaning of one. But our two national weaknesses do not make a political force. If years ago we had only studied our qualities instead of harping on our respective faults, Canada would probably not be a more united nation; but least it would have more strength to fight American pressures and to convince Canadians not to seek radical answers to difficult and long-standing problems.

Here I must confess that I am not very good at adopting a constitutional or juridical language to speak about our Canadian crisis. But I must say that even if the true spirit of the B.N.A. Act signed in 1867 did not allow for the presence of two political nations in Canada, it is no longer possible in 1967 to ignore the two branches of the Canadian tree. Quebec is not and never will be a province *comme les autres,* because four million human beings live, think, speak, and fight in a political and cultural climate completely different from that of the nine other provinces. Even when Donald Creighton, the high priest of constitutional matters, writes in arrogant anger, 'French-Canadian nationalism could be carried to the point at which English Canada would finally decide in disgust and indignation that it had had enough,' English Canada will still have to face the fact that we have survived, we are the second-largest majority in Canada, and we have the right to speak in our own country.

Since Quebec forms a society in constant evolution, her needs in 1967 cannot be fulfilled by a constitution ratified one hundred years ago. As long as Quebec will be compelled to act as a province, there will be tensions between our provincial government and the federal one, and within a few months we will come to a constitutional impasse endangering the life of the whole nation. Yes, independence for Quebec would be the ideal solution for those of us tired of not being able to feel at home in our own country. But English Canada is not ready to fight alone against the American giant; and Quebec is no more ready to assume alone the destiny of four million people, because these four million French Canadians have chosen to dream their fate rather than work to better it in their everyday lives.

This is why, if English Canada can never be my country because it refuses to accept my language and culture and refuses to share with me Canada's future, Quebec therefore is *ma patrie*. But Quebec is not yet a country. My own compatriots have not so far created structures for our political, cultural, and economic independence. If I analyse the failures of our societies, I cannot resist pointing out that we form two worlds in agony. An independent Quebec that in twenty years could no longer assume its liberty would die in the arms of irate Americans furious at being obliged to add our problems to theirs. And an English Canada economically weak could not survive if it were cut in two by Quebec's secession. In consequence, French and English Canadians who, for the sake of superiority, revenge, or racial prejudices refuse to accept the reality of our collective weaknesses will, tomorrow, be held responsible for Canada's death.

Yes, I am pessimistic, but I defy my reader to live for months among people who have nothing much in common and to come out of this experience without being morally bruised. Like all French-Canadian nationalists, I would love to write firmly that my country is Quebec, but again I face the problem that Quebec as a country does not exist. And I will not create it with words of anger, with dreams, with love or hatred; I will not invent a country by refusing to live in step with an Anglo-American rhythm, by justifying my hunger for freedom, or by seeking revenge because Ottawa has refused to give what I considered vital. Quebec will become a country only when the whole nation wants it…

I begin to suspect that the best solution for problems confronting us for years to come might be to adopt a special status that will eventually lead us to the concept of associate states modelled on the Federation of Switzerland. I already hear the loud protest of my English-speaking friends who will accuse me of wanting too much too quickly. But I feel that the time is ripe to ask for too much and very quickly. If English Canada does not give Quebec a more important place in the constitution, then yes, we will run to an independence for which neither French nor English Canada is prepared. I have no intentions of blackmailing anyone with these remarks; I have studied some facts and I simply give them their logical evaluation.

When I began this diary I stated: 'What I will write about Canada will not change Canada.' How little did I know on that night of February 1966 how much my trip would transform me. More than my publishers and my readers, I am fully conscious that the task of inventing solutions to unify a country divided into ten republics is too much for a single human being. I am also aware that though I have tried to remain serene and objective, I have probably not reported all I have heard and seen, nor have I been able to study extensively the imperatives for each province. But for more than six months, I have looked in all sincerity for a common denominator between French and English Canadians, and I have not found one.

Consequently, I have come back to my land, *ma Terre-Québec,* more *Québécoise* than *Canadienne,* because I have learned harshly, with pain and anguish, that to remain true to my past, to my culture, to my language, and to the very French individual that I have become, I must live in Quebec, in a Quebec that one day may yet become my *country.*

[Solange Chaput Rolland, My Country, Canada or Quebec? *(Toronto: MacMillan, 1966), pp. 115-118]*

René Lévesque and Sovereignty Association

There are key moments in the existence of a nation when boldness and quiet courage become the only form of prudence that can be applied.

If the nation does not then accept the calculated risk of major steps it can lose its destiny forever, exactly like a man who is afraid of life.

Nevertheless, on the road to guaranteed survival and permanent progress on which no nation can be allowed to stop, we have been moving for some time towards a crucial crossroads. It is up to us to choose the political status which suits us best; that is to say, the road which permits us the most sure and efficient way to accomplish the necessary steps.

On the one hand Quebec has attached itself in the last few years to an exhausting collective catching up in a large number of fields where backwardness had built up. As incomplete and imperfect as they are, these accomplishments have already allowed us to discover that the more we decide to undertake our "work" ourselves, the more we feel ourselves capable of succeeding as well as others.

This very normal feeling of being better served by ourselves, added to the inevitable pressures of unceasingly increasing needs and aspirations, has resulted in the establishment of a more and more precise plan which is still expanding; the plan of rights that Quebec realizes it can not do without and the instruments and resources which it needs to exercise them. This ever-important plan, which no one has a right to ignore, constitutes for us a strict minimum.

But on the other hand, it would seem that it would be dreaming to believe that for the rest of the country, this plan would not turn out to be a totally unacceptable maximum. From the viewpoint of a simple revision or even constitutional revamping, what we would have to ask, from all evidence surpasses not only the best of intentions shown in Ottawa and elsewhere but without doubt, also the ability of the present Federal regime to agree without fragmentation.

If Quebec was to engage and persist in talks to revise the present structures, it is clear that in 100 years it would still not be out of the woods. However, it is very probable that this nation which is now trying to make out of itself an acceptable homeland, would certainly not want to speak of the past. This would periodically bring the lamentable return to the old defensive battle and skirmishes during which we exhausted ourselves while neglecting the principle, as well as the falling back in electioneering at the two levels, harmful illusions of verbal nationalism and above all, the waste of energy that for us is surely the most nefarious aspect of the regime.

But this waste of energy is also felt on the English side of Canada. The regime also hinders the other majority in its efforts to simplify, rationalize and centralize as it would like to institutions which appear to be outdated.

This is proof that it endures a sense of frustration which from all evidence is in danger of soon becoming intolerable.

This parallel quest for two securities and two paths of collective progress, could not be continued in the present structures or anything close to it, without our ending up with a double paralysis.

Searching in the final analysis for the same thing—the chance to live life in one's own way according to one's needs and priorities—the two majorities would only continue to collide, always harder, one against the other, always hurting each other, creating mutual harm which would never end.

We believe it is possible to avoid this joint dead end by adapting to our situations the two big currents that dominate our era: that of the liberty of peoples and that of freely negotiated political and economical groupings.

Convinced among other things, that the danger is much less in a clear and distinct option rather than in the present hesitations and increasing instability which accompanies it, we propose the following:

First, we have to rid ourselves completely of the thoroughly-outdated federal regime. The problem can not resolve itself by the continuance or modification of the status quo.

That means that we will have to dare claim for ourselves the entire liberty of Quebec, its right to all the essential elements of independence, that is to say, the full control of each and every one of its principal collective decisions.

That means that Quebec should become a sovereign state.

Only in this way will we finally find security for our collective existence which otherwise would remain uncertain and crippled.

Only in this way will we finally have the chance and obligation to exert to the maximum our energies and our talents to solve, without excuse or loophole, all important questions that concern us.

In addition to being the only logical solution to the present Canadian impasse, it is also the sole common goal which can be overriding to the point of uniting us all, united strong enough to face all possible futures.

To English Canada we must then propose to maintain an association not only of neighbors but also of partners in a common enterprise without which it would be, for one as well as the other, impossible to preserve and develop on this continent, societies distinct from the United States.

This undertaking would be made up essentially of the ties, of the complementary activities of the innumerable economic inter-relationships within which we have learned to live. We would not destroy the framework in order to have to, sooner or later, maybe too late, rebuild it.

Such an association seems to us tailored to permit us, without the encumbrance of constitutional rigidities, to make common cause with permanent consultations, flexible adjustments and appropriate mechanisms which our common economic interest requires: Monetary union, a common tariff and co-ordination of fiscal policies. Nothing would prevent us—to the degree that we learn to understand each other better and to co-operate better in the context—from freely adding other areas where the same common action would seem mutually advantageous.

In short, we would have a regime within which two nations, one whose homeland would be Quebec, the other arranging the rest of the country to suit itself, would associate themselves in a new adaptation of the current formula of the common markets to form a new entity which could, for example, call itself the "Canadian Union."

[Summary statement of speech to Laurier Riding Association, presented to Quebec Liberal Federation, October 1967 (translated) in Canadian Annual Review 1967 *(Toronto: University of Toronto Press, 1968), pp. 64-65.]*

FLQ Manifesto, 8 October 1970 (translated)

The Front de libération du Québec is not a messiah, nor a modern day Robin Hood. It is a group of Quebec workers who have decided to use every means to make sure that the people of Quebec take control of their destiny.

The Front de libération du Québec wants the total independence of all Québécois, united in a free society, purged forever of the clique of voracious sharks, the patronizing "big bosses" and their henchmen who have made Quebec their hunting preserve for "cheap labour" and unscrupulous exploitation.

The Front de libération du Québec is not a movement of aggression, but is a response to the aggression organized by high finance and the puppet governments in Ottawa and Quebec (the Brinks "show," Bill 63, the electoral map, the so-called social progress tax, Power Corporation, "Doctors' insurance," the Lapalme guys...)

The Front de libération du Québec finances itself by "voluntary taxes" taken from the same enterprises that exploit the workers (banks, finance companies, etc...)

"The money power of the status quo, the majority of the traditional teachers of our people, have obtained the reaction they hoped for; a backward step rather than the change for which we have worked as never before, for which we will continue to work" (René Lévesque, April 29, 1970).

We believed once that perhaps it would be worth it to channel our energy and our impatience, as René Lévesque said so well, into the Parti québécois, but the Liberal victory clearly demonstrated that that which we call democracy in Quebec is nothing but the democracy of the rich. The Liberal party's victory was nothing but the victory of the election riggers, Simard-Cotroni. As a result, the British parliamentary system is finished and the Front de libération du Québec will never allow itself to be fooled by the pseudo-elections that the Anglo-Saxon capitalists toss to the people of Quebec every four years. A number of Québécois have understood and will act. In the coming year Bourassa will have to face reality; 100,000 revolutionary workers, armed and organized.

Yes, there are reasons for the Liberal victory. Yes, there are reasons for poverty, unemployment, slums, and for the fact that you, Mr Bergeron of Visitation Street and you, Mr Legendre of Laval who earn $10,000 a year, will not feel free in our country of Quebec.

Yes, there are reasons, and the guys at Lord know them, the fishermen of the Gaspé, the workers of the North Shore, the miners for the Iron Ore Company, Quebec Cartier Mining, and Noranda, also know these reasons. And the brave workers of Cabano that you tried to screw again know lots of reasons.

Yes, there are reasons why you, Mr Tremblay of Panet Street and you Mr Cloutier, who work in construction in St Jérôme, cannot pay for "Vaisseaux d'or" with all the jazz and oom-pa-pa like Drapeau the aristocrat, who is so concerned with slums that he puts coloured billboards in front of them to hide our misery from the tourists

Yes, there are reasons why you, Mrs Lemay of St Hyacinthe, can't pay for little trips to Florida like our dirty judges and parliamentary members do with our money.

The brave workers for Vickers and Davie Ship, who were thrown out and not given a reason, know these reasons. And the Murdochville men, who were attacked for the simple and sole reason that they wanted to organize a union and who were forced to pay $2 million by the dirty judges simply because they tried to exercise this basic right—they know justice and they know the reasons.

Yes, there are reasons why you, Mr Lachance of St Marguerite Street, must go and drown your sorrows in a bottle of that dog's beer, Molson. And you, Lachance's son, with your marijuana cigarettes...

Yes, there are reasons why you, the welfare recipients, are kept from generation to generation on social welfare. Yes, there are all sorts of reasons, and the Domtar workers in East Angus and Windsor know them well. And the workers at Squibb and Ayers, and the men at the Liquor Board and those at Seven-Up and Victoria Precision, and the blue collar workers in Laval and Montreal and the Lapalme boys know those reasons well.

The Dupont of Canada workers know them as well, even if soon they will only be able to express them in English (thus assimilated they will enlarge the number of immigrants and New Quebeckers, the darlings of Bill 63).

And the Montreal policemen, those strongarms of the system, should understand these reasons—they should have been able to see we live in a terrorized society because, without their force, without their violence, nothing could work on October 7.

We have had our fill of Canadian federalism which penalizes the Quebec milk producers to satisfy the needs of the Anglo-Saxons of the Commonwealth; the system which keeps the gallant Montreal taxi drivers in a state of semi-slavery to shamefully protect the exclusive monopoly of the nauseating Murray Hill and its proprietor—the murderer Charles Hershorn and his son Paul, who, on the night of October 7, repeatedly grabbed the twelve gauge shot gun from his employees hands to fire upon the taxi drivers and thereby mortally wound corporal Dumas, killed while demonstrating.

We have had our fill of a federal system which exercises a policy of heavy importation while turning out into the street the low wage-earners in the textile and shoe manufacturing trades, who are the most ill-treated in Quebec, for the benefit of a clutch of damned money-makers in their Cadillacs which rate the Quebec nation on the same level as other ethnic minorities in Canada.

We have had our fill, as have more and more Québécois, of a government which performs a-thousand-and-one acrobatics to charm American millionaires into investing in Quebec, La Belle Province, where thousands and thousands of square miles of forests, full of game and well-stocked lakes, are the exclusive preserve of the almighty twentieth century lords.

We have had our fill of a hypocrite like Bourassa who relies on Brinks armoured trucks, the living symbol of the foreign occupation of Quebec, to keep the poor natives of Quebec in the fear of misery and unemployment in which they are accustomed to living.

We have had our fill of taxes which the Ottawa representative to Quebec wants to give to the Anglophone bosses to encourage them to speak French, old boy, to negotiate in French: Repeat after me: "Cheap labour means man-power in a healthy market."

We have had our fill of promises of jobs and prosperity while we always remain the cowering servants and boot-lickers of the big shots who live in Westmount, Town of Mount Royal, Hampstead, and Outremont; all the fortresses of high finance on St James and Wall streets, while we, the Québécois, have not used all our means, including arms and dynamite, to rid ourselves of these economic and political bosses who are prepared to use every sort of sordid tactic to better screw us.

We live in a society of terrorized slaves, terrorized by the big bosses like Steinberg, Clark, Bronfman, Smith, Neaple, Timmins, Geoffrion, J.L. Lévesque, Hershorn, Thompson, Nesbitt, Desmarais, Kierans. Compared to them Rémi Popol the lousy no-good, Drapeau the Dog, Bourassa the lackey of the Simards, and Trudeau the fairy are peanuts.

We are terrorized by the capitalist Roman church, even though this seems less and less obvious (who owns the property on which the stock exchange stands?); by the payments to pay back Household Finance; by the publicity of the overlords of retail trade like Eaton, Simpson, Morgan, Steinberg, and General Motors; we are terrorized by the closed circles of science and culture which are the universities and by their bosses like Gaudry and Dorais and by the underling Robert Shaw.

The number of those who realize the oppression of this terrorist society are growing and the day will come when all the Westmounts of Quebec will disappear from the map.

Production workers, miners, foresters, teachers, students, and unemployed workers, take what belong to you, your jobs, your right to decide, and your liberty. And you, workers of General Electric, it's you who makes your factories run, only you are capable of production; without you General Electric is nothing!

Workers of Quebec, start today to take back what is yours; take for yourselves what belongs to you. Only you know your factories, your machines, your hotels, your universities, your unions. Don't wait for an organizational miracle.

Make your own revolution in your areas, in your places of work. And if you don't do it yourselves, other usurpers, technocrats and so on will replace the handful of cigar smokers we know, and everything will be the same again. Only you are able to build a free society.

We must fight, not singly, but together. We must fight until victory is ours with all the means at our disposal as did the patriots of 1837-38 (those whom our sacred Mother church excommunicated to sell out to the British interests).

In the four corners of Quebec, may those who have been contemptuously called lousy French and alcoholics start fighting their best against the enemies of liberty and justice and prevent all the professional swindlers and robbers, the bankers, the businessmen, the judges, and the sold-out politicators from causing harm.

We are the workers of Quebec and we will continue to the bitter end. We want to replace the slave society with a free society, functioning by itself and for itself; a society open to the world.

Our struggle can only lead to victory. You cannot hold an awakening people in misery and contempt indefinitely. Long live Free Quebec!

Long live our imprisoned political comrades.

Long live the Quebec revolution!

Long live the Front de libération du Québec.

[Canadian Annual Review 1970 (Toronto: University of Toronto Press, 1971), p. 46]

The Double Minority: French Canadians Outside Quebec Respond to the Election of the Parti Québécois

Manifesto

Our dreams have been shattered. We are going through a severe crisis which may even have been planned and deliberately cultivated. Francophones outside Quebec are like a family whose home has been destroyed by fire. We are without shelter, our eyes fixed on odd belongings scattered here and there. But we are still alive.

We the Francophones outside Quebec are a distressed people but we will no longer delude ourselves with the illusion that has for so long been fed to us: that we are the reason for this country's existence and that we have a special vocation to take an active part in the development of the two founding nations. These words are meaningless for people who no longer feel at home.

We have been manipulated without our knowledge. This was done so cleverly that we actually believed for a while that any opposition would be useless.

We know now why we are where we are. We, the French-speaking people of the Anglophone provinces, know now who we are. Actually, we suspected it for a long time but the dignity of silence now gives way to the dignity of speaking out. We want to make known our plight and explain why we refuse to be treated as pawns in a national chess game.

We are through with the deceitful words which cover up the wrong, through with the short-lived policies in which we so naively believed. We are also through with hiding our situation from everyone, afraid of admitting what we knew about ourselves. Finally, we are through with the thanks extracted from us by making us feel guilty.

The situation is clear now, the die is cast: if we survive, it will be because we have dared to speak out about ourselves and the injustice we suffer.

We face tremendous challenges. Today, our rights are illusory. Our schools are centres of assimilation. Access to our network of radio, television, and other communications systems is escaping us. Our national collectivity and soul is gradually vanishing.

Finally we must completely enter the economic sphere in all its dimensions so that we may abandon the image of ourselves as a quaint and obsolete folk culture.

Illusory rights

Whereas French has no definite and enforceable legal status across the country;
— French is not recognized in the Legislative Assemblies, except in three provinces (New Brunswick, Ontario and Quebec); French has received official recognition before the courts in only one province outside Quebec (New Brunswick);

- Integral parts of the legislation are still to be promulgated in the only province (New Brunswick), other than Quebec, where French has obtained official status in the Legislative Assembly;
- Full bilingual services in the Legislative Assembly are not available to Francophones, except in Quebec and New Brunswick;
- The official recognition of French in some provinces does not go beyond wishful thinking and statements of good intentions.

The Francophone communities outside Quebec must realize that they are the victims of a legal mirage.

Schools: Centres of alienation

It is not necessary to forbid French schools to ensure our alienation. Given enough time, we will eventually exhaust ourselves, grow more tired and will be forced to give up. Nor is it necessary to take away our schools. They can simply be granted to us only after long struggles and access to them can be made difficult. It is only necessary to wait and never provide for our most fundamental needs in the area of education. We do not have control of school boards. We are not perceived as landlords but tolerated tenants.

The so-called "bilingual" mixed schools do not ensure the transfer of our cultural identity from one generation to the other. They are not the centres of personal and collective development we would like them to be. On the contrary, for a number of reasons we will state, they have become a unique environment for the progressive and constant weakening of our identity. As a result, entire generations are lost.

Medium without a message
Ottawa (FFHQ) Francophones outside Quebec dissatisfied with the CBC

The FFHQ is greatly dissatisfied with the CBC's regional programming policy. The President of the Federation has announced that he will appeal to Parliament to obtain the implementation of the Accelerated Coverage Plan and the revision of all the programming policies of the Crown Corporation.

Francophones outside Quebec, he said, are very poorly served by the media. Their newspapers are in financial difficulty; French radio and television broadcasts are often unavailable and still do not meet the needs of a large segment of the French-speaking population outside Quebec.

The soul of a nation

A culture is made up of a number and variety of expressions of the life of a people. Ours is empty as we are. Why? The answer to this question lies in our everyday life. We are fed a North American culture which is necessarily Anglophone, a culture hardly Canadian, in which we see no reflection of what we are.

Twice a minority, Francophones outside Quebec lack the necessary resources to fill the gaps in a culture that is breaking up and losing its continuity. The consciousness that is manifested in our cultural expressions is not supported by those who nevertheless have promised to help the continued emergence of the vital forces of our communities. We could be on the threshold of a fuller development and expression of our collective life: we only lack the liberating spark.

Do you speak French?
We were born French Canadians. As a people, we must be able to live and develop in the French language, or else we are destined to disappear. The disappearance of our language would signal the collapse of our collective aspirations. We have seen the launching of institutional bilingualism programmes since the late sixties. But, limited to these programmes, the bilingualism policy is doomed to failure. Bilingualism cannot survive or expand without the advancement of the Francophone communities in Quebec and in each of the Canadian provinces.

The same old arguments
Before we determine our method of action and the minimum conditions for a real and complete solution to the problems of Francophone communities outside Quebec, we wish to point out that we are perfectly aware of the ready-made arguments likely to be advanced and of the attempts likely to be made to divert us from our objectives. The Francophone communities outside Quebec have anticipated this manoeuver and will not be fooled by the diversionary tactics of those who would try to minimize the strength of the one million people these communities represent. By now, we are well acquainted with all these tactics and only list them here to discourage anyone who might be tempted to use them.

"People don't want French."

"Francophones are apathetic and fail to get involved when something is done for them."

"Francophones are not united."

"You have rights but you don't use them."

"Things are fine... progress has been made. Don't you appreciate what we are doing for you?"

"You are too pessimistic. Things are not all that bad."

"You don't understand, you don't see the problem in the right light."

"You can't determine what you need because you lack the necessary analytical tools."

"Your structures and cultural associations are not responsible. They are inefficient."

"You ask for too much too soon... there are limits."

"We have tremendous administrative problems which complicate decision-making. We cannot proceed any faster."

"We must consider the multicultural Canadian mosaic. French Canadians are not the only people to be considered."

"You are full-fledged citizens. You have access to all government services in the same capacity as everyone else."

"You must understand that it is necessary to attract the moderate Anglophones to your cause."

We have repeated these arguments in our manifesto to denounce the attitude of those who make it their duty to repeat these fallacious statements and who, instead of hearing us, deny us the right to perceive and express our own drama.

The Condition
This final and public display of our collective disillusion may seem brutal. Yet, all our communities experience it. They have all analysed their true needs and have all determined the minimum conditions without which they would be unable to resist the pressures of the environment much longer.

These minimum conditions must be translated into a comprehensive, coherent and specific development policy for communities of French language and culture.

That is the ultimate criterion on which the judgment made on this country will be based.

> [*La Fédération des Francophones hors Québec*, The Heirs of Lord Durham: Manifesto of a Vanishing People *(Ottawa, 1978), pp. 19-20]*

Charter of the French Language (Bill 101)

Bill No. 101, 1977, assented to August 26, 1977

Preamble

WHEREAS the French language, the distinctive language of a people that is in the majority French-speaking, is the instrument by which that people has articulated its identity;

Whereas the Assemblée Nationale du Québec recognizes that Québecers wish to see the quality and influence of the French language assured; and is resolved therefore to make of French the language of Government and the Law, as well as the normal and everyday language of work, instruction, communication, commerce and business;

Whereas the Assemblée Nationale du Québec intends in this pursuit to deal fairly and openly with the ethnic minorities, whose valuable contribution to the development of Québec it readily acknowledges;

Whereas the Assemblée Nationale du Québec recognizes the right of the Amerinds and the Inuit of Québec, the first inhabitants of this land, to preserve and develop their original language and culture;

Whereas these observations and intentions are in keeping with a new perception of the worth of national cultures in all parts of the earth, and of the obligation of every people to contribute in its special way to the international community;

Therefore, Her Majesty, with the advice and consent of the Assemblée Nationale du Québec, enacts as follows:

TITLE I
Status of the French Language

CHAPTER I
The Official Language of Québec
[¶100]

Sec 1. [Official language].—French is the official language of Québec.

CHAPTER II
Fundamental Language Rights
[¶105]

Sec 2. [Right to French communications].—Every person has a right to have the civil administration, the health services and social services, the public utility firms, the professional corporations, the associations of employees and all business firms doing business in Québec communicate with him in French.

[¶ 110]

Sec. 3. [Deliberative assemblies].—In deliberative assembly, every person has a right to speak in French.

[¶115]

Sec. 4. [Workers' activities]. —Workers have a right to carry on their activities in French.

[¶120]

Sec. 5. [Consumers' rights]. —Consumers of goods and services have a right to be informed and served in French.

[¶125]

Sec. 6. [Education]. —Every person eligible for instruction in Québec has a right to receive that instruction in French.

CHAPTER III
The Language of the Legislature
and the Courts
[¶ 130]

Sec. 7. [Official language].—French is the language of the legislature and the courts in Québec.

[¶ 135]

Sec. 8. [Bills].—Legislative bills shall be drafted in the official language. They shall also be tabled in the National Assembly, passed and assented to in that language.

[¶140]

Sec. 9. [French official text]. —Only the French text of the statutes and regulations is official.

[¶ 145]

Sec. 10. [English version available].—An English version of every legislative bill, statute and regulation shall be printed and published by the civil administration.

[¶ 150]

Sec. 11. [Artificial persons' pleadings]. —Artificial persons addressing themselves to the courts and to bodies discharging judicial or quasi-judicial functions shall do so in the official language, and shall use the official language in pleading before them unless all the parties to the action agree to their pleading in English.

[¶ 155]

Sec. 12. [Procedural documents]. —Procedural documents issued by bodies discharging judicial or quasi-judicial functions or drawn up and sent by the advocates practising before them shall be drawn up in the official language. Such documents may, however, be drawn up in another language if the natural person for whose intention they are issued expressly consents thereto.

[¶160]

Sec. 13. [Official version of judgments]. —The judgments rendered in Québec by the courts and by bodies discharging judicial or quasi-judicial functions must be drawn up in French or be accompanied with a duly authenticated French version. Only the French version of the judgment is official.

CHAPTER IV
The Language of the Civil Administration

[¶165]

Sec. 14. [Designation in French only]. —The Government, the government departments, the other agencies of the civil administration and the services thereof shall be designated by their French names alone.

[¶170]

Sec. 15. [Language of texts and documents]. —The civil administration shall draw up and publish its texts and documents in the official language.

This section does not apply to relations with persons outside Québec, to publicity and communiqués carried by news media that publish in a language other than French or to correspondence between the civil administration and natural persons when the latter address it in a language other than French.

[¶175]

Sec. 16. [Communications with other governments, etc.]. —The civil administration shall use only the official language in its written communications with other governments and with artificial persons established in Québec.

[¶180]

Sec. 17. [Internal communications in French only]. —The Government, the government departments and the other agencies of the civil administration shall use only the official language in their written communications with each other.

[¶185]

Sec. 18. [Language of internal communications]. —French is the language of written internal communications in the Government, the government departments, and the other agencies of the civil administration.

[¶190]

Sec. 19. (Minutes, etc., of deliberative assemblies]. —The notices of meeting, agendas and minutes of all deliberative assemblies in the civil administration shall be drawn up in the official language.

[¶ 195]

Sec. 20. [Knowledge for appointment, etc.]. —In order to be appointed, transferred or promoted to an office in the civil administration, a knowledge of the official language appropriate to the office applied for is required.

For the application of the preceding paragraph, each agency of the civil administration shall establish criteria and procedures of verification and submit them to the Office de la langue française for approval, failing which the Office may establish them itself. If the Office considers the criteria and procedures unsatisfactory, it may either request the agency concerned to modify them or establish them itself.

[¶200]

Sec. 21. [Language of contracts]. —Contracts entered into by the civil administration, including the related sub-contracts, shall be drawn up in the official language. Such contracts and the related documents may be drawn up in another language when the civil administration enters into a contract with a party outside Québec.

[¶205]

Sec. 22. [Signs and posters]. —The civil administration shall use only French in signs and posters, except where reasons of public health or safety require the use of another language as well.

[¶210]

Sec. 23. [Health and social services]. —The health services and the social services must ensure that their services are available in the official language.

They must draw up their notices, communications and printed matter intended for the public in the official language.

Sec. 24. [Municipal and school bodies, etc.]. —The municipal and school bodies, the health services and social services and the other services recognized under paragraph (f) of section 113 may erect signs and posters in both French and another language, the French text predominating.

[¶1220]

Sec. 25. [Delay to comply]. —The municipal bodies, the health services and the social services recognized under paragraph (f) of section 113 must comply with sections 15 to 23 before the end of 1983 and, upon the coming into force of this act, must take the required measures to attain that objective.

[¶225]

Sec. 26. [Names and internal communications]. —The school bodies, the health services and the social services recognized under paragraph (f) of section 113 may use both the official language and another language in their names and in their internal communications.

[¶230]

Sec. 27. [Clinical records]. —In the health services and the social services, the documents filed in the clinical records shall be drafted in French or in English, as the person drafting them sees fit. However, each health service or social service may require such documents to be drafted in French alone. Resumés of clinical records must be furnished in French on demand to any person authorized to obtain them.

[¶235]

Sec. 28. [School bodies' internal communications]. —In the school bodies, the official language and the language of instruction may be used as the language of internal communication in departments entrusted with organizing or giving instruction in a language other than French.

[¶240]

Sec. 29. [Traffic signs]. —Only the official language shall be used on traffic signs. The French inscription may be complemented or replaced by symbols or pictographs.

*[Québec Charter of the French Language with Regulations
(CCH Canadian, 1977), pp. 7-9] Reproduced by permission of Publications
du Québec.*

The 1980 Referendum Question

THE GOVERNMENT OF QUEBEC HAS MADE PUBLIC ITS PROPOSAL TO NEGOTIATE A NEW AGREEMENT WITH THE REST OF CANADA BASED ON THE EQUALITY OF NATIONS;

THIS AGREEMENT WOULD ENABLE QUEBEC TO ACQUIRE THE EXCLUSIVE POWER TO MAKE ITS LAWS, LEVY ITS TAXES AND

ESTABLISH RELATIONS ABROAD—IN OTHER WORDS, SOVEREIGN-
TY—AND AT THE SAME TIME TO MAINTAIN WITH CANADA AN
ECONOMIC ASSOCIATION INCLUDING A COMMON CURRENCY;

NO CHANGE IN POLITICAL STATUS RESULTING FROM THESE NEGO-
TIATIONS WILL BE AFFECTED WITHOUT APPROVAL BY THE PEOPLE
THROUGH ANOTHER REFERENDUM;

ON THESE TERMS DO YOU GIVE THE GOVERNMENT OF QUEBEC THE
MANDATE TO NEGOTIATE THE PROPOSED AGREEMENT BETWEEN
QUEBEC AND CANADA?

> *[Marie-Hélène Bergeron et al, eds.,* The Question: The Debate on the
> Referendum Question, *National Assembly March 4-20 1980: Documents on
> the Debate (Kingston: Institute of Intergovernmental Relations, 1980), p. 4]*

Section B
The 1980s and Beyond

The federal government's responsibility for equalization of regional disparities was entrenched in the 1982 constitution. This impulse towards central-
ization was at odds with a general trend toward decentralization, as embodied in the Meech Lake Accord. Voices of dissent, whether they be the
Assembly of First Nations, Quebec, or anti-free traders, together joined the
chorus of a tumultuous period in public life.

The Macdonald Commission on Regional Development

This Commission believes that regional development must remain an essential
component of Canadian policy and, indeed, of the Confederation bargain as now
reflected in section 36 of the Constitution Act, 1982. It must be recognized, however, that policies intended to promote regional development have often hindered
the overall efficiency of the national economy in that they impeded inter-regional adjustment and distorted regional development. Canadians need to reconsider
the way in which we look at regional economic disparity, what we do to overcome
it, and the institutional mechanisms we bring to the task.

■ We recommend a new federal-provincial system of sharing regional development expenditures and responsibilities.

• The federal government should direct regional development programs
toward improving regional productivity and the efficiency of the labour market. To these ends, such programs should include measures to improve work-

er and management skills, enhance research and development efforts, ensure a high level of infrastructural support, and supply assistance for intra- and inter-regional mobility. The federal government should not only provide such programs on a national basis, but should also make a special effort in the less developed provinces. While it might make sense, too, for the federal government to provide assistance for plant modernization as a means to enhance regional productivity, we believe that it should provide this type of assistance on a national basis, if at all, or that the provincial governments should take on this responsibility on a regional basis.

• Under his arrangement, the federal government would end all explicit and direct regional employment-creation programs. While national schemes would continue, federal subsidies, tax breaks, and so on, intended only to generate jobs in, or attract firms to, a particular locale, would be eliminated. Similarly, the federal government would terminate regionally differentiated unemployment-insurance programs, tax credits, and other measures that tend to distort regional labour markets. Funds formerly allocated to these types of programs would instead become the source of Regional Economic Development Grants.

• Provinces that qualify for equalization payments would be eligible for Regional Economic Development Grants. The amounts of the grants would be determined by a formula on a per capita basis, and they would be proportionate to the degree of fiscal disparity identified by the equalization formula. As noted earlier, equalization payments are necessary to offset economic disparities, while the purpose of these new grants would be to reduce future disparities. They would be renegotiated every five years.

• Provinces would assume full responsibility for local or place-specific employment measures as part of their own approach to regional development. They would be free to use the Regional Economic Development Grants for this purpose, subject only to two conditions:

– Each recipient province would sign an Economic and Regional Development Agreement (ERDA) with the federal government, which would set out a broad economic development plan for the province (and for each other province) and would indicate the measures to be carried out by both orders of government. Some elements of these packages might take the form of shared-cost programs or federal contributions to provincial activities; in general, however, Commissioners recommend that under the ERDA umbrella, each government remain responsible for the implementation and delivery of its own programs, in order to enhance accountability.

– The recipient province would be required to sign the proposed Code of Economic Conduct to improve the functioning of the Canadian economic union.

■ While recognizing the immediate need for financial prudence at the federal level, Commissioners believe that the total federal financial commitment to regional development—combining the Regional Economic Development

Grants and other funds spent through ERDAs—should increase significantly over the next few years.

- The federal government would continue to play an important role in other development efforts which have significant regional impacts such as:
  - A reformed equalization system
  - The proposed Universal Income Security Program and the Transitional Adjustment Assistance Program
  - Sectoral policies, such as those pertaining to fisheries, agriculture, and forestry. These should be designed according to criteria for good sectoral policy (see Parts III and IV of this Report), but they ought to also be developed in close consultation with provincial governments where these are affected to an important degree.

■ A sustained federal commitment to regional development requires that a single central agency be responsible for injecting regional concerns into the programs of individual federal departments, and for co-ordinating federal efforts. It would appear to Commissioners that the Federal-Provincial Relations Office (FPRO) reporting to the Prime Minister, would be the appropriate existing body. We believe also that the Federal Economic Development Co-ordinator (FEDC) or other senior officials resident in each province could help to co-ordinate federal activities within each province, interacting with the provincial government and establishing links with local economic interests. The federal government should enlarge the responsibilities of such federal regional officials, who should report directly to FPRO.

[Privy Council Office, Canada, Report of the Royal Commission on the Economic Union and Development Prospects for Canada Vol. III (Ottawa, 1985) Compendium of Conclusions and Recommendations, Part VI: The Institutional Context, pp. 467-471] Reproduced with the permission of the Minister of Public Works and Government Services, Canada, 1997.

Text of the Meech Lake Accord

1987 CONSTITUTIONAL ACCORD
JUNE 3, 1987

WHEREAS first ministers, assembled in Ottawa, have arrived at a unanimous accord on constitutional amendments that would bring about the full and active participation of Quebec in Canada's constitutional evolution, would recognize the principle of equality of all provinces, would provide new arrangements to foster greater harmony and cooperation between the Government of Canada and the governments of the provinces and would require that annual constitutional conferences composed of first ministers be convened not later than December 31, 1988;

AND WHEREAS first ministers have also reached unanimous agreement on certain additional commitments in relation to some of those amendments;

NOW THEREFORE the Prime Minister of Canada and the first ministers of the provinces commit themselves and the governments they represent to the following:

1. The Prime Minister of Canada will lay or cause to be laid before the Senate and House of Commons, and the first ministers of the provinces will lay or cause to be laid before their legislative assemblies, as soon as possible, a resolution, in the form appended hereto, to authorize a proclamation to be issued by the Governor General under the Great Seal of Canada to amend the Constitution of Canada.

2. The Government of Canada will, as soon as possible, conclude an agreement with the Government of Quebec that would

(a) incorporate the principles of the Cullen-Couture agreement on the selection abroad and in Canada of independent immigrants, visitors for medical treatment, students and temporary workers, and on the selection of refugees abroad and economic criteria for family reunification and assisted relatives,

(b) guarantee that Quebec will receive a number of immigrants, including refugees, within the annual total established by the federal government for all of Canada proportionate to its share of the population of Canada, with the right to exceed that figure by five per cent for demographic reasons, and

(c) provide an undertaking by Canada to withdraw services (except citizenship services) for the reception and integration (including linguistic and cultural) of all foreign nationals wishing to settle in Quebec where services are to be provided by Quebec, with such withdrawal to be accompanied by reasonable compensation, and the Government of Canada and the Government of Quebec will take the necessary steps to give the agreement the force of law under the proposed amendment relating to such agreements.

3. Nothing in this Accord should be construed as preventing the negotiation of similar agreements with other provinces relating to immigration and the temporary admission of aliens.

4. Until the proposed amendment relating to appointments to the Senate comes into force, any person summoned to fill a vacancy in the Senate shall be chosen from among persons whose names have been submitted by the government of the province to which the vacancy relates and must be acceptable to the Queen's Privy Council for Canada.

Motion for a Resolution to authorize
an amendment to the Constitution of Canada

WHEREAS the Constitution Act, 1982 came into force on April 17, 1982, following an agreement between Canada and all the provinces except Quebec;

AND WHEREAS the Government of Quebec has established a set of five proposals for constitutional change and has stated that amendments to give effect to those proposals would enable Quebec to resume a full role in the constitutional councils of Canada;

AND WHEREAS the amendment proposed in the schedule hereto sets out the basis on which Quebec's five constitutional proposals may be met;

AND WHEREAS the amendment proposed in the schedule hereto also recognizes the principle of the equality of all the provinces, provides new arrangements to foster greater harmony and cooperation between the Government of Canada and the governments of the provinces and requires that conferences be convened to consider important constitutional, economic and other issues;

AND WHEREAS certain portions of the amendment proposed in the schedule hereto relate to matters referred to in section 41 of the Constitution Act, 1982;

AND WHEREAS section 41 of the Constitution Act, 1982 provides that an amendment to the Constitution of Canada may be made by proclamation issued by the Governor General under the Great Seal of Canada where so authorized by resolutions of the Senate and the House of Commons and of the legislative assembly of each province;

NOW THEREFORE the (Senate) (House of Commons) (legislative assembly) resolves that an amendment to the Constitution of Canada be authorized to be made by proclamation issued by Her Excellency the Governor General under the Great Seal of Canada in accordance with the schedule hereto.

SCHEDULE
CONSTITUTION AMENDMENT, 1987
Constitution Act, 1867

1. The *Constitution Act, 1867* is amended by adding thereto, immediately after section 1 thereof, the following section:

2. (1) The Constitution of Canada shall be interpreted in a manner consistent with

(*a*) the recognition that the existence of French-speaking Canadians, centered in Quebec but also present elsewhere in Canada, and English-speaking Canadians, concentrated outside Quebec but also present in Quebec, constitutes a fundamental characteristic of Canada; and

(*b*) the recognition that Quebec constitutes within Canada a distinct society.

(2) The role of the Parliament of Canada and the provincial legislatures to preserve the fundamental; characteristic of Canada referred to in paragraph (1) (*a*) is affirmed.

(3) The role of the legislature and Government of Quebec to preserve and promote the distinct identity of Quebec referred to in paragraph (1) (*b*) is affirmed.

(4) Nothing in this section derogates from the powers, rights or privileges of Parliament or the Government of Canada, or of the legislatures or governments of the provinces, including any powers, rights or privileges relating to language.

2. The said Act is further amended by adding thereto, immediately after section 24 thereof, the following section:

25. (1) Where a vacancy occurs in the Senate, the government of the province to which the vacancy relates may, in relation to that vacancy, submit to the Queen's Privy Council for Canada the names of persons who may be summoned to the Senate.

(2) Until an amendment to the Constitution of Canada is made in relation to the Senate pursuant to section 41 of the *Constitution Act, 1982,* the person summoned to fill a vacancy in the Senate shall be chosen from among persons whose names have been submitted under subsection (1) by the government of the province to which the vacancy relates and must be acceptable to the Queen's Privy Council for Canada...

[Privy Council Office, Canada, Constitution Amendment, 1987] Reproduced with the permission of the Minister of Public Works and Government Services, 1997.

Elijah Harper in the Manitoba House

Mr. Elijah Harper: (Cree spoken, translation unavailable)

Mr. Speaker, we are united to meet our objectives. The fight that we are fighting is not with Quebec. We support their aspirations. We support the distinct society. We support the right for them to protect their culture, to be self-determining, a self-government. Those are the very same goals that we as aboriginal people are trying to achieve. We were unable to protect our own culture, our own languages, our own institutions, our own self-government, because we as aboriginal people have never bargained away the right to self government.

As I mentioned before, the federal Government has determined what our rights, what our participation should be in Canada. We have an Act, an Indian Act, that has shackled Indian people. This human bondage must be done away with. I believe that aboriginal people will some day obtain self-government, but that is with the co-operation from other governments.

We will continue to fight for our own destiny; we were not able to control our own destiny. We have been told that because we do not support Meech Lake that there will be economic consequences, that there will be a backlash, and that Quebec will separate. I do not believe that for a moment, because Quebec's goals are the same goals for aboriginal people...

As I mentioned, our fight is not with Quebec, if Quebec is to separate, it is not because English Canada rejected Meech Lake Accord, but rather the aboriginal people want to have a rightful place in Canadian society. I do not think Quebec has that moral authority to separate from Canada. We have never denied Quebec their rightful place in the Canadian society.

Mr. Speaker, we have a relationship with the Canadian Government, a special relationship, not in a sense that we are a special group of people, not that we are better than any other group of people, but because of the treaties we have signed with the federal Government. Many of those treaties have not been upheld. Here in Manitoba we have treaty land entitlement that is still outstanding. . .

I know the Prime Minister sent a letter to us, to the chiefs, a few days ago, hoping that we will support Meech Lake. The chiefs indicated that they were willing to hear the Prime Minister himself or his delegates to see what they had to offer. Of course, the Prime Minister's office sent a delegation to offer us some things which were unacceptable to the Manitoba chiefs, because we have heard it before.

We have been promised from the governments as to their intentions as to what they want to do. One of them is they want to invite the chiefs to sit at the constitutional conferences, but we are not really assured whether they would be a voice around those discussions. Another one we should define treaties, but the federal Government has that obligation already, if Meech Lake fails they still have that obligation. They still need to define what those treaty rights are...

I hope the Canadian people will listen seriously to the greatest contributions we made to this country, the positive contributions we made to this country. There is no one group in Canada that can claim that they have made the greatest contribution except the aboriginal people, for the land and resources so the other people may live within Canada. We are a rich country, a wealthy country, but we have not received these benefits.

We are prepared to fight so long as we can. If we sign Meech Lake tomorrow, I do not think conditions will improve. If we sign it in five years time, I am not sure whether anything will improve. We are prepared to live with the consequences of our actions, but I do not believe the Canadian people will support the actions of governments, a backlash from governments against aboriginal people. The disastrous situation in those communities is just horrendous. As one reporter asked me, what disastrous consequences would there be if we do not support Meech Lake? I mentioned, what more disastrous conditions can there exist on reserves as they are now? It cannot get any worse.

We are prepared to live for the rights that we are fighting for. We are prepared to hurt a little. We are prepared to wait 10 years; we are prepared to wait 15 years; we are prepared to wait 25 years, because we believe in what we are fighting for. We are not interested in short-term solutions. What we are fighting for is for our people, for our children, for the future of our children, for our culture, for our heritage and what we believe in. Most of all we are fighting for our rightful place in Canadian society and also fighting for democracy for aboriginal people and indeed all Canadians. Thank you.

[Second Session, Thirty-Fourth Legislature of the Legislative Assembly of Manitoba, Debates and Proceedings, 38-39 Elizabeth II, 21 June 1990: 6017-6019]

Charter of the Assembly of First Nations[1]

PREAMBLE

WE THE CHIEFS OF THE INDIAN FIRST NATIONS IN CANADA HAVING DECLARED:

THAT our peoples are the original peoples of this land having been put here by the Creator;

THAT the Creator gave us laws that govern all our relationships for us to live in harmony with nature and mankind;

THAT the laws of the Creator defined our rights and responsibilities;

THAT the Creator gave us our spiritual beliefs, our languages, our cultures, and a place on Mother Earth which provided us with all our needs;

THAT we have maintained our freedom, our languages, and our traditions from time immemorial;

THAT we continue to exercise the rights and fulfill the responsibilities and obligations given to us by the Creator for the land upon which we were placed;

THAT the Creator has given us the right to govern ourselves and the right to self-determination;

THAT the rights and responsibilities given to us by the Creator cannot be altered or taken away by any other nation;

THAT our aboriginal title, aboriginal rights and international treaty rights exist and are recognized by international law;

THAT the Royal Proclamation of 7 October 1763 is binding on both the Crowns of the United Kingdom and of Canada;

THAT the Constitution of Canada protects our aboriginal title, aboriginal rights (both collective and individual) and international treaty rights;

THAT our governmental powers and responsibilities exist; and

THAT our nations are part of the international community

ARE DETERMINED:

To protect our succeeding generations from colonialism;

To reaffirm our faith in fundamental human rights, in the dignity and worth of the human person, in the equal rights of men and women of our First Nations large and small;

---

[1] The original version of this Charter was adopted at Vancouver, British Columbia, on 31 July 1985. For the ease of writing only, the masculine gender is used in this Charter. Whenever the masculine gender occurs it is intended to include the feminine gender.

To establish conditions under which justice and respect for the obligations arising from our international treaties and from international law can be maintained; and

To promote social progress and better standards of life among our peoples,

AND FOR THESE ENDS,

To respect our diversity,

To practise tolerance and work together as good neighbours,

To unite our strength to maintain our security, and

To employ national and international machinery for the promotion of the political, economic and social advancement of our peoples

SO, WE HAVE RESOLVED TO COMBINE OUR EFFORTS TO ACCOMPLISH COMMON AIMS.

ACCORDINGLY, our respective Governments, through the chiefs assembled in the City of Penticton in 1982, agreed to establish a national organisation known as the Assembly of First Nations (AFN) and now agree in the City of Vancouver in 1985 to the present Charter of the Assembly of First Nations.

IDEALS
ARTICLE 1

Diplomatic and political relations between First Nations in all of the Assembly of First Nations shall be guided by the following ideals:

(a) By virtue of their rich heritage, historical experience and contemporary circumstances, First Nations possess common interests and aspirations to exercise their political will in common and to develop a collective struggle or cause based upon the Indian values of trust, confidence and toleration.

(b) By virtue of the recognition and affirmation of their mutual freedom and self-determination, First Nations possess the knowledge and political will to respect the sovereignty of each First Nation.

(c) By virtue of the recognition and respect for their mutual sovereign equality, First Nations can establish collective political relations based upon respect for diversity.

(d) By virtue of their mutual belief in justice, First Nations can establish collective political relations that will not render a single First Nation to suffer or benefit as a direct result of privilege, favouritism, preferential treatment or the abuse of power.

PRINCIPLES
ARTICLE 2

First Nations, in the pursuit of the ideals stated in Article 1, shall subscribe to and maintain these Principles:

1. First Nations involved in diplomatic and political relations within the Assembly of First Nations recognize that collective political power and action is a practical imperative for the preservation and integrity of the right of self-determination for each First Nation.

2. In order to achieve political solidarity, diplomatic and political relations between First Nations involved in the Assembly of First Nations shall be characterized by the principles of co-existence and diversity.

3. The purpose, authority, responsibilities and jurisdiction of the Assembly of First Nations shall be derivative in nature and scope. All actions or initiatives in excess of the delegation from First Nations shall be null and void and of no force or effect.

4. All delegated power, mandates or responsibility derive from the sovereignty of First Nations, and the persons or institutions entrusted to exercise such delegation have a sacred trust and duty, in performance, to comply strictly with the nature and quality of the delegation.

5. The Assembly of First Nations shall remain at all times an instrument to advance the aspirations of First Nations and shall not become greater in strength, power, resources or jurisdiction than the First Nations for which it was established to serve.

6. Any decision or direction on a subject matter of a fundamental nature that may affect the jurisdiction, rights and survival of First Nations, may be undertaken as a national or international matter provided the First Nations-in-Assembly have reached a consensus to grant delegated power, mandate or responsibility to the Assembly of First Nations. When all efforts at achieving a consensus have been exhausted without success, a positive vote of 60% of the Chiefs and other designated representatives of First Nations shall be sufficient for the Assembly of First Nations to undertake any subject matter of a fundamental nature as a national or international matter.

7. The resources allocated to the Assembly of First Nations Secretariat shall be distributed and utilized for the greater benefit of all Member First Nations in efforts that are truly in form and substance national in scope and for which consensus has been achieved by the member First Nations.

ROLE AND FUNCTION
ARTICLE 3

The role and function of the Assembly of First Nations is:

(a) To be a national delegated forum for determining and harmonising effective collective and co-operative measures on any subject matters which the First Nations delegate for review, study, response or action.

(b) To be a national delegated forum of First Nations which, by virtue of their sovereignty, are the sole legitimate source for what it is, does or may become in the future.

(c) To be a national delegated forum for the purpose of advancing the aspirations of First Nations and to remain subordinate in strength, power and resources to the First Nations jurisdiction for which it is established to serve.

(d) To perform and adhere strictly, as a sacred trust and duty, to the nature, scope and extent of the delegation granted from time to time by First Nations.

(e) To seek, utilize and distribute resources for the greater benefit of all First Nations in endeavours that are truly in form and substance national or international in nature and scope and for which delegation has been granted by First Nations.

MEMBERSHIP
ARTICLE 4

All First Nations in Canada have the right to be Members of the Assembly of First Nations...

[Adopted at Vancouver, BC, 31 July 1985, pp. 1–5]

Fighting Words in the 1990s

Living Under Economic Occupation

Canada is the most economically occupied country in the industrial world; no other country even comes close. More than half of our manufacturing sector is under foreign control. We have learned from years of experience that, left to their own devices, foreign corporations may act contrary to Canadian economic interests, destroying more jobs than they create, and killing off Canadian competitors. They import more, export less, and are less likely to use local suppliers than are Canadian firms. Three-quarters of U.S. exports to Canada are transfers from U.S. parents to their Canadian subsidiaries, rather than exchanges on the open market.

The purpose of foreign-investment regulations was to give government the leverage to ensure that transnational corporations made commitments that benefited the Canadian economy. It was also to reduce gradually the level of foreign ownership in Canada.

. Free trade replaced the national market with a continental market and greatly hampered the ability of government to regulate corporations. Not only did they no longer have to be good corporate citizens while in Canada, they didn't even have to stay in order to sell into the Canadian market.

The withdrawal of the obligation on foreign companies to produce in Canada has dramatically changed U.S. subsidiaries here. Rather than becoming export platforms into the new continental market, branch manufacturing plants are simply shutting down. If they leave anything behind, it is just a warehouse or a sales office. The Canadian market can now be supplied merely by adding an extra shift or by filling unused capacity at a U.S. or Mexican plant. As Adam Zimmerman, vice-chairman of Noranda Inc., said "if you can move a plant, why would you stay here?" Scores of companies have closed their Canadian purchasing or marketing divisions. Many have eliminated their Canadian boards of directors and absorbed their subsidiary so that it is no longer a separate legal entity.

The consequences of this transformation are evident in the enormous casualties in the manufacturing sector. Services closely linked to manufacturing, such as computing, engineering, advertising, and other business services, are also hurting.

The Corporate Agenda

The Conservative/corporate action plan to dismantle the country has been devious and convoluted in its implementation. However, the concept itself is really quite simple. For convenience we have broken it into seven strands that are intricately woven into a fabric. The strands reinforce one another, and the effect is greater than the sum of its parts.

Here is their action plan.

1. Tie the Canadian economy by a free-trade agreement to the most powerful economy in the world, in which the corporate sector controls the government's agenda and an unfettered "free-market ideology" is firmly entrenched. This free-trade agreement is a constitution of corporate rights that reduces and circumscribes the power of governments, an international treaty that protects this new order from change or reversal by subsequent governments. Say the agreement will make Canada stronger. Say it will create jobs.

Use the integration of the two economies as a lever to reshape the Canadian economy in the U.S. image. Integration of the smaller into the larger leaves no choice, as the economies must mirror each other. Force "economic restructuring," i.e., cut jobs. Force "alignment of cost structures," i.e., force down wages, weaken union bargaining power, force down labour laws and environmental standards, force down taxes, force down government spending on social programs, etc. Do it in the name of harmonization. To harmonize means to Americanize.

2. Use monetary policy, that is, interest rates and exchange rates, to speed up restructuring. To weed out "weak" companies, accelerate the loss of jobs and the downward pressure on wages by speeding up import competition and creating a recession. Nothing will produce mass unemployment as fast as a high-interest-rate policy combined with a policy to cut public spending. High unemployment keeps wage demands low. Also, a high-interest-rate policy is a good way to transfer more wealth to those who have wealth.

In the name of fighting the deficit, use high interest rates to increase the deficit. Focus public attention on the "urgency" to reduce the deficit as a smokescreen to hide the slashing of public spending.

3. Bring in tax subsidies for high-income earners and large corporations. Say the purpose is to free up private savings and unleash the entrepreneurial energies of Canadian business. Increase taxes for middle-income earners and the working poor. Where possible, do it surreptitiously through mechanisms such as the inflation de-indexing of tax brackets.

4. Cut back social programs, especially the universal ones. Do it in the name of targeting those who need them most. Delink programs from cost-of-living increases, so that they lose value automatically and gradually. Shift the burden of providing these programs to the provinces. Apologize, but say the deficit crisis leaves no choice. Get the provinces on side by giving them more power.

Weakening social protections and creating high unemployment produce a more fearful and more compliant work-force—willing to work at low-skill, low-pay jobs; willing to work at part-time or temporary jobs; and willing to move to where the jobs are. A "flexible," undemanding work-force increases competitiveness.

5. In the name of fighting inflation, strengthen measures such as sales taxes (GST) and high interest rates, which actually increase inflation. As inflation rises, weaken the bargaining power of workers to keep wages apace. Do this directly to public-sector employees by imposing a wage freeze.

6. Privatize profitable public-sector enterprises. Return them at attractive prices to the corporate sector or offer shares to high-income Canadians. Deregulate sectors of the economy. Privatization and deregulation, while bolstering corporate profits, usually result in higher prices to consumers or poorer-quality products, or both. They also kill jobs, depress wages, and weaken unions.

7. Bring in all these policies in the name of international competitiveness. Say competitiveness will bring more jobs and greater prosperity, but be vague about when. Also say that, to be competitive, Canadian workers have to reduce wages and social protections. Argue that, in an increasingly competitive world, we have no choice, we must adjust. Place the burden of adjustment on ordinary Canadians who are disrupted and dislocated by this corporate-driven adjustment process.

[Maud Barlow and Bruce Campbell, Take Back the Nation, *(Toronto: Key Porter Books, 1991), pp. 9-15]*

The 1995 Referendum Question

The question that will appear on the ballot paper is:

Do you agree that Québec should become sovereign, after having made a formal offer to Canada for a new Economic and Political Partnership, within the scope of the Bill respecting the future of Québec and of the agreement signed on June 12, 1995?

[Resolution of the Québec Assemblée Nationale, 20 September 1995]

Arguments of the Official 'Yes' and 'No' Committees, 1995

YES... AND IT ALL BECOMES POSSIBLE

The forces for change are presenting a proposal that breaks with a political status quo that has been rejected by Quebecers. Since any reform of the federal regime that would accommodate the legitimate interests and needs of Québec is impossible, only sovereignty can answer, now and for the future, Quebecers' desire for autonomy. While they express this aspiration with persistence and conviction, they also wish to maintain flexible ties with their Canadian neighbours by maintaining a common economic space and political institutions. The partnership offer which shall be made to Canada, following a YES victory in the referendum, is inspired by values of openness and respect for two peoples called by geography and history to live side-by-side as good neighbours.

A YES on the night of October 30 will finally make it possible for Québec to attain the political status its linguistic and cultural specificity leads it to. This initiative is resolutely respectful of the identity of First Nations and the anglophone community.

The Constitution of a sovereign Québec will recognize the right of First Nations to self-government on lands over which they will have full ownership, and their existing constitutional rights will be confirmed. The Constitution will also guarantee the anglophone community the preservation of its identity and institutions, notably in the fields of education, health, and social services. The constitutional measures regarding the anglophone community and the First Nations will be defined with the participation of their representatives, and it will not be possible to change the resulting provisions without following rules previously agreed to.

All of us have received the text of the proposed law defining the new political status of Québec, and the text of the agreement signed June 12, 1995. They describe a clear, modern, and open project, which appeals to the heart as well as the mind. It is with pride and enthusiasm that Quebecers will say YES to change and that the new sovereign country of Québec will soon come into being.

NO TO A WEAKER QUÉBEC

Separation would exact a heavy economic price. A lengthy period of uncertainty would begin the day after a Yes vote. Would separation unfold as painlessly as its proponents suggest? Would an independent Québec state be able to meet its obligations to its citizens and lenders? What would happen to our dollar and to interest rates? What would happen to those who depend on Canadian markets, and those who benefit from federal programs and services?

Quebecers have always exerted substantial influence and leadership in the Parliament of Canada and in the federal government. Separation means a loss of representation for the defence of our interests.

As part of Canada, we have opened markets, signed agreements and partici-pated in the most exclusive and effective forums in the international community, such as the G7. As a separate country, these doors would be closed.

Separation will result in countless arguments over issues which currently are not in dispute. With all the acrimony following the breakup, these sterile debates could go on for years...

The Place of Québec in Canada

Québec is a distinct society within the Canadian federation. Our history, our fran-cophone majority, our culture, our laws and our institutions are testimony to this.

Two recent attempts to amend the Canadian constitution were not successful. While an important issue, this regrettable situation does not justify the break-up of Canada...

[Le Directeur Général des Elections du Québec, Oui/Non Référendum Québec 1995 (Quebec, 1995), pp. 21-22, 23-24]

QUESTIONS

1. How did Solange Chaput Rolland identify her dilemma in 1966?

2. What were the arguments for what has become known as 'Sovereignty Association' presented by René Lévesque in 1967?

3. What are the recommendations of the Macdonald Commission on Regional Development? Are there connections with the ideas found in the Meech Lake Accord?

4. How did Elijah Harper understand the Meech Lake Accord?

5. Why are Maud Barlow and Bruce Campbell opposed to what they describe as the 'Free trade Conservative/corporate agenda?'

READINGS

Keith Banting and Richard Simeon, *And No One Cheered: Federalism, Democracy and the Constitution Act* (Toronto: Methuen, 1983)

Michael Behiels, ed., *The Meech Lake Primer: Conflicting Views of the 1987 Constitution Accord* (Ottawa: University of Ottawa Press, 1989)

Deborah Coyne, *Roll the Dice: Working with Clyde Wells during the Meech Lake Negotiations* (Toronto: James Lorimer, 1992)

René Lévesque, *Memoirs* (Toronto: McClelland and Stewart, 1986)

Paul-André Linteau et al, *Québec Since 1930: A History* (Toronto: Lorimer, 1991)

Ovide Mercredi and Mary Ellen Turpel, *In the Rapids: Navigating the Future of First Nations* (Toronto: Viking, 1993)

Pierre Vallières, *White Niggers of America* (Toronto: McClelland and Stewart, 1971)